Family FAITH

A Devotional on Family Dynamics

DRS. CLAUDIO and PAMELA CONSUEGRA

Pacific Press®
Publishing Association
Nampa, Idaho | Oshawa, Ontario, Canada
www.pacificpress.com

Cover design by Gerald Lee Monks
Cover design resources from iStockphoto.com
Inside design by Aaron Troia

The authors assume full responsibility for the accuracy of all facts and quotations as cited in this book.

You can obtain additional copies of this book by calling toll-free 1-800-765-6955 or by visiting http://www.adventistbookcenter.com.

Library of Congress Cataloging-in-Publication Data
Names: Conseugra, Claudio, 1958- author.
Title: Family faith : a devotional on family dynamics / Drs. Claudio and
    Pamela Consuegra.
Description: Nampa : Pacific Press Pub., 2016. | Includes index.
Identifiers: LCCN 2016019907 | ISBN 9780816361250 (hard cover)
Subjects: LCSH: Devotional calendars--Seventh-Day Adventists.
Classification: LCC BV4810 .C555 2016 | DDC 249—dc23 LC record available at
https://lccn.loc.gov/2016019907

July 2016

January

The Marriage Resolution

"But from the beginning of the creation, God 'made them male and female.'"
—*Mark 10:6, NKJV*

On January 1, your whole life can be transformed. For one day at least, all your good intentions can be jump-started and all your bad habits unplugged. But January 1 is inevitably followed by January 2 and January 3. Someday soon, you will opt for snuggling in a cozy bed a few more minutes rather than plunging out into the cold on that jog. Pretty soon, candy wrappers will pop up in your desk drawer again. By January 4 or 5, you will have lost your temper over a bad driver, a broken glass, or a stubbed toe. By the 7th, your socks have a permanent place on the bathroom floor and your dental floss is collecting dust. By the 10th, you fall asleep before you can even get the Bible open.

For all but a few of us, most New Year's resolutions get packed away with the last of the Christmas decorations. The problem with most of our resolutions is that they are too safe, too sensible, and too self-centered. We resolve to make tiny cosmetic changes in our lifestyles but refuse to consider restructuring our lives and changing the paradigms by which we live.

For those of us who are married, what if this year we resolve to make a real, lasting, drastic change? Let us resolve to be a new and improved husband or wife. The changes we have to make don't have to be extraordinary. Here are three suggestions for you. First of all, go deeply into the Word of God. Spending time daily for your individual walk with Him will not only draw you closer to your heavenly Father, it will help you grow closer to your spouse in the journey of marriage. Secondly, set daily time aside for just the two of you—clearing the clutter from your busy schedule so you may serve your spouse instead. And finally, recommit daily to each other as you did on your wedding day.

Most of the resolutions we will make this year have to do with ourselves: our weight, our exercise program, our school, our work, and so on. Let's make a different type of resolution this year, one that will bless our spouses, our marriage, and ultimately, our relationship with God.

Father God, at the doors of the new year I recommit myself to You. May my walk with You this year draw me close to You and to those I love.

Begin and End With Prayer

*"And they burn to the L*ORD *every morning and every evening
burnt sacrifices and sweet incense."*
—2 Chronicles 13:11, NKJV

In a sense the father is the priest of the household, laying upon the family altar the morning and evening sacrifice. In the morning before he leaves home for his daily labor, let the father gather his children about him and, bowing before God, commit them to the care of the Father in heaven. When the cares of the day are past, let the family unite in offering grateful prayer and raising the song of praise, in acknowledgment of divine care during the day.

"Fathers and mothers, however pressing your business, do not fail to gather your family around God's altar. Ask for the guardianship of holy angels in your home. Remember that your dear ones are exposed to temptations. Daily annoyances beset the path of young and old. Those who would live patient, loving, cheerful lives must pray. Only by receiving constant help from God can we gain the victory over self.

"Home should be a place where cheerfulness, courtesy, and love abide; and where these graces dwell, there will abide happiness and peace. Troubles may invade, but these are the lot of humanity. Let patience, gratitude, and love keep sunshine in the heart, though the day may be ever so cloudy. In such homes angels of God abide.

"Let the husband and wife study each other's happiness, never failing in the small courtesies and little kindly acts that cheer and brighten the life. Perfect confidence should exist between husband and wife. Together they should consider their responsibilities. Together they should work for the highest good of their children. Never should they in the presence of the children criticize each other's plans or question each other's judgment. Let the wife be careful not to make the husband's work for the children more difficult. Let the husband hold up the hands of his wife, giving her wise counsel and loving encouragement.

"Let parents become acquainted with their children, seeking to understand their tastes and dispositions, entering into their feelings, and drawing out what is in their hearts."—*The Ministry of Healing,* 392–394.

Dear Lord, please help us begin and end each day with prayer, for we want our home to be a place where angels love to dwell.

Taking Care of the Widows

When the Lord saw her, He had compassion on her and said to her,
"Do not weep."—Luke 7:13, NKJV

Jesus left Capernaum, where He had healed the servant of a centurion, and a large crowd followed Him to the nearby city of Nain. There they met the funeral procession for a young man who was the only son of a widow. It is hard for us to recognize the context of this woman's loss. As a widow, she had already lost her husband, and in a land where men were the breadwinners, she'd lost her financial stability, her social status, and her future security. And now her only son was dead too. Her heart broke with the overwhelming loss. Jesus was moved with compassion and, raising the young man to life, gave him back to his mother.

There are many examples throughout the Bible where we find God showing special care for widows. Both Old and New Testaments contain instruction on how He expects His children to care for the widows in their midst. In Exodus 22:22, He says, "You shall not afflict any widow or fatherless child" (NKJV).

God has compassion on widows and asks that we show them the same regard. "Pure and undefiled religion before God and the Father is this: to visit orphans and widows in their trouble" (James 1:27, NKJV). The early church had a policy of supporting its widows and orphans, while in Old Testament times, the law provided for widows through a special tithe, and there was a policy of leaving gleanings during harvest time. When a nation and its leaders take care of the widows, they are promised a blessing (Deuteronomy 14:29). The person or nation that does not is cursed (27:19).

Jesus' own mother was widowed. He knew by watching her mourn the death of her life companion what pain she had gone through. This explains why, while hanging on the cross, Jesus made careful provision for Mary by asking His closest friend, John, to take care of her.

Widowed people are among the singles in our congregations that we sometimes overlook. Because they have family, we sometimes forget that they have special needs. It is our responsibility and privilege to see that they are visited and their welfare taken care of. Both widows and widowers have similar, but different needs.

Father, please open our eyes to the needs of the widows and widowers in our congregations and in our community, and may we be an extension of Your love for them.

Why God Hates Divorce

"For the LORD God of Israel says that He hates divorce, for it covers one's garment with violence," says the LORD of hosts. "Therefore take heed to your spirit, that you do not deal treacherously." —Malachi 2:16, NKJV

In order to safeguard His relationship with His people, God commanded them not to intermarry with the surrounding nations who worshiped other gods. But this forbidden practice had become so widespread that the prophet Malachi could legitimately say that the whole nation of Judah had profaned the Lord's institution. God's covenant relationship with His people was being contaminated by the men of the nation treating their marriages so casually and by marrying women who worshiped foreign gods.

To make things worse, the men of Israel were divorcing their wives so they could be joined in these mixed marriages. This blatant disregard for marriage prompted God to say that He hates divorce, for it violates His ideal.

We may be tempted to think that what happens in our homes has no bearing on the rest of life, but family life influences every other part of our lives. In America half of the children born this year to parents who are married will see their parents divorce before they turn eighteen. The devastating physical, emotional, educational, spiritual, and financial effects that divorce will have on these children will last well into adulthood and affect future generations. Even an amicable divorce tears apart the fundamental unit of society.

If you are in the middle of a contentious relationship, you may feel the only way out is divorce. Here is something to consider. "University of Chicago sociologist Dr. Linda Waite says, 'For most people, marital unhappiness is not permanent.'"* Recent findings indicate that two-thirds of all unhappy marriages are repaired within five years. When the unhappy spouses were surveyed five years later, those who had remained married were more likely than the divorced subjects to state that they were happy.

God hates divorce because of what it does to His children and what it does to their relationship with Him. Don't give up on your marriage; fight for it as if your very life and salvation depended on it.

Father, please help those couples who are in the midst of the difficult decision to separate and divorce. Give them Your wisdom and grace. Heal their homes and help them to mend their relationship. For Your honor and glory.

---

* The Church Initiative, "Causes of Divorce," Growthtrac, accessed March 1, 2016, http://www.growthtrac.com/causes-of-divorce/#.VtXe12dGV9A.

Our Heavenly Parent

"If a son asks for bread from any father among you, will he give him a stone? Or if he asks for a fish, will he give him a serpent instead of a fish? Or if he asks for an egg, will he offer him a scorpion? If you then, being evil, know how to give good gifts to your children, how much more will your heavenly Father give the Holy Spirit to those who ask Him!"—Luke 11:11–13, NKJV

The relationship between a parent and child is one of life's most important factors when considering the physical, emotional, and spiritual development of children.

From the physical point of view, human children are totally helpless and dependent on others from the time they are born. Without the physical nurture they receive from their parents, or caregivers, children would simply die shortly after their birth. As children grow, parents are responsible for providing them with healthy, nutritious food if they want their children to be strong and healthy.

Regarding emotional health, babies and children who experience closeness and safe physical touch from their parents develop good emotional health. The words children hear from their parents will greatly affect their psychological well-being. Children who grow up hearing loving, encouraging, and affirming words from their parents are more inclined to develop a strong emotional foundation that will help them develop into healthier and more successful adults.

Finally, regarding spiritual health, the relationship a child has with its parents will either lead them closer to or further from God. The Bible uses a mother's love toward her child as an example of the tender care God has for His children. The relationship of fathers toward their children is also used to demonstrate the love between us and our heavenly Father. Today's text states that God's goodness to us is greater than even the best a parent can give their child.

How encouraging to realize that as parents, regardless of how we may have been parented, we have a heavenly Father who loves us with compassion. He gives us the best example of what it means to be a good parent, and He will give us the wisdom we need as we journey through the adventure of parenting.

Thank You for loving us the way You do, Father. Give us grace to be forgiving of any parenting mistakes we may have experienced as children. Your example of parental love serves to comfort and instruct us as we strive to be good parents to our children.

Finding Rest

"Come to Me, all you who labor and are heavy laden, and I will give you rest.
Take My yoke upon you and learn from Me, for I am gentle and lowly in heart,
and you will find rest for your souls. For My yoke is easy and My burden is light."
—Matthew 11:28–30, NKJV

John, who baptized Jesus, was in prison. While there, his faith must have been tested severely. He sent some of his disciples to ask Jesus if He was indeed the Messiah, as he believed Him to be, or if it was time to look for someone else. Jesus responded to John's disciples by telling them to look at the evidence of His ministry. He then began to teach and minister to the people, while John's followers watched.

As Jesus ministered, He must have been thinking deeply of His cousin and the struggles he was facing after being thrown in prison for standing and proclaiming what is right and true. Jesus may well have been thinking of His many disciples, who would also soon experience persecution, imprisonment, and even death because of their convictions.

How do Jesus' words above apply to those who find themselves in a difficult marriage or to those faced with challenging family situations? To them, and to each of us, Jesus promises that He is ready to carry their heavy burdens if they will take His yoke and learn of Him. His yoke is made to fit each one and is so much lighter to bear. Jesus invites us to bring to Him whatever situation we're going through today and promises to take them off our shoulders and give us something much better in their place.

Perhaps this is Jesus' way of saying, "Don't give up on your relationship!" You see, He wants to do much more than just carry our burdens. He wants to give us rest. He doesn't want us to remain in a sad and miserable relationship. "Give it to Me," He says, "and I'll bless you and fill you with peace and rest." Rather than settling and "accepting what life has dealt you," accept what Jesus offers and enjoy life abundantly.

Dear Father, thank You that whatever challenges we may face in our married lives or in our families, they do not have to be unbearable, for Jesus promises to bear all our burdens and give us what we can easily carry. Take our burdens, dear Jesus, and help us to walk each day close beside You.

It Begins in the Home

"Return to your own house, and tell what great things God has done for you."
And he went his way and proclaimed throughout the whole city what great
things Jesus had done for him.—Luke 8:39, NKJV

Until Jesus cast the demons out, this man had been away from his family and had made his home in a cemetery. People were afraid of him because of his violent behavior, probably his foul language, and his horrible appearance.

After Jesus released him from the demons, his immediate reaction was to follow Jesus. But Jesus wanted more than the heart and life of this one man. He also wanted the man's family, friends, and neighbors to come to know the freedom from sin He was offering. So Jesus sent him as a missionary to his own home.

Can you imagine the look of surprise on the faces of everyone when they saw their beloved husband, father, and friend? He was no longer wild but fully whole. He was filled with peace and joy. He didn't have to take them through a whole set of Bible studies or preach an evangelistic series. All he had to do was tell them what Jesus had done for him. It was the most powerful sermon he could preach.

Ellen White writes, "No sooner is one converted than there is born within him a desire to make known to others what a precious friend he has found in Jesus. The saving and sanctifying truth cannot be shut up in his heart" (*The Desire of Ages*, 141). We all have stories of what God has done in our lives, and we need to remember that our mission field does not have to take us to the other side of the world. It should begin at home—with our loved ones. Again, Ellen White writes, "Our work for Christ is to begin with the family, in the home. . . .There is no missionary field more important than this" (*The Adventist Home*, 35).

When others see what God has done in our lives, when our behavior and our words testify of Him in kind, gentle words, it is then that others will see the evidence of what God has done in our lives. Let's be mindful of how we live so that others, particularly our family, may see the God who lives in us.

Father, reflect Your love through me that others may see You shining through me and come to know You, love You, and serve You too.

The Importance of Ordering Priorities

"Therefore, brethren, seek out from among you seven men of good reputation, full of the Holy Spirit and wisdom, whom we may appoint over this business; but we will give ourselves continually to prayer and to the ministry of the word."
—Acts 6:3, 4, NKJV

In the early church, it became evident that the apostles could not do everything that was expected of them. They were overwhelmed by the many demands for their service. Recognizing they were being stretched beyond the limit, they delegated some of their responsibilities to godly men who were able to handle those many demands. They chose Stephen and others to perform many of the day-to-day services, so they could have the time they needed to devote their lives "to prayer and to the ministry of the word" (Acts 6:4, NKJV).

We know what it means to be too busy. Stretched too thin. We understand how the disciples must have felt. And, just as they needed to make some important changes, the same may be true for us today. How often do we allow all the busyness of the day to push aside time for personal devotions? How often do we have worship together as a family? Are there better ways of managing our schedules so that every member of the family has time with Jesus? Forsaking time with God, even when you spend that time with your family, can leave you empty and ineffective. Are we so busy running here and there that there is no time left in the day to sit at Jesus' feet and spend time in prayer and the Word?

The best way to nurture family relationships is to spend time together. The same is true of our relationship with Jesus. Our spiritual lives will grow in proportion to the amount of time we spend in the study of His Word and in talking to Him. And as we grow closer to God, our hearts are also drawn closer to our family members.

Remember, as parents, we model to our children how to set priorities and manage our time. If we are not spending time with Jesus, our little ones will think it is not important either. Why don't we take an inventory today and see if perhaps there are things that we need to reorder?

Dear Lord, I want to develop a closer relationship with You. Show me areas of my life where change is needed in order to make time with You my first priority.

Jesus' Recipe for a Happy Marriage

"Judge not, and you will not be judged; condemn not, and you will not be condemned; forgive, and you will be forgiven; give, and it will be given to you."
—Luke 6:37, 38, ESV

In this narrative of Jesus' ministry, Luke describes the time when Jesus chose, from a larger group of followers, the Twelve who would be His disciples. Once He had chosen the Twelve, Jesus began the process of training and preparing them for the work they would undertake, once He returned to His Father in heaven.

We are Jesus' disciples at all times, in all places, and to all people. Nowhere is this truer than at home, with our family. Here are three things we need to practice daily:

Do not judge. The most basic problem with communication in marriage is the inability to listen attentively. We jump to conclusions. Make quick decisions about what we think our spouse meant and often fail to give them the benefit of the doubt. We misinterpret their words or actions and assume they're being careless, hateful, or unloving toward us. Jesus teaches us a better way. We need to actively break that judgmental cycle. He urges us, "Don't judge and you will not be judged."

Do not condemn. When a judgmental attitude is fed daily, the next step many take is to attack their spouse emotionally, verbally, and at times even physically. The best solution to the problem of condemning each other is to be reminded of God's grace. Since Jesus died for us, we are no longer condemned (Romans 8:1). Jesus died for our spouse, too, so they are also no longer condemned. A disciple of Jesus has been given God's grace and must extend it to their spouse. In marriage, instead of condemnation, offer grace.

Forgive. We know that in every relationship there will be times when we say or do things that are unkind or unloving. We may judge our spouse. We may even condemn our spouse, and in turn, receive their condemnation. We have the choice to perpetuate a judgmental, condemning spirit, and thus strengthen a destructive cycle that will destroy our love and the happiness of our home, or we can begin breaking that cycle by forgiving one another.

Jesus' recipe for a good, healthy marriage begins with these three simple ingredients: Don't judge, don't condemn. Instead, choose to forgive.

Lord, thank You for extending Your love, Your grace, and Your forgiveness to us. May we be as loving, gracious, and forgiving toward our spouse.

Logs and Specks

"Why do you see the speck that is in your brother's eye, but do not notice the log that is in your own eye? How can you say to your brother, 'Brother, let me take out the speck that is in your eye,' when you yourself do not see the log that is in your own eye?" —Luke 6:41, 42, ESV

From the very beginning, after Adam and Eve sinned and God confronted them with what they had done, Adam pointed the finger of blame at Eve. He also indirectly pointed a finger at God who had created her. And in turn Eve pointed her finger at the serpent.

Many marriages begin in a loving way but turn into a hotbed of mutual criticism. A husband finds every reason to fault his wife, comparing her to other women. Ellen White wrote about such men: "Many husbands do not sufficiently understand and appreciate the cares and perplexities which their wives endure, generally confined all day to an unceasing round of household duties. They frequently come to their homes with clouded brows, bringing no sunshine to the family circle. If the meals are not on time, the tired wife, who is frequently housekeeper, nurse, cook, and housemaid, all in one, is greeted with faultfinding" (*The Adventist Home*, 224).

Wives express little appreciation for their husbands and fail to affirm them for anything they do for them or for their home. They think that if they nag them enough it will encourage their husbands to do more and be better.

Here's good counsel for those tempted to find fault in their spouse: "The heart of his wife should be the grave for the faults of the husband, and the heart of the husband the grave for his wife's faults. . . . I have been shown that there should be a sacred shield around every family" (Ibid., 177).

Jesus made it clear. When you have a beam in your own eye, how can you possibly tell your spouse about the speck of dust in their eye? Ellen White says, "Let the husband and wife talk things all over together. Renew the early attentions to each other, acknowledge your faults to each other. . . . Be determined that you will be all that it is possible for you to be to each other, and the bonds of wedlock will be the most desirable of ties" (*In Heavenly Places*, 203).

Father, please help me to look for what is good and praiseworthy in my spouse. Help me to appreciate all they bring into my life and for being Your gift to me.

How to Build on the Rock

*"Everyone who comes to me and hears my words and does them, I will show
you what he is like: he is like a man building a house, who dug deep and laid the
foundation on the rock. And when a flood arose, the stream broke against that
house and could not shake it, because it had been well built."*
—Luke 6:47, 48, ESV

Ellen White describes the scene where these words of Jesus were spoken:
"As the people sat upon the hillside, listening to the words of Christ, they
could see valleys and ravines through which the mountain streams found
their way to the sea. In summer these streams often wholly disappeared,
leaving only a dry and dusty channel. But when the wintry storms burst upon
the hills, the rivers became fierce, raging torrents, at times overspreading the
valleys, and bearing everything away on their resistless flood. Often, then,
the hovels reared by the peasants on the grassy plain, apparently beyond
reach of danger, were swept away. But high upon the hill were houses built
upon the rock. In some parts of the land were dwellings built wholly of rock,
and many of them had withstood the tempests of a thousand years. These
houses were reared with toil and great difficulty. They were not easy of access,
and their location appeared less easy of access than the grassy plain. But they
were founded upon the rock; and wind and flood and tempest beat upon
them in vain" (*This Day With God*, 215).

While the words of Jesus apply to our own personal life and underscore
the importance of our establishing a true foundation on the Rock, Jesus
Christ, His words also show the importance of our homes being built on that
same foundation. Daily devotional and prayer times are to be more than a
tradition or habit. They should form the foundation of our spiritual lives.

Ellen White further states: "Had Adam and Eve heeded the words that
God spoke to them in the beginning, they would not have fallen from their
first estate" (Ibid.). The foundation for a strong marriage and family is the
same: the Rock, Jesus Christ. When the storms of life come, that sure foundation will hold the family together.

*Father, help us to build our foundation daily on Your Son, Jesus Christ, and
when the storms of life come and threaten to destroy us, may His strength be
ours, and may He keep us together while the world tries to tear us apart.*

The Golden Chain of Love

For this cause shall a man leave his father and mother, and cleave to his wife.
—Mark 10:7, KJV

Too often the marriage relation is entered into without proper consideration. None should marry in uncertainty. But if they have not been properly considerate in this matter, and after marriage find themselves dissimilar in character, and liable to reap unhappiness in the place of joy, let them not breathe into another's mind the fact that their marriage was unwise. . . . The evil is always increased when either the wife or the husband, finding some one who appears to be a congenial spirit, ventures to whisper to this trusted one the secrets of the married life. The very act of making known the secret confirms the existence of a condition of things that would not be at all necessary if the husband and wife loved God supremely. . . .

"In many cases where these difficulties are thought to exist, the cause is imaginary. . . . If the husband and wife would freely talk over the matter with each other in the spirit of Christ, the difficulty would be healed. . . . If they loved God supremely, their hearts would be so filled, so satisfied, with His love, that they would not be consumed with longing for affection to be manifested in acts toward themselves.

"Many have mistaken the true duty of the wife to the husband and the husband to the wife. Self becomes all absorbing, and Satan . . . has his net all ready to draw about the human soul, to get it so entangled by human imaginations that it seems impossible for human wisdom to disentangle the meshes of his finely woven snares.

"But what human wisdom cannot do the wisdom of God can do through the surrender of the will, the mind, the soul, the strength, the entire being, to God. His providence can unite hearts in bonds that are of heavenly origin. But the result will not be a mere external interchange of affection in soft and flattering words. There will be a new experience; the loom of heaven weaves with warp and woof finer, yet more firm, than those of earth. The material is not a mere tissue fabric, but a texture that will bear the wear and test of trial; heart is bound firmly to heart in the golden chain of a love that is genuine" (*In Heavenly Places*, 205).

Father, please bind our hearts together in love.

Close Your Eyes

"The lamp of the body is the eye. Therefore, when your eye is good, your whole body also is full of light. But when your eye is bad, your body also is full of darkness. Therefore take heed that the light which is in you is not darkness. If then your whole body is full of light, having no part dark, the whole body will be full of light, as when the bright shining of a lamp gives you light."
—Luke 11:34–36, NKJV

Men tend to be highly visual, and this is one of the reasons why pornography is mostly used by men—although recent research shows that women are increasingly using pornography. One of the problems with pornography is that it deepens a sense of emptiness in the user. This drives him back to look for more, which, in turn, is what develops his dependence or addiction to it. The more he watches, the more he will begin to long for his wife to imitate what he's watching, and when she doesn't, he becomes frustrated and goes back to watching more pornography. This promotes a vicious cycle of frustration, loneliness, desire, and continued use. Another problem is that his wife will never be able to compare with the women he's watching on screen, and he will grow increasingly dissatisfied with her.

Though women may be disgusted with men's use of pornography, many are reading romantic novels that are descriptive of sexual situations. Women often watch movies and TV programs with fictitious plots, romantic encounters, and couples falling in love within minutes of meeting and also having sex shortly thereafter. The effect of this material constantly being viewed will be an effect similar to pornography on women by creating a world of fantasy that no man can possibly fulfill.

How can one be free of these habits or addictions? Our scripture for today tells us that Jesus cast out a demon from a man that kept him unable to speak. How encouraging, for though he couldn't ask for Jesus' help, Jesus heard the unspoken longing of this man's heart and acted on it. For those of us who seem unable to break away from sin, this story should lift our spirits with the knowledge that God hears our innermost longing for Him, and that He helps us even when we feel helpless.

Father God, please hear our plea for deliverance from the habits and addictions against which we battle, and deliver us from the world of fantasy and the resulting sins into which we fall.

Who Do You Love Most?

"Do not think that I came to bring peace on earth. I did not come to bring peace but a sword. . . . He who loves father or mother more than Me is not worthy of Me. And he who loves son or daughter more than Me is not worthy of Me."
—Matthew 10:34–37, NKJV

These verses are known as one of the hard sayings of Jesus. The *Andrews Study Bible* provides this insight. "Rather than contradicting Himself, [Jesus] is making two points: First, He is saying that the gospel at times engenders conflict because of the deep differences and disagreements that arise by those who accept it and those who don't. Second, family and its place in society are redefined in its popular social understanding. The blood family is no longer at the top of the hierarchy in the setting of the gospel. Acceptance of, and love for, Jesus must be primary. To be sure, the Scripture teaches the importance of the family bond; but not at the expense of following Jesus."

Conflict is part of any human relationship. It is especially sad when that conflict exists due to our differences in religious beliefs and convictions. This is what Jesus is addressing in the passage. However, it is not Jesus who causes conflict in the home, but at times it is the acceptance of His teachings that may set us in opposition to family members. Consequently, they may reject those who have a different understanding of Jesus' teachings.

One of the most important lessons we can learn from this section, however, is that Jesus demands that He have first place in our lives. In the Ten Commandments, we read, "I am the Lord your God, who brought you out of the land of Egypt, out of the house of bondage. You shall have no other gods before Me" (Exodus 20:2, 3, NKJV). Anyone, or anything, who takes first place in our lives becomes our god. For the Christian, the first place can only be occupied by God.

Does this mean we stop loving our family? Never! Rather, when we make God first in our lives, our relationship with our family changes and our family takes on a more exalted place. No longer are they simply blood relatives, they are now also faith relatives.

Father, by placing You first in my life I am not relegating my family to last but rather giving You, and them, the place each rightly deserves. Father, be first in our lives, always and forever.

When Families Need Help

When Jesus heard that, He said to them, "Those who are well have no need of a physician, but those who are sick."—Matthew 9:12, NKJV

The Russian poet and author Ivan Andreevich Krylov wrote a story in 1814 about a man who went to visit a museum. He was enthralled with the number of items to be seen and was particularly drawn to the many small objects on display—so much so that he neglected to notice the elephant exhibition. This is where the expression "the elephant in the room" originates, and it refers to a situation that everyone is aware of but no one wants to acknowledge or deal with.

When we ignore problems rather than resolving them, they only become more complicated. Avoidance never ends well. If you find yourself continually sidestepping a chronic issue in your home, ask yourself, *Why?* In the text for today Jesus tells the Pharisees that people who are healthy have no need of a doctor, unlike those who are ill. Before you can receive help for your problem, you have to recognize that the problem exists. You have to acknowledge the elephant in the room.

Some people get stuck by believing they're a failure if they admit to having a problem. The trouble with thinking that way is that ignoring a problem doesn't make it go away and avoidance can be fatal to a marriage and devastating to a family. It takes courage to say, "I need help," but saying it can become the first step toward healing and recovery. Asking for help is not a weakness. In fact, it may be the best gift you can give yourself and your family.

In a survey conducted by the National Fatherhood Institute, one of the top reasons given for divorce in the United States across all demographics is too much arguing. Continual fighting is a strong indicator that there's an elephant in the room. Beware of becoming so distracted by the arguments that you fail to notice the source of your disagreements. Perhaps it's time to take a long, close look at your marriage. Instead of feeling hopeless or overwhelmed by the weight of the situation, choose to do something about it. Do you need help? Be courageous and acknowledge that the problem is beyond your ability to handle. Ask for help today.

Father, please give us the courage to acknowledge the elephant in the room and guide us as we seek healing for our marriage and our home. Thank You.

God Desires Mercy

" 'I desire mercy, and not sacrifice.' "
—Matthew 12:7, ESV

This chapter begins with Matthew recalling the time Jesus and His disciples were walking through the grain fields on the Sabbath. They were hungry, so they plucked some of the grain and ate it as they continued on to their destination. The Pharisees wasted no time leveling their criticism toward Jesus for allowing His disciples to do something they considered contrary to how the Sabbath should be kept. They implied that Jesus should be able to have better control over the behavior of His disciples.

Jesus responded by reminding them of the time David, when fleeing from King Saul, entered the house of God with some of his men and ate of the consecrated shewbread, which was forbidden. Jesus then said, "If you had known what these words mean, 'I desire mercy, not sacrifice,' you would not have condemned the innocent. For the Son of Man is Lord of the Sabbath" (Matthew 12:7, 8, NIV).

How does this apply to our families? In our homes we can sometimes fall into the trap of being very strict with rules, traditions, and expectations with our spouse and children. While children need a clear structure with well-defined, fair boundaries so they know how to conduct themselves at home and outside, the rules need to be applied with gentle consistency. It is important to be compassionate and to exercise flexibility with them as they grow up. It is possible to do this and not compromise. A very strict rule of law that does not allow for any options or freedom to grow and make mistakes can produce children who rebel and resent their parents and the way they were brought up.

When setting guidelines for the family, the temperaments of the children need to be considered. While some children require firm guidance, others can be trained more readily. Regardless of temperament, however, a kind and gentle spirit between parent and child will help establish healthy family relations that will last a lifetime.

In marriage, as well, spouses need to be gracious and merciful with each other. Remember, we are all bound to make mistakes at some point or another. Particularly early in the marriage, as couples learn to live together, there needs to be more mutual flexibility, mercy, and compassion.

Father God, help us to remember Your mercy toward us, and extend ours toward our spouse and children so that we may have a close relationship toward one another and with You.

Can We Glory in Tribulation?

And not only that, but we also glory in tribulations, knowing that tribulation produces perseverance; and perseverance, character; and character, hope. Now hope does not disappoint, because the love of God has been poured out in our hearts by the Holy Spirit who was given to us.—Romans 5:3–5, NKJV

I don't know about you, but I find it hard to be happy about troubles that come my way. It is often hard to see the blessings in the midst of the trials. And yet Scripture reminds us that tribulations produce perseverance. In other words, good can come from situations that seem absolutely bad at the time. It is hard enough when we as adults go through tough times, but it's really hard to watch our children suffer.

When that happens, whether from their own bad choices or those of someone else, we want to rescue them from the situation. We want to fix it. In fact, if possible, we would gladly take their pain on our own shoulders. But God has another plan: to perfect them through their trials. Character-building lessons are rarely learned from the triumphs in life. It is the trials that teach us how to persevere despite the pain. Taking trials away from our kids deprives them of the chance to grow, build character, and trust in God. The best character-building lessons are learned when our children get up after they have fallen. Don't inhibit your child's growth by rescuing them from or taking over difficult situations. Instead, give them the tools they need to pick themselves up.

When our children look at us with tear-filled eyes and ask, "Why?" we need to admit that even parents do not always have the answers. More important than having the perfect answer is to teach them to trust Jesus. Even when we do not understand, we need to trust Jesus to open the next door and show us the way out.

As parents, do you feel the need to always rescue your child? How do you help your child deal with disappointments? Perhaps the best thing we can do as parents is to kneel down beside our children and teach them to take their troubles to the Lord in prayer.

Lord, help me to see the blessings among the trials. Help me to teach my child that good things can come out of the bad. Even when we do not understand all of the reasons or have all of the answers, help us as a family to trust You.

Love and Lead

"Most assuredly, I say to you, the Son can do nothing of Himself, but what He sees the Father do; for whatever He does, the Son also does in like manner. For the Father loves the Son, and shows Him all things that He Himself does."
—John 5:19, 20, NKJV

The relationship between God the Father and Jesus is unique to Them— the triune God. But in His humanity, Jesus lived His life in such a way as to teach us how fathers and their children can have a close relationship based on mutual love, respect, and obedience. There are two important lessons we fathers can learn from this.

First, fathers must lead by example, not just command with words. Jesus said He did what He saw the Father do. Children watch every action, hear every word, and imitate what they observe. For a child, their father is a larger-than-life figure whose example they want to emulate, and whose love and recognition they crave. Their way to seek attention is through copying what they see their fathers do.

Ellen White writes, "Fathers, spend as much time as possible with your children. Seek to become acquainted with their various dispositions, that you may know how to train them in harmony with the word of God. Never should a word of discouragement pass your lips. Do not bring darkness into the home. Be pleasant, kind, and affectionate toward your children, but not foolishly indulgent. Let them bear their little disappointments, as every one must. Do not encourage them to come to you with their petty complaints of one another. Teach them to bear with one another and to seek to maintain each other's confidence and respect.

". . . Fathers, . . . combine affection with authority, kindness and sympathy with firm restraint" (*The Adventist Home,* 222).

Second, not only does Jesus do what He sees the Father do, but the Father loves the Son. It isn't enough to show our children what to do; we must show them that we love them. This can be challenging for fathers who did not experience their own father's love as children, but God can heal our wounds and restore what was lost. As we receive our heavenly Father's love, we will learn how to love our children well and how to show them they are loved.

Dear Father, help us to first love and imitate You so that we may love and lead our own children, so that ultimately they may follow You, their loving Father.

The Sweetest Words

*Pleasant words are like a honeycomb, sweetness to
the soul and health to the bones.—Proverbs 16:24, NKJV*

Kind words are always better than harsh words. Faultfinding can make both the speaker and the hearer sick with anger and resentment. On the other hand, appropriately spoken words that encourage and soothe can be uplifting, even to the point of improving physical health.

Ellen White wrote, "Do you dislike to have harsh words spoken to you? Remember that when you speak such words others feel the sting. Let your praiseworthy example, your peaceable words and unselfish deeds, be a savor of life unto life" (*The Voice in Speech and Song*, 64).

In a world filled with competition, anger, and rudeness, the sweet, kind words spoken and heard at home can be refreshing and even therapeutic. White continues, "Pleasant, cheery words cost no more than unpleasant, moody words. Sharp words wound and bruise the soul. In this life everyone has difficulties with which to wrestle. Everyone meets with grievances and disappointments. Shall we not bring sunshine instead of gloom into the lives of those with whom we come in contact? Shall we not speak words that will help and bless? They will be just as much a blessing to us as to those to whom they are spoken" (ibid.).

One way to use kind words toward our loved ones is to make an ongoing list of the things you appreciate about them. Periodically review this list and tell them how you feel about what they said or did. For instance, after your wife fixes you a good meal, tell her how much you appreciated it, write it down on the list, and then, one day, instead of expressing frustration for something she might have done, remind yourself and thank her again for her great cooking skills. Or if your husband hung a picture you asked him to hang, tell him thank you for doing it and that you like how it looks on the wall. Let him know that every time you look at the picture, you think of him and how good he is with his hands. Kind words make others feel affirmed and loved. They are indeed healing to the body, mind, and heart.

Father, help me to maintain a positive attitude and to express words that are pleasant, kind, and gracious so that what I say may be sweet like honey to my family and those around me.

The Most Painful Death

While He was still speaking, someone came from the ruler of the synagogue's house, saying to him, "Your daughter is dead. Do not trouble the Teacher." But when Jesus heard it, He answered him, saying, "Do not be afraid; only believe, and she will be made well." —Luke 8:49, 50, NKJV

Though it is never easy to deal with the death of a loved one, it has been said there is no death more painful to accept than the death of a child. We anticipate losing our parents, maybe even our siblings to death, and although it's never welcome, we expect the chances are good that we will likely have to attend their funerals. But none of us expect our children, or grandchildren, to die before we do.

Ellen White experienced the death of two of her children. It is from sad experience that she writes of the death of her fourth child, three-month-old John Herbert. "After we returned from the funeral, my home seemed lonely. I felt reconciled to the will of God, yet despondency and gloom settled upon me" (*Testimonies for the Church,* 1:246).

Jairus likely experienced something of that gloom, and how he must have clung to Jesus' words, "Do not be afraid; only believe, and she will be made well." Jairus was one of only a few who were blessed to receive a child back from the grip of death. The widow of Nain was another one. How gratefully she received her son back from the dead!

Every other parent has to wait for that blessed hope to be made reality on resurrection morning, when they will experience the joy of holding their children once more. Ellen White describes that awesome moment when "little children are borne by holy angels to their mothers' arms" (*Child Guidance,* 566). While there is nothing that can remove the staggering grief experienced by parents dealing with the death of a child, Jesus' words to Jairus come as a sweet promise: "Do not be afraid; only believe." The hope and the certainty of the resurrection and the joyous reunions that will occur are as sure as God's promise. Joy *will* come in the morning!

Father, may we as parents never have to experience the pain and sorrow that comes from losing a child. But if that time were to come, remind us of the family reunion that will take place when Jesus returns so we can look forward to that glorious event with even greater anticipation.

Trust Like a Child

Trust GOD from the bottom of your heart;
don't try to figure out everything on your own.
Listen for GOD's voice in everything you do, everywhere you go;
he's the one who will keep you on track.
—*Proverbs 3:5, 6*, The Message

When we take into our hands the management of things with which we have to do, and depend upon our own wisdom for success, we are taking a burden which God has not given us, and are trying to bear it without His aid. We are taking upon ourselves the responsibility that belongs to God, and thus are really putting ourselves in His place. We may well have anxiety and anticipate danger and loss, for it is certain to befall us. But when we really believe that God loves us and means to do us good we shall cease to worry about the future. We shall trust God as a child trusts a loving parent. Then our troubles and torments will disappear, for our will is swallowed up in the will of God.

"Christ has given us no promise of help in bearing today the burdens of tomorrow. He has said, 'My grace is sufficient for thee' (2 Corinthians 12:9); but, like the manna given in the wilderness, His grace is bestowed daily, for the day's need. Like the hosts of Israel in their pilgrim life, we may find morning by morning the bread of heaven for the day's supply.

"One day alone is ours, and during this day we are to live for God. For this one day we are to place in the hand of Christ, in solemn service, all our purposes and plans, casting all our care upon Him, for He careth for us. 'I know the thoughts that I think toward you, saith the Lord, thoughts of peace, and not of evil, to give you an expected end.' 'In returning and rest shall ye be saved; in quietness and in confidence shall be your strength.' Jeremiah 29:11; Isaiah 30:15.

"If you will seek the Lord and be converted every day; if you will of your own spiritual choice be free and joyous in God; if with gladsome consent of heart to His gracious call you come wearing the yoke of Christ,—the yoke of obedience and service,—all your murmurings will be stilled, all your difficulties will be removed, all the perplexing problems that now confront you will be solved" (*Thoughts From the Mount of Blessing*, 100, 101).

Help me, dear Lord, to trust like a child.

Healing the Pain of Grief

When Jesus heard it, He departed from there by boat to a
deserted place by Himself. —Matthew 14:13, NKJV

When Jesus heard of the death of John the Baptist, He departed to a deserted place. Keep in mind that John was not only Jesus' forerunner, the one who baptized Him, and a powerful, compelling speaker; he was also Jesus' cousin. In losing John, Jesus lost more than a colleague in ministry; He lost a close family member.

Ellen White writes, "In a life wholly devoted to the good of others, the Saviour found it necessary to turn aside from ceaseless activity and contact with human needs, to seek retirement and unbroken communion with His Father. As the throng that had followed Him depart, He goes into the mountains, and there, alone with God, pours out His soul in prayer for these suffering, sinful, needy ones" (*The Ministry of Healing*, 58).

As a police and hospice chaplain, I have had to attend to people who have just lost a loved one. Many are surrounded by well-meaning relatives and friends who say things such as, "I know how you feel," or "You should be glad. At least they're not suffering anymore." I wish they would understand that in moments of sorrow, it is your caring presence and willingness to listen that can be the greatest gift to those who are grieving.

Jesus' example on grieving is worth noting. In His grief, He took some time to be alone. Too often we neglect to take time to grieve well. Jesus understood that His disciples also needed time alone to grieve. They were exhausted after their missionary travels and the news of John's death, and the constant pressure of being with the people threatened their health and well-being. So Jesus took them aside and had them rest for a while.

We need to remember Jesus' wisdom and come aside and rest after dealing with a traumatic situation. We need time to grieve. Time to recharge our emotional batteries, to feel the pain and experience the void left by our loss. Time to sorrow and mourn. This is part of the normal process of grieving and healing.

Father, thank You for allowing us to see a glimpse of Jesus' humanity and the sorrow He felt at the death of John. During our time of sorrow, help us to feel and to live out our pain so that healing will come naturally and faster than if we suppress it all.

Being Like-Minded

Now may the God of patience and comfort grant you to be like-minded toward one another, according to Christ Jesus, that you may with one mind and one mouth glorify the God and Father of our Lord Jesus Christ.
—*Romans 15:5, 6, NKJV*

We all bring certain baggage with us on our wedding day. These include issues arising from our upbringing as well as things we've experienced in life, both good and bad. Some of the baggage may be light, while some may be heavy and weigh us down. Regardless, we all bring baggage into our newly formed marriage.

These issues can become more pronounced as we enter the realm of parenting. How we were raised affects the parenting style that we naturally gravitate toward. Often, a husband and wife each have a different set of values and expectations, and children are very quick to pick up on these differences and use them to their benefit. It is amazing how quickly they realize which parent will agree to their requests and which one is more apt to deny them. If allowed, they will play one parent against the other.

Scripture tells us that we need to be like-minded. Talk about your expectations before you have children. Discuss important issues such as church attendance, school choice, worship in the home, and media choices. Discussing and making decisions on some key things before baby arrives will help you as parents to be united in child rearing.

However, if you're grappling with some key differences in parenting styles, it is not too late to have important conversations now. Just make sure that you have them in private, out of earshot of your children. Each parent should take some time to make a list of key parenting issues. Compare the lists and then discuss each item until you reach an agreement.

This may be difficult, but pray together for resolution and come to a decision you both can support so that you have a united front before your children. When confronted with a situation you had not anticipated, tell your child that you must first talk to your spouse and that you will get back to them as soon as you both agree on a course of action. Consider the message this sends to your children. You have made it clear that Mom and Dad will both agree on the decision.

Lord, where there are two or more, there are differences. Help us to be united as one with You. Lead us to be like-minded according to Your will.

The Father's Heart

"So he got up and went to his father. But while he was still a long way from home his father saw him, and his heart went out to him; he ran and hugged his son and kissed him." —Luke 15:20, NET

As much as we would love to have our children remain obedient, loving, and eager to follow our instructions, as they grow and gain their independence they will likely make choices that are contrary to something, and sometimes everything, we have taught them. Nothing breaks the hearts of parents more than to see their children turn their backs on their faith and beliefs, and to watch them live a life contrary to the principles they were taught from childhood. At the same time, nothing brings parents more joy than to see their wayward children return.

Children are more likely to return home if they have experienced the unconditional love of their parents. While we may not like the decisions they reach or agree with the choices they make, we can give them the assurance that nothing will keep us from loving them—even as nothing can separate us from the love of God.

The parable of the prodigal son is probably one of the best-known, best-loved stories of all time. But it is more than a lovely story—it's a beautiful allegory of the love and forgiveness that God extends to us, His children. While we tend to focus on the father's forgiveness for the wayward son, we often overlook the father's love and forgiveness for the older son. In reality he loved both of his children, the one who left and the one who stayed. And each of them, in their own way, failed to love their father. The younger son, by asking for his portion of the inheritance, was basically expressing his wish that the father were dead. The older son, with his angry and unforgiving spirit, did not recognize how generous his father had been with him all his life. The younger son, selfish though he was, accepted the father's generous offer of love and forgiveness, while the older son, self-righteous as he was, rejected his father's love.

Father, it's tough being a parent! Help us to trust our children to You. Help us to love them unconditionally, and thank You for Your generous love and forgiveness toward us. Help us to be as generous with our love and forgiveness toward our children as You are.

Jesus Loved Them

Now Jesus loved Martha and her sister and Lazarus.
—John 11:5, NKJV

We can draw many lessons from this precious story. We could talk about the foretaste of the resurrection day, when Jesus returns, and how families will be reunited with their loved ones. We could talk about Jesus' empathy, not just sympathy, for these two sisters. He didn't simply feel for them, He felt with them, and He cried. We could talk about the hardness of the hearts of those Jewish leaders who, in spite of being witnesses to the most powerful of all of Jesus' miracles, refused to believe in Him and instead went out to plot His destruction.

Instead, let's focus on the words, "Jesus loved Martha and her sister [Mary] and Lazarus." Evidently they knew Jesus loved them, and when Lazarus became ill, they didn't hesitate to call on Jesus for help. It was Jesus who was a favorite Friend to them. They loved to have Him in their home. Their love for Jesus was the natural response to His love for them and His forgiveness and deliverance on behalf of Mary. The tears with which she later washed His feet demonstrated her love for Him.

At the same time, the fact that Jesus loved them does not mean that death would not visit them; that sorrow and hardship would never knock on their door; that pain and suffering would be absent from their lives. And this is one of the most important lessons from this story. No matter who we are, or how well we are loved, we will be touched with pain, suffering, sickness, and even death at some point during our lives. This reality does not mean that God has forsaken us, that He is ignoring us, that He is too busy tending to the needs of others. On the contrary, this story teaches us that Jesus loves us before, in the midst of, and after we experience pain and sorrow, and even death. It was the knowledge of that love that encouraged Mary and Martha even as their hearts were breaking. We, too, can bask in His love for us even while our minds worry and our hearts break!

Dear Father, thank You for surrounding us with Your love even during those times when we have a hard time seeing You and when the tears covering our eyes feel as if they are about to drown our hearts. Help us to feel that love when we feel so lonely, helpless, and hopeless.

Two-getherness

Two people are better off than one, for they can help each other succeed.
—Ecclesiastes 4:9, NLT

In the book of Genesis, God told Adam and Eve that the two of them should become one; after all, the two had come from the one. That is what marriage is all about. Togetherness becomes "two-getherness" when two "mes" join together, and become one "us." As a result, you become stronger, producing greater results for each other, and are less lonely and less stressed.

It's undeniable what you two can accomplish in your marriage when you work together. Among many things, you help each other in your weaknesses and benefit from each other's strengths. We are reminded that "two are better than one, because they have a good reward for their labor. For if they fall, one will lift up his companion. But woe to him who is alone when he falls, for he has no one to help him up. Again, if two lie down together, they will keep warm; but how can one be warm alone? Though one may be overpowered by another, two can withstand him" (Ecclesiastes 4:9–12, NKJV).

What areas will help you to maintain a strong, healthy "two-getherness"? First of all, and above all, your individual relationship with God. If both of you enjoy a strong spiritual experience, as you are drawn closer to Jesus in the process you will come closer to one another. In addition, I would suggest you should look for agreement on the following areas:

1. Commitment to your marriage
2. Communication
3. Conflict resolution
4. Finances
5. Decision-making
6. Goals for the future
7. Child rearing, education, and discipline
8. Household roles and responsibilities
9. Sexual relationship
10. Honesty and openness
11. Spiritual, physical, and emotional health
12. Relationship with the extended family/in-laws

Keep your marriage "two-gether" for the long haul.

Father God, bless us so that as we maintain our individuality we may live in unity and "two-getherness."

Servant Leadership

"The greatest among you will be your servant."
—Matthew 23:11, NET

In one of the most significant passages in the New Testament dealing with marriage, Paul writes these words: "Wives, submit to your husbands as to the Lord, because the husband is the head of the wife as also Christ is the head of the church—he himself being the savior of the body. But as the church submits to Christ, so also wives should submit to their husbands in everything" (Ephesians 5:22–24, NET).

These words, isolated from their immediate context and the larger biblical context, have been grossly misused and have led to the abuse of women. These words have been used to misrepresent what Paul, and God, intended to say about the relationship of a woman toward her husband, insisting that the wife should be no more than a slave, a doormat, and a servant ready to fulfill her husband's every wish, desire, and command.

Let's use today's passage in conjunction with Ephesians 5 and draw up some biblical guidelines for a healthy marital relationship.

1. The husband is the head of the wife. While some see this as a man holding a higher position than his wife, Paul describes it as a relationship of mutual submission and dependence. He writes, "and submitting to one another out of reverence for Christ" (Ephesians 5:21, NET). The head cannot survive without the body any more than the body can survive without the head.

2. Wives, submit to your husbands as to the Lord. Paul does not say that the husbands *are* their lords, but rather that they should act toward their husbands in the same attitude of submission as they would to the Lord Jesus. When a husband acts like Jesus, as a servant-leader, then the wife finds it easy to submit to him. This mutual attitude of respect and servanthood is what Paul spoke about in verse 21.

The words of Paul in Ephesians 5:22–24 should in no way give men reason to mistreat their wives or to require strict "obedience" from them. After all, Paul continued his instructions to men by telling them to love their wives, *"just as Christ loved the church"* (verse 25, NET; emphasis added). Jesus served the church by dying for it; therefore, husbands should do everything to serve their wives, even to the point of dying for them, if it became necessary.

Father, teach us to be humble servants of our spouses and to treat each other with the same love that Your Son has for us, which He showed by dying on the cross.

Watch and Pray

Then He came to the disciples and found them sleeping, and said to Peter,
"What! Could you not watch with Me one hour? Watch and pray, lest you enter
into temptation. The spirit indeed is willing, but the flesh is weak."
—Matthew 26:40, 41, NKJV

K nowing what the disciples would be facing, Jesus went away to pray for them, and He encouraged them to spend time in prayer for themselves. While wrestling with the bitter cup from which He was about to drink, Jesus returned to find His disciples sleeping. Jesus knew how important it was for His disciples to spend time in prayer, because the events they were about to witness would try their faith and, if they were not prepared, could lead them to forsake their faith.

In marriage, God knows everything we will ever face. He knows how important it is for us to spend time together, as husbands and wives, in prayer. That's probably one of the reasons God's enemy wants to keep us so busy and distracted that we don't find time to pray together.

I sometimes wonder what our marriages would be like if we knew ahead of time the challenges we would face in the future. Would it overwhelm and perplex us beyond our limits? Perhaps it is in His mercy that He has not given us the ability to see our future so we would not be discouraged.

If we are not spending time praying together as husband and wife, we need to follow Jesus' example and begin to pray. Though it may seem challenging at first, we must not fall asleep on the job, as did the disciples. Whether first thing in the morning, or the last thing at night, or if praying together during the day or over the phone, we must make time each day to pray for each other, for our marriages, our families, our children, and for help during the challenges that will inevitably come in the future. If you still have children at home, it is important to spend time praying together as a family. That daily habit will help your children incorporate prayer as a part of their daily life and routine.

Father, thank You that we can spend this time in conversation together as a couple and as a family with You, knowing that You are pleased to hear from us and to talk to us. Help us, Father, to maintain this time as sacred as we do other obligations in our lives.

Marital Disputes

A dispute also started among them over which of them was to be regarded as the greatest. So Jesus said to them, ". . . The one who is greatest among you must become like the youngest, and the leader like the one who serves. For who is greater, the one who is seated at the table, or the one who serves? Is it not the one who is seated at the table? But I am among you as one who serves."
—Luke 22:24–27, NET

A lot of marital discord stems from this desire to be the greatest. This is nothing new. Soon after the Fall, God told Eve, "You will want to control your husband, but he will dominate you" (Genesis 3:16b, NET). One of the effects of the entrance of sin into the world was the desire for supremacy, even among those who were literally one flesh—Adam and Eve. God forewarned them that this dispute for control would be present in marriage and in society.

Jesus changes the paradigm and tells His disciples that in His kingdom it is not the greatest who is the one that is served, but rather it is the greatest who serves. In marriage we should look for ways to help and serve one another, starting with our spouse and children. Imagine a world in which the husbands and wives work hard at outdoing each other in how they serve one another! Well, Jesus says we should not only imagine such a world but that such is His kingdom of which He wants us to be a part.

Look for ways to serve your husband or wife out of love for them and out of love for Jesus. They may not always act in a way deserving of this courtesy, but it's at those times that you need to put forth every effort to show your love through acts of service. The disciples sure were not acting very loving on that last Passover night, and they sure didn't deserve to be served; but in His love for them, Jesus served them, and, "having loved his own who were in the world, he now loved them to the very end" (John 13:1, NET). Follow the example of Jesus, and love your spouse to the end.

Father, help us to love and serve one another to the end because, by so doing, we act as Your disciples, because it shows Your spirit working in our hearts, and because by doing so we know Your love abides in us and in our marriage.

Never Alone

"Yet, I'm not all alone, because the Father is with me. I've told you this so that my peace will be with you. In the world you'll have trouble. But cheer up! I have overcome the world." —John 16:32, 33, GW

As humans, living in this world of sin, it is inevitable that we will experience trouble at some point in our lives. That trouble may come in the form of illness, our own or a loved one's; loss of employment; inclement weather—a hurricane, a tornado, an earthquake, excessive snow or ice; accidents—at work, on the road, at home; problems with a co-worker, a supervisor, or the boss; problems at school—with a teacher, a classmate, or the administration. Even at church, a place where we are surrounded by people who believe in God, we can run into trouble with other church members for a host of reasons, some of their doing, some of our doing.

Marriage and the family are not exempt from trouble either. In marriage, the challenges that come from being raised in different families, environments, and cultures, and the fact that we have different personalities and temperaments is bound to bring about some friction sooner or later. The longer we live together, the more we learn to adapt to our differences as we create our own culture and feel more comfortable with each other. With life comes change that results in a shifting of family dynamics. There will always be a constant need to adapt, stretch, and grow.

We need to remember that even Jesus suffered trouble at the hands of His own people, even from His own disciples. And yet, He reminds His disciples that He was never left alone through any of those troubles and that the Father was with Him through it all. He gives His followers the assurance that we will not be alone either in our trials and tribulations. And the best assurance that we will not be consumed or destroyed by them is that He has overcome them all. That's why He can encourage us and tell us to "cheer up."

It's good to be reminded to cheer up! Don't give up on each other, on your relationship, on your family, because He has overcome and He is with you! We have good reason for courage and for cheer.

Father, thank You that even though we experience trouble in this world, You never leave us. May Your presence lift us up from the valley of despair and into the mountain of cheer.

Noah Saves His Family

Then the LORD said to Noah, "Come into the ark, you and all your household,
because I have seen that you are righteous before Me in this generation."
—Genesis 7:1, NKJV

The world before the Flood had become totally corrupt. In describing mankind at that time in history, Moses wrote, "Every intent of the thoughts of his heart was only evil continually" (Genesis 6:5, NKJV).

Ellen White describes what the antediluvians were doing to cause such sorrow to God. "Extensive groves, that retained their foliage throughout the year, were dedicated to the worship of false gods. With these groves were connected beautiful gardens, their long, winding avenues overhung with fruit-bearing trees of all descriptions, adorned with statuary, and furnished with all that could delight the senses or minister to the voluptuous desires of the people, and thus allure them to participate in the idolatrous worship" (*Patriarchs and Prophets*, 91). They also practiced polygamy and human sacrifices.

In spite of living in the midst of this decaying culture, "Noah was a just man, perfect in his generations. Noah walked with God" (Genesis 6:9, NKJV). But his example and powerful messages of warning did not yield a large harvest of souls. Ultimately, only his wife and their three sons and their wives were saved in the ark.

Though some might consider Noah a total failure, Ellen White writes, "Amid the prevailing corruption, Methuselah, Noah, and many others labored to keep alive the knowledge of the true God and to stay the tide of moral evil. . . . Enoch had repeated to his children what God had shown him in regard to the Flood, and Methuselah and his sons, who lived to hear the preaching of Noah, assisted in building the ark" (ibid., 92).

Although Noah's warnings were rejected by the world, his example resulted in blessings to his family. "As a reward for his faithfulness and integrity, God saved all the members of his family with him. What encouragement to parental fidelity!" (ibid., 98). Noah found grace in the eyes of the Lord, but most important, he became the instrument of salvation for his own family. Though no one hear and accept our message that the world is again coming to an end, I pray our own families will be saved not because of our "preaching," but because of the way we live before God.

Father, help us to live in such a way that our children will be saved because they see You reflected in us.

February

Train Up a Child

Train up a child in the way he should go, and when he is old he will not depart from it. —Proverbs 22:6, NKJV

Fathers, do not discourage your children. Combine affection with authority, kindness and sympathy with firm restraint. Give some of your leisure hours to your children; become acquainted with them; associate with them in their work and in their sports, and win their confidence. Cultivate friendship with them, especially with your sons. In this way you will be a strong influence for good.

"The father should do his part toward making home happy. Whatever his cares and business perplexities, they should not be permitted to overshadow his family; he should enter his home with smiles and pleasant words. . . .

"Parents, let your children see that you love them and will do all in your power to make them happy. If you do so, your necessary restrictions will have far greater weight in their young minds. Rule your children with tenderness and compassion, remembering that 'their angels do always behold the face of My Father which is in heaven.' Matthew 18:10. If you desire the angels to do for your children the work given them of God, co-operate with them by doing your part.

"Brought up under the wise and loving guidance of a true home, children will have no desire to wander away in search of pleasure and companionship. Evil will not attract them. The spirit that prevails in the home will mold their characters; they will form habits and principles that will be a strong defense against temptation when they shall leave the home shelter and take their place in the world.

"Children as well as parents have important duties in the home. They should be taught that they are a part of the home firm. They are fed and clothed and loved and cared for, and they should respond to these many mercies by bearing their share of the home burdens and bringing all the happiness possible into the family of which they are members.

"Children are sometimes tempted to chafe under restraint; but in afterlife they will bless their parents for the faithful care and strict watchfulness that guarded and guided them in their years of inexperience" (*The Ministry of Healing*, 391, 392, 394).

Heavenly Father, may we look to You each day, and experience a fresh understanding of what it means to be Your child. And may we learn to be good fathers by watching You at work.

Filled With the Spirit

When the Day of Pentecost had fully come, they were all with one accord in one place. . . . And they were all filled with the Holy Spirit and began to speak with other tongues, as the Spirit gave them utterance. —Acts 2:1, 4, NKJV

It was the work of the Holy Spirit on each of the disciple's hearts that brought them together in one accord. Once the Holy Spirit was poured on the disciples, they began to speak in the languages of the people who had come from many parts of the world and had gathered in Jerusalem for the festival.

The same Holy Spirit also wants to bring unity to our families. Conflict, stress, and the pressures of this world continually threaten to divide us. The divorce rates in the United States and in many countries of the world attest to the fact that marriages are breaking apart. The witness of these broken marriages leads many to believe that if God can't keep the marriages of Christians intact, then what's the point of following Him? On the other hand, when there is unity in a Christian marriage, or in the family, those within it are a living witness to its very members and to those outside the family circle.

One of the results of the outpouring of the Holy Spirit was that the disciples were able to speak in other languages. Gary Chapman has become well known for his books on the Five Love Languages, in which he explains the need to learn to speak our spouse's love language. When the Holy Spirit falls on us, as a result of us being in unity, we then will have the ability to speak our spouse's love language with greater ease. What may be foreign to us at first, with the aid of the Holy Spirit, will become natural, and our relationship will be strengthened.

Let us submit ourselves to the working of the Holy Spirit in our hearts and lives and homes, so He can strengthen our marriages and our families and speak to others through the example we show.

Loving Father, pour Your Spirit on us as a couple and as a family that the unity You desire for us may become a daily reality. May Your Spirit enable us each to speak the love language of the other and communicate our love for one another. May we bring glory and not reproach through our example of Christianity in the home.

Healing a Broken Relationship

"Repent therefore and be converted, that your sins may be blotted out, so that times of refreshing may come from the presence of the Lord."
—*Acts 3:19, NKJV*

Today's text comes from Peter's sermon on the Day of Pentecost. The people had gathered in Jerusalem from many nations around the world and heard the disciples speak in their own language. They misunderstood the cause, however, and instead of attributing this miracle to God, they said the disciples were drunk. Peter wasted no time in setting the record straight and went on to preach the good news of salvation in the power of the Holy Spirit to those gathered there.

When brokenness enters a marital relationship, it often happens that the couple allows things to fester and infect the entire relationship until an amputation—divorce—seems to be the only way to save them individually. They often feel helpless and see no way to restore intimacy to their relationship. The result of sin is always separation and a breakdown in relationships, whether between us and God or between husband and wife.

Peter's message brings hope to families everywhere. For just as our relationship with God can be restored when there is repentance, so can our marriages be healed when there is genuine repentance. This repentance must include full confession and a true recognition of what was done was wrong. There should be no excusing the event, no rationalizing, no blaming one another, but a sincere recognition of what happened and of the pain it caused the other.

The promise from Peter to those that repent is that the "times of refreshing" will come. Peter's words offer encouragement that God can restore our broken relationship with Him, and with one another, no matter how grievous our sin and brokenness. And while the hurt feelings may take a long time to heal, and trust may be slow in being rebuilt, if there is genuine repentance the healing will come and the relationship can be as good, or maybe even better, than it was before. It is the Holy Spirit that brings conviction of our wrongdoing and takes our unspoken longings and heart cries for forgiveness before the Father, making them beautiful.

Father, thank You for restoring our relationship with You and making it even better than before. May that experience be the same in our relationship as spouses and as parents so that when we hurt or fail each other, You will restore us and bring us back to the "times of refreshing" You promise.

Choices and Consequences

*All who were possessors of lands or houses sold them, and brought the proceeds
of the things that were sold, and laid them at the apostles' feet; and they
distributed to each as anyone had need. —Acts 4:34, 35, NKJV*

Ananias and Sapphira were members of the early Christian Church. They
most likely started off with good intentions, but evidently when they
realized how much they'd be giving to the church, they decided to give only
part of the proceeds. Ananias came first to present what he thought was a
sizeable offering, only to be confronted by Peter to tell the truth. He had a
choice: tell the truth or lie. When he lied, he died. Sapphira then came and
was given the opportunity to tell the truth, but she, too, chose to lie and also
died.

Ellen White describes these events. "Ananias and Sapphira grieved the
Holy Spirit by yielding to feelings of covetousness. . . . They thought they had
been too hasty, that they ought to reconsider their decision. They talked the
matter over, and decided not to fulfill their pledge. They saw, however, that
those who parted with their possessions to supply the needs of their poorer
brethren, were held in high esteem among the believers; and ashamed to
have their brethren know that their selfish souls grudged that which they had
solemnly dedicated to God, they deliberately decided to sell their property
and pretend to give all the proceeds into the general fund, but really to keep
a large share for themselves. Thus they would secure their living from the
common store and at the same time gain the high esteem of their brethren"
(*The Acts of the Apostles*, 72).

The influence of a spouse can serve as a great blessing or a horrible curse.
When one spouse takes a step in the direction opposite to God's will, the
consequences can have devastating results for the family. Our first allegiance
should always be to God. The first of the Ten Commandments states it clearly:
"I am the LORD your God, who brought you out of the land of Egypt, out of
the house of bondage. You shall have no other gods before Me" (Exodus 20:2,
3, NKJV). Jesus made it clear that in our list of priorities God should always
take first place.

*Father, help us to remember that our choices have consequences that will
affect not only ourselves but those we love the most. Help us keep our priorities
aligned correctly and to make You our first love.*

When Two Agree

Then Peter said to her, "How is it that you have agreed together to test the Spirit of the Lord? Look, the feet of those who have buried your husband are at the door, and they will carry you out." —Acts 5:9, NKJV

In marriage, it is the responsibility of the husband and wife individually to make God their first priority. Even above one another. If one spouse steps away from making God first, then the other spouse must make a choice: go along with their partner or stand true to the Lord's command to have no other gods before Him. One of the areas where couples can fail to do this is illustrated in the story of Ananias and Sapphira. When it comes to returning God's tithe to Him and presenting offering to the church to further its ministry, many couples have disagreements and in many cases defraud God.

Ellen White writes, "The same sin was often repeated in the afterhistory of the church, and it is committed by many in our time; but though not attended with the visible manifestation of God's displeasure, it is no less heinous in His sight now than in the apostles' time. The warning has been given, God has clearly manifested His abhorrence of this sin, and all who pursue a similar course of action may be sure that they are destroying their own souls" (*Counsels on Stewardship*, 312).

The spouses should agree early in their marriage, in fact before their marriage, what portion of their finances belongs to God and what part they will give to the church, and then both should encourage each other to be faithful to that commitment. If the time comes when one chooses to go back on that commitment, the other should not simply go along but they should remain faithful to God. By doing so, not only are they keeping their individual commitment of generosity and obedience to God, thus protecting their eternal salvation, but they would also be serving as an example to their spouse that they may repent and return to their walk with God. Agreeing in what is wrong could spell out devastation and death not just to one of the spouses but to both, to their marriage, and ultimately to their children.

Father, help us to remain faithful and true to You first and always, and may we help each other, as spouses, to keep You first in each other's life for each other's sake and for the sake of our children and others.

The Gifts of Confession and Prayer

Confess your trespasses to one another, and pray for one another, that you may be healed. The effective, fervent prayer of a righteous man avails much.
—James 5:16, NKJV

While James's advice is for members of the church at large, his words apply to the home and to the relationship between husband and wife. When we say or do anything that hurts a member of the family, we need to confess directly to them, and do it as soon as possible, before the pain festers into anger.

Ellen White writes, "I am instructed to urge upon our people most earnestly the necessity of religion in the home. Among the members of the household there is ever to be a kind, thoughtful consideration. Morning and evening let all hearts be united in reverent worship. At the season of evening worship let every member of the family search well his own heart. Let every wrong that has been committed be made right. If during the day, one has wronged another or spoken unkindly, let the transgressor seek pardon of the one he has injured. Often grievances are cherished in the mind, and misunderstandings and heartaches are created that need not be. If the one who is suspected of wrong be given an opportunity, he might be able to make explanations that would bring relief to other members of the family" (*My Life Today,* 32).

The second part of James's instruction is to "pray for one another." While confession should take place when harm has been done, prayer is something that should happen daily. We need to carve time out of our daily lives to pray together as a couple and as a family. We make time to eat when we're hungry. We make time to rest when we're weary. We make time for reading, to watch TV, to check out Facebook, to talk on the phone, to play, to travel, to do anything that we want to do. And it is these very things that distract us and keep us from doing the one thing we most need to do—pray together.

It is prayer that strengthens and heals our hearts and our homes. Let us, then, confess our sins to one another, forgive one another, and pray for each other.

Father, please give us the grace to be humble enough to confess our sins to one another, and help us to make time to pray together and to pray for one another.

The Example of a Godly Father

There was a certain man in Caesarea called Cornelius, a centurion of what was called the Italian Regiment, a devout man and one who feared God with all his household, who gave alms generously to the people, and prayed to God always.
—Acts 10:1, 2, NKJV

Cornelius was a Roman centurion, in charge of one hundred men. Although he was not Jewish, he believed in God and led his household, including his children, accordingly. Ellen White writes that he was "a man of wealth and noble birth, and his position was one of trust and honor. A heathen by birth, training, and education, through contact with the Jews he had gained a knowledge of God, and he worshiped Him with a true heart, showing the sincerity of his faith by compassion to the poor. He was known far and near for his beneficence, and his righteous life made him of good repute among both Jews and Gentiles. His influence was a blessing to all with whom he came in contact" (*The Acts of the Apostles,* 132, 133).

Because of his devout spirit, God sent an angel to tell him to send for Peter. At the same time, God sent Peter a vision which would teach him that God does not make racial or ethnic distinctions but offers His grace and salvation to all people. As a result of Peter's visit, Cornelius and his entire household were all baptized.

Cornelius is a powerful example of the influence a good man holds in his family. Ellen White writes, "He was faithful to Jehovah in his home life and in his official duties. He had erected the altar of God in his home, for he dared not attempt to carry out his plans or to bear his responsibilities without the help of God" (ibid., 133).

What a wonderful example of the critical role fathers play in their children's spiritual lives. It is through the life and example of their fathers that children come to know and love God. If the fathers fail to live a godly life, the chances that their children will follow God are greatly reduced, and in many cases it may not even happen.

Father, may we realize the importance of living a life worthy of Your calling, knowing that our lives and examples may well determine the eternal destiny of our children. Thank You that we can come to You for wisdom to lead our children to follow You.

The Adoption Option

Even so we, when we were children, were in bondage under the elements of the world. But when the fullness of the time had come, God sent forth His Son, born of a woman, born under the law, to redeem those who were under the law, that we might receive the adoption as sons. —Galatians 4:3–5, NKJV

Many years ago, during my internship at a counseling center, my supervisor told me of a conversation he had with his daughter. He told her, "If there were a hundred children standing against a wall and you were one of them, and I was asked to choose any of them to be mine, I would still choose you." Though his daughter was not adopted, he wanted to assure her that as parents they treasured her as a precious member of their family. She was a joy, not an obligation, to them.

Children of adoption have a special place in the hearts of their adoptive parents. They were chosen specifically by people who wanted to be their parents. They could have been raised in an orphanage or in the foster care system, but instead they were chosen to live in a home to be loved and raised by parents who wanted them. At some point in their lives, however, they may want to know why their biological parents didn't want them. That is normal for many children and should not be feared by the adoptive parents.

When is the best time to tell children of their adoption? The consensus among experts is that children should be told as they grow up as part of their normal life experience. As long as they are always surrounded by the love of their parents, their adoption will not be a shock to them. They can be taught of the great joy and privilege of having been chosen and raised by two very special people who wanted to have children to love.

Allow your child to feel safe when asking questions. Give them as much information as is appropriate for their age and maturity level. All children need to be reassured they are loved. Share with them that we have all been adopted into God's family and He loves us all very much.

Father, thank You for adopting us as Your children. Give us tender hearts and much wisdom as we help our children navigate the sometimes difficult waters of adoption. And may we show compassion and support toward the adoptive parents and their children within our church family.

Standing Watch

I will stand my watch and set myself on the rampart, and watch to see what He
will say to me, and what I will answer when I am corrected.
—Habakkuk 2:1, NKJV

There are three important points in this verse, all of which we can relate to the attitude of fathers as they come before the Lord and seek wisdom in their role as head of their home.

First, *stand my watch.* Like prophets of old, fathers are to be watchmen, waiting and watching with patient intensity all that comes within their view. The words Habakkuk uses imply watching with persevering fixity of attention.

Second, *what He will say to me.* The literal expression means "in me." God speaks not simply to a father's outward ear but rather *inwardly.* When we have prayed to God, we need to wait and listen to what answers God gives by His Word, His Spirit, through others, and through events that take place—what some would call providences.

Finally, *what I will answer when I am corrected.* In other words, what attitude will I show toward God when in answer to my prayers He chastises me, corrects me, or reproves me? If God answers our prayers just the way we want Him to, we express our thanks to Him. But what do we say when in answer to our prayers He reproves us? This can be an important growth point for a man.

In his role as father and head of the home a man is to be a seer, an old term to describe part of the role of the prophet, standing and watching, earnestly and patiently, to see what God will tell him, for wisdom to know how to lead his home and his children, for guidance from God that he can impart to his own household.

His role is also as God's spokesman. But that role does not give men the right to speak as if they were infallible, flawless, or perfect. In fact, Habakkuk reminds men that if they are open to God's leading, there will be times when He will use reproof. When that happens, a man's humble attitude will teach important lessons about submission to God and the acknowledgment that God knows what is best for us.

Father God, may we as parents keep watch faithfully. Give us humble hearts that we may accept Your guidance and reproof graciously, trusting Your love, and showing our children who You are through the example of our lives.

Can This Marriage Be Saved?

"Go, take yourself a wife of harlotry and children of harlotry."
—*Hosea 1:2, NKJV*

The prophet Hosea lived his life as an object lesson demonstrating God's faithfulness in spite of the unfaithfulness of His people. God instructed him to marry Gomer, who was a harlot, and to adopt her children, born of other fathers. The lesson in this book, told through Hosea's life story, is that God still chooses to be our "husband," even though we turn our backs on Him again and again and commit adultery with His enemy.

People often ask, "Can this marriage be saved?" after the devastation of adultery. They go on to cite Jesus, who said that the only acceptable cause for divorce was adultery. The first thing we must understand is that while Jesus said adultery can be the justification for divorce, He did not say that in the case of adultery the couple must divorce.

Adultery does not have to be the death blow to a marriage. While there may be few things as damaging to a marriage, it is possible for a marriage to be saved and the relationship restored after the tragedy of adultery. In fact, it is possible for the marriage to become even stronger after going through this trauma. How is this possible? Several things need to take place. These include:

1. There must be total openness and disclosure, to the extent that the injured party is prepared to listen. Any secrets will ultimately lead to another fall. Sin thrives in an atmosphere of secrecy and shrivels in a spirit of openness and honesty. Willard Harley, author of the books *His Needs, Her Needs,* and *Love Busters,* advocates the policy of radical honesty, which involves being honest about the past; present honesty; emotional honesty; and future honesty.

2. Forgiveness must take place. A good description of forgiveness is that it's not an event but a journey. A tough journey, to be sure, and one that includes feeling and acknowledging the pain, and even the hatred, but pressing onward through it, until harmony is restored. The extent of forgiveness will need to match the depth of the injury. This can take time and will require patience and grace on the part of both the husband and wife.

Father, may Your grace and forgiveness give us the courage and the strength to rebuild our relationship. Please make us strong in all the weak places for the sake of our children and for Your honor and glory.

After Adultery

*"Israel, I will make you my wife forever. I will be honest and faithful to you.
I will show you my love and compassion. I will be true to you, my wife.
Then you will know the Lord." —Hosea 2:19, 20, GW*

In spite of the devastation that comes as a result of infidelity, God is still our Healer, and He longs to restore to us the things that are broken. But He does more than merely restore. He makes all things beautiful. A broken marriage can be turned into something of matchless beauty, reflecting the relationship He longs to have with His people.

Here are five more things that are needed to help restore a broken relationship.

1. Make a recommitment to God and to the marriage covenant. It can be a public or a private commitment, but it is important to do something to commemorate and celebrate a new beginning.
2. Trust must be rebuilt. Like with forgiveness, this may take time and will require patience. Trust is one of the foundational aspects of a healthy marriage and must be nurtured to full maturity.
3. Accountability. The spouse who sinned must rely on their spouse and others to serve as accountability partners; building an extra layer of protection around the marriage to protect against another fall.
4. Put a complete end to any relationship and connection with the outside party involved in the affair. This may mean changing jobs, moving, changing phone numbers, or giving the spouse all Internet passwords. Don't give even the smallest opportunity for sin to slip in again.
5. Focus on rebuilding the marriage. What was it that led one or both partners to seek a relationship outside of their marriage? Both husband and wife must become intentional in strengthening their marriage by drawing closer to the Lord, praying together daily, going to a marriage counselor who may help them discover the underlying problems in their marriage, attending marriage retreats and conferences, reading marriage and relationship books together, and discussing what they're learning and applying the principles to their relationship.

Don't lose hope. A good marriage is worth fighting for!

Dear Lord, we look to You, our hearts filled with hope. You are our Redeemer and Savior. Draw near, for we need You so much. Thank You for Your unfailing faithfulness. Thank You for teaching us how to be faithful.

Practice What You Preach

Therefore I run thus: not with uncertainty. Thus I fight: not as one who beats the air. But I discipline my body and bring it into subjection, lest, when I have preached to others, I myself should become disqualified.
—1 Corinthians 9:26, 27, NKJV

Paul lived with purpose and was certain he would reach his goal. It mattered to him that he lived what he preached. He set a high standard, Christlikeness, and depended on God to live out His love through him, "lest, when I have preached to others," he said, "I myself should become disqualified."

How does that apply to parenting? Our children depend on us to set the standard and to show it by our actions. Our words are important, but if they don't align with our actions, then they are wasted. Do we show our children by our actions that Jesus is our best Friend? Do our children see us spending time in God's Word? Do they hear us praying? Do they enjoy having family worship together?

When it comes to media, are we practicing the same principles that we want them to emulate? As they watch us flip through the channels on the television, choosing what to watch, do our actions reinforce what we tell them, about watching only those things that are good? They listen to the same music we do. Are we making good choices?

Are Sabbath mornings a delight in our homes or a time to dread? Our children witness our eagerness, or lack of enthusiasm, on Sabbath morning as we wake up and prepare to go to Sabbath School and church. Is Sabbath truly a happy day, or is it filled with "don'ts"? Do our children look forward to Sabbath? In essence, are we making the same choices that we're teaching our children to make?

The sermons we live will preach louder than our words. Do our actions match our words? Remember, what our mothers told us is true: actions really do speak louder than words. Yes, parents make mistakes too. But perhaps one of the best things we can model for our children is a willingness to admit when we have failed and to seek forgiveness from them and from God.

Lord, help me reflect You to my child. May my actions match my words, and when I fail, please help me to acknowledge that to You and to my children. You have entrusted me to show You to my children, and that is an awesome responsibility.

A Message to Parents

And these words, which I command thee this day, shall be in thine heart: and thou shalt teach them diligently unto thy children, and shalt talk of them when thou sittest in thine house, and when thou walkest by the way, and when thou liest down, and when thou risest up. —Deuteronomy 6:6, 7, KJV

Parents should be united in their faith, that they may be united in their efforts to bring their children up in the belief of the truth. Upon the mother in a special sense rests the work of molding the minds of the young children. . . . Business matters often keep the father much from home and prevent him from taking an equal share in the training of the children, but whenever he can, he should unite with the mother in this work. Let parents work unitedly, instilling into their children's hearts the principles of righteousness.

"There has been too little definite work done in preparing our children for the tests that all must meet in their contact with the world and its influences. They have not been helped as they should to form characters strong enough to resist temptation and stand firm for the principles of right, in the terrible issues before all who remain faithful to the commandments of God and the testimony of Jesus Christ.

"Parents need to understand the temptations that the youth must daily meet, that they may teach them how to overcome them. There are influences in the school and in the world that parents need to guard against. God wants us to turn our eyes from the vanities and pleasures and ambitions of the world, and set them on the glorious and immortal reward of those who run with patience the race set before them in the gospel. He wants us to educate our children to avoid the influences that would draw them away from Christ. The Lord is soon coming, and we must prepare for this solemn event. . . . Let your daily life in the home reveal the living principles of the Word of God. Heavenly agencies will cooperate with you as you seek to reach the standard of perfection and as you seek to teach your children how to conform their lives to the principles of righteousness" (*In Heavenly Places*, 208).

Heavenly Father, we ask that you send the Holy Spirit to teach us the deep things of God, with wisdom and discernment, that we may guide our children in safe paths.

No More War

They shall beat their swords into plowshares, and their spears into pruning hooks; nation shall not lift up sword against nation, neither shall they learn war anymore. —Micah 4:3, NKJV

Sometimes we look at this verse and apply it to sometime in the distant future. When we do that, we fail to realize that the application begins with each of us. When God establishes His kingdom on earth, He first establishes it in the heart of each of His children. It is when He abides in our hearts, minds, and in our lives, that the principles of justice and peace flow naturally from us to others.

The question is, Why do we think we must wait until the second coming of Jesus for this experience to take place in our lives, in our marriages, and in our families? In practical terms, how can we apply this concept to our homes and our families?

First, instead of looking for ways to show that we are right and others are wrong, we can bring our disagreements to God so He can bring conviction of wrongdoing to each of us. Sometimes conflict arises when a husband tries to show that the fault lies with his wife. It happens the other way around as well. But when we submit ourselves to God and allow Him to show us where we have erred, then we can ask Him to help us eliminate our judgmental attitude toward one another.

Secondly, while we don't have physical swords in our homes, at times our tongues can be sharper than any sword. We can use our words to cut each other down or build each other up. Allowing God to live in our hearts will help us to control our tongues so that we don't use them to hurt our loved ones.

Finally, there will be "no more war" in our marriages and families when God reigns in our hearts and we learn to deal with conflict in a constructive way. The goal is not to eliminate all conflict, because as individuals, we each have the right to feel and think differently. The goal is to manage conflict in a positive way, in a way that benefits the couple and the family.

Father God, come into our hearts today and establish the principles of Your kingdom there, so that Your justice will reign in our lives, and our words will build up and not tear down, and even our disagreements will become stepping-stones toward a stronger marriage.

With Whose God Do You Walk?

For all people walk each in the name of his god, but we will walk in the name of the Lord our God forever and ever. —Micah 4:5, NKJV

False gods were easier to recognize back in the day when they had strange-sounding names and were carved of wood or crafted from silver and gold. But false gods still abound today, and they carry very ordinary-sounding names. Here are a few examples: work, money, beauty, power, prestige, toys, and knowledge. It's easier than we think to become caught up in the pursuit of these gods and to teach our children to do the same.

Many parents sacrifice quality family time together by keeping their children in a never-ending whirl of activity. Wanting their kids to have the edge, the advantage, the fast start that will put them ahead of the other kids, life becomes a blur of soccer, karate, music lessons, dance, theater, cheerleading, and beauty contests. While parents believe they're enriching their children's lives, the children are often left exhausted at the end of each day, and as the weekend approaches, instead of rest and worship, another set of fun activities—camping, games, parties—keeps driving them forward. The frantic pace of their lives, the lack of downtime, the absence of family time leaves everyone depleted of energy for each other, much less for their time with God.

As parents the buck stops with us. We need to slow down and take time to reset our priorities. Are we spending time, quality time, alone with the Lord? Let us establish a personal connection with God. Following that, let's set time aside to seek the Lord as a couple, and from there, spend time as a family together with God. If we think we're too busy to do this, then we're just too busy, and will most likely need to ask the Lord to help us realign our priorities.

This is how Eugene Peterson paraphrases Micah 4:5 in *The Message*: "Meanwhile, all the other people live however they wish, picking and choosing their gods. But we live honoring God, and we're loyal to our God forever and ever." Teach us to live this, Lord!

Father God, help us to maintain a personal daily connection with You, as well as couple and family time with each other and with You. Bless us and keep us as the gods of this world call our attention away from You. May we walk with You alone.

Choose to Agree

"Can two walk together, unless they are agreed?"
—Amos 3:3, NKJV

In the history of God's people, false prophets freely gave counsel and assured kings and people alike that the words were straight from Jehovah. God did not always intervene to save His children. There were times they had to deal with the consequences of their choices. Exile and captivity were often the bitter fruits that resulted from listening to those who did not walk with the Lord.

God's faithful messengers continued to call and lead the people back to God. Though the message of God's true prophets was not always popular or gladly accepted, Amos 3:1–8 shows that God and His prophets were in agreement, and it was God who gave the messages for His people. Incredibly, sixty-six books authored by some forty prophets, written over a period of fourteen hundred years yet containing a common theme and harmony, clearly shows God was the One inspiring all of His prophets.

Marriage counselors say that couples preparing for marriage need to have agreement on at least four major areas: religion, in-law relations, parenting, and finances. The idea that love is all you need and that love will overlook any differences or difficulties may be a romantic way of looking at things, but it can grow old very quickly. Any couple hoping to establish a strong foundation for a lifetime of living together will soon find out that romantic love is not enough to hold a marriage together. It's like the frosting on a wedding cake, sweet and lovely, but it doesn't replace the cake. Neither can it replace the nuts and bolts of a dynamic relationship in which each has learned to work through challenges together.

While some argue that opposites attract, and there is some truth to that, it is also true that the disagreements that come about from being opposites can ultimately undo a relationship. Her habit of being late may at first seem like a cute eccentricity, but after a while it can begin to irritate and then infuriate her husband. His habit of leaving his shoes and socks in the middle of the room may go almost unnoticed in the beginning, until she trips over them a couple times and eventually starts to fling them at him.

While two people should not agree on everything, it is important to learn to come to agreement on the things that matter.

Father God, bless me and my (future) spouse that we may treasure those things we have in common, especially our faith in You.

Seek God and Live

*For thus says the L*ORD *to the house of Israel: "Seek Me and live."*
—Amos 5:4, NKJV

In my homeland of Colombia, in the capital city of Bogotá, there is a mountain above the city. It is called Monserrate and is part of the Andes mountain range. On top of the mountain is a cathedral built in honor of the lord of Monserrate. The story goes that the lord of Monserrate will perform miracles and answer the prayers of those who make a pilgrimage to the top of the mountain. Each day people can be seen crawling on their hands and knees to the top of the mountain. They arrive some twenty-five hundred feet above the city, bloodied, scraped, and exhausted, desperately hoping their suffering will move the heart of the lord to respond to their pleas for help. What extraordinary lengths people will go to, yet they neglect the simple gospel message that invites, "Seek Me and live."

Jesus makes it clear that all God requires is for people to humble themselves and come to Him and they will find rest (see Matthew 11:28). While we would never think of climbing a mountain on our hands and knees to get God's attention, there is still a warning for us in this story. Don't allow the acts of worship, church attendance and activities, the busyness associated with being a Christian to ever be a substitute for simply seeking and following Jesus.

Many of us are "cultural" Christians. We grew up in the faith, and it is the only thing we know. Doing all the things mentioned above can so easily become second nature. We can do them without even thinking about the reasons why we are doing them. But God is not impressed with anything, no matter how good it is, that doesn't flow from a heart grounded in love for Him. There are no extra points awarded for bloodied hands and knees.

It's so much better to just do what Jesus asks of us! So let us seek God and live. Seek God and have life abundant. Seek God and remember that marriage, our marriage, was given as a reflection of God's relationship with His people. Seek God and lead your children to seek Him too. Seek God and share Him with others. Seek God and live!

Father God, thank You for Your patience with us. Thank You for desiring more than the outward forms that come so naturally when we're being simply religious. You desire a personal relationship with us. May we seek You—and live!

Learn From Others

For whatever things were written before were written for our learning, that we through the patience and comfort of the Scriptures might have hope.
—Romans 15:4, NKJV

Paul tells us that the Old Testament was written to teach us and to give us hope. He reminds us that God's Word is as relevant to us today as it was when first written. In the devotional *Conflict and Courage*, Ellen White writes, "The lives recorded in the Bible are authentic histories of actual individuals. From Adam down through successive generations to the times of the apostles we have a plain, unvarnished account of what actually occurred and the genuine experience of real characters" (*Conflict and Courage*, 7).

Life can be hard at times. One encouraging aspect of the Bible is that in its pages we find stories of people who've also gone through hard times. Their experiences may not alleviate our own pain, but knowing others have faced similar challenges reminds us that we are not alone. Adam and Even lost one son at the hands of another. David's son, Absalom, rebelled against his father, dethroned him, and even persecuted him. We read of friends betraying friends, spouses lying to each other or committing adultery, and many more examples of humanity gone wrong.

"Men whom God favored, and to whom He entrusted great responsibilities, were sometimes overcome by temptation and committed sins, even as we of the present day strive, waver, and frequently fall into error. But it is encouraging to desponding hearts to know that through God's grace they could gain fresh vigor to again rise above their evil natures; and, remembering this, we are ready to renew the conflict ourselves" (ibid.).

As dark as those passages are, it brings comfort to know that God does not forsake His children. We are not left to struggle alone. We can find encouragement in knowing that God still loves us in spite of our failures and is willing and able to help us when we fall and fail and to give us the strength to carry on.

Father God, as we study Your Word daily, may we find help and inspiration from the stories of old, and help us to learn from the lives of Your children that our own lives, our marriages, and our families can be victorious!

Just Say "No"

So Moses' father-in-law said to him, "The thing that you do is not good. Both you and these people who are with you will surely wear yourselves out. For this thing is too much for you; you are not able to perform it by yourself."
—Exodus 18:17, 18, NKJV

Moses' father-in-law was a wise man who had sound counsel for his son-in-law. As he watched Moses going to work every day as the sole judge over all the tribes of Israel, he saw what Moses was too busy to see. The number of people demanding his time was so great that even though he worked from dawn until dusk, he wasn't making a dent in his workload. Jethro immediately recognized that Moses was a man who had not learned how to say "No" to requests for his time. His recommendation? He suggested Moses focus on only two things—representing the people before God, and handling only the most difficult of the disputes. The rest of the work could be delegated to capable men he appointed.

Moses listened, delegated, and discovered something amazing. He was able to accomplish more than ever before, and he was doing it in much less time. By narrowing his focus and doing only that which he was called to do, Moses grew in his effectiveness as a leader. If this advice worked for Moses, can it work for us?

In order to fulfill our God-given responsibilities, we must learn to set appropriate boundaries. As parents, we are responsible for setting limits for ourselves so we have time for doing what God calls us to do—being the primary disciple-maker for our children. If you are too busy to spend quality time with your children, it's time to take a moment to review your to-do list. What actions do you need to take to ensure that your career or anything else does not push your children to the end of your priority list? Moses had resources all around him that he was not utilizing. He was trying to be everything to everyone. Are there resources that you can take better advantage of? Are there ways that you can work smarter instead of harder? It's time to take inventory and consider the same counsel that was given to Moses long ago. After all, Jethro's wise counsel is timeless.

Lord, what are my priorities today? Show me what to delegate, what can wait, and what it is You would have me accomplish on this day.

The gift of companionship

Two are better than one, because they have a good reward for their labor. For if they fall, one will lift up his companion. But woe to him who is alone when he falls, for he has no one to help him up. Again, if two lie down together, they will keep warm; but how can one be warm alone? —Ecclesiastes 4:9–11, NKJV

Former Secretary-General of the United Nations Dag Hammarskjöld once wrote, "What makes loneliness an anguish is not that I have no one to share my burden, but this: I have only my own burden to bear." And an ancient Jewish proverb says, "A friendless man is like a left hand bereft of the right." We were created for relationship. Life is something to be shared with a friend.

Solomon speaks of the warmth of human relationships. His picture is very practical, and while it can obviously be a reference to marriage, it must also be noted that in those days travelers often slept together on cold nights. It was not only a practical way to keep warm, it was a necessity. Traveling with a companion also served as protection from the dangers on the road as we see in Jesus' story of the good Samaritan.

Traveling through life with a good life companion and friends is important for many reasons. George Eliot described a best friend as a "well-spring in the wilderness." God designed that man should not be alone and thus created an equal companion for Adam. One of the greatest blessings of marriage is the companionship, and the friendship, two people can offer each other. But friendship is equally important to us whether we're single or married, and seeking such company is a benefit not only for ourselves but also brings joy and meaning to others.

Two are better than one, for if one falls he has a friend to lift him up—and how often we need someone to walk beside us and pick us up when we fall. An encouraging word, a smile, sometimes a good, old-fashioned bear hug can make all the difference when we're feeling low. And the wonderful thing about friendship is that we can be there for our friend when they're the one needing a hug. Solomon teaches us the value of true friendship and the importance of treasuring our friends!

Father God, thank You for the gift of friendship and companionship. Bless us with that true friend in our lives, and may we bless others with our friendship.

I Am Very Content

Actually, I don't have a sense of needing anything personally. I've learned by now to be quite content whatever my circumstances.
—Philippians 4:11, The Message

I recently rode in a taxi in my homeland of Colombia, South America. As we stopped at the first red light, a woman stood beside another taxi, yelling at a man inside the vehicle. My driver commented, "The things that alcohol will make people do. I've never had a drink in my life." Since it was only 8:00 a.m., I was curious what made him conclude that the passengers of the other taxi were drunk. The light changed and I asked him why he'd never had alcohol. I'm not sure what answer I expected, but certainly not the one he gave me. The rest of the journey was spent listening to his very sad life story.

He began by describing his family as "very strange." He was one of thirteen siblings. His father was a police officer who never allowed any of them to play outside as children. He was kicked out of school unjustly for something done by another student. As an adult he was fired twice from companies without being given a reason. He married and had children, but his wife divorced him, and now neither his wife nor children speak to him. His siblings have a combined total of twenty university degrees including several medical degrees. Most of them never married. They don't speak to one another, and none of them know where he lives. His closing words, as he dropped me off, were, "Since my youth I have often thought of suicide. Most days I really don't care if I live or die."

I am rarely speechless, but my heart was so broken for this man that I could not find words to say. If he didn't need to keep working his taxi, I might have asked him to stop so we could talk more, but he needed to stay on the clock.

His story made me realize how blessed I am. But am I content in *all* things? Paul was in jail but could joyfully declare that he was content! Regardless of our circumstances, Jesus offers to live within us, and that is the source of our contentment.

Father God, help us to appreciate the goodness with which our lives are filled. Help us to truly appreciate the abundance that is ours. And perhaps more important, help us to be content whatever situation we find ourselves facing.

How to Know What to Pray

Likewise the Spirit also helps in our weaknesses. For we do not know what we should pray for as we ought, but the Spirit Himself makes intercession for us with groanings which cannot be uttered. —Romans 8:26, NKJV

Jews often pray with their eyes open and their faces turned upward, their bodies turned toward Jerusalem. Muslims pray five times each day, facing Mecca, with their heads to the ground. People in other faith traditions burn incense, beat drums, and perform many other acts as part of their prayer rituals. Christians of different faiths will recite prayers, close their eyes, clasp their hands, stand or kneel, all as part of their prayer traditions.

Paul is more concerned about the content of our prayers than our posture. He recognizes how very limited our prayers are because of our weakened, selfish natures, and so he encourages us by reminding us that God still hears our prayers because the Holy Spirit takes them and utters them on our behalf.

Often we petition God for something important to us. We forget Paul's words that we *don't* know what to pray for. We pray for healing for our loved ones facing chronic illness or even death. As a hospice chaplain, I worked with patients who had no hope of recovery but listened as their loved ones continued to pray for a miracle that would keep them alive. While it's normal to want our loved ones to live as long as possible, is it what's best for them?

The Jewish people teach that some prayers should never be uttered. For instance, if you're driving home and you see that a house is on fire, you should not pray, "God, please don't let it be mine." Such a prayer is equal to saying, "God, please make sure it's someone else's home that's on fire."

Today's text assures us that in spite of our poorly phrased prayers, and the spirit which sometimes accompanies them, the Holy Spirit still speaks on our behalf, praying for us with an agony that we ourselves rarely experience. He filters them and strengthens them through His own pleading on our behalf. So don't stop praying for your spouse, your family and friends, and for others, and let the Spirit do His work on our behalf.

Father God, thank You that we have not only an Intercessor in Jesus but an Interpreter in the Holy Spirit. Thank You for the assurance that You hear us and that You answer us in our need.

Man the Fort!

He who scatters has come up before your face. Man the fort! Watch the road!
Strengthen your flanks! Fortify your power mightily.
—Nahum 2:1, NKJV

Our marriages and families are under attack from many directions. Society tries to tell us that divorce is a good option when our relationship no longer makes us happy. Politically, marriage is under attack by those who believe people of the same gender should have the right to be married. Some social scientists believe living together before marriage is good, in spite of evidence that shows many problems springing from this lifestyle.

Nahum's words seem to place the responsibility for fighting to protect the city/family on the men. "Man the fort!" writes Nahum. As husbands, we must "man the home"! We cannot sit back passively while so many forces threaten to destroy it. We must assume the responsibility for the health and well-being of our wives and children. This means we must assume and practice our role as the priest of the home by initiating the family morning and evening devotions. Nothing should take the place of these divine appointments.

"Watch the road!" The study of the Scriptures, particularly the prophetic passages, should tell us as husbands what is approaching so we can make proper preparation for those events. Personal preparation can't be done by anybody else or relegated to others.

"Strengthen your flanks!" Look to see what may be causing our marriage or family to experience weakness. Is the programing on TV leading us closer to each other or further apart? Is the Internet, and what it brings into the home and into our lives, helping us or hurting us? What controls should be applied to the access we or our children have to all this technology?

"Fortify your power mightily." All we have to do is to watch the commercials on TV that show men as weak, foolish, unreliable, and dumb. These are the images young boys are growing up with. As men, we need to portray men as being strong, smart, driven, committed to God and to their wives and their families, decisive, passionate, and compassionate.

Nahum's challenge to Nineveh, facing the attack of the enemy, is our challenge as men today, when our homes and families face even more fierce attacks. Man the fort!

Father, help us to be the type of men You created us to be, in Your image: strong, courageous, wise, compassionate, and committed to You as well as to our wives and to our families.

I'm Responsible for Me!

So then each of us shall give account of himself to God. Therefore let us not judge one another anymore, but rather resolve this, not to put a stumbling block or a cause to fall in our brother's way. —Romans 14:12, 13, NKJV

Paul tells us in Romans 14:10 that we will all have to appear before God's judgment court. Back in the Greco-Roman world, it was common for officials like Pilate to make known their judgments from a *bema* or rostrum. When Paul speaks of God judging all people before His throne, Paul was using a common image that the Jewish mind could easily grasp. His counsel for us to "not judge one another" is important. What does this look like in the context of marriage?

Since there is only one perfect Person, Jesus, that makes it impossible for anyone to find a perfect person to marry. In the same way, it is impossible for us to be a perfect match for someone else. And yet it is all too human for us to start finding fault in our spouse. Ironically, we typically imagine that they're the only one with faults—like seeing a speck in someone else while ignoring the log in our own eye. That's why Paul's counsel should be of particular interest to us, because we will all have to give account of ourselves. Here are a few things we should keep in mind:

1. We will have to give an account of *ourselves,* not our spouse, so we should focus on the changes we need to make.
2. We are not the judge—God is—and He does not need for us, nor does He give us the right, to judge others.
3. When we judge others, rather than helping them, we become a stumbling block and prevent them from growing in the image of Christ.

Instead of judging others, let's find ways to help each other to imitate Christ and thus become more like Him. Judging my spouse will only make me less satisfied with them and bring unhappiness into the home. On the other hand, if I help my spouse to be more like Christ, in reality I am helping myself have the best spouse possible, and we will both be happier with the person He's given us to be our helpmeet.

Dear Lord, please help me to be less judgmental of others, particularly my spouse, and instead may I give them the love and support they need to become more like Jesus Christ.

Mercy in Marriage

*"For I desire mercy and not sacrifice, and the knowledge of God
more than burnt offerings."—Hosea 6:6, NKJV*

This is one of the best known, most often quoted passages of the Old
Testament. The word *mercy* is the same word translated as "love" or
"faithfulness." It describes the steadfast love shown by God in His covenant
with Israel. In place of burnt offerings, He would prefer a genuine, deep,
personal relationship with Him.

A marriage relationship that follows God's pattern of steadfast love should
be one in which love, faithfulness, and mercy are foundational. Let's look
first of all at *love*. Genuine love is the giving of oneself completely to another
person, with an unselfish devotion that seeks the best for the other person.
Secondly, *faithfulness* is the commitment to not betray the other person's
trust and to remain with them regardless of the difficulty or the number of
challenges that come our way. And finally, *mercy* is accepting the faults of the
other person, knowing that, like us, they are not perfect, yet we are perfect
for each other.

Our relationship with God is reflected in our relationship with one another. His desire is that we draw close to Him, that we love Him, that we
remain faithful to Him, because the result of such a relationship is that we'll
be more loving toward one another, faithful in our relationship with one
another, and that we will extend mercy to one another. To most of us, it
is more natural to be judgmental of others while excusing ourselves. God's
order of things encourages us to look at ourselves before we look at the faults
of others and to be merciful with others as God has been merciful with us.

It is well for us to remember what Jesus said: "Judge not, that you be not
judged. For with what judgment you judge, you will be judged; and with the
measure you use, it will be measured back to you. And why do you look at
the speck in your brother's eye, but do not consider the plank in your own
eye? Or how can you say to your brother, 'Let me remove the speck from
your eye'; and look, a plank is in your own eye? Hypocrite! First remove the
plank from your own eye, and then you will see clearly to remove the speck
from your brother's eye" (Matthew 7:1–5, NKJV).

*Father, please help me to be less judgmental of others and to be more merci-
ful, especially with those closest to me.*

Healing Words

"But I would strengthen you with my mouth, and the comfort of my lips would relieve your grief."—Job 16:5, NKJV

Job had lost all of his property, but what hurt him most was the loss of his children. Ultimately, he was struck with a dreadful skin disease and stung with discouraging words from his own wife. To add insult to injury, his friends, who'd supposedly come to encourage him, spent most of their time hurling accusations and calling on him to repent.

The text above is Job's response to Eliphaz's so-called consolations. Job longed for words that would strengthen him, words spoken from the heart with love. He was hungry for words that would bring true comfort and consolation.

I know that for the most part, people have good intentions when trying to encourage their friends. Still, I have heard people say things at funerals or to bereaved families that make me cringe. Probably the most commonly used words are, "I know just how you feel." Although they may have experienced a similar heartbreak, the reality is that no one can possibly know what we're feeling because pain is a very personal experience.

Have you heard someone say to a parent whose child has died, "Well, at least you have other children"? Or, "You're still young! You can have more children"? Or have your heard someone tell a person whose relationship has ended, "There are plenty more fish in the ocean"? Oh, how we need to weigh our words and think twice before speaking. Our careless words, intended to bring consolation, often do more harm than we possibly realize.

When dealing with people who have experienced great loss, it's good for us to remember that simply being with them in their pain is often more helpful than any words we may say. Later, after the funeral, when visiting those who are still going through the grieving process, another gift we can give them is to let them talk about their loved one. In fact, encouraging them to speak and share their favorite memories, to use the name of the one who's died, is extremely comforting. Too soon they are left to grieve alone. It is at these times that our presence and love in encouraging them to express their feelings and to talk about their loved ones can become one of the most helpful tools for healing.

Father, help us to become instruments of healing through our presence and through our heartfelt words.

The Wise Listen

Let the wise listen and add to their learning,
and let the discerning get guidance.
—Proverbs 1:5, NIV

Many years ago I read a book titled *The Lost Art of Listening*. It may seem strange that someone would write a book about listening when it is such a basic skill. One person talks—the other listens. The truth is, it's so basic that we take it for granted. Unfortunately, most of us think of ourselves as better listeners than we actually are. Why do we so often fail to connect when speaking with others? One reason is that we're often so busy thinking of our response to what's being said that we are not really listening to the one who is speaking.

The writer of the book of Proverbs reminds us that "the wise listen and add to their learning." We actually become wiser by listening, much more so than by talking. When we listen to try and understand the message the other person is trying to convey, we will have a better chance of actually hearing the message correctly. Someone wrote, "We hear only half of what is said to us, understand only half of that, believe only half of that, and remember only half of that." No wonder we have such difficulty communicating with others.

How can we become more effective listeners? Let us start by determining to listen, truly listen, not only to what is being said but also to the emotions behind what's being said. Pay attention to the feelings conveyed. Then, instead of trying to interpret what we think we heard, repeat their words back to them and ask if you heard what they meant to say. Very often, the acknowledgment of those feelings and repeating back what you heard can burst the doors wide open to better communication.

Pray for discernment to hear the words that are not being said. Sometimes, what remains unspoken lies at the heart of what a person is trying to say. It could be that they are waiting to see if they can trust us enough to share at a deeper level. If we're only giving them half of our attention, they'll get the message that they're not that important to us. Miscommunication happens too easily. Let's be careful to listen, slow to speak, and quick to learn.

Father, helps us to use our ears, our minds, and our hearts more often than we use our mouths so that we may hear, listen, and understand what our loved ones are trying to tell us.

The Tongue That Cuts or Heals

There is one who speaks like the piercings of a sword,
but the tongue of the wise promotes health.
—Proverbs 12:18, NKJV

We've probably all experienced piercing words being spoken. It's not a pleasant experience. Those who speak "like the piercings of a sword" speak hastily and in a reckless manner. The opposite is the tongue of the wise who uses soothing and gentle language.

The Seventh-day Adventist Bible Commentary explains, "The simile is particularly striking in Hebrew, since the edge of a sword is called its mouth. The hasty, impatient mouth speaks words that wound the hearts of friends and lead to great suffering and sorrow. Tactless words often prick the tender hearts of those who mourn or are in difficulty, but the wise man knows what to say to comfort the sorrowing, soothe the angry, and cheer the despondent [see Proverbs 10:11]" (3:989).

The words we use either encourage or discourage, they can heal or hurt, they can restore hope or destroy life. Ellen White wrote, "The voice and tongue are gifts from God, and if rightly used, they are a power for God. Words mean very much. They may express love, devotion, praise, melody to God, or hatred and revenge. Words reveal the sentiments of the heart. They may be a savor of life unto life or of death unto death. The tongue is a world of blessing, or a world of iniquity" (Manuscript 40, December 31, 1896).

Let's make a special effort to eliminate from our speech words that tear down or criticize or wound the other person. Instead, let's begin a new habit of using positive, encouraging words, words that build up and bring encouragement and cheer. Instead of catching others when they're doing something bad and wounding them with our words, let's catch them doing what is good, and express our appreciation for those things. That's an effective way to reinforce good behavior.

Express appreciation for even the smallest actions or words of others. Tell your wife you appreciate the meal she prepared for you, or how well she keeps the house. Compliment her for the way she looks and how she takes care of herself, of your children, and of you. Thank your husband for mowing the lawn, for keeping the cars in good working condition, or for painting the house. Each of those words can be like healing balm for your relationship.

Father, helps us to use our words to strengthen, encourage, and build up those around us.

March

Training for Service

As thou hast sent me into the world, even so have I also sent them into the world.
—John 17:18, KJV

Every son and daughter of God is called to be a missionary; we are called to the service of God and our fellow men; and to fit us for this service should be the object of our education.

"This object should ever be kept in view by Christian parents and teachers. We know not in what line our children may serve. They may spend their lives within the circle of the home; they may engage in life's common vocations, or go as teachers of the gospel to heathen lands; but all are alike called to be missionaries for God, ministers of mercy to the world.

"The children and youth, with their fresh talent, energy, and courage, their quick susceptibilities, are loved of God, and He desires to bring them into harmony with divine agencies. They are to obtain an education that will help them to stand by the side of Christ in unselfish service. . . .

"Our children stand, as it were, at the parting of the ways. On every hand the world's enticements to self-seeking and self-indulgence call them away from the path cast up for the ransomed of the Lord. Whether their lives shall be a blessing or a curse depends upon the choice they make. . . .

"God's word does not repress activity, but guides it aright. God does not bid the youth to be less aspiring. The elements of character that make a man truly successful and honored among men—the irrepressible desire for some greater good, the indomitable will, the strenuous application, the untiring perseverance—are not to be discouraged. By the grace of God they are to be directed to the attainment of objects as much higher than mere selfish and worldly interests as the heavens are higher than the earth.

"With us as parents and as Christians it rests to give our children right direction. They are to be carefully, wisely, tenderly guided into paths of Christlike ministry. We are under sacred covenant with God to rear our children for His service. To surround them with such influences as shall lead them to choose a life of service, and to give them the training needed, is our first duty" (*The Ministry of Healing*, 395, 396).

Dear Lord, keep us from losing sight of the fact that You have called us to make You known. Grant us a heart that finds fulfillment in serving You.

Love Covers All

*Most important of all, continue to show deep love for each other,
for love covers a multitude of sins. —1 Peter 4:8, NLT*

Shaunti Feldhahn, in her book *The Surprising Secrets of Highly Happy Marriages,* writes about the power of a positive, loving attitude that happy couples have toward their relationship and toward their spouse. "Highly happy spouses choose to believe their mate cares for them—no matter what they're seeing from their spouse or feeling at the time—and they act accordingly." She adds, "It turns out that positive changes in a marriage rarely depend on one difficult spouse suddenly becoming an altogether different person. Usually, the opposite is true. Change—even in challenging marriages—most often starts with one immediate, practical, and surprising choice. A choice made by just one partner. And you can make it. The day you put one surprising secret to work in your relationship—and then another— may go unnoticed by your partner. But you have launched an insurrection against mediocrity and unhappiness."

Feldhahn's research, which is supported extensively in the area of cognitive behavioral psychology, reveals that when we choose to love our spouse and we show it through word and action, our thinking toward them changes. As our thinking changes, eventually our feelings will change as well. It begins with the thoughts on which we allow ourselves to dwell.

What does this mean? God is not asking us to wait until we *feel* loving toward our spouse. He wants us to *act* lovingly in spite of what we may be feeling at the moment. While it may be tempting to wait for our partner to change and become more loving before we respond to them lovingly, what God says and challenges us to do is that we should be the ones to take that first step. This may require some time and patience on our part. A sense of humor can also be helpful. And when we act lovingly, then often wonderful and surprising things can happen.

Peter counsels us to "continue to show deep love for each other." This is a love that does not needlessly expose the weaknesses or sins of the one we love, a love that protects the reputation and good name of our spouse even as we would like for them to protect our name and honor.

Father God, help us to act lovingly even when we don't feel it. May Your love permeate our lives and our relationships so that it will cover us and bless us with a better future.

Finish What You Start

So finish what you began to do. Then your willingness will be
matched by what you accomplish. —2 Corinthians 8:11, GW

Like all sports, Formula 1 Grand Prix racing has very specific rules that must be strictly adhered. Thirty minutes before the race begins, drivers are free to complete a reconnaissance lap of the circuit before taking up their grid positions. If a driver wishes to complete additional reconnaissance laps, he must pass through the pit lane each time in order to bypass the grid. The pit lane closes fifteen minutes prior to the formation lap. Drivers still in the pit lane at this time are required to start the race from there.

Ten minutes before the start, the grid must be cleared except for team technical staff, race officials, and drivers. With three minutes to go, all cars must have their wheels fitted. Any car not complying will receive a ten-second time penalty. With a minute to go, all cars must have their engines running. All personnel must leave the grid at least fifteen seconds before the green lights come on that signal the start of the formation lap.

All these rules, and several more, are there to ensure the safety of the drivers and their team, but also to ensure that the race will start correctly and fairly for all the participants. Of course, even when everything goes just right, every race is different, depending on the weather conditions, the men driving those powerful machines, the condition of each car, the support team that changes the tires and fills the gas tank at every pit stop, and other variables. In the end, the team that works best will prove to be the winner. The champion is not just the driver who crosses the finish line in first place; it is the entire team that helped him or her get there.

Marriage and family life is a team sport. It is what we do together to ensure we are all winners that will help us to achieve the goals we set for ourselves. It is not only how we begin this race we call family life that's important, but that we stay the course and cross the finish line together. Keeping the end in mind will help us reach those goals and realize Paul's advice to "finish what you began to do."

Father God, thank You for our families. Help us to finish the race together, and receive the trophy of eternal life from Your hand when we cross the finish line.

All Things New

*Now I saw a new heaven and a new earth, for the first heaven and the first earth
had passed away. Also there was no more sea. Then I, John, saw the holy city,
New Jerusalem, coming down out of heaven from God, prepared as a bride
adorned for her husband. And I heard a loud voice from heaven saying, "Behold,
the tabernacle of God is with men, and He will dwell with them, and they shall
be His people. God Himself will be with them and be their God. And God will
wipe away every tear from their eyes; there shall be no more death, nor sorrow,
nor crying. There shall be no more pain, for the former things have passed away."
Then He who sat on the throne said, "Behold, I make all things new."
—Revelation 21:1–5, NKJV*

These words from the apostle John are filled with such promise. They
remind us that this world, with all its challenges, is temporary and will
not last forever. The promise of a land where there are no tears, no pain, no
death, where all things will be made new, gives us hope as we deal with life's
trials here on earth.

There will be an end to the pain that makes our hearts ache as we watch
our children struggle in school, or when they grapple with being betrayed by
a friend. Those parents whose children have physical or mental challenges
will watch with awe as their young ones run and play on streets of gold. For
parents who've known the indescribable heartbreak of having lost a child to
death, who can imagine the joy at being reunited? I wonder if Jesus, looking
down through time, thought of that as He raised Jairus's little girl back to
life? What joy it must have been for Him to give those parents a foretaste of
heaven. Oh, just imagine the family reunions that await us in heaven!

But until that time we must keep our eyes fixed toward heaven. Though
He tarries, He will not forever delay His coming. And one day soon, perhaps
sooner than we can imagine, He will make all things new!

*Dear Lord, keep my eyes looking up and focused on You. I look forward to
that day in heaven when all will be made new. My tears will be dried by Your
loving hand and my night will be turned into an eternal day. Thank You for the
heavenly home that is waiting for me.*

Keep Me From Stumbling

Now to Him who is able to keep you from stumbling, and to present you faultless before the presence of His glory with exceeding joy, to God our Savior, who alone is wise, be glory and majesty, dominion and power, both now and forever. Amen.
—Jude 1:24, 25, NKJV

Have you ever felt at your wit's end? Frustrated beyond belief by your inability to do the thing you know you should do. The thing you honestly *want* to do. But you've messed up yet again! Take heart because help is promised. When you have reached the brink, ask for His help. Ask that He will stand by you and keep you from falling, giving you the ability to respond in a manner that would glorify His name.

We have all been guilty of doing the opposite. Our tempers often get the best of us, and even as the words are exiting our mouths we experience regret. The good news in those times is to remember that God is there to help us get up again. With His help we can keep walking forward and lean on Him to prevent us from stumbling again. When you have stumbled, don't be too hard on yourself. Ask God to forgive you and ask your spouse or children to do the same.

As difficult and humbling as they can be, these times of stumbling can be opportunities to give powerful spiritual lessons to our children of God's forgiveness and of His willingness to keep us from falling again. Seeing God at work in the lives of their parents provides an incredibly powerful example for our children. They get to see Christianity in real life. Let's face it, life can get real messy, and when we show our children what it looks like to be a Christian in those situations—in real life—we show them that they can depend on Jesus just like Mom and Dad.

Jude directs us to focus our thoughts on "Him who is able." That's another way of saying, "Trust in the One who has the power to keep you from falling," our best Friend, Jesus. Don't ever forget that in our struggles we are not alone. We have a promised partnership with God. Claim that promise today and walk with your hand firmly held in His—for He is the only One who can keep you from falling.

Dear Lord, keep me from stumbling today. Give me patience and help me to endure. Show me a better way. Your way, Lord.

Ministry Begins at Home

For this reason I left you in Crete, that you should set in order the things that are lacking, and appoint elders in every city as I commanded you—if a man is blameless, the husband of one wife, having faithful children not accused of dissipation or insubordination. —Titus 1:5, 6, NKJV

It is interesting to note that Paul, in writing to Titus, states that the qualifications for deacons and elders in the early church begin on the home front. Paul did not make a high standing in the community or elevated position on the career ladder as a qualifier. Instead, of far greater importance was what was happening behind the closed doors of the home. What were the relationships like within the home walls? What words described the husband/wife relationship? Were the children expected to be obedient? Was the home a faithful witness of Jesus to others?

I wonder if we have failed to realize that our homes are indeed major centers of evangelism. And, what happens outside the church and in our homes often speaks louder of Jesus than what happens behind the pulpit. Others are watching us. They see our interactions with family members in the grocery store, at the gas station, and in restaurants. They notice as our family takes the time to hold hands, bow heads, and say a prayer of thanksgiving in the restaurant. They see the husband open the car door for his wife in the parking lot. And, they hear the tone of our voices as we speak to our little ones.

Does this mean we have to show that we're a perfect family? No! For there is no such thing as a perfect family. But a happy family that shows respect to one another and a genuine happiness in being together—that should happen naturally when we make Jesus first and as we teach our children to do the same.

What message are we telling the world through our families? Would our homes stand up to this test? Do your neighbors know that Jesus is the center of your home? Jesus should not be a hidden guest in our homes. He should have a place of honor. He should be invited to go with our families wherever we go. Others should see Him as we reflect Him in our homes and family interactions.

Dear Lord, may my home be an evangelistic center. May my neighbors, friends, and family members see You. May my home testify of Your mercy, Your love, Your forgiveness, and Your grace.

I Need to See You

Hear my prayer, O Lord, and let my cry come to You. Do not hide Your face from me in the day of my trouble; incline Your ear to me; in the day that I call, answer me speedily. For my days are consumed like smoke, and my bones are burned like a hearth.... This will be written for the generation to come, that a people yet to be created may praise the Lord. —Psalm 102:1–3, 18, NKJV

A mud slide devastates a community, destroying homes and killing scores of people. An airliner crashes, killing all on board and leaving hundreds of families to grieve their loss. A child is diagnosed with terminal cancer and her life ends almost before it's really begun. Three firefighters die while fighting an apartment fire in a large city. A building collapses and kills most of its residents. Five soldiers are killed by a road-side bomb.

We read, hear, or see stories like these almost every day in the news. In fact, we hear them so often that they have begun to lose their impact. It's as if we're becoming immunized to the bad news a little at a time until it happens to us or to someone we know personally. It's one thing to hear of a plane crash, but quite another thing to know one of the passengers. It's one thing to hear of a police officer killed while on duty, but it's another thing to have known him personally and to attend his funeral and see a widow's tears. It's one thing to hear of the young cancer victim, but it's another thing to be her pastor, her parents, or her grandparents.

For any one of us experiencing deep pain and sorrow, David's words become ours. While we're going through the darkest moments in our lives, it can sometimes feel as though God were not there. We cry out, "God, please, don't hide from me in my pain!" But the psalmist's words are also very encouraging. God is not hiding His face from us in our pain and sorrow. On the contrary, His face shines in our times of darkness, His warmth surrounds us when we feel alone, and at the end we will sing His praises.

Father God, thank You for always being next to us in our pain and sorrow. We trust You, and we trust that one day we will be able to praise Your name and tell others of Your love and faithfulness during our darkest hours.

No More Fix-It Lists for God

I thank my God always, making mention of you in my prayers.
—Philemon 1:4, NASB

If I were to ask, "Do you see your child as a gift from God?" I've no doubt you would tell me that your child is one of the greatest treasures you have ever known. I don't doubt it. And yet I wonder, if we were to take inventory on our words and on the messages we communicate to our children, what do they hear? Is it possible for us to love our children while failing to let them know how much we love them?

As parents we feel responsible for training up our children. That's a good thing. But it's possible for us to end up focusing too much on the things that need fixing in their lives. Complaining and griping is one of Satan's tactics that we use and, unfortunately, it can infect all our interactions with our family. Do you often find yourself speaking negatively about your child? It is easy for our daily prayers to sound like a fix-it list. That list becomes long as we spend prayer time asking God to fix our children and our spouse.

We gladly hand to God His to-do list every day. And as our prayers ascend to the heavenly throne, they sound something like this: "Lord, fix John's grumbling, make Katie quit fighting with her little sister. Help Michael to stop being such a slacker, may he study harder and make better grades. And please, please, Lord, let Susie start sleeping through the night. Every night!"

When was the last time that we devoted prayer time exclusively to thanking God for each member of our family? Mention them by name and thank God for specific things about each one. And, don't forget to tell them too. Knowing that you have been a praise on someone's prayer list can be a powerful blessing. By focusing on the positives, our daily fix-it lists can become times of thanksgiving and praise. "Lord, thank You for John's ability to see things that need changing, thank You that little Katie can stand up for herself when she sees injustice, thank You that Michael enjoys being out in Your creation, and thank You for little Susie's energy."

Dear Lord, thank You for my children. Thank You for the awesome privilege of being their parent. Thank You for the gifts You've given them, and help me to be quick to recognize and affirm those gifts in the lives of my children.

God Is Not Finished Yet!

God is the one who began this good work in you, and I am certain that he won't
stop before it is complete on the day that Christ Jesus returns.
—*Philippians 1:6, CEV*

It takes time to grow. Trees can take years before they start to bear fruit. Just like trees, children take time to grow. In the busyness of raising them we can overlook that fact. We need to give them all the time they need to grow without becoming impatient. The years of childhood are so precious and so fleeting that we need to treasure them and not place unrealistic expectations on our little ones. The same holds true for our older ones.

We struggle with our own shortcomings and tend to be hard on ourselves, forgetting that God is not finished working with us yet. Today's text reminds us that it is God who began this work of growth in us—and any work that God begins, He finishes. And He finishes it well. We will continue to grow and mature spiritually throughout our lifetime. So will our children. We need to let go of the unfair expectations we have for them and give God the time and space He needs to do His work in their lives.

Let's focus on the positives. Though we're not blind to the areas in which they need to grow, let's look for areas where we do see growth occurring and take the time to affirm that in our children. It not only encourages them, it reinforces the new behavior. If all they hear about is their faults, they will become discouraged. Out of that discouragement, poor self-esteem will develop and they will become unmotivated and quit attempting new things for fear of failure. When they do fail, remind them that it is through our failures that we all learn. It is only in falling that we learn how to get up.

I'm thankful that I serve a God who never gives up on me. And, we should never give up on our children. The verse above is a promise which assures me that God won't stop until He's finished. Christ keeps working on my heart and my attitudes day after day. He loves me and continually forgives me and allows me to start anew. Now that's great news for us and for our children!

Dear Lord, please help me to exercise patience with my children. I trust You to finish the work that You have started in them, and in me.

A Handsome Child

So the woman conceived and bore a son. And when she saw
that he was a beautiful child, she hid him three months.
—Exodus 2:2, NKJV

What mother doesn't think their child is handsome? In a poll conducted in the United Kingdom, one thousand parents revealed their reactions when they first saw their babies. Of the 18 percent who admitted being disappointed by the looks of their child, more than half had discussed their feelings with their partners but only 8 percent said they had spoken to anyone else about it. Instead it seems the vast majority suffer their disappointment in silence, choosing to put on the brave face society expects.

As human beings we are wired to love our babies. That's how God made us. But regardless of whether we see our babies as beautiful or plain, the poll overwhelmingly supports the theory that we all fall in love with our children at first sight. It appears that every parent feels a pressure to say their new baby is beautiful, but only four out of five actually believe it. And yet, the remaining fifth who secretly feel their baby is ugly don't love them any less and may even feel the need to spoil them more than they would a good-looking baby.

Often babies are born with misshapen heads as a result of the trauma of going through the birth canal. That can be a shock if you're not expecting it. But with time their head assumes the proper shape and will eventually be covered with hair.

Were you a little disappointed with your child's looks when you first laid eyes on him? Did she seem less lovely than you imagined or hoped? That may have less to do with what your baby actually looks like and more to do with the world's idea of what constitutes a beautiful baby. We have seen the Gerber baby on so many baby food jars, posters, and commercials that we expect ours to look just like that baby. But the reality is that our children are beautiful because they are ours.

Regardless of whether or not our baby is beautiful by the world's standards, we fall in love with them more and more every day. Let your baby know he is loved. Cherish her smiles. Before long, they will no longer be babies.

Father God, thank You for our children, Your gift to us. May they experience our love toward them in the same way we experience Your love toward us.

In-Laws or Out-Laws?

When Esau was forty years old, he took as wives Judith the daughter of Beeri the Hittite, and Basemath the daughter of Elon the Hittite. And they were a grief of mind to Isaac and Rebekah.
—Genesis 26:34, 35, NKJV

Parents often have conflict with their children over their potential mate, particularly if it's one whose beliefs and lifestyle are contrary to the way they raised their children. Shakespeare immortalized this conflict in Romeo and Juliet, and it is the theme of many dramas in literature, stage, and screen.

Fortunately, there are less drastic solutions than the romantic death scene in Romeo and Juliet. Like Tevye in *Fiddler on the Roof,* or Robert in *Downton Abbey,* there are parents who eventually accept their adult children's choices and even give their blessing. But it takes work and willingness. Here are several suggestions to help you navigate through troubled waters:

1. Pray for wisdom to be gracious and kind. It's amazing how kindness has the power to break down barriers.
2. Avoid criticism, and when things are tough, don't ever say, "I told you this wasn't going to work."
3. Treat both your child and their spouse with respect. At the end of the day we all long to be loved and accepted by those we love, even when our choices are less than stellar.
4. Don't side with your child when they're arguing.
5. Keep an open-door policy in your home. Let the front door always be a welcoming place for them to step through.

The choice of life partner lies ultimately with your child. Many parents begin to pray for that choice long before their children are even dating because it's that important a decision. Guiding your children in making sound life choices as they are growing up will help establish a pattern of wise decision-making that can stand them in good stead in the years to come.

Your child's choice of marriage partner may always bring heartache. In that case, continue in prayer for them and for yourselves, that you can be as Christ to them and that He will win them in the end.

Father, bless our children and help them to choose a life partner who has the same values and beliefs that we raised them to uphold. Give us wisdom and grace, and bless us that we may always have a close, positive relationship with them and their chosen spouse.

One Husband and One Wife

The LORD God said, "It is not good that the man should be alone; I will make him a help meet for him." —Genesis 2:18, JPS

When God created Eve, His plan was not that the man and the woman would be in competition for supremacy. That came later and was a result of sin. God's plan was that they would be equal in His image and that they would serve one another. This principle is stated later by Paul in Ephesians 5:21, where he wrote, "Submitting to one another in the fear of God" (NKJV).

The fact that Eve was created after Adam, and formed from part of his body, does not indicate that God meant her to be inferior to Adam. On the contrary. Some Jewish commentators note that it was to show the marked difference between humankind and the animal world. Among animals, it is common for them to mate and then move on to the next partner. God meant for Adam and Eve to always be close to one another in an exclusive relationship. There was no room in God's plan for anything less than monogamy.

From the beginning, God intended that one man and one woman would make up the marital unit. Polygamy, or even a series of spouses, which some call serial monogamy, was not God's intention—even if it was permitted for some and for certain seasons. God's best plan for us as individuals is to be married to only one individual, and for a lifetime.

Ellen White makes a most sublime observation when she writes, "God Himself gave Adam a companion. He provided 'an help meet for him'—a helper corresponding to him—one who was fitted to be his companion, and who could be one with him in love and sympathy. . . . A part of man, bone of his bone, and flesh of his flesh, she was his second self; showing the close union and the affectionate attachment that should exist in this relation" (*The Adventist Home*, 25). It was God's intention to establish only the very best for Eden's first family—only that which would guarantee their happiness.

Father God, thank You for designing marriage of one man and one woman as Your ideal, knowing that it would be best for both husband and wife, and for our family. Help us to have love and sympathy one for the other and to be the true helpmate You designed for us to be.

Bring Your Children to Christ Daily

*One day some parents brought their children to Jesus so he could touch
and bless them. But the disciples scolded the parents for bothering him.*
—Mark 10:13, NLT

This is a favorite verse to use at baby dedications, and rightly so, for the image of Jesus blessing the little children is beautiful. During a dedication service the child is blessed and prayed over and the parents are affirmed for making the important decision to commit to raising their children to love and follow Jesus. A baby dedication tells everyone that the child belongs to the Lord, and the church family are encouraged to come alongside the parents and support them in prayer as they raise their child in the knowledge of the Lord.

Jesus blessing the children is a good story to remember not just at a dedication but throughout our days as parents. We can bring our children before the Lord in prayer every day. Ellen White writes, "In your work for your children take hold of the mighty power of God. Commit your children to the Lord in prayer. Work earnestly and untiringly for them. God will hear your prayers and will draw them to Himself. Then, at the last great day, you can bring them to God, saying, 'Here am I, and the children whom Thou hast given me' " (*The Adventist Home*, 536).

Children who are prayed for in this manner every day are truly blessed and will prove to be a blessing to the world. At times we will have to make difficult decisions as we raise them. There will certainly be more than a few decisions they will challenge as they're growing up, but the power of a consistent, praying parent is a wonderful thing, and will do more good for the successful raising of our children than anything else. It is our privilege, our responsibility, our joy, to bring our children before the Lord in prayer each day, no matter their age. And on the day of final account, the "child who has been brought up in a faithful way has been a light in the world . . . and the parents hear the 'Well done' of the Master" (ibid.).

Father God, I lift my children up to You today. Thank You for understanding the longing in my heart for them to know You, to love You, to serve You. May they honor You and serve You all the days of their lives. Keep them and save them for eternity, Lord.

Turn Humbly Toward God

But I, the LORD, won't destroy any of your people
who are truly humble and turn to me for safety.
—*Zephaniah 3:12, CEV*

Insurance companies have termed catastrophic events in nature, such as tornadoes, earthquakes, and hurricanes, as "acts of God." In a sense, Satan has successfully worked to spread the lie that God is to blame for all the pain and destruction in the world. How diabolical when it is Satan himself and all his evil angels who work to bring death and darkness upon the earth and on all living things.

As I think of all the marriages and families falling apart, my heart aches at the destruction the devil has caused in bringing pain and havoc to countless innocent children. The security and safety of their homes, the loving atmosphere of their parents' marriage, the peace and comfort they should enjoy during their growing years have been exchanged for yelling, anger, and other horrible abuses. It is no wonder that many children, raised in such homes, don't appear to have any interest in God, in His people, or the things He has planned for them.

In spite of the harsh realities of life on planet Earth, because the promises of God are sure, we can have hope. Listen to the vibrant heartthrob of His love in these words: "But I, the Lord, won't destroy any of your people who are truly humble and turn to me for safety." When we turn humbly toward God, we will find in Him our safety zone. Commit yourself and your family to God every day, humbly submit to His power and His guidance, and rest confident in His protection. This includes protection over everything concerning us, our finances, our home, and our family.

The key word used here is *humbly*. Our sense of self, our wounded pride, all want to prove that we can be strong and independent. But God wants us to learn that true strength comes when we learn to depend on Him. We want to be self-reliant, but God offers to help us if we rely on Him. Humbly submitting to God may be the hardest thing we have to do, but also the best thing for us and for our family.

Dear Lord, give us the humble spirit that we need. Please draw near and provide us with the protection and the safety that we desperately need. We pray for Your hand to be over our finances, our home, and our family. Thank You, Lord.

Ministry for All!

*"And it shall come to pass afterward that I will pour out My Spirit on all flesh;
your sons and your daughters shall prophesy, your old men shall dream dreams,
your young men shall see visions."*
—Joel 2:28, NKJV

Since I began in the pastoral ministry nearly thirty years ago, my wife has been by my side. We have had to move many times due to the opportunities of ministry or because we were asked to serve a congregation in another area. Each time I took a new church, my wife had to leave her job as a teacher and apply for a job in the new location. We were blessed each time that she was able to find a teaching position nearby.

There's something I've learned about ministry through the years. Ministry, whether pastoral or teaching, is not something you choose. Rather, it's something that God calls you to do. I have also learned and have been a witness to the fact that God calls both men and women, as He wishes, and equips them through His Holy Spirit. In addition, I have learned that when God calls somebody, and they allow Him to lead, the results become evident in the fruit that is borne through their ministry. For instance, as a pastor you see positive changes in the congregation you serve, you witness growth, both numerical and spiritual, and you see changed lives as a result of God working through you and in the lives of your congregants.

As a teacher, you witness the very same things—spiritual and numeric growth in the school, positive changes in finances and in the school facilities, and you see the changed lives that result from the work of dedicated ministers in the teaching ministry. The Holy Spirit is the same, the call is the same, and the ministry is the same. In fact, Paul wrote to the Ephesians that God gave His church the gift—not gifts—of "pastors and teachers." Not two separate gifts but one.

In marriage, when the husband and wife work together, as the spiritual ministers of their home, everyone benefits, everyone is blessed. Ellen White says, "Missionaries for the Master are best prepared for work abroad in the Christian household, where God is feared, where God is loved, where God is worshiped" (*The Adventist Home*, 35).

Father God, thank You for calling us, equipping us, and using us to minister to others. May we remember to minister to our families as well, for ministry begins in the home.

I Lay Me Down

I lay down and slept, yet I woke up in safety,
for the LORD was watching over me.
—Psalm 3:5, NLT

David represents himself as in danger of attack at any moment during the night, hunted and cursed by his enemies, nevertheless able to lie down in peace and sleep, so great was his trust in God. Since everything was in God's hands, he had a sense of complete protection. His sleep was not mere weariness or indolence or presumption; it was an act of faith. Internal calm nerved him for the next day's fight.

"**The Lord sustained me.** The first waking thought is one of recognition that God had honored the trust placed in Him, even as his last thought on going to sleep had been one of complete confidence. The psalmist is strengthened to meet the needs of the day. The last thoughts of the night are often the first thoughts of the day. Note the sudden dramatic change from depression to triumph. Such is the benediction of the night and the promise of the new day" (*The Seventh-day Adventist Bible Commentary*, 3:637).

The psalmist writes a morning prayer in which he thanks God for keeping him safe and for watching over him throughout the night. Many children struggle with being scared to go to sleep at night. Some imagine there is something terrifying hiding under their beds or in their closets, and they feel vulnerable and afraid. While their fears are childish and unfounded, we should not dismiss them but see in them an opportunity to teach our little ones to bring all their cares and concerns to the Lord in prayer. These precious lessons, learned in childhood, will stand them in good stead in the days ahead, when their fears are far from unfounded.

"To neglect the duty of praying with our children is to lose one of the greatest blessings within our reach. . . .

"The power of a mother's prayers cannot be too highly estimated. She who kneels beside her son and daughter through the vicissitudes of childhood, through the perils of youth, will never know till the judgment the influence of her prayers upon the life of her children" (*The Adventist Home*, 266).

First thing in the morning, pray with them so they can thank Him for His protection overnight, teaching them gratitude for each new day.

Father God, thank You for a new day of life and health, and thank You for watching over us as we sleep at night.

He Can Hold It Together

*God's Son has all the brightness of God's own glory and is like him
in every way. By his own mighty word, he holds the universe together.
After the Son had washed away our sins, he sat down at the right side
of the glorious God in heaven.* —Hebrews 1:3, CEV

It is estimated that there are four hundred billion stars in our galaxy.
Scientists estimate that in the Milky Way alone there are five hundred
million potential planets, other than the earth, where life could exist. If these
numbers are applied to all the galaxies in the universe, there would be a
staggering variety of planets capable of supporting life. It is all speculation,
of course, but several branches of mathematics, quantum mechanics, and
astrophysics have all come to similar conclusions: our universe is just one of
many.

There's another universe, much closer to home, that is just as vast—the
human brain. Our brains are remarkably complex objects with a hundred
billion neurons and quadrillion connections. Though we've made huge
progress at understanding and mapping how the brain works, we still know
very little about the intricacies of how this organic supercomputer operates.
But we do know the human brain is the most complicated thing we have
yet discovered. It is the brain where we have everything we need to give us
the ability to form language and culture, consciousness, the idea of self, the
ability to learn, and the capacity to understand the universe and to reflect on
our place within it.

The vast expanse of the universe moves, expands, contracts, all in a uniform, organized fashion. It is God who holds the universe together. The vast
universe of the human brain is also held by God. We don't understand how
it happens, how it all works, but we know that it does. So, if God holds the
universe together, and He knows everything about how our brain works,
doesn't He also know how families work?

"The sweetest type of heaven is a home where the Spirit of the Lord pre-
sides. If the will of God is fulfilled, the husband and wife will respect each
other and cultivate love and confidence" (*The Adventist Home*, 15). With
Christ at the center of our homes, we can know His order, blessing, and joy.

*Father God, thank You for holding everything under Your hands' control. I
submit myself, my marriage, and my family to Your control. Please bless us and
help our home to be a little heaven on earth.*

A Treasured Friendship

Then Jonathan said to David, . . . "May the Lord be between you and me, and between your descendants and my descendants, forever."
—1 Samuel 20:42, NKJV

The friendship between David and Jonathan is a favorite among the hundreds of stories found in God's Word. There is another story of antiquity that has become a classic illustration of true friendship: the story of Damon and Pythias.

These young men loved each other so dearly that they were hardly ever seen apart. Pythias somehow roused the anger of the tyrant who imprisoned him and condemned him to die. Damon desperately tried to obtain his friend's pardon and release. Now, Pythias's mother was very old, and lived far away with her daughter, and Pythias was anxious about leaving them alone. Damon went to see the tyrant and asked to take his friend's place, even to the point of death if need be, if only Pythias were allowed to visit his family one last time.

The tyrant Dionysius had heard of the young men's friendship and hated them both simply because they were good, yet he allowed them to change places, warning that if Pythias were not back in time, Damon would have to die in his stead. Pythias hastened home, found a husband for his sister, and provided for his mother. On his return, he fell into the hands of thieves and, after hours of struggling, he managed to get free and sped along his way. Regardless of his pains, Pythias pressed anxiously onward, across a plain where the hot rays of the sun and the burning sands greatly increased his fatigue and faintness, and almost caused him die of thirst. Onward he sped, for the sun was sinking fast, and he knew that his friend would die if he were not back by sunset.

The last hour came, and Damon was led to the place of crucifixion.

Just as the guards were about to nail Damon to the cross, Pythias dashed up, bloodstained and disheveled. With a sob of relief he loosened his friend's bonds and bade the guards bind him instead. Dionysius was so touched by this true friendship that for once he forgot his cruelty and let both young men go free, saying that he would not have believed such devotion possible had he not seen it with his own eyes.

Jesus is our best Friend. He died in our place so that one day we might go home with Him for eternity.

Father, thank You for Jesus. My Friend. My Savior.

What Type of Person Are You?

Therefore, since all these things will be dissolved, what manner of persons ought you to be in holy conduct and godliness . . . ?
—2 Peter 3:11, NKJV

Here Peter reveals that his great concern is not with events but with men, that is, with the characters of his readers. He has gone into detail about last-day events in order to bring before them the imperative need for holiness, and now devotes the remainder of his epistle to impressing this need upon them" (*The Seventh-day Adventist Bible Commentary*, 7:616).

Have you ever felt as though it is easier at times to be nice to strangers than it is to those you live with? Why is that? Why is it that the ones to whom we should speak the most lovingly and act the most loving toward often get to see the worst of us? It is relatively easy to be pleasant around strangers, at least for a time. It's not difficult to keep our guard up around them, and after all, we have a reputation to uphold.

Answer this question honestly: What would others think if they could peak inside your home throughout the day? Would you want them to hear how you talk to your spouse and to your children? The truth is that unseen angels do see inside our homes! Jesus sees and hears too. And so do our children. We may not think about it much, but our children are watching us all the time. They see how we respond to stress and how we react to frustrating situations.

And think about this: our sons will tend to treat their wives in the same way they see their fathers treating their mothers. Our little girls will communicate to their husbands the way that they witness their mothers speaking to their fathers. And, even if you are single, your child will grow up to reflect the same communication style and conflict resolution that you use. The importance of modeling "holy conduct and godliness" cannot be underestimated.

It is in these unnoticed and seemingly unimportant moments in our everyday lives that our characters are revealed. So, how do we respond to the issue raised in our scriptural text for today? What kind of person should we be? Does it match the person we are? Or do we need to change something?

Dear Lord, please help me guard my tongue, my thoughts, and my actions. Help me to reflect You to everyone I meet, but most of all, help my family to see You in me today.

Reading Scripture From Childhood

From childhood you have known the Holy Scriptures, which are able to make
you wise for salvation through faith which is in Christ Jesus.
—2 Timothy 3:15, NKJV

One of the most important things that you can do with your child is to read to them. Literacy development is the number one predictor of academic success in children. So, the number one thing that you can do to impact literacy development is to read to your child every day. Imagine, something as simple as reading to your child can have a profound effect on them. Yes, it does take time. But the rewards not only help assure academic success, they just may be eternal.

Why not combine reading to your child every day with having daily family worship? Consider the choices of available reading material. You may read those precious Bible stories of Daniel in the lions' den, Noah's ark, or David and Goliath. You can take an entire week of family devotions, read the same story each night, and then do various things each night to make that story come alive for your little one. As a family you may reenact the story, each one playing a different role, illustrate the story in a family mural using finger paints or bright crayons, have a puppet show, or write a song. The possibilities are endless.

Dedicate a specific time each day to family worship. Make sure everyone in the house knows the time and the place to get together. It should be at the same time every day so that it becomes a daily habit for everyone in the family. Once you determine to do this, you'll probably be inundated with interruptions. In fact, you can count on it. But don't let that discourage you, and don't allow busyness to push aside this important time together. You will never regret time spent worshiping with one another as a family.

Make sure those biblical lessons and stories are age appropriate for your child. Family worship should be something that they look forward to all day long. Involve them in selecting the weekly story of emphasis and in planning the activities. Those simple stories that a young child listens to you read to them will become great life lessons that they will carry with them into adulthood, and their memories of the time spent together will be priceless.

Dear Lord, help me as a parent to teach my child to love Your Word. May they learn by watching me spend time with You in Your Word.

How to Keep Love Alive

Giving thanks always for all things unto God and the Father in the name of our Lord Jesus Christ; submitting yourselves one to another in the fear of God.
—Ephesians 5:20, 21, KJV

How much trouble and what a tide of woe and unhappiness would be saved if men, and women also, would continue to cultivate the regard, attention, and kind words of appreciation and little courtesies of life which kept love alive, and which they felt were necessary in gaining the companions of their choice. If the husband and wife would only continue to cultivate these attentions which nourish love, they would be happy in each other's society and would have a sanctifying influence upon their families. They would have in themselves a little world of happiness and would not desire to go outside this world for new attractions and new objects of love. . . .

"If the hearts were kept tender in our families, if there were a noble, generous deference to each other's tastes and opinions, if the wife were seeking opportunities to express her love by actions in her courtesies to her husband, and the husband manifesting the same consideration and kindly regard for the wife, the children would partake of the same spirit. The influence would pervade the household, and what a tide of misery would be saved in families! Men would not go from home to find happiness; and women would not pine for love, and lose courage and self-respect, and become lifelong invalids. Only one life lease is granted us, and with care, painstaking, and self-control it can be made endurable, pleasant, and even happy.

"Every couple who unite their life interest should seek to make the life of each as happy as possible. That which we prize we seek to preserve and make more valuable, if we can. In the marriage contract men and women have made a trade, an investment for life, and they should do their utmost to control their words of impatience and fretfulness, even more carefully than they did before their marriage, for now their destinies are united for life as husband and wife, and each is valued in exact proportion to the amount of painstaking and effort put forth to retain and keep fresh the love so eagerly sought for and prized before marriage" (*This Day With God*, 335).

Dear Lord, please fill our hearts and our homes with a spirit of thanksgiving and praise. May we look for ways to bring joy to one another.

Keep Your Eyes on the Goal

Keep your eyes on Jesus, who both began and finished this race we're in.
Study how he did it. Because he never lost sight of where he was headed—
that exhilarating finish in and with God—he could put up with
anything along the way: Cross, shame, whatever.
—Hebrews 12:2, The Message

One of those famous quotes from New York Yankees' catcher Yogi Berra, or a Yogism, goes like this: "If you don't know where you are going, you'll end up someplace else." While it sounds funny, and kind of silly, it is actually very profound. He demonstrates the fact that if we don't set goals for our life we will probably end up someplace, but not where we had hoped to be. I may wish I had a doctoral degree, but if I don't make that a firm and measurable goal, and plan accordingly, chances are that I will reach the end of my life without that doctoral degree. We could say the same for owning a house. If we don't make that a goal, and work, save, and plan accordingly, we won't be homeowners.

It is the same way with marriage. You may enter into marriage with dreams and romantic ideals, wearing rose-tinted glasses, hoping things work out for you and your spouse. If that's all you do, however, you may hit some rocky times down the road. How much better it would be to set a number of goals and move together in the direction of reaching them. Then when you hit the tough times, you will be in a better position to pull through them. Some of the goals you could set for your marriage should include such things as owning a home, retiring from work at a certain age, setting the number of children you would like to have, saving money for the kids' education, going on mission experiences together.

Of course, the most important goal is to remain married until death comes or Jesus returns. With this goal in mind, you can recruit His help knowing Jesus will help you reach that goal successfully and happily. Our text today encourages us to keep our eyes on the goal, as Jesus did. That's how He was able to put up with the constant challenges He faced to the end.

Father God, thank You for teaching us the importance of setting goals. Help us to set lifelong goals for our marriage and family, and help us to keep looking to You as we reach them successfully.

A Daily Drink

Jesus answered and said to her, "Whoever drinks of this water will thirst again, but whoever drinks of the water that I shall give him will never thirst. But the water that I shall give him will become in him a fountain of water springing up into everlasting life." —John 4:13, 14, NKJV

We all recognize, and science confirms it, that in order to have the best of health we need to work at maintaining healthy habits. The Weimar Institute developed what is known as NEWSTART, which is an acronym for Nutrition, Exercise, Water, Sunlight, Temperance, Air, Rest, and Trust in Divine Power. These seven elements help us to have better health, but they don't simply happen in our lives; we must be intentional, we must work at it, we must ensure that these eight principles are part of our lives.

In the world of athletics or sports, we recognize that the best of the best have natural abilities but also work hard to be successful. In the realm of work, most people who work hard accomplish many things for their company and for themselves. In the arts, artists, musicians, and performers have to work hard, and for a long time, to perfect their skills until they are recognized and rewarded for them.

In the spiritual realm the same is true. We recognize that spiritual growth takes place when we read the Bible, pray, and share or witness to others. Bible study is one of the vehicles God uses to communicate His will to us, to teach about Him and His plan for our lives. Prayer is how we communicate with Him and how we develop a close relationship with Him. Witnessing or sharing is the way we exercise our faith, the way we are strengthened and grow.

If we work hard at being good in our studies, at work, in sports or the arts, why do we think that a good marriage happens without any effort on our part? If we must study the Bible, pray, and help make disciples of others not just for their benefit but for our own, shouldn't we also make the same effort in order to have a good, healthy, and strong marriage?

Today's passage reminds us that as much as we must drink water daily, and pray daily, so also do we need to work daily at making and keeping our marriages healthy and strong.

Father God, help us to make that daily effort to maintain strong, healthy relationships with You, with our spouse, with our family, and with others in our lives.

He Is So Close!

". . . so that they should seek the Lord, in the hope that they might grope for Him and find Him, though He is not far from each one of us; for in Him we live and move and have our being, as also some of your own poets have said, 'For we are also His offspring.' " —Acts 17:27, 28, NKJV

Sometimes God feels so far away. Just when we need Him most, it seems as though He is nowhere to be found. If it's any consolation, even Jesus felt that way once while hanging from the cross at Calvary. With the weight of the sins of the world on His shoulders, it seemed to Jesus as though He had been abandoned by His own Father with whom He had shared eternity. And maybe that scene gives us an indication of why we feel so far away from God; sin makes us feel far from Him even when He is so close to us.

That's why these words from the apostle Paul, declared to the Greek philosophers, are so encouraging. "There is no doubt expressed in Paul's words; he is rather making a positive statement of fact. The Lord is near to men, even when they do not acknowledge Him. This makes it a comparatively simple matter for men to find God, for He is by their side, awaiting their awakening and aiding their efforts to discover Him. God can and does reveal Himself according to the measure of zeal and earnestness shown by those who seek Him" (*The Seventh-day Adventist Bible Commentary*, 6:353).

Paul wasn't reminding some Christians that God is near to us; he was telling those who didn't even know or believe in God. What that tells me is that God is near to each of us even when we reject Him, deny Him, or even rebel against Him. He reminds of His presence with words such as, "I will never leave you nor forsake you" (Hebrews 13:5, NKJV) or, "I am with you always, even unto the end of the world" (Matthew 28:20, ASV).

On days when you feel alone, remind yourself of these words and be encouraged by knowing that God is very close, that He will never leave us, that He will be with us every step of the way until the end of this race.

Father God, thank You for being with us, very near to us, even when we don't feel close to You. And thank You because You never abandon us in spite of ourselves.

A Gradual Change

But we all, with unveiled face, beholding as in a mirror the glory of the Lord, are being transformed into the same image from glory to glory, just as by the Spirit of the Lord.—2 Corinthians 3:18, NKJV

We've all probably noticed that couples who've been married for many years start to look like one another. Even scientists have concluded that indeed people begin to resemble the person to whom they are married for a long time. Whether that is true, or just our impression, I'm not quite sure, but even if people don't look alike, they surely act alike, talk alike, and think alike. It's as though being married to a person for so many years changes us to the point that we adopt many of their mannerisms, words, and ideas.

That's what happened to Jesus' disciples after spending just a little over three years with Him. People could recognize that Peter had changed and even spoke like Jesus. That's why it is important for us to also spend time with Jesus, so that we can be changed daily to resemble Him more each day. "The contemplation of the image of Christ acts upon the moral and spiritual nature as the presence of God did upon the face of Moses. The humblest Christian who constantly looks to Christ as his Redeemer will reflect in his own life something of the glory of Christ. If he faithfully continues to do so, he will go on 'from glory to glory' in his personal Christian experience" (*The Seventh-day Adventist Bible Commentary*, 6:851).

Here's where this idea impacts our marriages: instead of trying to change our spouse to match what we'd like them to be, we should try to emulate Jesus and be the person He wants us to be. While we're thinking about that, we should probably ask ourselves why we want our spouse to change. Didn't we fall in love with them because of who they are? But if there really are areas where they need to grow, why not trust Jesus to change them? He knows them best and knows who He created them to be. The interesting thing is that when we both allow Jesus to change us, individually, not only do we resemble Him more but we're also drawn closer to each other. Contemplating the image of Christ has a remarkable effect on our lives, our marriages, and our homes.

Father God, change me from within that I may resemble Your Son, especially to my spouse.

The Solution for Desire?

But I say to the unmarried and to the widows: It is good for them if they remain even as I am; but if they cannot exercise self-control, let them marry. For it is better to marry than to burn with passion.
—1 Corinthians 7:8, 9, NKJV

I've considered the words of this text often. At first sight, Paul seems to recommend marriage as a way to handle sexual desire. If you are burning with sexual desire, it seems to dictate, then marry so all your sexual needs will be met. But I'm not sure that's what Paul had in mind. Should that be the main reason you marry someone? So that you can have your sexual desires met?

I think what Paul is advocating is sexual purity. We find examples of people in the Bible who didn't simply give in to their sexual needs but who chose to remain sexually pure as a way to honor God. Joseph is a good example. While a slave, serving in Potiphar's house, he was repeatedly tempted by his master's wife to have sexual relations with her. His response is exemplary and one for which he is well remembered, "How then can I do this great wickedness, and sin against God?" (Genesis 39:9, NKJV).

So Paul is not advocating marriage as a way to avoid sexual temptation or sexual immorality. Instead, what Paul is advocating is sexual purity among those who are not married, as well as for those who are married. Whether married or single, don't let lust and passion control your life; rather, let Jesus have control of your passions. "The strongest temptation is no excuse for sin. No matter how severe the pressure brought to bear upon you, sin is your own act. The seat of the difficulty is the unrenewed heart" (*The Adventist Home*, 331).

Father God, help me to yield my passion to Your control that my love may be pure and blameless.

Have Hope, Be Patient, and Pray

Rejoice in hope, be patient in suffering, persevere in prayer.
—*Romans 12:12, NRSV*

Romans 12 is rich in guidance and instruction from the apostle Paul to the members of the church in Rome, and to all of us. Paul probably understood the challenges that were coming to the Christian church. To prepare them for the coming persecution and the falling away of the faith, Paul tells them to rejoice, to be patient, and to persevere in prayer.

This is great, practical advice for marriage. As good as a relationship may be, there will be good and bad days, and there will be challenges that come to interrupt the peace and calm we enjoy. Some may even come to the place where they feel it's best to call it quits, separate, or get a divorce. They would rather take the seemingly easy exit than do the hard work of staying in their relationship and making it work.

Consider Paul's advice:

1. *Rejoice in hope.* Recent research shows that when couples who are considering divorce choose to remain together, they report a higher level of satisfaction just five years later than they experienced during the time when they'd considered ending their marriage. This tells us that there is hope if we choose to remain together and fight for our marriage. So rejoice in that hope.
2. *Be patient in suffering.* Patience, in the original Greek of the New Testament, is not simply sitting passively, waiting for good things to happen. Patience is more like the tenacity you need in the midst of strong winds. You don't just sit there praying the winds will cease; you hang on for dear life. Patience in the suffering that may come to your marriage means hanging on to the relationship until the dark days pass.
3. *Persevere in prayer.* During the darkest hours of our lives, no matter what causes that darkness, we can't cease from praying, we don't give up praying, we don't lose our hold on God's hand. It is during those most challenging days that we hang on to Him even more tenaciously.

Take to heart this advice from Paul and see your relationship survive and thrive.

Father God, bless us during the challenging days, that we may see the hope beyond the darkness until we experience the sunshine of love and peace in our marriage.

A Common Goal

*You must get along with each other. You must learn to be
considerate of one another, cultivating a life in common.*
—*1 Corinthians 1:10,* The Message

The New King James Version renders our text for today this way: "that you be perfectly joined together in the same mind and in the same judgment." As I read these words, I was reminded of the marriage injunction repeated three times in the Bible: "Therefore a man shall leave his father and mother and be joined to his wife, and they shall become one flesh" (Genesis 2:24, NKJV; see also Matthew 19:5; Ephesians 5:3). God's desire for marriage is that the man and the woman who come together in this union will be not simply be joined legally or physically but that they will surrender themselves completely to Him in all things and that their lives will consist of like mind and judgment.

What does this mean in practical terms? Does it mean that they both have to do the same things, think the same, and speak the same words? Eugene Peterson, in his paraphrase of the Bible, *The Message,* has captured the essence in three principles:

1. *Get along with each other.* This includes accepting the fact that each of us is unique, and enjoying and appreciating the other person. At the same time, it means that we should be careful to not be overbearing with our own thoughts, actions, and words, but rather be careful that our thoughts and actions don't cause harm to our spouse.
2. *Be considerate of one another.* This reflects the words of Paul, that love does not demand its own way (see 1 Corinthians 13:5, 6). Loving spouses don't want their way all the time but rather think of what the other person may like, need, or want.
3. *Cultivate a life in common.* One of the many advantages of marriage is that the couple looks after the well-being of the family. What this means is that they plan together for their future, they save money so that they may be able to retire one day, they buy a house or a car by consulting with each other, they encourage each other to go to the doctor because they want to make sure their spouse has good health.

Learn and practice these three principles in your marriage daily, and you will enjoy the blessings for a lifetime.

Father God, help us to look to You for strength to live by these principles so that our marriage can be stronger and healthier each day.

Look to Give, Not to Get

"Give, and you will receive. Your gift will return to you in full—pressed down, shaken together to make room for more, running over, and poured into your lap. The amount you give will determine the amount you get back."
—Luke 6:38, NLT

As I look at this statement from Jesus, it strikes me that He could have simply said something like, "Give and you will get in return." Instead, Jesus describes the superabundance which comes as a result of being generous. We repeat often the words of Jesus that "it is more blessed to give than to receive" (Acts 20:35, NKJV). We believe the principle behind these words and have even seen it in practice when we gather things or food to give to those in need. And yet, sometimes we forget that simply giving things and food to the needy is not the only time the principle of generosity should be applied, but it should also include our relationship with our spouse.

In the marriage relationship, after the honeymoon period ends, there's a period of accommodation during which each spouse tries in some way to bring their newly formed family more in line to the family in which they grew up. We all feel more comfortable with those practices, with the food, or with the habits of our family of origin and we think that's the way things should naturally progress in our marriage and in our homes. We believe the words that "the two shall become one." But the question is, "Which one?"

Jesus tells us in today's text that when we practice generosity at home, starting with our spouse, the result will be a more harmonious relationship that exceeds our expectations. He encourages us to practice generosity in helping around the house; generosity in serving and helping our spouse; generosity in how much we compliment them; generosity in our words of love, affirmation, and appreciation; generosity in our intimacy with them; generosity in forgiveness; generosity in patience; generosity in kindness. And what He promises is a greater gift in return. If both spouses aim to be generous with each other, the result will be a strong and abiding love for one another that will continue for as long as they are together and be a blessing to their family, their church, and their community.

Father God, help us to give generously of ourselves to our marriage, our home, and our families. Thank You so much for Your abundant generosity and for giving to us without measure.

Like a Kiss

An honest answer is like a kiss of friendship.
—Proverbs 24:26, NLT

Kissing has inspired people through the ages to write stirring poems and beautiful sayings. Ingrid Bergman said, "A kiss is a lovely trick designed by nature to stop speech when words become superfluous." I was curious to see what has been written about kissing and found three quotes particularly interesting, because they all relate to our text for today.

Let's read them:

1. "A kiss is a secret which takes the lips for the ear."—Edmond Rostand.
2. "Never close your lips to those whom you have already opened your heart."—Charles Dickens
3. "The mouth is made for communication, and nothing is more articulate than a kiss."—Jarod Kintz.

So how does this apply to the wise man's words found in Proverbs, "An honest answer is like a kiss of friendship"? Many have written about the importance of honesty and openness as being one of the most important ingredients in healthy relationships. This honesty refers to telling the truth but also tells us that it is important that we not withhold the truth. It means telling what one feels and also that we should not keep those feelings to ourselves. This is incredibly important in marriage. Speaking honestly to the one we love the most helps keep the relationship alive and dynamic. That's why the writer of Proverbs writes that being honest is like a kiss—a good, warm kiss from someone you love. There's no room for a relationship to grow stagnant and stale when filled with love of this kind.

Honesty is like sharing a secret with someone you love by taking their lips for the ear, as Edmond Rostand describes in his play, *Cyrano de Bergerac*. Opening your heart to the person you love is like opening your lips to them, inviting them to open their hearts to you and sealing the union with a kiss, as Dickens might say. And communicating honestly, like a kiss, is the most articulate way to express our love, as Jarod Kintz describes.

So, kiss. Kiss your loved one often and long. And kiss them with an open, honest heart. There is not another person in the world that we give ourselves to so unreservedly as when we draw close and kiss our spouse.

Father God, help us to be honest and open with each other, and help us to express those feelings often to each other through our words and kisses.

The Rest We Need

Then Jesus said, "Come to me, all of you who are weary and carry heavy
burdens, and I will give you rest. Take my yoke upon you. Let me teach you,
because I am humble and gentle at heart, and you will find rest for your souls."
—Matthew 11:28, 29, NLT

Everyone, without exception, knows how it feels to bear heavy burdens. Sickness creeps into every home, uninvited and unwelcome. Others are burdened by unemployment or a job that pays an inadequate wage. Some struggle with unresolved family problems that strangle any chance of celebrating holidays together or growing old with those who know and love us. Yes, we all face challenges and carry burdens in this life, and we also know how it feels to be weary from the weight of it all. Where can we find relief?

Today's scripture reading contains some of the best-known, best-loved words of Jesus. "Come to me," He invites, "and I will give you rest." These words remind us that no matter what our burdens may be, or how heavy they are, Jesus wants to lift them up off our shoulders and give us true rest. Will He give us back the job we lost, or restore to us the foreclosed home? Perhaps. Perhaps not. The rest Jesus promises is greater than our fears and bigger than our needs. He offers to walk by our side to help us carry our burdens so we don't have to do it alone and so they won't crush us.

In my practice as a hospice chaplain and a grief and bereavement counselor, I encouraged people who were grieving the illness or the loss of their loved one to tell me stories and share memories of their loved ones. I walked alongside them as they shared both the good and the bad. I told them often that "pain shared is pain halved." And it's true. When we share our pain with someone who cares, it somehow grows smaller and becomes more bearable. It also brings others into our life that will help carry our pain so we don't have to do it alone.

That's what Jesus offers us. "Let me teach you," He says, and as we do, we discover that there is no one better to share our pain and our burdens than Jesus. And as we do, He lifts our load and gives rest to our weary hearts.

Father God, thank You for Jesus, who promises to help us carry our burdens
so they don't have to crush us.

April

We Are Here for a Purpose

And walk in love, as Christ also has loved us and given Himself for us, an offering and a sacrifice to God for a sweet-smelling aroma.
—Ephesians 5:2, NKJV

Let the youth be impressed with the thought that they are not their own. They belong to Christ. They are the purchase of His blood, the claim of His love. They live because He keeps them by His power. Their time, their strength, their capabilities are His, to be developed, to be trained, to be used for Him.

"Next to the angelic beings, the human family, formed in the image of God, are the noblest of His created works. God desires them to become all that He has made it possible for them to be, and to do their very best with the powers He has given them. . . .

"Before us God places eternity, with its solemn realities, and gives us a grasp on immortal, imperishable themes. He presents valuable, ennobling truth, that we may advance in a safe and sure path, in pursuit of an object worthy of the earnest engagement of all our capabilities.

"God looks into the tiny seed that He Himself has formed, and sees wrapped within it the beautiful flower, the shrub, or the lofty, wide-spreading tree. So does He see the possibilities in every human being. We are here for a purpose. God has given us His plan for our life, and He desires us to reach the highest standard of development.

"He desires that we shall constantly be growing in holiness, in happiness, in usefulness. All have capabilities which they must be taught to regard as sacred endowments, to appreciate as the Lord's gifts, and rightly to employ. He desires the youth to cultivate every power of their being, and to bring every faculty into active exercise. He desires them to enjoy all that is useful and precious in this life, to be good and to do good, laying up a heavenly treasure for the future life.

"It should be their ambition to excel in all things that are unselfish, high, and noble. Let them look to Christ as the pattern after which they are to be fashioned. The holy ambition that He revealed in His life they are to cherish—an ambition to make the world better for their having lived in it. This is the work to which they are called" (*The Ministry of Healing*, 396–398).

Father, may we find our greatest purpose and deepest joy in serving others in Your name.

He Understands!

Jesus understands every weakness of ours, because he was tempted in every way that we are. But he did not sin! So whenever we are in need, we should come bravely before the throne of our merciful God. There we will be treated with undeserved kindness, and we will find help.
—Hebrews 4:15, 16, CEV

Although people mean well when they tell someone who's grieving the loss of a loved one, "I know how you feel," what they really mean is that they, too, have experienced loss and so they know how it feels. But no one can truly know how the experience feels for another person. While their intentions are good, their words seldom help the other person feel better. The reality is that very few words, if any, will make a person feel better about their loss.

For any of us on the receiving end of such sentiments, we smile, we express appreciation, but deep inside we wish there was an answer to our pain. We long to have a sympathetic heart do more than sympathize. We long for them to be able to remove our pain. At the same time, while we want the pain to go away, we don't want the memories of our loved one to fade. It's not uncommon to think that if the pain goes away, so will our memories. One of the things we fear the most is that our loved one will be forgotten, that nothing will remain to remind the world that they were here. They lived. They existed. They mattered.

Our text for today reminds us that Jesus is the only One who can truly sympathize with us. In other words, He is the only One who can truly feel what we do. Now, while we know and understand that concept, it's much easier to believe it when things in life are going well. But it's when we are in the midst of the day-to-day pain and agony that those words really make a difference and begin to bring the healing we so desperately need.

If you know someone who is grieving and you're afraid of saying the wrong thing, don't let your fear keep you silent. Remember, it is your love, your presence, and your kindness toward the grieving that will prove to be more valuable than anything you might have to say.

Lord, thank You for understanding our pain. Although You are the only One who knows how we feel—You are enough. In You we find solace, comfort, and lasting peace.

When It All Falls Apart

*God's Son has all the brightness of God's own glory and is like
him in every way. By his own mighty word, he holds the universe
together. After the Son had washed away our sins, he sat down at the
right side of the glorious God in heaven. —Hebrews 1:3, CEV*

Have you ever felt like your marriage was unraveling before you, spinning out of control, heading down the drain, and you were unable to stop it from being lost forever? Maybe you feel helpless to do anything to change its course. You don't want your marriage to come to an end, but you seem to be totally unable to prevent it from doing so. The pain feels unbearable, the stress overwhelming, and the sadness is crushing. You never intended for your marriage to end in divorce. You started, like every other couple, with dreams of a lifetime of love and happiness together. But now you wonder if you'll be able to make it through even one more day together.

What a desperately sad picture this paints. Unfortunately, too many couples have come to me and have shared their version of this story. They are at the end of their rope and are looking one last time to see if there might be a life jacket floating around for them to grab before they drown.

Paul brings us some wonderful news: It is Jesus who holds the universe together! And because we are part of His universe, He can hold our marriage together. Just as He brought healing to the blind, the sick, and the lame, He can bring healing to our relationship. Just as He brought the dead back to life, He can also bring our dead marriage back to life and make it vibrant and exciting again.

Commit yourself anew to Him today. Commit your marriage to Him once more. Redouble your prayers for your spouse, for your relationship, for your home. And then take the next crucially important step: act lovingly toward your spouse. In fact, act toward them as though you were going through the most wonderful time in your relationship. And then, expect that Jesus will hold your marriage together. He holds the universe together. Can He not hold your marriage together as well?

Father God, we are so tired of the struggle to hold our marriage together. Today we commit ourselves and our relationship to You. Please bring healing, peace, love, and laughter back, and hold our home together for eternity.

In Quietness and Confidence

For thus says the Lord God, the Holy One of Israel: "In returning and rest you shall be saved; in quietness and confidence shall be your strength." But you would not. —Isaiah 30:15, NKJV

Rest? When was the last time you could honestly say that you felt completely rested? And yet, Jesus calls us to come apart with Him and in quietness receive the rest He has promised. Take another look at the verse. Note the last four words: "But you would not." Why does it always seem that if something has to be dropped from our schedules, spending time with Jesus is usually the first thing we drop? We become dazed by our to-do list. There are meals to prepare and serve, laundry that needs to be washed, put in the dryer, folded, and put away. And an endless round of trips to the doctor for check-ups, dental visits, and grocery store runs. The list seems endless.

Perhaps one of the biggest reasons we fail to spend time regularly with Jesus is that we think we need to carve out large blocks of time. Just the thought of it is daunting. But who said it had to be big blocks of time? There's nothing wrong with starting small. Even a few quiet moments spent intentionally and consistently every day will reap big rewards. Fit it in wherever you can. Try the morning meditations, midday minutes, or moonlit moments. The important thing is to spend some time every day, intentionally choosing to quietly reflect on Jesus.

"In quietness and confidence shall be your strength." If it's been a while since you last tried it, I invite you to take Jesus at His word. Test Him—and see what happens. Perhaps those few minutes alone with Him will stretch all the other hours in your day. When you spend time with the Lord, your strength and energy will be renewed and you will be able to face whatever comes your way during the day. And, don't be surprised when the sweetness of your time together lingers with you throughout the day, so that you find it continuing even as you bathe your baby, rock him to sleep, prepare a meal, or go on your errands. Your strength for today is promised. The secret to securing it lies in communion with Jesus.

Dear Lord, in the busyness of life please help me to stop and listen to You. I need rest. I need quietness, and I need Your strength to meet the challenges that this day will bring.

The Author and Finisher

*Keep your eyes on Jesus, who both began and finished this race we're in.
Study how he did it. Because he never lost sight of where he was headed—
that exhilarating finish in and with God—he could put up with anything along
the way: cross, shame, whatever. —Hebrews 12:2, The Message*

Sometimes I wonder if we really believe in Jesus' power and ability to help us, or in His willingness to help us. Many people rush into relationships that are not healthy or good instead of waiting for God to bring into their lives the right person, at the right time, according to His will for them.

If we truly believe that God has the power and ability to do anything, we need to learn to trust Him with our relationships. If He is responsible for the start of a friendship, why not allow Him to help that friendship grow into a meaningful, lasting relationship? And if that friendship grows into courtship and eventually into a marital relationship, why not allow Him the freedom to do His work in our lives—in His way and in His time?

Of course, the problem with trust in the area of relationships is not limited to those who are single. I have met many married people who set out to change their spouse, often only a short time after saying their "I Dos." They end up destroying what could have been a wonderful marriage just because they don't trust that the One who brought them together knew what He was doing, and they think they can improve on His work. But if we believe God is the Author of our relationship, why not trust Him to make it grow into something strong, vibrant, and beautiful?

Let us determine to keep our eyes on Jesus and not on one another. Why not trust the One who called forth order in the midst of the chaos of creation? Why not trust that He can bring forth something beautiful in our relationships? Let us not lose sight of the direction we want our marriage and our family to go, and with Him, as the Author and Finisher of our faith, as our Guide, we can enjoy the journey of life together.

Father God, we entrust all the relationships in our life, especially our marriage and our family, into Your hands. Because You are the Author, we trust You also to be the Finisher of all that You do in us.

No Condemnation

There is therefore now no condemnation to those who are in Christ Jesus, who do not walk according to the flesh, but according to the Spirit.
—Romans 8:1, NKJV

One of the most moving stories from the life of Jesus is the story of the woman caught in adultery. Jesus was teaching the people in the temple when the scribes and Pharisees brought a woman and set her in front of everyone. Trying to trap Jesus, they said, "Teacher, this woman was caught in adultery, in the very act. Now Moses, in the law, commanded us that such should be stoned. But what do You say?" Without a word, Jesus stooped down and wrote on the ground with His finger, and then He said to them, "He who is without sin among you, let him throw a stone at her first." Eventually, Jesus was left alone with the woman. When He asked, "Woman, where are those accusers of yours? Has no one condemned you?" She said, "No one, Lord." And Jesus responded, "Neither do I condemn you; go and sin no more" (see John 8:2–11, NKJV).

The fact that only the woman was brought to Jesus makes it clear that it was a set-up on the part of the Pharisees. When they would not stone her, Jesus pronounced those precious words, "Neither do I condemn you." What hope and comfort these words have brought to so many through the centuries. Paul echoes the same sentiment when he proclaims, "There is therefore now no condemnation to those who are in Christ Jesus." It was not only the woman caught in adultery that Jesus did not condemn, but also every one of us, who find forgiveness in Him.

If, in His purity, He does not condemn us, why do we think it's OK to condemn one another? Our spouse, when they make a mistake that hurts us; our children, when they disappoint us and fail to live up to our expectations; our friends when they betray our trust and let us down. Let us learn from Jesus how to treat one another. May we be quick to forgive, gracious, and patient. Let's choose not to carry a grudge or hold onto a spirit of bitterness or resentment. May those we love hear us say, "Neither do I condemn you." And may we show, by our actions, that we have forgiven.

Father God, thank You for not condemning us but instead showering Your love on each of us. Help us to share the same love with those around us. May we be more gracious, condemn less, and love more.

True Love

Many waters cannot quench love, nor can rivers drown it. If a man tried to buy love with all his wealth, his offer would be utterly scorned.
—Song of Solomon 8:7, NLT.

Pure love is such that nothing can destroy it. It cannot be bought. The highest offer would be completely scorned. It's a theme that has been explored in books, movies, poems, stories, and songs since the beginning of time, and yet it somehow remains so poorly understood. Not surprising when you realize that we speak of loving pizza, ice cream, a new sweater, or taking a nap. You name it. We *love* it. No wonder there is some confusion when it comes to defining and understanding what true love actually is—and what it's not.

The best place to find a definition of true love is God's Word. In it, Solomon describes love as something that cannot be bought. True love, he writes, cannot be quenched or drowned. The reason is that true love is not a feeling, although it makes us feel good. True love is a decision to love, trust, and commit to another person, which is followed with consistent, loving actions, regardless of how we may feel at any given moment.

Paul also wrote about the subject of love. In his first letter to the church members in Corinth, he writes extensively about love in the thirteenth chapter, where he describes love in terms of action: what love does and what love does not do. First, love is patient, love is kind. Love rejoices in the truth, it bears all things, believes all things, hopes all things, and endures all things. In other words, love is faithful and consistent; love is based on more than feelings and emotions.

Second, Paul outlines some of the things love does not do. Love does not envy, is not boastful, and is not conceited. True love does not act improperly, is not selfish, is not provoked, and does not keep a record of wrongs. Love finds no joy in unrighteousness. Love does not react out of anger, jealousy, or deceit. Is this the way we love?

Take courage! It is Christ in us that gives us the desire and the power to love. When we make the decision to follow Him, true love and actions will flow naturally from our lives.

Dear Lord, the only way we can love the way You do is to have You in our lives. May Your love shine out to others because it cannot be quenched!

The Greatest Joy

I have no greater joy than this: to hear that my children
are living according to the truth.
—3 John 1:4, NET

Those who have gone through the unimaginable grief experienced from the death of a child tell me that there is no greater pain. As painful as death is, the accepted pattern of life dictates that parents don't outlive their children. While we anticipate burying our parents one day, as traumatic as that can be, none of us expects to bury our children.

Probably the second most painful experience for a Christian parent is to watch their child walk away from the faith in which they were raised. To see the love for God expressed in the life of a child wither and die carries its own unique grief. When our hope and longing for our children to grow up believing in, loving, and serving God is dashed, when they seem to turn their backs on Him, it breaks our hearts. We know that their decision will impact more than just their life in the here and now. It will determine their eternal destiny.

The apostle John sums up the feeling we have when our children continue to walk in the path we laid out for them, the path that leads them to know and love God supremely, when he says, "I have *no greater joy* than this: to hear that my children are living according to the truth" (italics added). There are few things in life more rewarding than to see our children take a stand for what is right, when they make life commitments such as baptism, and when they choose godly people with whom to associate, and eventually to marry.

How important it is for us to consistently set a godly example for them from the time they are small. Even when we are unaware, they are watching, observing to see if our actions match our words. Do we practice what we preach? However, even when we do set a good example, our children ultimately have the freedom to choose their own paths. At times that leads them away from God. But as long as we have breath, we cannot give up on them. We are called to love them, to pray for them, and to trust them to our faithful Father, who alone can read their hearts.

Father, we place our children in Your hands and trust them to Your care and keeping. We know our example falls short. Please shine Your love through us and help us to love our children well.

The Appropriate Time

To everything there is a season, a time for every purpose under heaven.
—Ecclesiastes 3:1, NKJV

D r. Scott Stanley, marriage researcher from the University of Colorado in Denver, speaks about the changes that have occurred in the last seventy or so years. Before the 1960s, the normal order of events for most people would be to date, then get married, and only then to enter into a sexual relationship. When the 1960s came, and with it the sexual revolution, the order of things began to change. At that time, it became the norm for people to date, then have sex, and then perhaps get married. In the late 1990s and into the beginning of the twenty-first century, there's a new pattern that is being set by many couples; they now meet and have sex, from that experience they decide if they want to date, and then they either choose to live together or get married to each other.

While there is no such thing as *dating* in the Bible, God's Word reserves sexual intimacy for marriage, not before, and not outside the boundaries of this sacred union. Even the Song of Solomon, a beautiful description of the marriage relationship, describes the order of events as God planned for a couple. Three times Shulamite, the bride, expresses her advice to her young friends with the words, "Do not stir up or awaken love until the appropriate time" (Song of Solomon 2:7; 3:5, HCSB).

When God says there is an appropriate time for everything, He also means for sexual intimacy. Rushing to have sex before marriage makes the relationship more complicated, clouds the judgment, and does not help the couple make sound decisions concerning their future. In fact, premarital sex often leads to what Stanley calls "sliding into cohabitation." This means that most cohabiting couples don't sit down to talk about the reasons they have for moving in together but simply slide into that arrangement a little at a time. Unfortunately, much research shows that people in cohabiting relationships often don't marry the person they are living with; many experience higher levels of physical abuse than married couples; and they have a much higher probability of divorce if they choose to marry.

We are blessed to have sound counsel to follow as prescribed in the Bible. God, our Designer and Creator, knows what is best for us and our future.

Father God, in Your wisdom You have given us a pattern for our happiness. Help us to follow the path that leads to a long, healthy relationship.

Your Children's Faith

*I rejoiced greatly because I have found some of your children living
according to the truth, just as the Father commanded us.*
—*2 John 1:4, NET*

At first glance, this text almost seems to indicate that perhaps not all of the children in this family were faithful, as John says that he rejoiced over those who were living according to the truth. The original language, however, tells us it's likely John meant that the children he knew about were faithful. As parents, we want to know that all our kids are living in such a way that they are faithful not just in the eyes of other people but in the eyes of God. How can we ensure our kids will grow up to love and follow God?

1. Pray for them daily. When we think about the book of Job, we probably remember the disasters that came on him. He lost everything, his children were killed, and he got really sick. But one great example from his life was his constant prayers for his children. The Bible states, "So it was, when the days of feasting had run their course, that Job would send and sanctify them, and he would rise early in the morning and offer burnt offerings according to the number of them all. For Job said, 'It may be that my sons have sinned and cursed God in their hearts.' Thus Job did regularly" (Job 1:5, NKJV). Rise early in the morning and pray for your children. Pray for them throughout the day, and let the last words on your lips at night be prayers for them.

2. Worship with them daily and weekly. One cannot estimate the value of daily family worship, morning and evening, and of attending church together as a family. Even as the kids grow up into adults, attending church together continues to bring the family closer to each other at the same time as they come closer to God.

3. Serve together. Research and experience show that acts of service deepen the spiritual experience of people. For children and young people, it is more valuable when the family devotes time in service together than when the parents send them or pay for them to go to do it.

May it be said about our children that they are living according to the truth just as the Father commanded us.

Father God, bless our children this day, and may they be faithful to You today and each day of their lives.

Imitate What Is Good

Dear friend, do not imitate what is bad but what is good.
—3 John 1:11, NET

How do we teach our children to imitate what is good instead of what is bad? As with most everything we want our children to learn, it all begins with the example we as parents give. When children see their father being rude, unkind, or abusive toward his wife, they are learning that it's acceptable for men to treat women poorly. On the other hand, when they see their father treating their mother with respect, kindness, and love, they discover the gold standard for how a man should treat a woman. When a man cheats on his taxes, steals things from work, or regularly breaks the law, he is teaching his children to do the same. When a father respects other people's property, respects the law of the land, and maintains ethically correct conduct, he is showing his children the proper way to live.

The way a woman cares for her husband shows her daughters the proper care of their father and how they should care for the man who will one day be their husband. She does not have to deny her individuality nor consider herself less important or lower than her husband, when God created her in His image as much as He created her husband in His image. By the way she acts she teaches her daughters to value and respect themselves, which is important to them as they relate to men in their lives. But when children see their mother imitate the women on TV or the movies, and live in such a way that she allows others to disrespect her, or her husband to abuse her, children learn that it is as much as a woman can hope for in a relationship. If she doesn't care for her home or her family, she is teaching her children to do the same thing.

Who are we imitating in our relationship as a couple? In the example of family living, who do we resemble? Let's take care not to imitate those who don't live godly lives. Let us imitate those who provide good examples of what a man and husband, a woman and wife should be to one another and to their children.

Father God, our children watch our every move, listen to our every word, and observe everything we do. Please help us to imitate those who live upright lives because by doing so we are giving our children a godly example to imitate for themselves.

Forsaken and Reviled

*"You will be betrayed even by parents, brothers, relatives, and friends,
and they will have some of you put to death."*
—Luke 21:16, NET

What would drive family members to turn against each other? How does this happen in Christians families? I remember when I first made a commitment to follow Jesus and to walk in the light He'd given me. It meant leaving the church I had grown up in, and that left my family and friends angry. They found every opportunity to criticize me and point out where they thought I had fallen, or where my life didn't completely match their views as it had in the past. The Bible states that we have "a cloud of witnesses," but I felt as though I had a cloud of spies.

As the years have gone by, I have lost the friendship of friends and the love of family. It is hard to ignore their hurtful actions and words, and yet Jesus points out that the worst is yet to come. When we choose to be born again and follow Jesus, the devil is not happy with the changes in our life. He brings criticism, attacks, anger, and animosity against us, and he knows it is more effective when it comes from those we love the most. Our consolation and hope is in knowing that even if every hand turns against us, the hand of Jesus still has us in His grasp.

Ellen White writes, "We shall find that we must let loose of all hands except the hand of Jesus Christ. Friends will prove treacherous, and will betray us. Relatives, deceived by the enemy, will think they do God service in opposing us and putting forth the utmost efforts to bring us into hard places, hoping we will deny our faith. But we may trust our hand in the hand of Christ amid darkness and peril.

"The followers of Christ must expect to encounter sneers. They will be reviled; their words and their faith will be misrepresented. Coldness and contempt may be harder to endure than martyrdom. . . .

"Parents will turn harshly against their children who accept unpopular truth. . . . The words of the apostle will be verified in the near future: 'All that will live godly in Christ Jesus shall suffer persecution' " (*Maranatha*, 197).

Father God, I plead for strength and courage to face these challenges. May we not be surprised or overwhelmed by them. Thank You for holding us in Your unfailing grasp.

Anyone Can Fall

Don't be so naive and self-confident. You're not exempt. You could fall flat on your face as easily as anyone else. Forget about self-confidence; it's useless. Cultivate God-confidence. —1 Corinthians 10:12, The Message

In the news we read frequently about people who are having an extra-marital affair. A husband or wife has left their spouse for somebody else and is now in a new relationship. It happens so often anymore that it seems we have stopped being shocked. Sadly, it seems to have become a normal part of life. So normal, in fact, that we hardly blink when we hear about it anymore.

One of the dangers of such a careless attitude is that we forget it could happen to any of us. In fact, the moment we begin to think, "It will never happen to me," we begin to lower our guard and are in danger of falling into the same situation. Self-confidence is dangerous. Peter thought that nothing could cause him to deny his allegiance to Christ, and yet in the moment of temptation, he caved, just as Jesus told him he would.

We don't have to become paranoid, distancing ourselves from everyone lest we sin, but we should all be on guard continually, so we are not deceived into thinking that we are so spiritually strong that we could never be overcome by temptation. It is part of Satan's deception to get us to believe that we can take care of ourselves and that we have the situation under control. How often the Bible tells us to "take heed," and there's a reason for that frequent counsel. Spiritual pride is hard to recognize in ourselves. The truth is that we can't handle temptation by ourselves—nor do we need to.

Apart from recognizing our reliance on God, another way to help ensure we don't fall is to have someone to hold us accountable. For a married person, that would be their spouse. For a single person, it could be a trusted friend, preferably of the same gender. What's important is that we don't fall into the trap of becoming overconfident in ourselves, or naive, thinking that we would never fall. Instead, recognize that we have a wily foe and only God's grace and the love of faithful friends can keep that from happening.

Father God, help us to realize that we are all fallible and could fall. Keep us from spiritual pride and help us to draw closer to You for strength and to others for encouragement and accountability.

He'll Finish What He Began

God is the one who began this good work in you, and I am certain that he won't
stop before it is complete on the day that Christ Jesus returns.
—Philippians 1:6, CEV

At some point in the history of the church, people began to teach and believe that our salvation is dependent on our doing our very best to lead good and holy lives. While still early in my Christian walk, I remember hearing, "If I do my best, then God will do the rest." With these words I was taught that I have to do everything in my power to earn my salvation, and when I fell short of God's goal, He would then make up the difference. While it sounds like an attractive proposition, it stops being so attractive when I realize even my best efforts are simply not good enough—and they never will be. That's an important reality check.

Fortunately, the truth of the Bible gives us a totally different perspective. It is not my effort plus God's grace which guarantees that I will have salvation; God's grace, which results in salvation, is totally, completely, and uniquely God's gift to us, regardless of anything we do or try to do. It has always been this way, and it will always continue to be true.

Are there any other areas in life in which we try to do our best only to fail repeatedly? Have we tried to live as husband and wife depending on our own best efforts and hoping that God will make up for our deficiencies? Wouldn't we be better off giving our lives and marriage completely over to God and allowing Him to do His great work in us and submit ourselves to His guiding power? Paul's promise tells us that it is God who began the good work in us. So, do we truly believe that God brought us together? If so, the promise ends with Paul's words that what God began, He will finish. In other words, if God began by bringing you two together, He can bring you two through the challenges in marriage until a happy, healthy end.

Commit yourself and your marriage daily to God that He may use you individually and as a couple to accomplish His great purpose in You.

Father God, bless us as individuals and as a couple, and finish the good work You began in us until Your ultimate purpose is accomplished in our lives and marriage.

The Power of Love

*Beloved, let us love one another, for love is of God; and everyone
who loves is born of God and knows God.*
—1 John 4:7, NKJV

Love is power. Intellectual and moral strength are involved in this principle and cannot be separated from it. The power of wealth has a tendency to corrupt and destroy; the power of force is strong to do hurt; but the excellence and value of pure love consist in its efficiency to do good, and to do nothing else than good.

"Whatsoever is done out of pure love, be it ever so little or contemptible in the sight of men, is wholly fruitful; for God regards more with how much love one worketh than the amount he doeth.

"Love is of God. The unconverted heart cannot originate nor produce this plant of heavenly growth, which lives and flourishes only where Christ reigns.

"Love works not for profit nor reward; yet God has ordained that great gain shall be the certain result of every labor of love. It is diffusive in its nature and quiet in its operation, yet strong and mighty in its purpose to overcome great evils. It is melting and transforming in its influence, and will take hold of the lives of the sinful and affect their hearts when every other means has proved unsuccessful.

"Pure love is simple in its operations, and is distinct from any other principle of action. The love of influence and the desire for the esteem of others may produce a well-ordered life and frequently a blameless conversation. Self-respect may lead us to avoid the appearance of evil. A selfish heart may perform generous actions, acknowledge the present truth, and express humility and affection in an outward manner, yet the motives may be deceptive and impure; the actions that flow from such a heart may be destitute of the savor of life and the fruits of true holiness, being destitute of the principles of pure love.

"Love should be cherished and cultivated, for its influence is divine" (*Letters to Young Lovers*, 31–33).

Father, there are many things that masquerade as love in the world today. Sometimes even Your children can become confused. So help us to look to You—the Source of Love—and direct our lives accordingly.

Be Willing to the End

So finish what you began to do. Then your willingness
will be matched by what you accomplish.
—*2 Corinthians 8:11, GW*

I often hear people say, "I wish things were different" or, "I'd like it if . . ." While the desire to see improvements in life and in our relationships is good, it's useless unless it's followed with a willingness to do whatever it takes to make it happen. It's not enough to *want* things to be different. We must be willing to work toward accomplishing whatever is needed to reach our goals.

"I'd like to have more education," must be followed by looking for the school where your program of study is offered, and filling out the applications necessary. Once enrolled, doing all the homework and studying for the tests in order to receive the grades needed to pass the class will ensure that we will eventually receive the degree we're pursuing.

"I wish I had a better job," must be followed with looking for other possibilities, getting the training and experience necessary. Then we must apply for another job, prepare our résumé, and make the proper contacts. Showing up for job interviews and pursuing our goal until we're successful will help land us the job we're passionate about.

It is no different when it comes to marriage. "I wish my marriage were better," must be followed with a willingness to make personal changes, getting professional counseling where needed. That can be followed by implementing new ideas and learning to communicate more effectively. If we truly wish for change, we must do whatever is necessary to achieve the end results of a better relationship. While it might be easy to believe that our spouse is the only one who needs to make changes, an improved relationship always takes the work of both parties. As long as we believe there's no great effort required on our part, then the end result will likely not be what we had wished for. Good outcomes require a willing spirit followed by action.

If you're struggling in this area, then take the words of our text today and make them part of your life and marriage: "Finish what you began to do. Then your willingness will be matched by what you accomplish."

Father God, plant in our hearts not only the desire to make things better in our marriage, but help that seed of desire sprout into a willingness to do all we can to see that desire bloom into positive changes in our relationship.

Fountains of Water

"But the water that I shall give him will become in him a fountain
of water springing up into everlasting life."
—John 4:14, NKJV

Family expert William Doherty writes that couples can stay connected by being intentional about family life through daily rituals. He describes an intentional family as having a working plan that will help build and maintain family connections, and goes on to explain that certain rituals are repeated activities or interactions that are meaningful to a couple and that offer everyday opportunities for couple bonding. Meals, morning and bedtime routines, and the comings and goings of spouses can all be part of those rituals of connection. For example, couples might create a ritual where they prepare breakfast together and clean up together. They might make prayer before each meal a ritual. Couples will find that if they are intentional about connecting with one another, their marriage will be stronger and more satisfying. Here are two rituals you can begin today and practice daily.

1. Be positive. Research shows that spouses who express more positive thoughts and feelings about each other than negative ones are more satisfied with their marriages, have a lower risk of divorce, and experience less conflict in their marriage. In fact, research shows that happy couples tend to have a ratio of five positives to every one negative. Negative interactions include criticism and sarcasm, while positive interactions include saying, "I love you," "You look nice today," or "Thank you."

2. Be appreciative. For many couples, just realizing that they shouldn't take their everyday interactions for granted can make an enormous difference in their relationship. Spouses can show appreciation by saying thank you, giving a hug, or doing something kind. Expressing appreciation for a spouse's daily kindnesses makes it more likely he or she will continue those efforts.

Just like the daily spiritual rituals of Bible study and prayer are important to maintaining a strong relationship with God, a healthy marriage requires something from us daily. As we drink water from the fountain, we are drawn closer to Jesus. As we draw closer to Him, we will draw closer to one another.

Father God, help us to make a daily concerted effort to build each other up and to strengthen our marriage through those simple daily rituals which are so positive and encouraging.

Change Is Good

But we all, with unveiled face, beholding as in a mirror the glory of the Lord, are being transformed into the same image from glory to glory, just as by the Spirit of the Lord.—2 Corinthians 3:18, NKJV

I've heard people say that when a man marries, he thinks, "She's the one I've been waiting for. She'll never change." And she always does. At the same time, a woman looks at her man and thinks, "He just needs a little work; after we're married, I'll help him change." And he never does.

In reality, both will change with the passing of time. We have learned from biology that every seven years all the cells in our bodies are replaced with new ones. At the same time, our ideas, politics, and interests also evolve over the years. Sometimes conflict in marriage arises when we change at a different pace from one another. The reality is that all of us are a work in progress. While we may want to encourage some changes in our spouse's behavior, nagging and arguing will get us nowhere and will leave us feeling miserable.

Successful people recognize that the only person we can change is ourselves, but it doesn't mean we have to do it all by ourselves. We can enlist the help of our spouse. When we are willing and ready to change some behavior, we can tell our spouse about our plan and enlist their support. Our request for help could be the energy for marital growth we need to make the changes we desire.

What if our spouse doesn't want to change? This is where the most powerful tool of marital change comes into play if we are going to have a healthy marriage: acceptance. When spouses show each other love and acceptance, they respond more quickly to each other's changes. Be ready to support any effort your partner makes toward change, no matter how tentative or incomplete that effort is. If he or she discloses a desire to change, be ready to help instead of hindering the process. It may be that either one or both of you may need professional help, but our role as helpmate is indispensable. We must become our spouse's greatest cheerleader!

Father God, we long to be changed into the image of Jesus Christ. Help us in that process and help us to be more accepting and more supportive of one another. May we recognize that we're each a work in progress—and be patient with one another.

There's No Better Time Than Now!

For he says, "At the acceptable time I have listened to you, and helped you on the day of salvation." Behold, now is the acceptable time; behold, now is the day of salvation. —2 Corinthians 6:2, RSV

When it comes to making changes to improve our marriage relationship, there's no better time to begin than today. Too many couples wait for one another to change their behavior or attitude, or for the children to grow a little older, or for something else to happen before they commit to working on their marriage. But if we keep putting it off, something else will always come up, and one day we'll wake up to find shattered lives and a marriage in ruins.

It's good to be reminded that it should never be our goal to change our spouse. Rather, the starting point should be that we become a more loving person. Harry Stack Sullivan, a noted American psychiatrist, suggests that love exists when the satisfaction and security of another person becomes as significant to one as one's own satisfaction and security. In this definition, love is an action undertaken to benefit another person. An important key to improving an intimate relationship is to give more and demand less from your spouse. If we want to improve our marriage, we must be willing to improve ourselves. Here is something we can do.

First, change our behavior. Remember Jesus' parable of the speck of dust and the beam, where He states that we should first examine our own faults before we criticize the faults of our spouse. Here are three steps to take.

1. Have patience with our spouse's faults and annoying habits. Drop the insistence that he or she must change.
2. Take responsibility to change ourselves and improve the relationship. Instead of blaming our partner for our unhappiness, or focusing attention on their mistakes, we must take the first step to improve things. We need to determine what is within our power to do—and do it. We should take the first step. We need to show love first!
3. The hope is that as we act in loving ways, our spouse will reciprocate; but even if they don't, we will have acted like Christ expects His disciples to act.

Father, it's so easy to read through a list of steps for change, but actually putting them into action is so much harder. Please give me a heart that is tender and forgiving. You know how much I long for Your love to fill our hearts and our home. Please help us, Lord.

A New Beginning

"I will give you a new heart and put a new spirit within you; I will take the heart of stone out of your flesh and give you a heart of flesh."
—Ezekiel 36:26, NKJV

We're focusing on ways to take responsibility for improving our marriage relationship. After first being willing to change our behavior, the second thing we need to do is to change our attitude. It could take some time to learn to stop focusing on their negatives and instead train our minds to focus on the positives. We can learn to overlook the few small things we may not like about our spouse and continually remind ourselves of the things we like and appreciate in them.

It might be helpful to make a list of everything we like and appreciate about them; include all the things they do for us and our family, and then start a new habit of thanking them for all they do. Be sincere in thanking them for what they do, and as you compliment and praise them for their strengths, you will be less likely to notice their weaknesses and faults.

The third thing we need to change is our heart. One of the wonderful things that social scientists have learned is that when we change our behavior, our attitude begins to change, and as a result our feelings also begin to change. This is a powerful truth. When we worship and serve God in true and healthy ways, we become more loving and less selfish. An unselfish person is much more likely to build a happy and satisfying marital relationship. His thoughts and actions are more often directed to the welfare of family members rather than upon his own personal wants and desires. And that's what loving like Jesus is all about.

Let's not wait for a better time. Recognize that *now* is the time. Let's ask God to take out our hearts of stone and give us hearts that are tender, compassionate, and loving. He will do it! Ask Him, and commit to taking these three simple steps:

1. Change our behaviors
2. Change our attitudes
3. Change our hearts

And the only way we can do that consistently is to daily ask God for His help.

Father, help me to begin right now to make the changes in my life that will help change our relationship and our home.

Change Your Mind!

Let the Spirit change your way of thinking.
—Ephesians 4:23, CEV

Sometimes we mistakenly identify ourselves as being depressed when it could likely be what is known as situational sadness. For example, this is what we experience after the death of a loved one, or the loss of a job.

Depression, on the other hand, is a powerfully negative mood that interferes with our daily life. When we're depressed, we are sad, despondent, and lethargic. We feel hopeless or helpless. We want to cry frequently and may feel as if we absolutely cannot get out of bed in the morning. One of the concerns is that depression affects our bodies as well as our minds. We may eat less, or more, but less often. We may feel at night as if we're starting to come out of it, only to wake up in the morning feeling even worse. Depression may be the result of an adversity in life or it may seem to appear on its own. It can also be triggered by a change of season or a change of lifestyle, or for no apparent reason at all.

Depression can be life-threatening and may lead a person to feel suicidal. Many people suffering from depression find relief through medication. While some medication may indeed be helpful, the side effects and the addictive effects are not desirable outcomes. Other healthier approaches can be more beneficial in the long run. The good news is that as serious as it may be, depression is a state of mind and body that can be changed through a combination of things such as a change in nutrition and activity, intake of vitamins, Cognitive-Behavioral Therapy (CBT), and the help of God. CBT focuses on eliminating self-defeating behavior, replacing negative thinking patterns and self-talk with realistic beliefs about oneself and the world. CBT is the only form of psychotherapy that has been scientifically proven to work better than a placebo in treating major depression.

In Ephesians, Paul reminds us that with the help of the Holy Spirit we can change any thinking pattern that hurts us. We don't have to defeat ourselves with negative thought patterns, but with His help we can establish positive, healthy thoughts which lead to healthier behavior.

Holy Spirit, help us change the negative thoughts that defeat us even when we have good intentions and desires. Help us choose good, positive thoughts that will impact us every day in our lives, marriages, and families.

Time to Grow Up!

When I was a child, I spoke as a child, I understood as a child, I thought as a child; but when I became a man, I put away childish things.
—*1 Corinthians 13:11, NKJV*

Much recent research has demonstrated that the frontal lobe of the brain, the seat of decision making and judgment, is not fully developed until about the age of twenty-five. This indicates that most people are not mature enough to marry until that age. It's no wonder that the younger a couple, the higher the probability of divorce.

What is the difference between emotional maturity and immaturity? Following are a few signs of emotional immaturity.

1. Emotional volatility: the tendency for emotions to get out of control. This manifests as temper tantrums, screaming, yelling, breaking things, or hitting others; getting upset, inability to take criticism, extreme jealousy, unwillingness to forgive, and an unpredictable change of moods.
2. Lack of independence: being too reliant on others, needing someone around all the time, not having independent opinions or being willing/able to express them, being very easily influenced by others.
3. Seeking constant attention: being loyal only as long as a relationship is "useful," needing immediate gratification that may result in financial or personal problems, and impulsive behavior.
4. Extreme self-centeredness: making unreasonable demands, being constantly preoccupied with self, seeking out positive feedback or sympathy relentlessly, and tending to not accept responsibility for anything.

The emotionally immature person can't understand the needs and feelings of others, and has a difficult time being a partner or a parent. In contrast, here are some of the characteristics of an emotionally mature person.

1. The ability to give and receive love and affection
2. The ability to deal with reality
3. The ability to learn from experience and deal with frustration
4. The ability to accept constructive criticism constructively
5. Having optimism and self-confidence

Lord, help us to grow up into the mature adults that we need to be in order to have a healthy, successful marriage.

Faith and Love

For this reason, because I have heard of your faith in the Lord Jesus and your love for all the saints, I do not cease to give thanks for you when I remember you in my prayers. —Ephesians 1:15, 16, NET

Most of us don't realize how often others take note of us, our behavior, and our relationship with our family. In interacting with our spouse, do we walk ahead of them, or avoid holding the door open for them? When we sit separately in church, don't hold hands, or speak unkindly to each other, we may not notice, but others do. There's a danger that we may have done it that way for so long that it no longer registers with us. Often the ones who notice most are those closest to us—our own children.

The apostle Paul commended the members of the church at Ephesus because their faith and their love worked together. In fact, he not only commended them but thanked God for them and their attitude toward one another. He recognized their faith in action through their loving acts toward all the saints. They were not selectively nice to only some of the saints, but to all—the rich and the poor, the leaders and the followers. But most important, they were loving toward those saints who were members of their own household. Sometimes we forget that those closest to us are also part of God's family and therefore they are counted among God's saints.

Following the example of the Ephesians, then, our faith is not demonstrated in how many miracles we perform, if any, or if we are able to understand and teach complicated Bible passages, or whether we can guide others to a greater knowledge of God, all of which are good, but on whether our love for people reflects the faith we have in the God we love and serve. If Paul were alive today and he knew us and the church we attend on a regular basis, what would he say of us? If he knew how we relate to those closest to us, the saints who live with us, what would he say of our faith? I pray his words would be a strong commendation.

Father God, help our faith be reflected in our loving actions toward all the saints, particularly the ones within our own household. May our love be like Christ's love for us—and may others know that we are Christians by the way we love one another.

You Were Sealed!

And when you heard the word of truth (the gospel of your salvation)—when you believed in Christ—you were marked with the seal of the promised Holy Spirit.
—Ephesians 1:13, NET

Many years ago, I was asked to officiate at the marriage ceremony for a couple from Mexico. They asked if I would perform the rope ceremony. I told them I didn't know what they meant, so they explained that in the area where they lived it was the custom for the pastor to place a rope around the couple who were getting married as a symbol of the sacred bond of marriage. Once I understood the significance, I readily agreed to it, and it became a vivid memory I still treasure to this day.

There are many ceremonies that symbolize the union of husband and wife. We chose the unity candle—but with a variation. We chose to leave the two candles lit because, while we were becoming one, we were not losing our individuality. Other couples have used two pitchers of colorful sand or water to represent the symbolism of two merging to become one.

So what exactly is it that makes us one? Is it the common beliefs we share? Or the goals, values, or plans we have established together? Is it the commitment we are making to one another? While all of these certainly play a role in helping us become one, I believe the only thing that truly makes us one is the One who made us in the first place. God, our Creator, is the One who creates the miracle wherein two become one. Our text reminds us that we are sealed by the Holy Spirit when we believe in Jesus Christ. It is that individual belief and commitment to Him that makes it possible for us as individuals to become one. That is why the wedding ceremony is more than a legal requirement but a sacred service which seals the couple's commitment to God and to each other.

As you plan for your wedding, plan for God's presence and arrange the service accordingly. And for those already married, make it a point to remember that you are sealed by the same God who created you and brought you together and who now desires for you to remain together for a lifetime.

Father God, thank You for creating us and for making us one. Strengthen our bonds each day and may we honor You for the rest of our lives through our marriage.

Trust God With Your Life

Trust in the LORD with all your heart, and lean not on your own understanding;
in all your ways acknowledge Him, and He shall direct your paths.
—Proverbs 3:5, 6, NKJV

Here are a couple of questions we need to ask ourselves: Who do we trust when things go wrong in our marriage? Do we place our trust in ourselves, or do we run to our family or our friends and rush to tell them our side of the story? Some people run to therapists, counselors, divorce lawyers, coworkers, or friends. It is sometimes true that we run everywhere but toward God. Is it easier to talk to someone we can see, even when we recognize that many times they are not really trained or equipped to give us sound advice and guidance? Some have even gone through similar situations but did not resolve them in healthy ways. How can we look to someone to help fix our marital challenges when they gave up on theirs?

Now, I know that most people mean well when they offer advice, but not all advice is good, or even helpful. Our family and friends are already biased toward our side of things, and after hearing about our marital difficulties they may end up turning against our spouse. When the challenges have been ironed out within the marriage relationship, it may be difficult for these friends to then work through the feelings and biases they have developed toward our spouse.

I'm not suggesting we refrain from getting help when we need it. There are many gifted counselors who are used by the Lord. But I want to encourage seeking God's help first. When we place our confidence in God, it doesn't mean we lay aside our own intelligence and neglect the power of choice God has given to us. No! In fact, intelligence is necessary to discern the wisdom found in God's Word and from His guiding providences. God created and designed marriage. So then, why don't we trust Him first, before anybody else, with our marriage? From Him we can learn all the principles for a healthy, abundant, and blessing-filled marriage. We trust God with so many areas of our lives, why not trust Him with our marriage?

Heavenly Father, You can see the struggles we're dealing with today. As we look to You for wisdom and discernment, please help us to trust You with our marriage, with our home, and with every area of our lives. Thank You.

Wisdom Is Better Than Money

Wisdom is a shelter as money is a shelter, but the advantage of knowledge is this: wisdom preserves those who have it.
—Ecclesiastes 7:12, NIV

The wise man tells us that both wisdom and money can provide us with shelter. Money can shelter us from poverty, it can provide the help we need when we're ill or hungry. Wealth can secure for us an education that will open many doors of opportunity. But wealth cannot buy our salvation. It cannot give us the peace that passes understanding. It cannot purchase a relationship with God.

And when it comes to wealth, how certain can we be that it will always be available? We've all watched the stock market tank. It seems to come in cycles. Things soar economically and everyone believes that the good times will last forever. But they never do. Economies around the world seem to turn on a dime and can freefall without warning. Then rich and poor alike reel with the effects, and many give way to uncontrolled panic. Each economic crash brings news of investors taking their lives after losing their jobs, their homes, and even their marriages. When we place our trust in money or material things, we are bound to end up disappointed.

Wisdom, however, never disappoints. It is not fleeting as wealth is. Wisdom helps us to live through the seemingly unimaginable circumstances that life often throws our way. Wisdom helps us to manage even when our lives seem out of control. Wisdom helps us to look beyond disasters, work through difficulties, and walk through fiery situations. Wisdom helps us sort through crises, manage conflicts in a positive way, and find solutions even to the most challenging situations.

Money may never save our marriage, but wisdom can. Money will never provide the spiritual shelter we need when the hard times come. But wisdom will lead us to the Source of all wisdom—the wisdom solidly established on God's Word. The Bible contains sound counsel that will guide us in every situation. We can trust the wisdom it contains. It will never disappoint. Ever. And that's a promise we can take to the bank!

Father God, it's sometimes easy for us to think that money will solve all our problems. We know it won't—and so we ask You to give us the wisdom we need to help heal our marriage and our home. May we find our shelter and our safety in You and the wisdom that comes from You. Thank You, Lord.

Love No Matter What!

Do you think anyone is going to be able to drive a wedge between us and Christ's love for us? There is no way! Not trouble, not hard times, not hatred, not hunger, not homelessness, not bullying threats, not backstabbing, not even the worst sins listed in Scripture. —Romans 8:35, 36, The Message

These verses assure us that God's love for us is totally unconditional. Does that describe the love we have for our spouse? Do we love them at all times, not just when they act lovingly toward us? What if we acted lovingly toward them even when their actions weren't very kind or loving toward us? What if we spoke well to them even when their words toward us are hateful, mean, or unkind?

What if we lived with unconditional love toward our children? I believe every parent will experience sadness or disappointment at some time with their children. Like us, they are not perfect. They may well do things that are totally contrary to the way we have taught them. They may not mean to be hurtful. They may just be exercising their desire to be independent as part of the growing process. Even if their actions or words hurt us, our love for them should not be dependent on whether they act lovingly toward us. Our actions, words, and feelings should consistently communicate that we love them regardless. We should make it clear to them that our love for them is not conditional on their response toward us, but on God's love toward us; and since God's love toward us is unconditional, then so is our love for them.

Does this mean that we accept, condone, or encourage negative or harmful behavior? Unconditional love does not mean active support in the face of poor decisions. If my child chooses to use drugs, I would not tell them, "I'll support you in whatever you do." That would be illogical and would show lack of love, not true support. Unconditional love means loving them in spite of their choices. God's love calls us to love them even when they seem unresponsive to our love.

God calls us to love unconditionally our spouse and our children. And we can do this as we bask in the knowledge and the experience of His unconditional love for us. Do you know His love for you today?

Father, thank You for Your unconditional love for me. May Your love in me flow through to my family in ways that are consistent and unconditional.

Let Go

Their possessions will be taken, their homes left in ruins. They won't get to live in the houses they build, or drink wine from the grapes in their own vineyards.
—Zephaniah 1:13, CEV

Today's text describes people who pursue happiness by acquiring and keeping things. A very wealthy man was once asked how many dollars it would take for him to be completely happy. He responded by saying, "Just one more." Many live believing that if they could have one more dollar, one more car, another home, a larger paycheck, then they'd be happy. As a result, many have accumulated wealth but have not found the happiness they long for.

One of the safest and best things we can do for our family is to live in such a way that we teach them to love and depend on God and not on material things. A fire, an earthquake, a tornado, a hurricane, or a tsunami can wipe away everything we have in an instant. The collapse of the economy, a war, or the loss of employment may cause us to lose everything we have worked for, saved for, and lived for. And if our identity and happiness are tied to those things, when they're gone we lose our sense of self and meaning in life. But if our confidence is in God, who never changes, then we have real meaning in life. Someone once said that you never see a hearse pulling a U-Haul™ trailer. You can't take it with you to the grave.

I remember hearing the story of a rich man who was told by the angel of death that he had come to take him. The man asked if he could take something with him, to which the angel of death agreed. A few minutes later the man returned with a heavy suitcase. When he arrived at the pearly gates, Saint Peter asked the man to show him what was in the suitcase. He opened it up to reveal a mound of golden coins. Peter's response to the man was, "Why would you bring pavement to heaven?" The things we value here on earth don't have that same value in eternity. But character, values, principles, beliefs, the things that draw us closer to God, they are the real treasures we can take with us that will last through eternity.

Father, open our eyes and help us to see the things that are truly valuable. May our characters reflect Your loveliness and may our lives be centered in You.

Changing You From the Inside Out

For as he thinks within himself, so he is.
—Proverbs 23:7, NASB

Cognitive behavioral therapy, or CBT, is one of the most widely used therapeutic approaches in psychology today. Most therapists working with patients dealing with anxiety and depression use a blend of cognitive and behavioral therapy. CBT is "problem focused" and "action oriented." The therapist tries to assist the client in selecting specific strategies to help address those problems.

Today's text can be used as an illustration of how CBT works. We are and we behave according to the way that we think. This would be a concise presentation of both CBT and our text for today. The problem is that sometimes our thinking is not completely rational. For instance, when we focus on all the negative aspects or shortcomings of our spouse, our thinking becomes negative and we begin to "feel" miserable. The next "logical" step for us in this thought pattern is to seek happiness, and that most often means leaving our spouse and finding happiness in someone else.

Instead of giving up on your family, a better approach is to change your thought pattern about your spouse and your marriage. Begin by making a list of all the things you like and appreciate in your spouse. Don't overlook the smallest words or actions. If you like the outfit they're wearing, the fact they mowed the lawn, the lunch they fixed today, their smile, the fact they spent time with the kids helping them with their homework, how hard they work to provide for the needs of the family, then add those things to that list. The next step is to express appreciation toward them, each day, for at least one of the things on your list.

When you focus on the positives, your thinking pattern toward them will change, then your behavior toward them will change. It won't happen overnight. Be patient. Eventually, your feelings toward them will become more positive as well. The key is found within the words of our text today. "For as he thinks within himself, so he is." If you think loving thoughts and behave in a loving manner, you will feel loving. If we wait to "feel" loving before we begin to act lovingly—that may never happen. Changing our thoughts will produce a change in our behavior and will ultimately result in a change of our feelings.

Father, help us to change our thoughts toward our spouse, and to behave lovingly toward them. Renew our minds and renew our love.

In Unity

*Behold, how good and how pleasant it is for brethren
to dwell together in unity!—Psalm 133:1, KJV*

Marriage is a partnership between two equals, and the happiest ones are those in which there's unity in several important areas. These include the following.

1. Spiritual unity. This should be found at the core of the marriage relationship. When our walk with God is sound, we can build spiritual intimacy with our spouse that will further strengthen our own spiritual walk.

2. Emotional unity. This is the deep sense we have of sharing a connection with one another. When we experience emotional unity we feel loved, respected, and appreciated, and we instinctively respond by offering the same to our spouse.

3. Intellectual unity. This does not mean that we always agree with our spouse, or hold the same political persuasions. It does mean that we can communicate intellectually on a rational level, even when our opinions differ. Listening to the news together, reading the same books or magazines and discussing the thoughts and ideas they contain can go a long way to help forge intellectual unity. This exchange of ideas will help build the unity you need, even if you don't always agree.

4. Physical unity. It is an interesting fact that sexual intimacy cannot be separated from emotional, spiritual, and social unity and still be healthy or thrive. In fact, often the problems that arise in the sexual area of marriage have their origin when there are problems in the other areas. Physical unity goes far deeper than the physical act of love.

5. Social unity. This does not mean you must have all the same interests, but you should be able to enjoy at least a good number of activities together as the foundation for a strong relationship. Of course, the establishment of this foundation should begin during the dating period. You may want to try some things the other likes to see if you would enjoy doing them as well.

Behold, how good and how pleasant it is when husband and wife dwell together in unity. Celebrate your differences and enjoy the things you hold in common. Pray and work toward that end in your marriage, and your home will be a blessing to everyone it encompasses.

Father God, help us to have the type of unity that will help us build a strong, lasting, healthy, and happy marriage. May we recognize and appreciate the differences and strengths in our spouse, while drawing on the things we hold in common.

May

Courtesy Begins at Home

And be kind to one another.
—Ephesians 4:32, NKJV

The principle inculcated by the injunction, 'Be kindly affectioned one to another,' lies at the very foundation of domestic happiness. Christian courtesy should reign in every household. It is cheap, but it has power to soften natures which would grow hard and rough without it. The cultivation of a uniform courtesy, a willingness to do by others as we would like them to do by us, would banish half the ills of life.

"If we would have our children practice kindness, courtesy, and love, we ourselves must set them the example.

"Courtesy, even in little things, should be manifested by the parents toward each other. Universal kindness should be the law of the house. No rude language should be indulged; no bitter words should be spoken.

"All may possess a cheerful countenance, a gentle voice, a courteous manner; and these are elements of power. Children are attracted by a cheerful, sunny demeanor. Show them kindness and courtesy, and they will manifest the same spirit toward you and toward one another.

"By speaking kindly to their children and praising them when they try to do right, parents may encourage their efforts, make them very happy, and throw around the family circle a charm which will chase away very dark shadow and bring cheerful sunlight in. Mutual kindness and forbearance will make home a Paradise and attract holy angels into the family circle; but they will flee from a house where there are unpleasant words, fretfulness, and strife. Unkindness, complaining, and anger shut Jesus from the dwelling.

"The courtesies of everyday life and the affection that should exist between members of the same family do not depend upon outward circumstances.

"Pleasant voices, gentle manners, and sincere affection that finds expression in all the actions, together with industry, neatness, and economy, make even a hovel the happiest of homes. The Creator regards such a home with approbation.

"There are many who should live less for the outside world and more for the members of their own family circle. There should be less display of superficial politeness and affection toward strangers and visitors and more of the courtesy that springs from genuine love and sympathy toward the dear ones of our own firesides" (*The Adventist Home*, 421, 422).

Father, give us kind hearts and gentle words toward our families.

Shepherd Your Flock

Know the state of your flocks, and put your heart into caring for your herds.
—Proverbs 27:23, NLT

Two interesting responsibilities of ancient shepherds involved caring for their herds. In certain regions, a species of fly entered a sheep's brain through its ears and began to feed on the animal's brain. The pain caused the sheep to find a rock against which it would violently hit its head in an attempt to alleviate the pain. Eventually, the poor animal would fracture its skull and die. To prevent this, shepherds anointed their flocks with oil to keep flies from entering the sheep's brain through its ears.

As parents we protect our children through prayer. Daily we should anoint them with the oil of the Holy Spirit, asking Him to protect their minds from everything the devil is trying to use to distract and destroy them.

The second responsibility resulted in several shepherds bringing their flocks and merging them. Thus they shared the responsibility. This is a good principle for parents. Fathers can be an example for their boys and team up with other fathers in taking their sons camping or fishing. It's a great way to provide them with a sound example and model what healthy manhood looks like. Mothers can get together with other mothers to teach their daughters many of the fun, creative skills needed in running a home. It will be a blessing that the girls will one day use with their own children.

Today's text says that a good shepherd knows the state of his flock. That happens when the shepherd spends time with his flock. As parents, we need to spend time with our children, in order to know how they're doing and what challenges they're facing. Get to know their friends, enjoy family meals together, watch what they're watching—with them—and know what they're reading. When we develop a close relationship with our children, they will feel comfortable in sharing their lives with us and will be less likely to withhold harmful secrets, which could prove destructive if left unchecked.

Shepherding our children does not mean driving them with a stick to wherever we want them to go; it means leading them and lovingly teaching them how to follow in good and safe paths. It is protecting them from negative influences. It is shielding them from evil. It is rescuing them when they have fallen and leading them back home when they have wandered away.

Father God, help us to be faithful shepherds to the little flock You have entrusted to our care.

Laughter Is Good Medicine

A cheerful disposition is good for your health;
gloom and doom leave you bone-tired.
—Proverbs 17:22, The Message

So, now that we know the physical, emotional, and social benefits to be found in laughter, how do we incorporate more laughter into our lives? Can we learn to laugh more, or is it a case of "easier said than done"? Below are several ideas to help get you started on the pathway to better physical, mental, and social health through laughter:

1. Smile. Smiling is the beginning of laughter. Like laughter, it's contagious. Pioneers in "laugh therapy" find it's possible to laugh without even experiencing a funny event. The same holds for smiling. When you look at someone, practice smiling.
2. Count your blessings. Literally make a list. The simple act of considering the good things in your life will distance you from negative thoughts that are a barrier to humor and laughter. When you're in a state of sadness, you have further to travel to get to humor and laughter.
3. When you hear laughter, move toward it. Sometimes humor and laughter are private, a shared joke in a small group, but usually not. More often, people are very happy to share something funny because it gives them an opportunity to laugh again and feed off the humor you find in it. When you hear laughter, seek it out and ask, "What's funny?"
4. Spend time with fun, playful people. These are people who laugh easily— both at themselves and at life's absurdities—and who routinely find the humor in everyday events. Their laughter is contagious.
5. Bring humor into conversations. Ask people, "What's the funniest thing that happened to you today? This week? In your life?"

Bringing laughter and joy into your life can become a life-changing experience. And practice makes perfect. The more often you do it, the easier it becomes. As an added bonus, if you want to increase your own joy, bring laughter into the life of your spouse, your children, your family, your co-workers, and even strangers. Go ahead. Try it! Laughter is a gift. Be generous in sharing it, and you'll soon find out that it's a laughing matter.

Father God, thank You for the gift of laughter. Help us to experience it in our lives, and help us to share it with others so that its healing power may change their attitude and outlook into a more positive, joyful one.

Truth Is Love

[Love] rejoices in the truth.
—1 Corinthians 13:6, NKJV

It is very probable that if you are lying about one thing, then you are likely being untruthful in several other areas as well. After a while, what was once black and white becomes gray. You begin to believe that you're not really lying—more like fudging the truth, or telling a little white lie. And what's the harm in that? It's not like you're hurting anyone.

Marriages that are in trouble can often name dishonesty as one of the major issues even when it can take a while for most couples to recognize the fact. Dishonesty is insidious. It begins so innocently. Maybe you began telling lies because you didn't want to hurt your spouse's feelings. Since lying helped to smooth things over and avoid an argument, you convinced yourself into believing that the ends justified the means. But one lie always leads to another, and each time it becomes a little easier to be dishonest.

There are many ways to deceive one another. Avoiding an issue, distracting your spouse by focusing on an insignificant part of an issue, or any variant of these is being less than honest. Omitting information or deflecting the questions with a show of anger to avoid further discussion is also being dishonest. Giving one another the silent treatment is a particularly cruel form of deception—but deception nonetheless.

If your marital relationship is in bad shape, then the chances are good that dishonest communication has become part of your life. If that is the case, you must understand that honesty and open communication are essential if you want to prevent divorce and rescue your marriage. In fact, if you want to restore openness in your marriage, it is essential for you to understand that honesty is more than just the absence of lies. Breaking a well-established pattern of deceit is never easy and is always uncomfortable. Discuss with your spouse the options and strategies you both will agree to implement in order to restore honesty and openness in your marriage.

In order for it to work, you will both have to accept responsibility for being truthful. The apostle Paul made it clear that truth and honesty are a practical demonstration of love. Practice love by practicing truthfulness.

Father, help us to always speak the truth to each other, not just because it is good for us and our marriage, but because that's how we express love to one another.

Don't Keep a Record

[Love] thinks no evil.
—1 Corinthians 13:5, NKJV

The New King James Version of the Bible does not adequately convey the full meaning of what Paul evidently intended to say in this verse. Following is a sample of several other translations:

English Standard Version—"[Love] is not resentful" (does not count up wrongdoing)

New American Standard Bible—"Does not take into account a wrong suffered"

New International Version—"It keeps no record of wrongs"

The Message—"Doesn't keep score of the sins of others"

God's Word translation—"It doesn't keep track of wrongs."

The apostle Peter must have thought he would impress Jesus with his piety by asking Him, "Lord, how often shall my brother sin against me, and I forgive him? Up to seven times?" (Matthew 18:21, NKJV). He must have been taken aback when Jesus responded, "I do not say to you, up to seven times, but up to seventy times seven" (verse 22). Added up, that comes to 490. Did Jesus really mean we should forgive someone almost 500 times after they have hurt us? Who can possibly continue to forgive that many times without being taken advantage of, or even abused?

The Seventh-day Adventist Bible Commentary explains, "Of course, the number itself is not important, being only symbolic. . . . Forgiveness is not a matter of mathematics or legal regulations, but an attitude. He who harbors within himself the idea that at some future time he will not forgive, is far from extending true forgiveness even though he may go through the form of forgiving. If the spirit of forgiveness actuates the heart, a person will be as ready to forgive a repentant soul the eighth time as the first time, or the 491st time as the eighth. True forgiveness is not limited by numbers. . . . 'Nothing can justify an unforgiving spirit' " (5:449).

Paul and Jesus agree—love does not keep record of wrongs. Love forgives and removes the desire to punish or hurt the other person. This is the same way God forgives us and does not hold our past sin against us ever again. Love and forgiveness are a much better option in our marriages.

Father God, bless us that we may have a loving, forgiving spirit toward one another, so that harmony, peace, and love may reign in our home.

What Can I Do?

I can do all things through Christ who strengthens me.
—Philippians 4:13, NKJV

This promise is probably one of the best known and best loved of all the wonderful passages found in Paul's writings. We learn it, memorize it, quote it, and believe it. But what do we do with it when we are suddenly faced with unexpected marital difficulties? What do we do with this promise when thoughts of separation and divorce threaten to overwhelm and destroy everything we've worked for? Our home? Our family? Is there power in the promise when our relationship seems hopeless and we feel helpless? Can this promise make a difference when it matters most?

The cognitive-behavioral school of psychology teaches us that if we want to change our behavior we must first begin by changing our thinking. There are many ways they suggest this can be done, but in essence, genuine, lasting change becomes possible through the power and strength of Christ. As a marriage and family counselor, I have seen miraculous transformations. Marriages that had become like death sentences were revived. Families ravaged by infidelity had a renewal of their trust and their love. Marriages where abuse abounded experienced healing and became havens of peace and harmony. The changes were remarkable and nothing short of miraculous.

I would like to suggest that it is when we're going through the biggest challenges and difficulties in our marriage that we need to believe and hold on to the power in Paul's words. As we claim the promise, we allow the Holy Spirit to change our hearts and minds, and, ultimately, these changes will be reflected in our behavior. Things we once believed impossible can be accomplished by His grace. His Spirit working within us can transform and renew our minds, our lives, and our homes.

"In Christ there is strength to fulfill duty, power to resist temptation, vigor to endure affliction, patience to suffer without complaint. In Him there is grace for daily growth, courage for multiplied battles, energy for devoted service" (*The Seventh-day Adventist Bible Commentary*, 7:178).

Claim His power to change you today and every day. Claim His power to change your attitude toward your spouse and your marriage. Claim His power to transform your marriage from wherever it is today, to where He longs to take it. Until it becomes a foretaste of heaven.

Father God, change us with Your power. Bless our marriage so that it will be a foretaste of heaven, and give us great joy today and every day.

Belittling Your Neighbor

It is a sin to belittle one's neighbor; blessed are those who help the poor.
—Proverbs 14:21, NLT

One of the characteristics of a Christian is their desire to build others up, to help them reach the stature of Jesus Christ, and to reflect the image of Jesus. That is why it is so uncharacteristic of a Christian husband or wife to belittle, humiliate, or put their spouse down, either in public or in the privacy of their home.

The word *belittle* means to regard or portray as less impressive or important than appearances indicate; to depreciate or disparage. A synonym to depreciate is to take away their value. Another word that we use is to devalue or to invalidate your spouse. This is something critically important in marriage. Let's see how this hurts and destroys a relationship.

In Ephesians 5:33, Paul emphasizes the difference between husbands and wives by telling husbands to love their wives and instructing wives to respect their husbands. Paul understood that one of the most important emotional needs for a man is respect and affirmation, to feel valued, appreciated, admired, and encouraged by his wife. Hearing those words from her will build him up, encourage him to go out and fight the battles of life for his family, and strengthen him in the face of discouragement, stress, and even failure. It is a wise wife who expresses these feelings regularly and with authenticity.

Women have needs that are different from men. As a husband, you build your wife up and show her that you love her when you listen attentively to her, when you spend time with your children, playing, praying, and reading to them, when you help around the house, and when you are completely honest and trustworthy with her. If you look down on her as if she were inferior, when you lecture her instead of giving her a simple answer, or when you tell her she's dumb, stupid, ignorant, or worthless, you are stealing her God-given worth from her.

The text for today tells us that it is a sin to belittle our neighbor—which includes our spouse. Instead, God blesses those who help the poor—and that includes our spouse. Do all in your power to build your spouse up. You will both be blessed as a result.

Father, help me to be the kind of spouse who builds their spouse up. And may our words and actions become a blessing to our entire family. Thank You, Lord.

Three Ingredients for a Lasting Marriage

And now abide faith, hope, love, these three; but the greatest of these is love.
—1 Corinthians 13:13, NKJV.

The thirteenth chapter of First Corinthians has come to be known as "the love chapter," and even a hurried reading of the passage shows us the reason why. Today's verse is among the best known among believers and nonbelievers alike. Paul wraps up this section of his letter by stating that as important as prophecies and knowledge may be, at the end of the day there are only three things that will remain: "faith, hope, love . . . but the greatest of these is love." What implication do these words have for our homes? For our marriages? Let's consider them for a moment.

1. Faith. Researchers have found that successful couples who agree on four crucial areas tend to have more lasting, more satisfying relationships. The first of those four areas is spirituality. If we can't agree on our spirituality as a couple, the foundation for a long, strong relationship, and home, will be weak. It is our faith in God that helps us navigate the challenges and hardships that are an inevitable part of life. The other areas that are crucial to a stable marriage include agreement on how to handle finances, how to get along with the in-laws, and how to be a good parent.

2. Hope. Studies have shown that it is impossible for us to live without hope. In the many seasons of marriage, we can sometimes slip into a sense of complacency with our relationship. Very often we don't even realize we've done so until there is a crisis that shows how far we have drifted apart from each other. At that time of crisis, when there seems to be no way out and no reason to move forward, when the waters of despair seem to overwhelm us, it is hope that can help keep us together. Hope can provide the staying power that we need to hang on until the relationship is restored.

3. Love. The type of giving, unselfish, sacrificial love that Paul speaks about in this chapter is crucial for the well-being of a lasting marriage. Love brought us together, love has been with us through the ups and downs of life, and love will be glue that keeps us together.

Faith, hope, and love. When these are part of our marriage, we can survive even the toughest challenge.

Father God, may these three abide in our life and marriage, and may they keep us together for the long run.

Repetitive Communication

"And when you pray, do not use vain repetitions as the heathen do. For they think that they will be heard for their many words. Therefore do not be like them. For your Father knows the things you have need of before you ask Him."
—Matthew 6:7, 8, NKJV

Ellen White wrote, "Prayer is the opening of the heart to God as to a friend. Not that it is necessary in order to make known to God what we are, but in order to enable us to receive Him. Prayer does not bring God down to us, but brings us up to Him" (*Prayer,* 8). A conversation between friends that simply repeats the same words and thoughts over and over again will not only become tiresome but will discourage growth and depth in the relationship. Ultimately, it can lead to the end of the friendship.

This is especially true in a marriage. After the excitement of getting to know and love one another wears off, a couple can slip into a pattern of not communicating deeply. When life is busy with work and raising children, good conversation becomes even more important, and finding the time can be challenging. A healthy relationship requires ongoing sharing of thoughts and ideas. Growing marriages need to grow deeper and stronger—not just busier.

A good way to help ensure ongoing growth in our conversation with our spouse is to be sure that we are each growing in our walk with God. We need to both speak to Him from the depths of our hearts and also listen attentively to what He has to share with us at any given moment and in every situation. Often, the quality and content of our conversation with God impacts our conversation with others—including our spouse. As we spend time speaking with and listening to the Lord, we will experience greater closeness to our spouse and children, exchanging thoughts, feelings, and ideas, and listening for what they have to share.

This sharing often takes place during family meals, worship times, and fun times. Open your ears and your heart to what others have to say, and speak to them from the depths of your heart; that type of intimacy is what God designed marriage and the family to enjoy.

Father God, help us as we communicate our thoughts and feelings, our likes and dislikes, our fears and our joys with one another so that our sharing will forge a tighter bond between us.

The Bible, Our Light and Guide

And there followed another angel, saying, Babylon is fallen,
is fallen, that great city, because she made all nations drink of the
wine of the wrath of her fornication. —Revelation 14:8, KJV

Individually and as a people we have a most solemn work before us. There is a daily preparation of heart and mind to be gained in order that we may be fitted to work out the purposes of God for us. The perils of the last days are upon us, and at this time we are each determining what our destiny for eternity shall be. Individually we are to form characters that will stand the test of the judgment. Individually we are to give, in the church where we are, an example of faithfulness and consecration.

"The ministry of the Word is designed to prepare a people to stand in the times of temptation in which we live; and church members are to cooperate with the work of [the] ministry by revealing in the life the principles of the truth, that no word shall be spoken or act performed that will lead into false paths or create a condition of things that God cannot approve.

"There has been revealed to me the grave dangers we shall meet in these last days of peril and temptation. Our only reliable light and guide for this time is in the Word of God. We must take this Word as our counselor, and faithfully follow its instructions, or we shall find that we are being controlled by our own peculiar traits of character, and our lives will reveal a selfish work that will be a hindrance and not a blessing to our fellow men. . . .

"It is the duty of those who stand as leaders and teachers of the people to instruct church members how to labor in missionary lines. . . .

"The world is preparing for the closing work of the third angel's message. The truth is now to go forth with a power that it has not known for years. The message of present truth is to be proclaimed everywhere" (*The Upward Look*, 274).

O Lord, how easily we are distracted from this daily preparation of heart and mind. Please make us ever aware of the nearness of Your return and the work that must be done, not only in the world, but especially in our homes. May we not neglect to teach our children the importance of building their lives, their characters, on the Word of God.

"You Complete Me!"

For in Him dwells all the fullness of the Godhead bodily; and you are complete in Him, who is the head of all principality and power.
—Colossians 2:9, 10, NKJV

The movie *Jerry Maguire* had some memorable lines that have become truly cringe-worthy. Among them, the words spoken by Jerry to his girlfriend, "You complete me!" Some would argue that Tom Cruise could make any line work, and many find those words so romantic that they've borrowed them to express their devotion to their beloved. The concept behind those words hasn't worked too well for Cruise. At the time of filming *Jerry Maguire,* he was married to his second wife, Nicole Kidman. Five years later they divorced, and Cruise began a romantic relationship with Penelope Cruz. His third marriage, to Katie Holmes, ended a couple of years ago. The cynics among us would argue that Tom Cruise is still looking for someone to "complete" him.

This romantic view that we need another person to complete us began with the Greek philosopher Plato, who wrote about a "super race" of andro-gynous humans who attempted to overthrow the gods. These humans were both male and female. As they became more powerful, Zeus, the king of the gods, said, "I shall now cut each of them in two . . . and they will be both weaker and more useful to us through the increase in their numbers."

This forceful separation left both halves wandering the world, looking for their "soul mate," desperate to be reunited. When the two halves did finally find each other, all they could do was cling together, which sadly led to their deaths "because they were unwilling to do anything apart from one another." Zeus was no longer concerned about these once powerful beings because they were no longer a threat to the gods.

The Bible's view is very different. The truth is that because the fullness of the Godhead dwells in Jesus, our Creator, we are complete in Him! No other human being can complete us. They can, and do, add to our lives. But a human being, who is not perfect, cannot possibly meet all our needs. Jesus, because He is perfect, can and does complete us. So stop looking for another person to be your perfect soul mate. Submit first to Jesus. As you each do this, He will complete you both.

Father God, thank You that we can be complete in Jesus. Help us to draw closer to Him and, in that way, be blessed to draw closer to one another.

Generosity

Give freely and become more wealthy; be stingy and lose everything.
—Proverbs 11:24, NLT

Often we think of generosity exclusively in terms of money or possessions. While this can be true and accurate, it is far from exclusive. There are many nonmaterial things that God has blessed us with and that He invites us to share generously with those in need. This is an important lesson that He wants us to learn—give freely and become wealthier; be stingy and lose everything. Those who hoard their blessings end up paranoid that everyone is out to get them and rob them. The more they close themselves off from one another, the more often they end up sad, lonely, isolated individuals.

What are some of the nonmaterial things that we've been blessed to receive from the Lord? Typically, they're the very things we overlook as being too ordinary to share. I believe these words from Proverbs also refer to the time, the kindness, the attention, the help, and the love we give to those closest to us and even to those we are not related to. The wise man counsels us to not be stingy—starting with our spouse, our children, and our family. The paradox is that the more we give, the more we will receive. Perhaps it's because God loves a cheerful giver that He blesses us so abundantly.

Don't be like Ebenezer Scrooge and other hoarders like him. What is the point of being rich if you have no one to share and enjoy your blessings with? If we hoard our kindness, time, and compassion, the results will be similar to those who hoard their money: we will end up lonely and sad. So give generously of yourself. Starting with those closest to you, who for some reason are often the ones at the bottom of your list, be generous with your love; extravagant with your time; and cheerful in all your interactions.

May God be our example in giving to others—of ourselves and of our finances. Let us stop taking what we have for granted and look to see who needs our help. In giving to others, we are giving to the Lord. Let us give as unto the Lord. Generously. Let us not be stingy in our giving.

Father God, help us to recognize that everything belongs to You, and You give us so much more than we deserve. In return, Father, as You have blessed us, help us to be generous so we may share your blessings with others.

Swollen With Pride

"Behold the proud, his soul is not upright in him;
but the just shall live by his faith."
—Habakkuk 2:4, NKJV

When two people marry, there is a normal, automatic tension. Each person, because of their family of origin, tends to want to pull his or her spouse in the direction in which they were raised. They want to live in the way they were accustomed to. When those patterns were good and healthy, that can be a good, solid basis for building a new home. The problems begin when one or both partners had faulty or even unhealthy families of origin, and each wants the other to follow the same patterns. Tension and conflict will be the result.

The next issue that normally arises is an unwillingness to recognize wrongdoing. Pride takes over, and one or neither is willing to admit that those patterns set during their upbringing are bad. They feel that if the other person is not willing to accept their family of origin's patterns they are in reality attacking them, or at the very least rejecting them. They rise up to defend their family and initiate an attack on their partner's family.

While this tension and resulting conflict are natural in the process of adapting to life together, the biggest issue arises when one or both are unwilling to recognize their contribution to their problems and proudly stand their ground, even if it is not good, or even if it's detrimental to the relationship. "Like a bloated toad, these arrogant people hop along toward destruction."* Consciously or subconsciously, they run toward the precipice, taking their family with them until they plunge together into the death of their relationship.

Habakkuk offers a much better solution for you and for your family: "The just shall live by his faith." Set aside pride and arrogance and live with the knowledge of God's presence in your life and in your marriage, and learn to depend on Him to help you form a healthy relationship. When the horizon looks dark, let Him be your sunshine. When the ground seems shaky, let Him be your rock. When the storms of conflict and strife arrive in your marriage, let Him come and bring you peace. Instead of hopping along toward the destruction of your marriage, walk with God by faith so you and your family will have life, and life abundant.

Father God, come live in our lives, in our marriage, in our family, and eradicate all pride and sin from our relationship that we may live.

---

* Dallas Theological Seminary, *The Bible Knowledge Commentary: An Exposition of the Scriptures,* ed. J. F. Walvoord and R. B. Zuck (Wheaton, IL: Victor Books, 1985).

Pride Leads to Conflict

Pride leads to conflict; those who take advice are wise.
—Proverbs 13:10, NLT

Disagreements and arguments crop up in even the best marriages. It's not the absence of conflict but rather how conflict is handled that is an important key to marital success or failure. Some of the most current research confirms that poorly handled conflict can negatively influence mental, physical, and family health. Feelings of anger, bitterness, and unhappiness, which sometimes lead to separation and divorce, often result.

The question is, What causes conflict in marriage? Although no two situations are alike, there are some common patterns that often result in marital conflict and can lead to infidelity in marriage, or separation, or divorce. Following are four of those possible causes:

1. Unacknowledged or unresolved anger or resentment. Disagreements over finances, sex, parenting, in-laws, or spirituality are reported as some of the most common issues over which couples have conflict. Unless dealt with, anger and resentment may be the trigger for future conflict.

2. Taking each other for granted and becoming bored with the relationship. Sometimes couples settle for a comfortable relationship and don't strive to grow in intimacy. Unfortunately, many begin to focus on the negative things they see in their spouse and use them to criticize and even attack their perceived weaknesses.

3. A narcissistic personality style. This describes a spouse who is so excessively self-involved and ego-centric that he or she doesn't seem to have any regard or compassion for the needs or desires of others, including those of his or her spouse. They don't seem to feel any guilt, remorse, or shame for their hurtful or inappropriate behavior toward their spouse.

4. Pride. Today's text also teaches us that pride leads to conflict. Sinful human nature seeks control. As long as we allow our sinful nature, or pride, to control us, we will seek to control our spouse. If they also allow their sinful human nature to control them, they will seek to control us. The struggle for control inevitably leads to conflict (see Genesis 3:16). On the other hand, Christ's nature in us should lead us to be humble. Instead of trying to control the other, Christ's nature in us will lead us to want to serve our spouse.

Father God, help our nature to be more Christlike so that we may seek to serve one another and so that instead of having unhealthy conflict we may have loving harmony.

Why Worry?

*I'll search Jerusalem with lamps and punish those people who sit there
unworried while thinking, "The Lord won't do anything, good or bad."*
—Zephaniah 1:12, CEV

Sometimes we have a tendency to worry about everything until we become paralyzed. I'm not speaking of a pathological fear, but rather the daily worry about our job, and the traffic, the kids, finances, the weather, anything that concerns us. We may remember Jesus' words, "Don't worry about tomorrow. It will take care of itself. You have enough to worry about today" (Matthew 6:34, CEV). Jesus was not saying we should not worry at all. He was encouraging us to take life one day at a time.

Some people don't seem to be troubled by worry, either for today or tomorrow. They don't really plan for their future, simply choosing to do nothing but trust that everything will turn out well in the end. Solomon wrote, "How long will you lie there doing nothing at all? When are you going to get up and stop sleeping?" (Proverbs 6:9, CEV).

This attitude can have a devastating effect on homes. Too often, those who neglect their marriage and their family only realize there's a problem once it's too late. Some don't seem to realize that their marriage is falling apart a little at a time. Distracted by work, friends, watching or practicing sports, and whatever else entertains them, they can end up lonely and disconnected.

The sad result for many who hold to a "couldn't care less" attitude is the demise of their marriage and the loss of their children. After it's too late, they wonder what happened, and often begin to blame others for what happened—their spouse, the school, the church, or something else or someone else. They question, *Why did God allow this to happen? Why didn't He keep our family together? Why have our children rejected the church, and walked away from God?*

We would all do well to take inventory of our lives and our homes before it is too late. As needed, make the commitment to make changes and be intentional about spending time growing the success of your relationships. Successful homes are not an accident; they require people choosing to commit to a lifelong, healthy, happy relationship for the rest of their lives.

Father, while we don't want to worry unnecessarily about tomorrow, help us to do all in our power to see that our home is healthy. May we plan for the future and work toward making that future possible with Your blessing.

Don't Forget God

A bride could not forget to wear her jewelry to her wedding,
but you have forgotten me day after day.
—Jeremiah 2:32, CEV

Jeremiah presents a somewhat preposterous situation. On her wedding day, one of the most important days of her life, the bride is careful to have everything just perfect, but she's forgotten the groom.

To illustrate how important this day is for the bride, a news report shared the story of a bride who, on the day of her wedding, called 911 to report that her car, with her wedding gown inside, had been stolen. As the news played the 911 tape, one could hear the anguish in the bride's voice. Unexpectedly, the dispatcher asked the size of the dress, and when it turned out they were the same size, she quickly offered to lend the bride her own wedding gown. Not only that, she took it to the bride, who was able to wear it on her special day.

To get back to Jeremiah's message, while some brides may harbor an inner fear that they will be left standing at the altar, it would be preposterous to think that a bride who has gone to great lengths to have everything perfect on her wedding day would see to all the details and neglect to find a groom. How many brides have done everything in their power to be ready for their wedding except have a husband?

Jeremiah says that portrays our situation when we leave God out of our life and out of our family. It is preposterous! Yet it's done all the time. We go about our lives as though God doesn't even exist. We work, get a paycheck, spend it, travel, entertain, and live our lives while ignoring the fact that it is God who has made it possible for us to have life and work and money.

Jeremiah invites us to turn to God before it's too late. Pray for, and with, your spouse. Pray for God's guidance and blessings, for a resurgence of love, for the power to forgive, for the ability to make positive changes, for patience, for wisdom, for the ability to see the best in the other, for God to change us from the inside out. Turn to God before it is too late for your marriage and for your family.

Father God, help us to turn to You with all our hearts and not forget You. Bless our life and marriage by being at the center of all we are and all we do.

The Lasting Heritage

Behold, children are a heritage from the LORD, the fruit of the womb is a reward. Like arrows in the hand of a warrior, so are the children of one's youth. Happy is the man who has his quiver full of them; they shall not be ashamed, but shall speak with their enemies in the gate.—Psalm 127:3–5, NKJV

The word *heritage* is a well-known word, although it's not one we typically use every day. There are several definitions of the word *heritage*, and here are a few of them:

1. Something inherited at birth, such as personal characteristics, status, and possessions
2. Anything that has been transmitted from the past or handed down by tradition

The word *heritage* appears often in the Bible, where we find at least two usages of the word:

1. The Israelites regarded as belonging inalienably to God
2. The land of Canaan regarded as God's gift to the Israelites

A heritage, in general terms, is something given or left to someone's descendants. What is really interesting in the text for today is that the children, who will one day receive our heritage, are God's heritage to us. They are one way that God shows His love for us.

This can be challenging to remember when parenting young children. There are times when it can feel overwhelming. The demands of disciplining them, answering endless questions, ensuring they are doing their schoolwork, teaching them to do household chores, and countless other responsibilities often leave us feeling exhausted.

Having two young-adult daughters who don't live at home anymore, I can say we truly enjoy when they are home. What joy they bring to our hearts when they're here, and how painful it is when they leave. I have friends who have lost children through accidents or after an illness, and they have expressed the deep pain they experience and the longing to have them back.

Enjoy your children and their time at home. A friend of mine shared this powerful thought: "Learn to appreciate what you have before time makes you appreciate what you had."

Father God, thank You for giving us our children. Help us to appreciate that special gift and to leave to them the heritage of our love for them.

A Place of Rest

"But not so on Mount Zion—there's respite there! A safe and holy place!
The family of Jacob will take back their possessions from those who
took them from them." —Obadiah 1:17, The Message

The emotions that arise from thoughts of *home* have inspired countless expressions and songs that touch our hearts deeply. "Home, Sweet Home," "For there's no place like home for the holidays," and the list could go on.

We all need a place to call home—a place to come back to. The prodigal son felt that emptiness and regret and headed for home. Joseph, in the Old Testament, longed for home. The Israelites who were taken captive to Babylon cried alongside the river as they sang of home.

Those of us born in a faraway country miss the place we used to call home. Others now live across the country, far from family and friends, and treasure the memories they have of home. With the passing years we have the opportunity to build new memories with our families. Let's make them good ones! Memories that will help them understand how precious home is and that it is often the simple things in life that can end up being the most valuable—like sharing a meal of corn on the cob together on the back porch. It's not about having a lot of money to spend on making memories, but the time you take to make home a special place for your family.

For husbands and wives, creating a home that is a safe place to come to at the end of a busy workday is especially important. After battling with the challenges of business, home should be a place where both husband and wife can feel loved; where they can relax and disconnect from the stress of work-related responsibilities. Sharing in the tasks of preparing supper, helping the kids with homework, and getting ready for bedtime lighten the load for both husband and wife. Let's determine to place the nagging, complaining, and nitpicking out with the rest of trash. Let's not make space for them to fill our homes.

Let's make our homes a place of respite, a place where our families will feel loved and comfortable, and a place that they will want to come back to at the end of each day. Let's create homes that will give us a glimpse of heaven and be a blessing to the world.

Father God, help us to create in our home a place to come back to, a little foretaste of heaven.

Give Generously

*Do not withhold good from those who deserve it
when it's in your power to help them.*
—Proverbs 3:27, NLT

God made provision for the poor in His instructions to the ancient Israelites. One such provision was that farmers were not to go back and gather the grain that had fallen during the harvest, but to leave that grain in the fields for the poor to glean. This was how many provided for their needs when they had nowhere else to go for help.

Jesus gave special mention to the widow who gave everything she had as an offering in the temple. This example of sacrificial giving wasn't even noticed by the rich, who were too busy making sure everyone noticed how much they were giving. They may have given large amounts, but what they gave was only a portion of what they possessed. The widow, by contrast, gave everything she had.

A young man with cerebral palsy had received many donations to help with a surgery that would assist him greatly by providing more mobility. However, when he heard of a young child who also had cerebral palsy and needed surgery, he gave everything that had been donated for his own surgery so the young child could have it instead. What an act of generosity on his part!

How generous are we with those closest to us? I'm not referring only to financial generosity. How generous are we with expressing our appreciation for them? How generous are we in giving praise and affirmation for what they do? How often do we speak words that lift them up, encourage them, and bring joy to them? What good is it if we just think about what we'd like to say to them, but never get around to actually saying it? Our text today reminds us not to withhold good things from others when it is within our power to be helpful. This includes being kind and speaking well to our loved ones, to those closest to us, to those with whom we work, to our neighbors, or to those who go to school with us.

The Christian life should be characterized by a generous spirit—for God has been so generous with us! Let us shower others with words that will help them, encourage them, and strengthen them. The right word, at the right time, may just be what they need in their time of need.

Father God, help us to be generous in our praise of others that we may alleviate their burdens and encourage them when they're down.

Why Do You Work So Hard?

*It is useless for you to work so hard from early morning until late at night,
anxiously working for food to eat; for God gives rest to his loved ones.*
—Psalm 127:2, NLT

Psalm 127 is one of two wisdom poems authored by Solomon. Basically, Solomon is stating that life without God is meaningless. This is also the main theme of the book of Ecclesiastes. He emphasizes that all our work is futile unless God is at its center. This is a great reminder in light of a recent Gallup poll.

In the poll it was determined that the average work week in the United States is no longer forty hours but rather forty-seven hours. Only 40 percent of those polled said they worked an average of forty hours a week, and 50 percent reported that they worked more than forty hours. Salaried employees reported the highest number of hours worked each week. Americans are working longer hours than ever before, and yet only 13 percent expressed enjoyment in their work.

We admire people who are not afraid of hard work. Men and women who have a good work ethic are respected and sought after in the job market. Being busy, overworked, has almost become a badge of honor among many people. Yet Solomon says it's futile for us "to work so hard from early morning until late at night, anxiously working for food to eat." While we recognize the need, and the importance, of working to put food on the table, at what point does our overworking become futile? When we reach burnout? How does overwork impact our home life, and what effect does it have on our family relationships?

Working hard to provide for our family is important. So is time spent with them. Working so hard that we never see them—even if it is to provide them with some of life's comforts—does not make us better parents. How important that we find the balance between working hard to meet our needs and giving time to the equally important aspects of family life, such as resting and playing together; enjoying quality time together in service activities around our neighborhoods and in our communities. While working hard to provide for our families, let's ask God for wisdom to find that balance.

Father God, help me to have my priorities in the right order, and help me to understand that working simply to provide more things for my family is not as important as spending time with them.

Stand Up!

"Get up, for it is your duty to tell us how to proceed in setting things straight. We are behind you, so be strong and take action."
—Ezra 10:4, NLT

Every home must have a leader, the head of household, who the rest of the family may follow. The ideal is for the husband to assume that role and responsibility—that was God's original plan and design. But we can't ignore the reality that there are many women who have had to step up and assume the role of the head of household for many reasons, the most common being that they are single mothers or because their husband has abandoned his responsibility.

What does it mean to be the head of your household? Who are you called to be, and what are you called to do? Following are three responses to those important questions.

First, as the head of the home, it is your responsibility to see that your family follows, in obedience, the commands of God. Children instinctively copy what their parents do. If you are living in obedience to God's commands, your children are more likely to follow suit than if you say, "Do as I say—not as I do."

Second, you must lead. How do you know if you're leading effectively? One way is to ask yourself, "Is anyone following?" As General Norman Schwarzkopf once remarked, "If you are in command, then lead." Fortunately, we don't have to lead blindly. We can come to our heavenly Father for wisdom on how to be a good leader.

Thirdly, you should fill the role of protector, provider, and priest. As protector, you will protect the physical needs of your children as well as their emotional and spiritual needs. As provider, you will be a stabilizing influence in their lives and help meet their need for having a secure home and a sound education. Finally, as priest, you will be a person of prayer and live a life of obedience to God's Word, demonstrating consistency in all you do and say.

The myth of the perfect parent is just that—a myth. But a parent who steps up to the role as head of household and who, in God's strength and grace, strives to do their best each day will be blessed by the Lord. They will be a blessing, an example, and an inspiration to their children.

Father God, help us to lead our family to follow You through our own example of fair and loving leadership.

My Spouse, My Friend

"His mouth is full of sweetness. And he is wholly desirable. This is my beloved and this is my friend." —Song of Solomon 5:16, NASB

There are several important things to notice in this verse. First, the Shulamite who is speaking these words verbalizes her admiration of her beloved. Willard Harley, Christian psychologist and author of *His Needs, Her Needs* and *Love Busters,* writes that one of the most important emotional needs for most men is admiration. A man needs to know that his wife admires him and affirms him, that she is his biggest cheerleader, and that she expresses appreciation for who he is and what he does. Wives can make an ongoing list of the things their husbands do and express appreciation for them. Don't take him for granted, and don't assume that what he does, even the smallest of actions, is what he's supposed to do and that he therefore does not deserve to hear a sincere "thank you."

Passion and desire should be solely reserved for your spouse. Because men tend to be more visual than women, they find their wives desirable as they look at them: the way they dress and fix their hair, the way their bodies look, the way they walk, and their demeanor toward them. Women, on the other hand, find their husbands desirable when they initiate worship, when they are kind and polite, when they listen attentively, and when they spend quality time together. It is not things, money, or riches that we as husbands and wives desire so much as loving actions and words from our spouse.

Finally, friendship is vital for a good marriage. Someone once said that you should marry your best friend. Well, whether or not you marry your best friend, you can cultivate a relationship with your spouse so that they will ultimately become your best friend. That means they will be your confidant, the person you will trust with anything and everything you have and you know. It means that there will not be any secrets between you and that you will not be afraid to express your deepest thoughts and feelings to them.

Enjoy each day the love and friendship from your spouse, and make sure you make every day a positive experience for them. It will pay great dividends for your relationship, for your home, and for your family.

Father God, thank You for giving me my best friend to live with me as my spouse. Help me to be their best friend too.

Move Forward

But one thing I do, forgetting those things which are behind and reaching forward to those things which are ahead, I press toward the goal for the prize of the upward call of God in Christ Jesus. —Philippians 3:13, 14, NKJV

Looking back at the hurts in your relationship will only keep you stuck in the sinkhole of resentment. The word *resentment* comes from two Latin words which mean "to feel again." Looking back at the wounds makes you feel the pain again. What is the best way to deal with it? Following are five steps:

1. *Make the decision that you're going to stay married, no matter what.* Repeat it to yourself often. Say it out loud and figure out what you need to do so both of you can make that commitment work.

2. *Put time into your marriage.* Unless you are intentional about changing the future, you may repeat the mistakes of the past. Devote time to cultivating a strong relationship with your spouse. Make them feel special, and let them know they are the most important person in your life.

3. *Figure out what you get out of being resentful.* Does it make you feel better? Does it feel good to give your spouse a bit of their own medicine? Well, then what? What does remaining resentful accomplish, anyway? Besides driving a wedge between you and your spouse, what real benefit have you gained for your relationship? Nelson Mandela said, "Resentment is like drinking poison and then hoping it will kill your enemies."

4. *Figure out what specifically hurt you and what you need to do to forgive.* Sometimes we have a big challenge trying to forgive because we think about everything that has happened or that has been done to us. Often complex tasks are easier to complete if we do them one step at a time. You may need to forgive one offense at a time.

5. *If you're still feeling resentful, sit down and calmly tell your spouse how you feel and why, without pointing an accusing finger.* Use "I" statements rather than "you" statements. Ask for their help and support to stop doing what has caused you pain in the past. It's important to forgive, but it is also important to protect yourself and ensure that the same painful events will not happen again.

Father God, help us to forgive the past, stop looking back with resentment to what we cannot change, and look forward to the future by making the necessary changes today.

Pray That You May Not Be Tempted

He said to them, "Pray that you may not enter into temptation."... Then He said to them, "Why do you sleep? Rise and pray, lest you enter into temptation."
—Luke 22:40, 46, NKJV

This instruction from Jesus provides us with a powerful plan when it comes to dealing with temptation. Ellen White expands on the teaching here: "Temptations may be all around you, yet you are safe as long as you do not enter into them. Many of us are overcome by Satan because we walk right into temptation.... It is your business to keep aloof from everyone and everything which will have a tendency to lead you away from duty and divert your mind from God.... If compelled to be in the society of those who are evil, you are not compelled to enter into or engage in their evil. You can, by prayer and watching, remain unsullied by the evil manifested about you" (*Our High Calling*, 132).

Jesus knew it was critically important for the disciples to spend time in prayer. It is no less critical for believers today to engage in prayer—particularly as it impacts their homes, marriages, and families. How many couples are found sleeping instead of spending time in prayer? How many parents are doing the same instead of praying that their children may not enter into temptation?

Husbands and wives, set aside time in the morning, or at night before going to bed, to pray together with one another. Read a passage from the Bible and then pray together. Do the same thing with your children. If they are away from home, send them a text to remind them you love them and you are praying for them. Be specific about your prayers—"You're in my prayers today as you take that test."

Don't neglect to gather the family for morning and/or evening worship. Make it short, age appropriate, and enjoyable. Ellen White advises that "the prayer offered should be short and pointed. The one who leads in prayer should not pray about everything, but should express his needs in simple words and praise God with thanksgiving" (*Child Guidance*, 521).

Don't allow the busyness of life to become so wearying that you are overtaken by sleep.

Father God, awaken in us the desire to spend time with You in prayer, not simply as a habit but as a wonderful way to maintain the lines of communication between us open and strong, especially as we face temptation.

Created to Do Good

God planned for us to do good things and to live as he has always wanted
us to live. That's why he sent Christ to make us what we are.
—Ephesians 2:10, CEV

God's plan when He created us was not for us to simply live for ourselves but rather that we would give to others of all the abundance that we have received from Him. The quality of unselfishness is a central characteristic in the life of a Christian. The standard for living that God has given to us is Jesus Christ. No one has given us a clearer demonstration of living a selfless life than Jesus. We fall short daily, but Jesus stands by ready to help as we ask Him.

As husbands, one of the areas where we need to do better is when it comes to how we treat our wives. Paul writes in Ephesians 5:25, 26, "Husbands, love your wives, just as Christ also loved the church and gave Himself for her, that He might sanctify and cleanse her" (NKJV). We need to stop and think about how Jesus has treated His bride. He lived for her and ultimately He willingly died for her. Jesus demonstrated His love by laying down His life for His friends. Do we love our spouse to that degree?

A good question to ask ourselves as we consider Jesus' relationship with the church is this: Is there anything that Jesus *didn't* do for, or to, His bride? The list is endless. He has never hurt, abused, neglected, or abandoned His bride. Nor will He. His promise is sure—"I will *never* leave you, nor forsake you!"

Our effort, as husbands, should be in imitating Jesus, by loving our wives selflessly. Every action and word should bless and help them. Now, I'm the first to confess that I have fallen far short of that goal, which is the reason I must continue to draw closer to Christ that I may imitate Him and be changed more into His image so that my words and actions will not just be mine but His through me.

The same is true in our relationship with our children. Jesus loved children and made them feel loved and accepted through His words and actions. May we be a better reflection of Christ to our wives and children.

Father God, help us to better reflect Your image in and through us to our wives (or husbands) and children that they may get a better of picture of You because of how we love and treat them.

Why Get Married?

That you may with one mind and one mouth glorify
the God and Father of our Lord Jesus Christ.
—Romans 15:6, NKJV

According to Pew Research, Americans believe that love is the main foundation of marriage. Most who never have been married say they would like to be at some point in their lives, but statistics show Americans aren't rushing to the altar, and the U.S. marriage rate is at an all-time low—only 51 percent of adults were married in 2011, according to U.S. Census Bureau statistics. So, while many choose not to marry, what are some of the common reasons why people choose to get married rather than stay living together?

One reason is the financial stability that occurs with two people bringing home a paycheck. With many young adults paying down college loans, the additional financial help can make purchasing and running a home affordable. The combined income can help provide a comfortable lifestyle and a better standard of living. Unexpected expenses, emergency surgeries, or motor vehicle accidents can have a devastating effect on people but can typically be weathered far better when there are two people to work through the challenges together.

Love is the number one reason why people choose to marry. Being married gives you a lifelong companion. Someone to love and be loved by. Someone to share your life with—a friend to help weather the storms that inevitably come to us all. Someone to share your joys and triumphs. When you start a family, you'll have a partner to work with in raising your children.

While these are good and valid reasons for getting married, for Christians, though, marriage is more than a nice arrangement that helps us financially, emotionally, and socially. Marriage is an opportunity to fulfill God's plan for our lives, to live His love and grace through us, to illustrate the type of relationship He desires to have with us, and that together we may love, worship, and serve Him. In Paul's words, marriage helps so that we "may with one mind and one mouth glorify the God and Father of our Lord Jesus Christ." What an awesome opportunity we have, as husband and wife, and together with our children, to glorify God.

Father God, may our lives as husbands and wives, and as parents and children, be lived in such a way that we will glorify You daily because You deserve it but also so that others may come to know You and the love You have for them.

Abide in Me

"Abide in Me, and I in you. As the branch cannot bear fruit of itself,
unless it abides in the vine, neither can you, unless you abide in Me."
—John 15:4, NKJV

Having our names on the church books does not guarantee that we will behave properly all the time. It does not guarantee that we will have the best of relationships. It does not guarantee that all will go well for us. We need more than membership. We need relationship—with Jesus Christ. When we are in close relationship with Jesus, then we are guaranteed that things will be different. We will be different. The way we act and talk will be more like Jesus, and our relationships will be healthier.

Ellen White made this interesting statement: "In your business, in companionship for leisure hours, and in alliance for life, let all the associations you form be entered upon with earnest, humble prayer. You will thus show that you honor God, and God will honor you. Pray when you are fainthearted. When you are desponding, close the lips firmly to men; do not shadow the path of others; but tell everything to Jesus. Reach up your hands for help. In your weakness lay hold of infinite strength. Ask for humility, wisdom, courage, increase of faith, that you may see light in God's light and rejoice in His love" (*The Ministry of Healing*, 513).

Those who have a close relationship with Christ, however, will not be looking for fault in their spouse. One of the evidences of an abiding Savior is that we will look for the best in the other instead of looking for things to criticize. When we are close to Jesus, we will desire for Him to change us and not tell Him how to change our spouse to meet our needs. Our prayers for our spouse should be that God would bless them as they come to know and love Him more fully.

When we are discouraged because our relationship is not all that we wish it were, when the problems and challenges we face seem to overwhelm us, we can lay hold of God's strength. Ask for humility, wisdom, courage, and increase of faith. Commit your relationship to God and let Him handle it in His wisdom and might.

Father God, bless me with humility, wisdom, and courage to fight for my marriage and for my family, and help me to draw close to You so that I may receive these blessings from Your hands daily.

I Don't Do It on Purpose

For what I am doing, I do not understand. For what I will to do,
that I do not practice; but what I hate, that I do.... For the good
that I will to do, I do not do; but the evil I will not to do, that
I practice.... O wretched man that I am!
—*Romans 7:15, 19, 24, NKJV*

P aul's experience is one we all have identified with at some point. We each struggle with different issues. Some battles we win. Some we lose. And often this becomes most evident in our homes and in our marriages.

Husbands and wives love each other, but sometimes they battle for supremacy in the relationship. They can be unkind, even rude or abusive toward one another. They don't like doing it, they reproach themselves for their behavior, yet they continue to do it. Done long enough, it becomes a habit, and the longer a habit is repeated, the more entrenched it becomes and the harder it is to overcome. The damage to the marriage can become irreparable.

God has created each of us with an amazing brain. While the experts used to believe that our brains were hardwired for certain behaviors, new research has uncovered the discovery of plasticity of the brain. That is, the ability for the brain to "reprogram" itself. Our brain has the capacity for building new neural pathways. Our thoughts travel along these pathways and can result in new and healthier behaviors. If you have a habit that is hurting your relationship, establish a new pattern, a new and healthier habit, until the old pattern gets weaker and the new pattern gets stronger.

Of course, we must not forget the last part of today's verses. While we can try to make changes in our attitudes and behaviors, in our words and in our actions, and while we may be successful up to a certain point, we must realize that ultimate and lasting victory can only be achieved through Jesus Christ. As we surrender our will to Him, as we contemplate His life, little by little we are changed to resemble Him more and us less. Serving Him is establishing a new pattern for our lives, a better way of living, and a healthier way of life.

Father God, help me to overcome the bad habits that are destroying me and the relationships with the people around me. Please help me to establish new patterns and a new lifestyle that promotes health, happiness, and wholeness in my marriage.

Enough Is Enough

"You have sown much, and bring in little; you eat, but do not have enough; you drink, but you are not filled with drink; you clothe yourselves, but no one is warm; and he who earns wages, earns wages to put into a bag with holes." . . . *"You looked for much, but indeed it came to little; and when you brought it home, I blew it away. Why?" says the* Lord *of hosts. "Because of My house that is in ruins, while every one of you runs to his own house."*
—*Haggai 1:6, 9, NKJV*

People work themselves to death in order to have the bigger house, the newer car, the latest electronic gadget, the finest clothes, and the largest bank account. In a desperate search for the good life, many think they have to be number one, the most famous, the fastest, and the best. And while pursuing this impossible dream, they neglect, and ultimately destroy, what is really most important. Athletes, movie stars, and musicians are adored by millions, yet many of them have the same struggles as their fans. They are in and out of rehabilitation centers and sometimes choose to end their lives.

At our place of work, there are people willing to do anything to rise to the top. They will lie, cheat, betray coworkers, take credit for the work others have done, and anything else to be considered for higher positions in the company. At school, some students plagiarize assignments, pay others to do their work, or cheat on exams so they can have the best of grades.

Even in church we sometimes see the same thing—people who want to be the head deacon, the head elder, or the leader in some department. Some will even try to undermine the pastor or the church leaders in their pursuit of power, position, and control. It seems as though the thought of being any-where else but at the top is unbearable. In their thinking, happiness comes from being number one.

Haggai puts things into perspective. The pursuit of happiness through wealth, power, control, fame, or anything else apart from God does not, and will never, bring lasting satisfaction or true happiness. Looking to ourselves, or to others, rather than outside ourselves brings hopelessness and despair. It is in looking outside of ourselves, to God, that we can find true satisfaction, true joy, and true happiness.

Father God, help us to remove the focus from ourselves and to turn our eyes toward You and toward the pursuit of helping others find You.

Hypocrisy in Marriage

"Therefore, when you do a charitable deed, do not sound a trumpet before you as the hypocrites do in the synagogues and in the streets, that they may have glory from men. Assuredly, I say to you, they have their reward."
—Matthew 6:2, NKJV

We have all seen people who are very unkind and rude to others in public. They don't seem to care where they are or who hears them when they make their snide remarks. This can be particularly uncomfortable for others when a husband and wife use sarcasm, or even yell at each other, seeming not to care that they're being observed. It is disconcerting, and actually, it's truly sad and even scary to see how two people who live together, who've committed their lives to one another, can end up treating each other so badly.

At the same time, I worry about those couples who look so good on the outside, who treat each other respectfully, maybe even cordially, in public, but who are living a totally different life behind closed doors. I know of couples that make sweet, loving, appreciative posts on social media—which is wonderful—but my heart aches for them when they send me private messages, telling of their pain and suffering at home.

Now, I'm not suggesting you leave your spouse or your marriage because things are bad at home. I am saying that we should aim at not being one type of person at home and someone different outside the home—any more than we should be one type of person at church and a different one away from church. If our words and actions are different in different places, it may be an indication that we have not had a true change of heart by God. We may like certain behaviors and practices some of the time, but deep inside, darkness lurks inside our hearts, and that darkness shows up and shows through when we are with those closest to us. That's why Jesus refers to these types of people as "whitewashed tombs" (Matthew 23:27, NKJV). While they may look good on the outside, they contain only death, darkness, and decay on the inside.

Let's make sure that we are pure inside. Then our lives, our behavior, will be the same inside the home as well as outside the home, and our words and actions toward our loved ones will reflect the relationship we have with Christ.

Father God, change us from the inside so that we may treat each other just as You treat us, lovingly and kindly.

We Need Patience . . . Right Now!

Love is patient.
—1 Corinthians 13:4, NIV

We have all heard the saying, "God, give me patience . . . and do it right now!" While we laugh about it, secretly we may wish for it to be true. We long to be more patient but don't have the patience to wait for this process to take place in our lives or marriages. When those who have been married for many years are asked the secret of marital success, many identify patience as a key ingredient. It's the indispensable virtue for living together day after day in harmony, without constantly struggling with one another or trying to change each other into being the person who would be most convenient and easy to live with.

In marriage, patience means knowing what needs to be changed and when, and what we need to learn to accept. Many couples on their wedding day probably considered their spouse practically perfect. As time passed, and they realized their spouse was human after all, they set out to change them. It's a tough moment when we realize that our spouse doesn't necessarily want to be changed. In fact, they have ideas for how they think we could improve!

We should indeed try to change. What we need to be clear about is that we need to try to make changes in our own life and behavior instead of trying to change our spouse. Change, however, takes time. In fact, it takes a lifetime, which is the reason why we need patience with ourselves, with our spouse, and with our marriage. But each day brings a small opportunity to cultivate the virtue and to grow one's marriage.

Healthy marriages grow and change. Social scientists point out that a couple can go through seven or more stages of marriage throughout a lifetime. Some stages hold excitement and promise: a child arrives or the couple moves into their dream home.

During this lifetime process of change there will inevitably be periods of disillusionment and boredom. They may find their spouse unappealing and wonder how they can ever spend the rest of their life with this person. Sometimes a couple may even consider divorce. These stages, although difficult, are normal. With patience, a couple can work through them and emerge into the next stage with a deeper appreciation of each other and of their marriage.

Father God, bless us with ever increasing amounts of patience with ourselves, and in particular with our spouse so our marriage will be healthier, stronger, and long-lasting.

June

Every Word Has an Influence

Let your speech always be with grace, seasoned with salt,
that you may know how you ought to answer each one.
—Colossians 4:6, NKJV

The voice is an entrusted talent, and it should be used to help and encourage and strengthen our fellow men. If parents will love God and keep the way of the Lord to do justice and judgment, their language will not savor of sickly sentimentalism. It will be of a sound, pure, edifying character. Whether they are at home or abroad, their words will be well chosen. They will descend to no cheapness. . . .

"Every word spoken by fathers and mothers has its influence over the children, for good or for evil. If the parents speak passionately, if they show the spirit shown by the children of this world, God counts them as the children of this world, not as His sons and daughters.

"A word spoken in due season may be as good seed in youthful minds and may result in leading little feet in the right path. But a wrong word may lead their feet in the path of ruin.

"Angels hear the words that are spoken in the home. Therefore, never scold; but let the influence of your words be such that it will ascend to heaven as fragrant incense.

"Parents should keep the atmosphere of the home pure and fragrant with kind words, with tender sympathy and love; but at the same time they are to be firm and unyielding in principle. If you are firm with your children, they may think that you do not love them. This you may expect, but never manifest harshness. Justice and mercy must clasp hands; there must be no wavering or impulsive movements. . . .

"Kind words are as dew and gentle showers to the soul. The Scripture says of Christ that grace was poured into His lips, that He might 'know how to speak a word in season to him that is weary.' And the Lord bids us, 'Let your speech be alway with grace,' 'that it may minister grace unto the hearers' " (*The Adventist Home*, 434, 435).

O Lord, please grant us the tongue of the learned, that we will know how to speak a word in season to him who is weary. Waken us, morning by morning, that we may hear all that You would say. May our words be sweet and kind, our homes joyful, and our hearts full of tender sympathy. May we not turn away from seeking and doing Your will.

At Daybreak

Oh, satisfy us early with Your mercy, that we may rejoice and
be glad all our days!—Psalm 90:14, NKJV

The Jewish Study Bible renders our verse for today this way: "Satisfy us at daybreak with Your steadfast love that we may sing for joy all our days." The commentators of the same Bible explain that "morning is the time of renewal, the time that God answers prayers" (Psalm 143:8). God doesn't answer prayers only in the morning, of course, for which I'm glad.

For those of us who are morning people, the time just after we get up is special because we're eager to begin the day, our minds are actively working, and we can enter into our time of prayer refreshed, before the distractions begin to pile up. At the same time, the evening is challenging for us. By the end of the day, our heads are clouded, and all we can think about is the moment when our heads will hit the pillow. The opposite is true for night people, of course. For them, the evening is when they do their best thinking, when they read, and their creativity is inspired. When they finally go to bed, it is usually several hours after other members of the family have called it a day.

The importance is not in when we set aside time for communion with God, but in ensuring that the time we offer to Him is when our minds are functioning most efficiently.

Regardless of when we pray, the psalmist calls us to spend some good quality time daily, speaking with God about our needs, our concerns, and our fears, pleading with Him for His mercy to cover us. It is time to rejoice and be glad, not just today, but all our days. We don't need to live in some sort of Christian utopia where we are always happy and never sad. What the psalmist tells us, however, is that in the midst of our challenges, and even in sorrow, we can find reasons to rejoice in God. That is something we need in all our relationships, because at some time or another, sorrow and pain will come to our lives.

May your daily prayers fill you with the assurance of God's mercy, and may He bring you gladness every day of your life.

Father God, help us to maintain communication, indeed communion, with You every day. That, in and of itself, will be what will bring us joy every day of our lives.

Better Than Wine

"How beautiful is your love, my sister, my bride! How much better is your love than wine, and the fragrance of your oils than all kinds of spices!"
—*Song of Solomon 4:10, NASB*

When we read the Song of Solomon, we discover in the story of the bride and groom a special, vibrant relationship between two people who obviously love one another deeply. Our Scripture for the day suggests that the care each took with their appearance and hygiene contributed to the vibrancy of their marriage. It is also important to note that the bride and groom are quick to praise one another.

In our own relationships, we should strive to be just as thoughtful and considerate. If your spouse loves a certain scent, a certain hairstyle, wear it for them often as an expression of your affection, and let them know how much you appreciate it when they do the same for you. We all need to hear words of praise and admiration from time to time.

What of our relationship with God? Can these same principles be applied to our walk with Him? Throughout Scripture, we see that purity of heart and goodness of character are invaluable to our heavenly Father. What are we doing to make ourselves more attractive to Him? Have we surrendered our sinful nature to His divine one? Are we, in communing with Him, allowing Him to change us into His likeness? Is the purity of our hearts like a pleasant aroma to the One who loves us so unconditionally? And how quick are we to praise Him, not just for what He has done for us, or because we hope to gain something by it, but because of who He is?

Take time today to reflect on who God is. What does Scripture tell us about His nature? How has He revealed Himself to you in your own life, and what does this say about who He is? Do you see Him? What is it about Him you love most? Now thank Him for it. The more we truly see Him, the more we will desire to be like Him. Just as our earthly relationships will flourish when carefully tended, so too will we draw closer to our heavenly Father when we take the time to live in His presence.

Father God, help us to express our love for one other, and for You, so that we may maintain a strong, healthy, and mutually satisfying relationship now and forever.

The Everlasting Treasure

"Do not lay up for yourselves treasures on earth, where moth and rust destroy
and where thieves break in and steal; but lay up for yourselves treasures in
heaven, where neither moth nor rust destroys and where thieves do not break in
and steal. For where your treasure is, there your heart will be also."
—Matthew 6:19–21, NKJV

I suppose some people will read the words of Jesus in today's text and conclude that we should live like hermits, perhaps in some sort of commune, and in a state of constant poverty.

I'm not sure that's what Jesus would want us to conclude. If we do, we are certain to reach retirement age and find ourselves impoverished, dependent on the charity of others, or working well into our senior years out of necessity.

I believe, rather, that Jesus was talking about the excessive accumulation of material things. There are people who, in pursuit of riches, have mistreated or even enslaved others. Jesus reminds us that no matter how much we may accumulate, it will do us no good in the end.

What does Jesus mean when He says, "Where your treasure is, there your heart will be also"? I would like to suggest at least three possibilities.

First, when we return faithfully God's tithe and give offerings to further His cause on earth, our hearts are responding to God's generosity toward us.

Secondly, when we spend quality time with our family, we are helping them in the development of their character for eternity. When we die, that will be the only lasting thing we can take with us. We will not wish, in our final moments, that we had spent more time at work, but we may well wish we had given more time to our family. Live without that regret, and invest in eternity by spending good quality time with them, starting today.

Finally, when we have enough to take care of our needs, we should consider using the rest to help others. There are many people in real need, and in caring for them, we are following God's command to "love one another," to "love your neighbor as yourself" (John 13:34; Matthew 22:39, NKJV).

Father God, please help us to keep our priorities in the proper order, to return
Your tithe and give offerings, to spend our time and money in such a way that
we help our loved ones prepare for eternity, and to help the needy and the poor.

Smoke and Mirrors

For now we see in a mirror, dimly, but then face to face. Now I know in part, but
then I shall know just as I also am known.
—1 Corinthians 13:12, NKJV

One of the most well-known characters in all of classic literature is Count Dracula, the ghoulish vampire created by Bram Stoker in 1897. Since then, vampires have been vividly portrayed in movies, cartoons, and even children's programs like *Sesame Street,* famous for their black capes and pointed fangs.

According to the tradition of these tales, killing a vampire is not an easy task. You must use either a crucifix, a silver bullet, or a wooden stake through the heart.

One of the most fascinating features of these dark tales is the idea that a vampire's reflection is never seen in a mirror.

How interesting . . . a vampire's reflection is never seen in a mirror. You might be wondering, What does this have to do with our relationships? Well, let's think about it. Emotionally, do you see your reflection in the mirror? Can your spouse see the real you? One of the many reasons why some couples have a difficult time resolving conflict in their relationship is that one spouse, or perhaps both, refuses to see him- or herself as part of the problem. They live in constant denial, even when someone points out their shortcomings. They don't realize when they have a bad attitude, or when they speak harshly toward others.

Dating is a time to get to know each other. Unfortunately, people put up "smoke screens" to protect themselves, at least for a while. It is only with time that we become more comfortable with one another, more vulnerable; that we open ourselves up to the other person and let them see us for who we really are. These mirrors, these masks, usually take about a year to come off, which is one of the reasons why we recommend that couples date at least that long before they begin to consider marriage.

If you wish to have a good, healthy relationship, show your real self. Be willing to make yourself vulnerable. Let there be no secrets, deception, or false impressions between you, but be true to yourself and to your spouse.

Father God, in our relationships with others, and in our walk with You, help
us to be sincere, open, and honest. Grant us the courage to be vulnerable, that
we may see ourselves and one another for who we really are.

I Hate Divorce

*"For I hate divorce!" says the L*ORD*, the God of Israel. "To divorce your
wife is to overwhelm her with cruelty," says the L*ORD *of Heaven's Armies.
"So guard your heart; do not be unfaithful to your wife."
—Malachi 2:16, NLT*

In a video that has recently gone viral, a thirty-year-old woman is seen kicking and screaming in the front seat of the car while her husband, who is driving, records the scene on his cell phone. He subsequently posted the video online in order to show the world what he had to live with, and to validate his decision to separate from and file a restraining order against his wife. She, on the other hand, claimed her husband was a bully who goaded her mercilessly until, finally, she had had enough.

What precipitated this tragic event? According to the woman, her husband had promised to take her out to the lake on their boat to meet up with some friends but changed his mind after they had a fight. Her husband often held the boat hostage, she said, and was forever coming up with reasons for them not to use it.

In his defense, the husband said he had worked a long week, and when he refused to take her out to the boat, she threw a fit, not for the first time. He added that in past tantrums, his wife had broken handles off the doors at their house, and that she shouted at him constantly while telling friends and family he was verbally abusing her.

"That was the last day I lived in our house," the man said of the scene he shared with the world. "I have moved out and filed a restraining order against her."

How sad that a marriage, which probably started with love, festivities, and lots of laughter, comes to an end with shouting and restraining orders. Chances are the relationship will end in divorce. Our text tells us God hates divorce because it overwhelms the spouse with cruelty. It causes long-lasting harm to everyone involved, especially the children. Some might watch this video and say, "Divorce is preferable to living in such a relationship." I would say it is better to fix the relationship than to live with the pain of divorce.

Father God, help us to maintain an atmosphere of love and forgiveness in our marriages. Where we encounter difficulty, grant us the willingness to work toward wholeness and understanding, that You may be honored in our relationships.

Love Is Not a Feeling

"This is My commandment, that you love one another as I have loved you. . . .
These things I command you, that you love one another."
—John 15:12, 17, NKJV

As a marriage counselor, I occasionally have clients tell me, "I just don't think I love him (or her) anymore." I can tell by talking with them, however, that deep inside there is still at least a seed of love. Part of the problem is that they mistake romance for love. So let us talk briefly about these.

When we first meet someone, our emotions are high. We are attracted to them for different reasons. It could be their looks, their personality, their warmth, their sense of humor, or a host of other reasons. The more time we spend with them, the more anxious we are to be with them again as soon as possible, for as long as possible. We get butterflies in our stomach when they walk in the room, when we see them in a crowd, when we see them on our wedding day, and we believe that these feelings are what love is all about. This is a dangerous mistake to make.

For many couples, the butterflies soon disappear and life becomes mundane. They wonder whether they made a mistake and begin to consider divorce, or worse, they begin illicit relationships with other people who awaken the butterflies in their stomach . . . until the doldrums come to the new relationship, and the cycle begins again and repeats with each subsequent relationship.

Jesus said, "This is My commandment, that you love one another." In this, He was trying to teach us that love is not an emotion. You cannot command a person to feel a certain way. That is not how it works. Jesus wants us to understand that love is a decision we make. When the feelings are gone, love remains a decision.

Research has confirmed something quite remarkable. When we choose to love someone, despite how we may feel, the romance we felt at the beginning of the relationship returns.

If you are feeling a bit detached from your spouse, begin by accepting Jesus' command to love them, regardless of your feelings. Love them, romance them, pray for them and with them, and wait to see how God awakens the feelings in response to your obedience.

Father God, we want to demonstrate that we love You by obeying You and by loving others, starting with our spouse. As we act lovingly toward them, rekindle our romance.

It's All About Control

Therefore let us pursue the things which make for peace and
the things by which one may edify another.
—Romans 14:19, NKJV

One of the easiest ways to destroy a marriage is to try to assert control over your spouse. Control can be subtle, and many are unaware of what they're doing. Here, I will discuss some of the more common forms of control encountered in relationships. As you read, consider whether you might be guilty of any of the following.

In the first example, a person persistently begs or demands something of their spouse, wearing them down until they give in. Children are very good at this. Another form of control is nagging. This is similar to persistence, except that it virtually always takes a very negative tone. Here, one spouse intentionally aggravates the other until they get their way. A common means of asserting control is to withdraw from the relationship either emotionally, physically, or both.

Giving in to passive-aggressive behavior is also something to avoid. Specific examples of such behavior include apathy, procrastination, stubbornness, sulking, and obstructing reconciliation. All of these are marked by a negative, passive resistance to interpersonal situations in the relationship.

Another form of control is punishment, which is typically manifested in two different ways. The first is withholding something that the other person needs, or upon which they have come to depend. This can include sex, fulfilling responsibilities, and so forth. The second is inflicting something negative or hurtful upon one's mate. This can include intentionally making their lives more difficult, or even subjecting them to physical or emotional abuse.

Withholding love is a form of punishment that deserves special mention. It is especially destructive because affection is a genuine need we have as human beings. Withholding it from your spouse will be very costly to your relationship. Rewarding your spouse with gifts or favors becomes a form of control if the intent is to manipulate. Sometimes rewarding is done as a type of appeasement in conjunction with intimidation or punishment.

The apostle Paul provides us with a better way to have a good, healthy marriage: "pursue the things which make for peace and the things by which one may edify another." Cultivate peace and build each other up.

Father God, grant us a desire for peace in our marriage. May we seek to build each other up so that our relationship will honor You.

The Head of the Household

"Then you shall say to the master of the house, 'The Teacher says to you, "Where is the guest room where I may eat the Passover with My disciples?" ' "
—Luke 22:11, NKJV

The New Testament has much to say about the responsibility of the husband, or the head of the household, but just a sample will suffice for now. The head of the home has an incredibly important responsibility to be "considerate" and "treat [family members] with respect" (1 Peter 3:7, NIV). Colossians 3:19 states an important principle of leadership when it admonishes, "Husbands, love your wives and do not be harsh with them" (NIV).

I imagine it was no accident that Jesus chose this man's home for the last meal He would have with His disciples before His death. I'm sure it was not because it was a luxurious, spacious room. Jesus never sought the comfort that the Jewish leaders were accustomed to. I have the feeling that this man exemplified what the spiritual head of the house should be like.

He was so in touch with God that when Jesus' disciples brought His request, he did not question it, but received it gladly. This is implied in the way the question is presented. Jesus didn't ask, "Do you have a room?" or "Would you be willing to make a room available?" Jesus' question was very direct and specific: "Where is *the* room?"

The head of the house was generous in his response to God. When Christ's disciples met with him, he didn't ask for any remuneration, but gladly showed them to the room.

In Luke's account of the Last Supper, we see that their host had made preparations for their arrival: "Then he will show you a large, furnished upper room" (Luke 22:12, NKJV). The room was already furnished. The only preparation that remained to the disciples was in the meal itself.

As head of the household, we have a tremendous amount of influence in the lives of those inside our home. Our decisions, actions, words, and attitudes will either help them to have a good, positive experience with God, or will lead to their rejection of Him. Let us pray today that we will open our homes for Jesus to come in, to feel comfortable inside, and to eat with us.

Father God, bless us as heads of our households, that our lives and examples would be such that those in our home may come to love You and serve You.

Who Is My Neighbor?

" 'You shall love the Lᴏʀᴅ your God with all your heart, with all your soul, with all your strength, and with all your mind,' and 'your neighbor as yourself.' " —Luke 10:27, NKJV

We are all familiar with the story of the Good Samaritan. We have read it countless times and heard innumerable sermons. We have looked at every detail of the story—the Jericho road, the man, the robbers, the priest, the Levite, the Samaritan, the inn. Some preachers have described the scene in such a way that we have felt as though we were there ourselves, watching it all play out.

When Jesus was asked, "Who is my neighbor?" He responded with this story. It would have been a shocking one to His audience. While we understand the principles taught in this parable, we may be limiting ourselves in its application. We read the story and look for ways to be nice to those different than us. We're willing to go to other lands as missionaries. We are happy to help in health clinics, teach Vacation Bible School classes, sing, build, or mingle with the locals, all with the goal of being good ambassadors of God . . . which is wonderful.

Today, however, I would suggest we need to be good Samaritans to those closest to us. In answer to the question, "Who is my neighbor?" Jesus' response was not "a good Samaritan," but rather, "a person who helps others in their time of need, whether there are differences between them or not." Instead of limiting ourselves to doing good outside of our home, shouldn't we start by helping those within it? I believe that if we were to ask Jesus today, "Who is my neighbor?" He would respond, "The spouse with whom you share your bed, the children who live under your roof, and those who live elsewhere; those closest to you." We are very good at applying His parable to those outside, but somehow we have neglected to follow its teachings with those inside.

It is a sad truth that sometimes we treat total strangers or guests better than we treat those who are closest to us. Let us read the parable again, and as we do so, may our hearts be changed. Let us treat those closest to our hearts as though they were guests in our home.

Father God, help us to treat the people closest to our hearts and lives in the same loving, courteous, polite manner we treat strangers when they come to our home.

By the Power of the Spirit

*So he answered and said to me: "This is the word of the L*ORD *to Zerubbabel: 'Not by might nor by power, but by My Spirit,' says the L*ORD *of hosts."*
—*Zechariah 4:6, NKJV*

Conflict is an almost inevitable part of any relationship. There will always be differences of opinion, and sometimes these differences take longer to resolve than others. When we find ourselves in the middle of ongoing conflict in our marriage, we can feel so hopeless. It seems as if there's no way out, no light at the end of the tunnel. Perhaps there are ongoing financial challenges as a result of loss of income, the pain of a spouse's infidelity, or a child struggling with harmful habits or involved in an abusive relationship.

When people come to me for marriage or family counseling, there are things I can suggest they do. There are many approaches to resolving couple and family conflict that a counselor may recommend. However, psychology alone will not solve all your problems. As Christians, we have much more than psychological techniques to help us. We have the Holy Spirit on our side.

Ellen White wrote, "In the great and measureless gift of the Holy Spirit are contained all of heaven's resources. It is not because of any restriction on the part of God that the riches of His grace do not flow earthward to men. If all were willing to receive, all would become filled with His Spirit" (*Christ's Object Lessons,* 419).

I love the descriptive words she uses in this excerpt. Let's look at a few of them. The Holy Spirit, she says, is a "great and measureless gift." God doesn't give us a little help. He gives us His all. Beyond the help of mankind, we have "all of heaven's resources" at our disposal through the Holy Spirit.

If we're willing to receive, we will be filled. God does not lack the desire to fill us with His Spirit. All He is waiting for is our willingness to open ourselves up to receiving it.

The Holy Spirit is not just the light at the end of our tunnel of trouble. He is the light that will guide us through to the other side.

Father, we need the help of Your Holy Spirit—in whom all the resources of heaven are found—to help us navigate our way out of the waters of conflict in our marriage and family.

Submit to Christ

Therefore, just as the church is subject to Christ,
so let the wives be to their own husbands in everything.
—Ephesians 5:24, NKJV

I am often asked to clarify Paul's words, "Wives, submit to your own husbands, as to the Lord" (Ephesians 5:22, NKJV). Many men have used this text to keep their wives in an oppressive, even abusive situation, but this was never Paul's intent. Jesus' words and His life teach us the form of leadership a husband should exercise at home. We might call it "servant leadership." Jesus taught, "He who is greatest among you shall be your servant" (Matthew 23:11, NKJV).

A husband who demands submission has not submitted himself to Christ's headship in his own life. Look carefully at Ellen White's insight into Ephesians 5:22:

"Many husbands stop at the words, 'Wives, submit yourselves,' but we will read the conclusion of the same injunction, which is, 'As it is fit in the Lord.'

"God requires that the wife shall keep the fear and glory of God ever before her. Entire submission is to be made only to the Lord Jesus Christ, who has purchased her as His own child by the infinite price of His life. God has given her a conscience, which she cannot violate with impunity. Her individuality cannot be merged into that of her husband, for she is the purchase of Christ. It is a mistake to imagine that with blind devotion she is to do exactly as her husband says in all things, when she knows that in so doing, injury would be worked for her body and her spirit, which have been ransomed from the slavery of Satan. There is One who stands higher than the husband to the wife; it is her Redeemer, and her submission to her husband is to be rendered as God has directed—'as it is fit in the Lord.'

"When husbands require the complete subjection of their wives, declaring that women have no voice or will in the family, but must render entire submission, they place their wives in a position contrary to the Scripture. In interpreting the Scripture in this way, they do violence to the design of the marriage institution" (*The Adventist Home*, 116).

Father God, may we never take advantage of our role in the home, but rather treat our spouse with the love and dignity You expect of us. May our marriages honor and glorify You.

Love, With a Servant's Heart

"But he who is greatest among you shall be your servant. And whoever exalts himself will be humbled, and he who humbles himself will be exalted."
—Matthew 23:11, 12, NKJV

Yesterday we looked at Ephesians 5:22 and sought to understand what Jesus and Ellen White have to say on the matter of a wife's submission to her husband. Let us continue our study now, where we left off with Mrs. White:

"The Lord Jesus has not been correctly represented in His relation to the church by many husbands in their relation to their wives, for they do not keep the way of the Lord. They declare that their wives must be subject to them in everything. But it was not the design of God that the husband should have control, as head of the house, when he himself does not submit to Christ. He must be under the rule of Christ that he may represent the relation of Christ to the church. If he is a coarse, rough, boisterous, egotistical, harsh, and overbearing man, let him never utter the word that the husband is the head of the wife, and that she must submit to him in everything; for he is not the Lord, he is not the husband in the true significance of the term. . . .

"Husbands should study the pattern and seek to know what is meant by the symbol presented in Ephesians, the relation Christ sustains to the church. The husband is to be as a Saviour in his family. Will he stand in his noble, God-given manhood, ever seeking to uplift his wife and children? Will he breathe about him a pure, sweet atmosphere? Will he not as assiduously cultivate the love of Jesus, making it an abiding principle in his home, as he will assert his claims to authority?

"Let every husband and father study to understand the words of Christ, not in a one-sided manner, merely dwelling upon the subjection of the wife to her husband, but in the light of the cross of Calvary, study as to his own position in the family circle" (*The Adventist Home*, 117).

I hope these words encourage us as husbands to show Christlike love to our wives, so that our marriages may honor Him.

Father God, may Your love for us flow through us to our wives, so that our marriages may be a reflection of the relationship between Jesus and His bride, the church.

A Family That Prays Together

Always keep on praying.
—1 Thessalonians 5:17, TLB

Perhaps you have heard the expression, "A family that prays together stays together." These words have been proven true over and over again. Praying is an outlet for our burdens and concerns and serves to strengthen our spirits. Praying with a partner has additional benefits because we can be united in our voices as they are lifted toward heaven. Just to know that someone else is joining us in prayer over an issue seems to lighten our burdens.

If you are married, I invite you to pray for and with your spouse on a daily basis. Together, lift your voices toward heaven. There is no sound so sweet as hearing your spouse praying for you. Bring to Jesus your joys as well as your sorrows, your blessings as well as your challenges, and allow His Spirit to soften any bitterness you may be harboring toward each other.

The day I became a parent, my personal prayer life received a big boost. I found myself constantly praying and interceding for my child. If you are married, the best person to partner with you in prayer over a parenting concern is your spouse. However, even single parents can ask another to be their prayer partner. Do you have a prayer partner? Do you pray daily that God will give you wisdom as you make parenting decisions? If ever parents needed to pray for guidance it is in today's world. If you are a grandparent, pray for your children as they raise your grandchildren. Mediate on their behalf.

As a family, do you have a daily devotional time? If not, today is a great time to start. Consider it a sacred commitment in your calendar. Do not allow other activities to rob you of family devotional time. If you have little ones, make sure your devotional activities are appropriate for their ages, and remember to encourage them to pray aloud as soon as they are able to talk. Their sweet, innocent prayers minister to the oldest members of the family.

Regardless of your family makeup: single parent, grandparent, married couple, or young single adult, make prayer a priority today. You have a Friend in Jesus who is waiting for you to talk to Him. He's listening!

Lord, thank You for the privilege of coming to You in prayer. Thank You for always being there to listen to our expressions of thanksgiving as well as our pleadings for help.

Children Are a Blessing

As a father pities his children, so the Lord *pities those who fear Him.*
—Psalm 103:13, NKJV

He who gave Eve to Adam as a helpmeet . . . ordained that men and women should be united in holy wedlock, to rear families whose members, crowned with honor, should be recognized as members of the family above.

"Children are the heritage of the Lord, and we are answerable to Him for our management of His property. . . . In love, faith, and prayer let parents work for their households, until with joy they can come to God saying, 'Behold, I and the children whom the Lord hath given me.' . . .

"I have a very tender interest in all children, for I became a sufferer at a very early age. I have taken many children to care for, and I have always felt that association with the simplicity of childhood was a great blessing to me. . . .

"The sympathy, forbearance, and love required in dealing with children would be a blessing in any household. They would soften and subdue set traits of character in those who need to be more cheerful and restful. The presence of a child in a home sweetens and refines. A child brought up in the fear of the Lord is a blessing.

"Care and affection for dependent children removes the roughness from our natures, makes us tender and sympathetic, and has an influence to develop the nobler elements of our character.

". . . After the birth of his first son, Enoch reached a higher experience; he was drawn into a closer relationship with God. He realized more fully his own obligations and responsibility as a son of God. And as he saw the child's love for its father, its simple trust in his protection; as he felt the deep, yearning tenderness of his own heart for that first-born son, he learned a precious lesson of the wonderful love of God to men in the gift of His Son, and the confidence which the children of God may repose in their heavenly Father.

". . . Children are committed to their parents as a precious trust, which God will one day require at their hands. We should give to their training more time, more care, and more prayer. . . .

"Remember that your sons and daughters are younger members of God's family. He has committed them to your care, to train and educate for heaven" (*The Adventist Home*, 159–161).

Thank You for loving us, as a Father!

Harmful Behaviors

But now you yourselves are to put off all these: anger, wrath, malice, blasphemy, filthy language out of your mouth. Do not lie to one another, since you have put off the old man with his deeds, and have put on the new man who is renewed in knowledge according to the image of Him who created him.
—Colossians 3:8–10, NKJV

The apostle Paul writes that our relationships should be different now that we have been changed from the inside by Jesus. Anger, malice, deceit—all the things that were so commonplace before, so second nature, should now give way to our new nature.

Think of how the words of Paul apply to your relationship with your spouse. Your old self won't be nearly as good a spouse as your new self. These verses from Colossians challenge us to set aside the poor behaviors that always get in the way of a healthy marriage and to put on the character of Christ instead.

You might find it helpful to sit down as a couple and, individually, compile a list of the negative traits you exhibit toward one another. Once you have done this, write a second list containing the opposite of each of these traits. This will give you somewhere to start as you consider how to "put on the new man." Practice the positive traits instead of simply fighting against the negative ones. Where you find yourself tempted to react in bitterness toward your spouse, use kindness instead. Where your tongue wishes to deliver a harsh word, speak with tenderness instead. Where resentment threatens to disrupt your peace, forgive instead.

It may sound like such a simple thing to do, as easy as putting on a coat, but it will take time and effort to implement. Be patient with yourself and with one another as you begin this process. Read the words of today's passage aloud together with your spouse and listen for that one sinful trait that is the hardest for you to get rid of, as well as for the one godly trait that is the hardest to clothe yourself in. Confess the ways you've failed, and ask your spouse to forgive you. Then pray together that God will give you the determination to put His character on again and again every day.

Father, help me today to put on the character of Jesus Christ so that I may be kinder, more gentle, more loving, and more forgiving toward my spouse.

Like the Grass

They are like a sleep. In the morning they are like grass which grows up.
—Psalm 90:5, NKJV

When compared to the infinity of God's existence, the mere seventy or eighty years we live are so minuscule. Maybe that is why the psalmist compares our life span to grass. Grass grows and dies so quickly—here today, gone tomorrow—and sometimes we don't even notice that cycle. The exception, of course, is when we have to mow it. When we have lots of rain, the grass grows unstoppably. It seems as though we have barely finished mowing it when it needs mowing again. And once the task is done, the grass clippings lie scattered across the rest of the grass, covering it like a thick, wilting blanket.

How many blades of grass are in my yard? I have no idea! And maybe that's another reason why the imagery of grass is used to describe the peoples of the world—so many are born, grow up, and eventually die that we take no notice of this endless cycle, unless it is a loved one who dies or brings a new life into the world.

It is easy to be discouraged at the brevity of our lives when we read this psalm, but there is encouragement to be found too. I love the imagery of death as nothing more than sleep—a dreamless, undisturbed sleep that ends the morning of the resurrection. There is hope that while we have but a few years to live, we will rise again one morning, never to wither again. We can also take from this psalm the reminder that as temporary as our existence is, our God is permanent. He has always been, and will always be, and through it all, He will be there beside us. There is no need to fear death, for God has promised that He will never leave us nor forsake us. He has been, and will be, "our dwelling place in all generations" (verse 1, NKJV).

The next time a loved one goes to his or her sleep of death, we can take comfort in the knowledge that God will be with us even as He has been with every other generation in the past.

Father God, thank You for the knowledge of Your permanence in our lives, for it removes our fear of the future and of death. Thank You for the hope we have that one day we will be renewed, never to wither again.

Earthly Treasures

*Do not love the world or the things in the world. If anyone loves
the world, the love of the Father is not in him.*
—*1 John 2:15, NKJV*

Look in the typical child's room, and you will see a toy box or a closet
filled with stuff, and yet, that same child will tell you they have nothing
to do. We have flooded our children with material possessions. There is
little need for imagination and creativity these days with children spending
the majority of their time plugged into some electronic gadget. The more
we buy, the more they want, as the newness seems to wear off in a short
time. Children tire easily, and as they grow and change, so do their likes and
dislikes. That toy they begged you for incessantly a few weeks ago is now
thrown into the back of their closet and forgotten. That electronic gadget
they had to have last month has now been replaced by a newer, up-to-date
model, and their list of wants is ever-growing.

Why not give your child gifts that can be renewed over and over again?
For example, art sets, wooden building blocks, scraps of cloth, containers of
buttons, marbles, and so on. Or, what about encouraging your child to start
a collection of rocks, bark, dried flowers, or leaves. A nature collection is
one that can last a lifetime. Who knows? Perhaps you will also take up a new
hobby or become a budding naturalist.

Take an inventory of your child's possessions. What unintended lesson
might you be teaching? Is there an adjustment you need to make? Is there a
new direction you can encourage your child to go in?

As parents, are we guilty of being bad role models? Do we also rush out
to buy the latest version of the iPhone or the big-screen television set? Do
we buy a new car when the old one still runs great? Do we ourselves pri-
oritize material goods? If so, it is no wonder that our children display the
same behavior. So, as we take inventory of our children's possessions, let's
first take inventory of our own. After all, our little ones will see value in the
same things that we treasure. Does your family's treasure chest contain more
things of this earth than it does heavenly goods?

*Lord, help me as a parent to model behavior that I want my children to
emulate. Help me to show them that the greatest wealth is in knowing and
loving You.*

Encourage Your Children

And suddenly a voice came from heaven, saying,
"This is My beloved Son, in whom I am well pleased."
—Matthew 3:17, NKJV

In reading about Jesus' baptism, it is easy to focus on the lessons provided by the baptism itself, or the manifestation of the Holy Spirit in the form of a dove. I would like us to consider the Father's words to Jesus. He could have simply stated, "This is My beloved Son," and the words would have confirmed the divinity of Jesus and His Messianic ministry, but it did not end there. The Father makes a point of expressing His delight in who Christ is. It is a lesson for us in the importance of affirming, encouraging, and strengthening our children as they grow.

First of all, God made it clear to Jesus, and to us since then, that He loved Him. Even though there was obviously no doubt in Jesus' mind, as He began His ministry the Father assured Him and confirmed His love for Him. The lesson for us is to affirm our children all the time of our love for them. Repeat those words regularly, never say goodbye without ending your conversation with those words, and even when they do something which is contrary to what you taught them and it breaks your heart, assure them of your love for them. They must know that even if they disappoint you, your love for them will not change.

The second word from God to Jesus, which we need to learn from, is the word *pleased,* or *delighted.* We sometimes have a tendency to focus on our children's misbehavior instead of emphasizing those times when they do well. One way to reinforce good behavior is by affirming our children when we "catch" them doing good. When your son picks up his toys, praise him immediately for that decision. A general word of affirmation such as "That's a good boy!" is not nearly as effective as words like, "Thank you for picking up your toys!" When your daughter hangs her clothes in the closet or helps set the table, express your feelings of delight and tell her how pleased you are with her actions.

Let the words of God toward His beloved Son be a lesson to us as parents as we express our delight in our children.

Father, thank You for teaching us through Your own example how we can affirm our children, and help us to express that delight, love, and appreciation to them often.

Promise of a Joyful Home

*He grants the barren woman a home, like a joyful
mother of children. Praise the LORD!*
—Psalm 113:9, NKJV

It amazes, shocks, and saddens me when I hear of a mother who killed her child or children! How can a mother do that to her own child? It is made even more shocking when we consider that so many women cannot conceive and would do anything to be able to bear a child of their own. Many watch their friends or relatives get pregnant. They see the joy it brings to them and to their families. They follow the progress, the changes, the baby shower, and the culmination of the many months of expectancy with the birth of their baby. And while they rejoice with the other person, at the same time, they feel the emptiness in their own heart.

Maybe that's why the verse in this psalm is so interesting to me. Some may read it as a promise to the barren that God will answer her prayers and she will bear children of her own. That is indeed very possible. I have known of some couples who had given up hope only to find themselves pregnant at last. I have known of couples that adopted a child or even several children and then had children of their own. So this possibility does exist.

Others may never conceive a child of their own, but they have the opportunity to adopt a child who has no family to love and instruct them. These couples love their adopted children just as much as they would have loved a child of their own flesh and blood, which is exactly as it should be.

Of course there are also some women who are content to remain childless. They are more than satisfied with having pets, or having a good, vibrant relationship with their husbands. They make good aunts, and that's as close to children as they want to be.

To every woman, whether she bears children of her own, adopts a child in need, or chooses not to have children at all, this psalm speaks the promise that God will give them a home, one just as joyful as a home in which children abound. Let God our Father provide you with that joyful home experience, regardless of your circumstances.

Father God, may our experience be such that whether we have children or not we will have a joyful home where we can experience love and share love with others.

181

Look and Wait

*Therefore I will look to the LORD; I will wait for
the God of my salvation; my God will hear me.*
—Micah 7:7, NKJV

A lot of pressure is put on young people these days to marry, and as the years progress and they find themselves still single, many find themselves so desperate to find a mate that they lower their standards to achieve their goal.

I like what Micah has to say here, and I think it is an important plan for singles to adopt for their lives. Micah says, "I will look to the Lord." Our focus in life should not be making money, gaining prestige, or even entering into marriage, but to have a relationship with God. Let singles find their fulfillment and satisfaction in God, regardless of the status of their social lives.

Micah also encourages us to "wait for . . . God." Society teaches us that time is short, and the sooner one marries the better. On the other hand, research says that those who marry before the age of twenty are two to three times more likely to divorce than those who wait. My conclusion is that it is better to wait to get married until a little later in life. Wait until your education is complete and you have entered the workforce. Wait for God to put you in touch with the right person rather than rushing into marriage with the first person who will have you. You will never regret the decision to trust in His timing.

Micah promises, "God will hear me." What that tells me is that when we pray, when we look to the Lord for guidance, and when we wait for God to show us the right partner, He will hear our plea. Now, that may mean we have to remain single for some time, or even for the rest of our lives. As one of my daughters told me once, "I'd rather be alone and single than alone and married." The wrong relationship can bring a lot of pain and unhappiness to a marriage and to the individuals involved.

So let's take Micah's words to heart. Look to the Lord, wait on the Lord, and remember that He will hear us.

Father God, we commit ourselves to look to You for guidance and fulfillment and to wait on You for an answer to our plea. Thank You for the promise that You will hear us and answer us. Until then, may we be patient.

A Mother's Love

Having so fond an affection for you, we were well-pleased to impart to you not only the gospel of God but also our own lives, because you had become very dear to us. —1 Thessalonians 2:8, NASB

The apostle Paul developed such a close, loving relationship with the people he brought to the knowledge of Jesus Christ that he considered them more like his children than his pupils. His affection for them, he writes, is comparable to the love that a mother has for her children.

About thirty-five years ago, social scientists began to teach about the importance of early bonding with babies. Experiments with animals showed that bonding is essential for a baby. Studies of newborn monkeys who were given mannequin mothers at birth showed that even when the mannequins were made of soft material and provided formula to the baby monkeys, the babies were better socialized when they had live mothers with whom they could interact. The baby monkeys with mannequin mothers also were more likely to suffer from despair. Scientists suspect that lack of bonding in human babies can cause similar problems.

Most babies are ready to bond immediately upon their birth. Parents, on the other hand, may have mixed feelings about it. Some parents feel an intense attachment within the first few minutes or days after their baby's birth, while for others, especially if the baby is adopted or has been placed in intensive care, it may take longer.

At any rate, bonding is a process, not something that takes place within minutes and not something that has to be limited to happening within a certain time period after birth. For many parents, bonding is a byproduct of caring for their baby on a daily basis. You may not even know it's taking place, but then you see your baby's first smile and suddenly you realize that you're filled with love and joy for that little child of yours.

This is not a skill you learn, it is a natural feeling that God places inside your heart automatically, for most people. Those of us who are parents love that feeling and relish the bond we have with our children. Enjoy every minute of the experience, today and as your children grow into youth and adulthood.

Father God, thank You for letting Your love shine through our hearts to our children. Help us to enjoy that experience as long as possible so that they, too, may experience Your love through us.

Unshakable Faith

Though the fig tree may not blossom, nor fruit be on the vines; though the labor of the olive may fail, and the fields yield no food; though the flock may be cut off from the fold, and there be no herd in the stalls—yet I will rejoice in the LORD, I will joy in the God of my salvation.
—Habakkuk 3:17, 18, NKJV

We find the response of Job to all his problems admirable. How could anyone lose all their possessions, all their children, and ultimately their health and yet not get angry or complain? How would we react if a friend found themselves in such a situation? How would they? Would we be surprised if they expressed their disdain, their frustration, their hopelessness? I think we would be more surprised if they didn't!

It would be only natural in this situation to have trouble accepting the circumstances, to live in denial of all the bad that has befallen us, yet this is the opposite of how Job responded. Studies have shown that people facing terminal illness go through several stages, the first being denial. The initial shock of such unexpected news leads people to deny that it is really happening.

In today's Scripture, Habakkuk is not in denial about his situation. He recognizes all that is happening to him, but, like Job, he does not allow it to shake his faith in God. He is able to maintain a positive attitude despite the circumstances because he remembers how God has blessed him in the past. He chooses to focus on the good things rather than simply giving up and dwelling on the bad things.

Every one of us will face challenging circumstances at some point in our lives. It may be the loss of a job, the unexpected loss of a child, finding ourselves with a terminal illness. In times like these, it is only natural to experience a time of denial, but we cannot remain there indefinitely. Remember that in Christ, we have the promise of eternal life and the assurance of a reunion with those we have lost. When we keep our trials in perspective and cling to God's promises, we can share the positive, grateful attitude of Job and Habakkuk, knowing our heavenly Father will take care of us.

Father, thank You for all You have done for us in the past. When things don't go well and the pain we experience seems unbearable, please remind us of all Your many blessings.

Offering Your Children to Idols

*"For when you offer your gifts and make your sons pass through the fire,
you defile yourselves with all your idols, even to this day. So shall I be
inquired of by you, O house of Israel? As I live," says the Lord GOD,
"I will not be inquired of by you."* —Ezekiel 20:31, NKJV

The thought of throwing our children into a fire is horrendous, even preposterous. It shocks us to think that people would do such a hideous thing to innocent children, yet today, parents throw their children to idols and don't think twice about it.

One way we do this is by giving our children unsupervised access to the Internet. This is, in fact, one of the biggest fires there is. While the Internet provides us with unlimited information, it also offers up avenues to sin, which were unthinkable just a few years ago. It is so easy and convenient for our children to access the dangerous aspects of the Internet along with the good.

Another way we may be throwing our children to idolatrous fire is by sending them to public schools. There are not Seventh-day Adventist schools everywhere, and for some parents, that is the only choice they have, yet I worry about those parents who had the option to send their children to an Adventist school and chose to send them instead to a public school, where they are taught things contrary to the Bible. They think that as long as they take their kids to church on Sabbath, their kids will be fine. But how can one to three hours a week at church have as strong an influence as forty hours a week at school? While no church school is perfect, it sure is a better alternative to a secular environment.

In what other ways might you be throwing your children into the fire?

I want to encourage you to look at the activities to which you are exposing your children. Please consider offering them as much time, if not more, in activities that teach them about God and provide them the opportunity to be of service to others. Learn to present your children to God instead of making them an offering to worldly idols.

Father God, we pause to present our children to You again just now, and ask that You bless them, protect them, and guide them as they grow. Help us to teach them the value of time spent in Your presence.

He'll Do It, If You Let Him

For it is God who works in you both to will and to do for His good pleasure.
—Philippians 2:13, NKJV

I often hear the expression, "I love him, but I am not in love with him." Perhaps they mean that they care about the other person, but the romance has left the relationship. The butterflies don't flutter in their stomach they once did. They have lost the excitement of yesterday, and so they come to me to see if I will permit them to separate or divorce.

I explain to them that love is not a feeling. It is a decision to care for one another even when the romantic feelings are no longer there. Amy Cuddy of Harvard University conducted research which showed that our behavior shapes our thinking and our feelings. (You can watch her presentation in a TED conference at http://www.ted.com/talks/amy_cuddy_your_body _language_shapes_who_you_are.html.) She explains that instead of waiting until we feel a certain way, we should begin to act as if we already felt that way. The feelings will eventually follow. In other words, if we don't have those romantic feelings toward our spouses, instead of waiting to feel romantic toward them we should start behaving in a romantic way toward them, and we will begin to think and feel romantically toward them, which is our ultimate desire.

Paul tells us that God not only works in us the desire to do something, He also helps us to do it. When we commit our life and marriage to God, He will help us to be loving toward our spouses.

You may not have those warm, fuzzy feelings you once had toward your spouse, but you can trust that God loves you and wants the best for you. What should you do? First, ask God to place in your heart the desire to act lovingly toward your spouse. Then submit yourself to God so that He will show His love through you toward your spouse. Finally, act lovingly toward your spouse even before you begin to feel it. The results will be that your attitude will follow your behavior, and your feelings will follow your attitude. You will find yourself experiencing a lasting, loving relationship, just as God designed it to be, rather than a momentary romance.

Father God, when the romance is gone, help me to want to love my spouse and to act lovingly toward them until the caring feelings return. May our marriage reflect our relationship with You.

Pleasant Words

Pleasant words are like a honeycomb,
sweetness to the soul and health to the bones.
—*Proverbs 16:24, NKJV*

The tongue can detect several different tastes: sweet, sour, salty, bitter. Some of us have a preference for one of three—sweet, salty, or sour. For instance, I prefer fruit that has a tart taste, but I also enjoy some sweet foods as well as some that are salty. In general terms, however, most of us don't care for things that have a bitter taste. The writer of this proverb understands that most of us, from the time we were children, have a preference for that which is sweet and pleasant and dislike that which is bitter.

In the book, *The Voice in Speech and Song,* we find some important guidance from Ellen White:

"Do you dislike to have harsh words spoken to you? Remember that when you speak such words others feel the sting. Let your praiseworthy example, your peaceable words and unselfish deeds, be a savor of life unto life.

"The talent of speech was given to be used for the benefit of all. Pleasant, cheery words cost no more than unpleasant, moody words. Sharp words wound and bruise the soul. In this life everyone has difficulties with which to wrestle. Everyone meets with grievances and disappointments. Shall we not bring sunshine instead of gloom into the lives of those with whom we come in contact? Shall we not speak words that will help and bless? They will be just as much a blessing to us as to those to whom they are spoken" (64).

A couple whose communication is founded on respect and sweet, pleasant words will experience a better, healthier relationship than one in which sarcasm, criticism, or bitter words are present. Children who hear their parents exchange pleasant, encouraging words with one another will develop a disposition far more pleasant than children whose tender ears are continually subjected to sharp words and constant criticism.

Let us practice daily the use of sweet, kind words toward each other. Our speech reflects our relationship with God, and when we choose kindness, our words invite others to experience a deeper relationship with Him.

Father God, help us to choose our words carefully, that they might bless others and draw them closer to You. May we speak to one another the way we would have our children speak, for they are always listening. May our words honor You.

Walk Humbly

*He has shown you, O man, what is good; and what does the L*ord *require of you*
but to do justly, to love mercy, and to walk humbly with your God?
—Micah 6:8, NKJV

There are three principles that Micah mentions in today's Scripture that, when applied to marriage and/or family life, can change the way in which we relate to one another. Let us think about them for a moment.

The first principle Micah gives us is to "do justly." It is possible that Micah mentions justice first because social injustice was the greatest sin that scarred the society of his day (cf. 3:1, 8). Practicing justice means to uphold what is right according to the will of God and, instead of offering animal sacrifices to atone for our sins, it requires the sacrifice of our own life. That is, we must be willing to give of ourselves in order to do what is right. Upholding justice might require the sacrifice of personal aims and ambitions, or an injury to our pride in exchange for the ability to see the other person's point of view. We should never pass judgment upon others on the basis of our personal thoughts and feelings alone.

The second principle Micah asks us to consider is to "love mercy." God desires that our justice be based on kindness and mercy. The Hebrew word *chesed* implies that those of us who have been recipients of God's mercy— that is, each and every one of us—should naturally extend that same mercy to others. To "love mercy" is an active command. It demands action on our part.

Our final principle of the day is to "walk humbly." The Hebrew verb *hatts-nea,* which translates to "make yourself humble," is used in only one other place in the Old Testament, in Proverbs 11:2: "When pride comes, then comes shame; but with the humble is wisdom" (NKJV). The term refers not so much to self-humiliation as to an attitude of humility and measured and careful conduct.

Today, and in the days to come, let each of us strive to relate to one another with justice, mercy, and the humble spirit which results from our relationship with God.

Father God, guide us in our relationships, so that our attitude toward each other would reflect our relationship with You. May we remember always to act justly, to love mercy, and to walk humbly before You and with those we love.

God's Solutions

And he said to them, "Pick me up and throw me into the sea; then the sea will become calm for you. For I know that this great tempest is because of me."
—Jonah 1:12, NKJV

We have all faced a situation at one time or another which we found so overwhelming we can't seem to find a clear solution, a way through it. Perhaps we have thought, "I wish I were not here," "I wish we were not married," or even, "I wish I were dead." Many have taken the easy way out, filing for divorce, abandoning the family, or committing suicide. While these steps might bring some relief, the results for those left behind are horrendous.

The effects of divorce, the breakup of a family, or suicide can be devastating to the children. I have known older adults who still struggle with the results of their parent's suicide decades later. There is a sense of guilt. *Was it something I did?* Rejection. *Why did they do that if they loved me? They must not have loved me!* Shame, a sense of abandonment, and endless questions as to why it all happened.

The wonderful thing about Jonah's story is how clear it is that God does not abandon us, even when we reject Him. God has an answer to our questions, a solution to our problems, and a plan for our lives. Even when we make bad decisions, God has a solution. God never intended to kill Jonah or the other people on board the ship, and even when Jonah tried to find the "easy" way out, God had already prepared his rescue—a large fish.

Just this morning I read these words again: "Though difficulties, perplexities, and discouragements may arise, let neither husband nor wife harbor the thought that their union is a mistake or a disappointment. Determine to be all that it is possible to be to each other. Continue the early attentions. In every way encourage each other in fighting the battles of life. Study to advance the happiness of each other. Let there be mutual love, mutual forbearance. Then marriage, instead of being the end of love, will be as it were the very beginning of love" (*The Faith I Live By*, 253).

Father God, remove all negative, harmful thoughts from our minds. As You gave Jonah a second chance, please grant us the opportunity to change, to make our lives better, to make our marriages healthier and happier.

More Mercy

*Oh, give thanks to the L*ord*, for He is good! For His mercy endures forever.*
—Psalm 136:1, NKJV

I suppose if we sang this psalm today it would be like a praise chorus or a responsive reading with the same words repeated again and again. There is probably a good reason for this repetition. Sometimes we forget or take for granted God's abundant mercy and His steadfast love for us. He simply will not give up on us! The psalmist had experienced God's overflowing mercy and expressed it repeatedly as a reminder to others, maybe even to himself.

The words "His mercy endures forever" are a key phrase that occurs twenty-six times in this poem in reference to God's goodness. The word translated "mercy" is *hesed*, which means, "divine love" "compassion," or "steadfast love."

I wonder if the psalmist also had in mind to teach us as married couples, as parents, as children, as families that we need to experience that steadfast love, that overflowing mercy, so that we can then extend it to our spouse, our children, our parents, our family! We seem to find it easier to practice judgment than mercy. Think about it. We are critical and unforgiving of our spouse's mistakes. We are impatient with our children when they do the opposite of what we want them to do, or when we have to repeat ourselves ten times before they hear us. As our parents age and their health begins to deteriorate, we become frustrated. Some even become abusive. This psalm speaks to us, urging us to give thanks to God for His steadfast love, His abundant mercy, His overwhelming compassion, and it urges us to extend the same to our loved ones. When we do, not only do we experience God in our lives, but we become the extension of His love toward our family and friends. They are His children, too, after all, just as we ourselves are.

Father God, thank You for Your mercy and love for us, which lasts forever. Thank You that You don't turn Your back on us. We are so grateful that You are slow to anger, that You do not become frustrated with us. Instead, You have compassion for us. You reach out to rescue us, to save us, to cover us with Your forgiveness and love. Help us to be more compassionate, more loving with others, especially those closest to us, and as we display Your love to one another, draw us closer to You.

In the Service of God

*The word of the L*ORD *came to Jonah son of Amittai: Go at once to Nineveh, that great city, and proclaim judgment upon it; for their wickedness has come before Me. Jonah, however, started out to flee to Tarshish from the L*ORD*'s service. He went down to Joppa and found a ship going to Tarshish. He paid the fare and went aboard to sail with the others to Tarshish, away from the service of the L*ORD*.—Jonah 1:1–3, JPS*

There seems to be this human tendency to want to do the opposite of what God commands. When He instructed Adam and Eve to offer animal sacrifices as a lesson and as a promise of the sacrifice of Jesus for our sins, Cain offered fruit instead. When God told the Israelites shortly after leaving Egypt to go in and take over the land He was giving them, they told Him they would not go in because they were afraid of the giants. When God told them they would not go in for forty years, they tried to go in anyway, and were routed by the people living there.

It seems as if this rebellious attitude is just as prevalent in dating and marriage as it is elsewhere. God already has certain guidelines, such as "Do not be unequally yoked together with unbelievers" (2 Corinthians 6:14, NKJV), yet hundreds upon hundreds totally disregard His guidance and enter into such relationships. This leads to disillusionment, frustration, and often divorce.

It is often the same in marriage. When the romantic feelings seem absent from their relationship, many want to flee back to the single life, or worse, into the arms of somebody else. I often hear words such as, "Don't I have the right to be happy?" or, "I made a mistake marrying him (or her)."

When you are married and there are conflicts, challenges, or difficulties in your relationship, instead of leaving, answer God's call to minister to your spouse for the soon second coming of Jesus (Ephesians 5:25, 26). Don't run away from God's service. Fulfill your God-given duties, do it joyfully and lovingly (1 Corinthians 13), and He will reward your efforts.

Father, at times we have taken our marriage as a convenient estate in life instead of a sacred duty. We forget that our relationship is meant to reflect our walk with You, and so we treat it lightly. Bless our marriage, and help me to be to my spouse the helpmeet You have called me to be.

July

The Effect of Harsh Words

A soft answer turns away wrath, but a harsh word stirs up anger.
—Proverbs 15:1, NKJV

In a home where harsh, fretful, scolding words are spoken, a child cries much; and upon its tender sensibilities are impressed the marks of unhappiness and discord. Then, mothers, let your countenance be full of sunshine. Smile, if you can, and the infant's mind and heart will reflect the light of your countenance as the polished plate of an artist portrays the human features. Be sure, mothers, to have an indwelling Christ so that on your child's plastic mind may be impressed the divine likeness.

". . . Allow nothing like strife or dissension to come into the home. Speak gently. Never raise your voice to harshness. Keep yourselves calm. Put away faultfinding and all untruthfulness. Tell the children that you want to help them to prepare for a holy heaven, where all is peace, where not one jarring note is heard. Be patient with them in their trials, which may look small to you but which are large to them. . . .

"We must subdue a hasty temper and control our words, and in this we shall gain great victories. Unless we control our words and temper, we are slaves to Satan. We are in subjection to him. He leads us captive. All jangling and unpleasant, impatient, fretful words are an offering presented to his satanic majesty. And it is a costly offering, more costly than any sacrifice we can make for God; for it destroys the peace and happiness of whole families, destroys health, and is eventually the cause of forfeiting an eternal life of happiness.

"It is important that children and youth should be trained to guard their words and deeds; for their course of action causes sunshine or shadow, not only in their own home, but also with all with whom they come in contact.

"Unhappiness is often caused by an unwise use of the talent of speech. The word of God does not authorize anyone to speak harshly, thereby creating disagreeable feelings and unhappiness in the family. The other members of the family lose their respect for the one who speaks thus, when if he would restrain his feelings, he might win the confidence and affection of all" (*The Adventist Home*, 436, 437).

Father, when we're tired it seems like the wrong words fly so easily from our mouths. May we find our rest in You so our words will be sweet and gentle.

Lord of Your Words

Let no corrupt word proceed out of your mouth, but what is good for necessary edification, that it may impart grace to the hearers.
—Ephesians 4:29, NKJV

The word *corrupt* in the original Greek language of the New Testament literally means "insipid," without *the salt of grace,* and therefore worthless. It reminds me of a story I once heard about a young man who told a much wiser man, "A mutual friend is speaking ill about you."

"Oh, really?" the older man responded. "Well, before you tell me what he was saying, be sure to let it pass through three doors."

"Three doors?"

"Yes. The first door is Truth. Are you certain that what you're about to tell me is absolutely true?"

"Well, no. I'm not certain. I heard it from some neighbors."

"The second door is Goodness. Can your information make it through the door Goodness? Will what you're about to tell me be good for me, or anybody else, to hear?"

"No, not really. In fact it would be exactly the opposite."

"The last door," said the wise man, "is called Necessary. Is it necessary for me to know what it is that is bothering you so much?"

"No," said the younger man quietly.

"Well, then," said his friend, "if it is not True, or Good, or Necessary, let us bury it in forgetfulness."

When it comes to our relationships with our spouse, loved ones, and friends, we must think carefully about what we're going to say before speaking. There's an expression that goes, "You are a slave of the words you say, but lord of the words you don't." While it may be difficult to hold back the words we want to say, it is impossible to bring back those that have already come out of our mouth. The apostle Paul reminds us of the importance of speaking words that edify and encourage others. Think of what positive things you can say to and about your spouse that will affirm them, encourage them, and strengthen them. Think of what you can do to help your children develop a good strong sense of self. Most important, think of what you can say to your loved ones and others that will help them experience God's grace in their lives. Don't be a slave of your words. Be their master.

Father God, help me to use all that I say to strengthen, encourage, and build others up, never to tear anyone down.

Taming the Tongue

Don't use foul or abusive language. Let everything you say be good and helpful,
so that your words will be an encouragement to those who hear them.
—Ephesians 4:29, NLT

Foul speech is the sign of a corrupt heart, "for out of the abundance of the heart the mouth speaketh" (Matthew 12:34, KJV). While it's easy to recognize profanity and obscenity as being foul, it is also true that frivolous and insipid conversation should not have any place in the life of a Christian. They are just as much evidence of an unregenerate spirit as is vulgarity. In comparison, words that are good and helpful tend to encourage, build up, and unify our churches, our homes, and our families.

While we know this is true, how many times have we uttered hurtful words that we have regretted later? Oh, the tongue is so hard to tame! There are many actions that can be undone, but we cannot put words back into our mouths. It is far too easy to speak first and think later. In so doing, however, we may end up leaving a path of destroyed relationships. Often the ones who get the worst of our words are our own families. It seems we have an easier time taming our tongues when we speak to others. Why do we let our guard down when we're at home?

The truth is that words spoken in the home are more important than those spoken anywhere else. Consider the consequences of a failure to follow the above scriptural advice in our homes. Ponder the importance of being a positive role model to our children. Would we want them to go to school and repeat the same words that we speak in our homes? Good communication skills are among the most important things that we can teach our little ones. Good communication is caught rather than taught. And communication is more than just the words we speak. Children catch on to the tone of our voices, the way we handle conflict, as well as our actual words.

Consider how you have communicated to your family this past week. Have your words been used to build up or to tear down? Have they been used to encourage or to discourage? Have they been helpful or hurtful? Perhaps we need to seek forgiveness from our family members and, with God's help, commit to using words that reflect the Lord we serve.

Lord, put a guard on my lips. May all that I say today be acceptable in Your sight!

Give Thanks for His Deliverance

Giving thanks to the Father who has qualified us to be partakers of the inheritance of the saints in the light. He has delivered us from the power of darkness and conveyed us into the kingdom of the Son of His love, in whom we have redemption through His blood, the forgiveness of sins.
—*Colossians 1:12–14, NKJV*

As spouses and parents, we need to cultivate a spirit of gratitude and thankfulness. If you're not already doing this, begin by expressing thanks for even the smallest, simplest things your spouse or children do. Show your appreciation when they mow the lawn, make supper, pick up toys, open the door of the car, or take out the garbage. Let's choose to never take each other for granted. When we make our family feel it is their obligation to be helpful, we take away their joy in serving one another.

When we develop a spirit of gratitude for the common, simple things in daily life, something will begin to happen that we may not realize at first: we will grow to appreciate even more all that God has done for us. Gratitude begets gratitude and joy begets joy. It's a simple, unavoidable fact. And with that in mind, we should give thanks for the three greatest gifts mentioned in the verses above.

First, that we have been redeemed through the shedding of Christ's blood, and our sins are forgiven, nevermore to be remembered. Remembering that truth, with thanksgiving, will keep it fresh in our mind and experience. Second, that we have been delivered and rescued from the penalty and power of sin. One of the most powerful truths we can claim is that Satan will never have power over us again. Finally, that we have been accepted into the kingdom of God for eternity. We are eternal citizens of heaven with a new passport and identification.

Paul urges us to always remember, with thanks, what Christ did for us on the cross. We should pray that our loved ones, our family, our children will remember to be thankful for these three great gifts every day. Joyfulness is a fruit of the Spirit and will be evident in the life of each Christian and every Christian home.

Father, thank You that You have rescued us, redeemed us, and that we have been accepted into Your kingdom, all through the life and death of Your Son and our Savior Jesus Christ. Help us to be grateful every day for these great gifts.

Be Patient, Persistent, and Joyful

Strengthened with all might, according to His glorious power,
for all patience and longsuffering with joy.
—Colossians 1:11, NKJV

One of the lessons our children must learn early in life is that of delayed gratification. When we quickly give in to our child's every whim and desire, we're only teaching them that they will always get what they want and do not need to exercise any patience whatsoever. On the other hand, when we teach our children from the time they are small that there are times when they need to wait, we are really teaching them the three principles mentioned in the text for today: spiritual strength is a result of knowing, and being obedient to, God's will. This strength produces great endurance and patience.

Here's an example. When your child asks for a toy, particularly one that costs a fair amount of money, you can make an agreement with them that if they save a certain amount of money toward that toy, you will help them with the final percentage. For instance, "If you save from your allowance until you have 80 percent of the cost, I will help you out with the final 20 percent." This teaches them to both be patient *and* persistent. If they truly want something, they can work toward that goal. If they don't want it badly enough they will probably give up before reaching the goal.

But if they persist, and save the agreed-on amount, one of several things will take place. In some cases, by the time they have saved that amount they have changed their minds and end up wanting something entirely different. But if they do persist in reaching their goal in buying whatever it is they've saved for, once they buy it they will experience greater appreciation and joy than if they had simply received it from us the moment they asked for it.

Don't fall into the mistaken belief that we must give our children whatever they long for. Don't answer every request immediately. Instead, let us work with them, teaching them the value of setting a goal and working hard toward reaching it. In doing so, they will learn from us the importance of patience, persistence, and appreciation for the joy that will come as a result.

Father God, bless my children that as they work to fulfill their wishes they may be patient. May they work toward their goal and be persistent, and experience the joy that comes with reaching a long-awaited goal.

Be Strong and Mighty

Strengthened with all might, according to His glorious power.
—Colossians 1:11, NKJV

One of the challenges that parents sometimes face is dealing with children who are, as James Dobson coined, "strong-willed children." These are the children who have a mind of their own and a fierce determination to follow wherever their minds dictate—which, it seems, is usually in the opposite direction to where their parents want them to go. A dictionary definition for strong-willed might be obstinate or stubborn, both of which have negative connotations.

Let's look at some of the positive aspects of being strong-willed. Someone with a strong will doesn't give up easily. A strong-willed person is determined, knows how to persevere, and is usually very focused on reaching their goals. A strong-willed child has a powerful will, and for many reasons that can be a good thing. If left without direction, however, it can become misguided and end up being a bad thing. For instance, a child who insists on going outside in the rain and throws a temper tantrum when called inside is strong-willed in a stubborn, immature way. Shaping and bending the will of such a child requires constant, consistent effort on the part of the parents, and yet it is vital to the future happiness of their child.

Someone with deeply held beliefs, who can stand up to the crowd, who will not be swayed by their peers, is strong-willed in a better, healthier way. A hero, someone who shows courage, someone who fights for what is right, is also strong-willed. It takes a strong will to stand up for what you believe in, particularly during difficult situations.

Dallas Cowboys coach Tom Landry used to say, "Don't pray for an easy life. Pray to be a strong person." This is exactly what Scripture is admonishing here. Pray each day that your family will be able to make tough decisions based on God's principles and will be able to remain strong and mighty.

Instead of praying that your child have an easy, trouble-free life, pray that they will be strong in their convictions, mighty in their beliefs, and powerful in their conscience—men and women of valor for God.

Father, while it might be easier to raise a child who is compliant, I pray that my child will be strong in the face of temptation and sin, mighty as they speak and live for You, and courageous even when the consequences may be painful for them.

Hunger to Know God

Increasing in the knowledge of God.
—Colossians 1:10, NKJV

The intent of this prayer is not that we should have a lot of knowledge about facts and information, as we would if trying to win a trivia contest of sorts. Paul's intention is for us to have more than a passing acquaintance with biblical doctrine, theology, and the deeper truths in God's Word. Paul prays that we might have the type of knowledge that grasps and penetrates an object. That we may be filled with the knowledge of God Himself. To know Him intimately and not just in theory or as a principle.

Many people study and investigate a subject they are passionate about. Archaeologists spend hours, days, months, and even years excavating ruins in faraway places so they can uncover the past and better understand the culture that once lived there. Researchers devote themselves to finding the cause and the cure for a disease. Athletes commit their lives to perfecting their skills and spend countless hours practicing in order to win championships, to establish records, and to make history.

Paul prays that all the saints would become possessors of this knowledge with the same kind of single-minded commitment. He wants us to know that this knowledge is available to all and is not a secret mystery that only a few can ever experience. This is what we should pray not only for ourselves but for our loved ones. That they would have that type of desire, and commitment, and passion for a personal relationship with God. Paul's longing is for the believers to be filled with a thorough knowledge of God's will.

And that is exactly what God longs for as well: He wants to have an intimate relationship with each of His children. When every member of the family hungers to know God intimately, their potential for success in life finds daily partnership with the heavenly Father. How wonderful it is to know the entire family is growing in intimacy with Christ each day.

What are you praying for your family's spiritual direction? Do you long for your children to know and experience a deeper knowledge of God? You can be sure this is a prayer that God loves to answer. Come to Him and ask that each member of your family may have that hunger, that passion to know God.

Father God, awaken in my family the hunger to know You so that they will come to know You and to experience You personally in their lives.

Live Fruitful Lives

Being fruitful in every good work.
—Colossians 1:10, NKJV

B earing fruit is one clear indication that we are walking with Jesus. It is a manifestation of a deep connection that believers have with God. But in order to bear fruit we must first be rooted and grounded in our relationship with God. One of the images we find in the Bible to illustrate this point is that of God's people being compared to a tree: "He shall be like a tree planted by the rivers of water, that brings forth its fruit in its season, whose leaf also shall not wither; and whatever he does shall prosper" (Psalm 1:3, NKJV). And the prophet Isaiah speaks of the remnant of God who are very fruitful because their roots go down deep: "And the remnant who have escaped of the house of Judah shall again take root downward, and bear fruit upward" (Isaiah 37:31, NKJV).

Another indication of a deep connection with God is service. Each year many young people dedicate their time and talents to serve others in countries around the world where the need is great. Student missionaries give at least one year of their lives to educate children and young adults. While learning about a different culture, into which they have immersed themselves, they teach their students about God. This experience of serving others often has such a profound effect that many of them return to the mission field after graduating, and continue to serve, doing so much to improve the quality of life in countries where conditions are often harsh. These young people may not be rich in worldly goods, as some of their contemporaries, but they are being "fruitful in every good work."

Pray for the young people in your life—that they will put down roots deep and strong as they walk with the Lord and serve Him through a life of service to others. Remember, they don't have to go to the mission field or outside of the country in order to bear good fruit. There are people in our neighborhood, at work, at school, that would benefit greatly from the love and service of dedicated Christians. And pray for yourself, too, that you will be an example to your family, in bearing fruit in every good work.

Father God, please bless my children, that they may be successfully rooted and grounded in You. And grant me the grace to provide a good example of love and service to others.

Walk Worthy

That you may walk worthy of the Lord.
—Colossians 1:10, NKJV

Webster's New International Dictionary of the English Language offers several definitions of the word *worthy*: possessing merit; excellent; virtuous; of high station; a man of eminent worth or value. And according to language scholar Kenneth Wuest, the word *worthy* in this verse of Colossians is best translated as *weight*. What Paul is praying, then, is that we might each go about our lives every day in such a manner that our words and actions *carry weight*.

When we pray for a loved one that they "walk worthy of the Lord," we are asking Him to help them in their conduct to demonstrate the character of Christ, so that everyone who meets them will clearly see that their word, their life, carries weight—that it is not easily moved by the winds of fashion, or opinion, or peer pressure.

In days gone by, people would put a lot of stock in a simple handshake or in giving their word to someone to seal an agreement. That small action carried all the weight of their character, of their family's name and reputation. Those who made that type of agreement would sooner die than fail to make good on their word. They would say things like, "My word is my bond," or, "My word is as good as money." We don't see much evidence of this nowadays. It used to be that a lawsuit was seldom heard of, but today we live in a highly litigious culture, where people wouldn't dream of sealing a deal without having a lawyer draw up and examine a contract of agreement. A handshake just doesn't count for much, or carry much weight, in today's world.

So, what does walking *worthy of the Lord* look like in your life? Would others describe you as a man or woman of eminent worth or value? As Christians, does our conduct demonstrate the character of the Christ we claim to follow? Do our words, our lives, carry weight that speaks of a life that is being walked worthy of God? And do we remember that our spouse and our children are watching how we are walking through life? No matter where we may be, we can come to the Lord and ask for His help in walking in such a manner that we honor Him.

Father God, please help us to walk in such a way before You that our lives will be marked by godly integrity. May our words and actions reflect Your character.

To Know God's Will

For this reason we also, since the day we heard it, do not cease to
pray for you, and to ask that you may be filled with the knowledge
of His will in all wisdom and spiritual understanding.
—Colossians 1:9, NKJV

When our children are young and they come to us asking for advice on what to do, it is a relatively easy thing to tell them what to do. With our years of life experience, we have gained a measure of wisdom, and can usually give them good counsel. As they grow older, however, it becomes more difficult. In spite of our experience, we don't have all the answers. We are not the all-knowing, all-wise sages that they once believed us to be. So what do we tell them when they come to us and ask how they can learn to know what God's will for them is?

At the risk of stating the obvious, Paul's recommendation is that we pray. Specifically that we pray for them to filled with the knowledge of God's will. The type of wisdom Paul refers to is godly wisdom—as opposed to a false philosophy or a show of wisdom. It is a wisdom that is saturated with spiritual understanding. When our children ask for advice, they may add, "I just wish I knew what to do!" Well, so do we! If we only knew what would be best for them in every instance. As challenging as life's tough questions can be, we can find confidence in praying that they—and we—would be filled with the knowledge of God's will; that they would live their lives with spiritual understanding as they come to know God's will.

Simply put, when we pray for our family members to know God's will, we are praying that they will be wise enough to know how to make good choices and do the right thing. To know God's will is to grow in a knowledge and experience of Him. What more important thing could we possibly pray for our children? Take a moment right now to pray for those you love most—your spouse, your children, and your friends—that all will be filled with the knowledge of God's will, and that He would grant them all wisdom and spiritual understanding in all matters concerning them.

Dear Lord, please bless my spouse, my children, and my friends, that they may be filled with the knowledge of Your will and that they may have the wisdom and spiritual understanding to follow it and live according to it.

Don't Think Too Highly of Yourself

For I say, through the grace given to me, to everyone who is among you, not to think of himself more highly than he ought to think, but to think soberly, as God has dealt to each one a measure of faith.
—Romans 12:3, NKJV

The message conveyed in the popular culture today is incredibly self-centered and self-serving. You can *be* more, *have* more, and *do* more. *You* are enough! This flies in the face of God's call for us to be servants if we want to be great in His kingdom. This desire for supremacy originated with Lucifer, who wanted to be equal with God. He presented that same desire to Eve and she embraced it. As a result of this rebellion, God told Adam and Eve that one of the consequences they would deal with would be a struggle for supremacy over one another.

Paul counsels believers not to think too highly of themselves. That doesn't mean we need to walk around with our heads bowed, telling ourselves how worthless we are. Rather, if we have truly accepted God's grace and have been born again, none of us will look down on anybody else, thinking ourselves better than everyone else. Sadly, many men and women misuse their God-given power to exert control over others. This is true even within some Christian homes. Satan is still selling his lie that we can be like the Most High.

Looking down on others is another way of saying that we think most highly of ourselves. No one else matches our caliber, and so our opinion, our decision, our point of view is always the only one that matters. Every time. Paul tells us to remember how God has dealt with each one of us, how He has extended His grace and mercy toward us. The very least we should do is to extend the same grace and mercy toward those we love. In God's sight, none of us are better than others. Again, Paul reminds us that "all have sinned, and come short of the glory of God" (Romans 3:23, KJV). There is no such thing as a better sinner, for all have sinned, and all fall short! And yet, God extends His mercy and grace to each one of us.

Father God, please help us to not think too highly of ourselves. May we rather have the heart of a servant in our attitude toward one another, most especially when it concerns those closest to us.

Each Child Is an Original

God has given each of us the ability to do certain things well.
—Romans 12:6, TLB

The scripture for today reminds us of a vital truth that we would do well to remember in our parenting: God has created each of us, and each of our children, with different abilities and gifts. This is not an accident. It is done to fulfill God's purpose for all of us as a body of believers. The same God who created each snowflake differently has made each one of His children as an original, unique, and precious individual. If everyone had the exact same gifts, just think how much poorer our life experiences would be and how much beauty would be lost to the world.

One of the best gifts we can give to our children is to recognize the originality and uniqueness of each one. While they may have similarities in personality or point of view, look for those gifts and talents that make them different. Celebrate their differences. Encourage and help them develop their different gifts, strengths, and interests. How sad when children grow up longing to be someone else. Teach them to recognize that God has gifted and created them to be who they are and that they are precious in His sight. Let them know that they have been given their specific individuality to shine God's love into this world in their own unique way.

Just as Paul was appointed to be an apostle and other believers were chosen to be prophets, teachers, miracle workers, healers of the sick, and so on, God has called, chosen, and gifted our children to help meet the many different needs in the world, and to spread the gospel to every nation, tongue, and people. This should inspire our children and help prepare them for a life of service in God's cause.

What a privilege we have as parents to nurture these God-given gifts in each child. As we walk in step with the Lord, we will be able to watch the Holy Spirit at work in the lives of our children. Teach them well: there is a hurting world in need of the very gifts and abilities with which God has blessed them. Encourage them as they seek to use their gifts to serve the Lord, and watch as He opens heaven's gates and pours out His blessing.

Dear Lord, help me to see my children as You do, and to prepare them for the work to which You have gifted and called them.

Stop Lying

Therefore, putting away lying, "Let each one of you speak truth with his
neighbor," for we are members of one another.
—Ephesians 4:25, NKJV

One of the most important emotional needs for women is the need for honesty and openness in the relationships that matter most. It is particularly difficult for a woman to feel that her husband is not being truthful, that he's lying, or hiding something from her. This doesn't typically come from a place of obsessive neediness but is simply an important part of a healthy relationship from a woman's perspective. In fact, honesty and truthfulness are important in all of our relationships.

For many people, lying has become so much a part of life that they are not even aware of the inroads it has made into their relationships. The danger lies in the subtlety or *necessity* of the lie—which is then easily justifiable. It often begins with little white lies, which are told to keep from hurting the feelings of the other person. A husband says he enjoyed the meal his wife prepared; she pretends to enjoy spending an entire afternoon watching the game with him; he doesn't tell her that the dress really does make her look fat; and she keeps quiet about or minimizes how disappointed she is when he spends so much time at the office.

No matter how small or insignificant the lie may seem, it will create a barrier that will eventually prevent true intimacy and honesty from taking place. It is so much easier to determine not to have any secrets from each other and to always speak the truth. The secret to maintaining truthfulness in a relationship is to learn to speak the truth in love. When we do so, there's never a need to fear we will needlessly hurt one another. Sometimes speaking the truth in love will bring pain—but faithful and true are the wounds of a friend. It is when we don't speak the truth that we cause the deeper hurt to each other, which can result in the ultimate deterioration of the marriage relationship. So, let's determine to follow Paul's advice and to decidedly put away lying once and for all!

O Lord, please teach me how to speak the truth in love. Give me the courage to put away lying once and for all. May our conversations always be honest and kind, and as our intimacy grows, we will give You all the praise and honor.

He Praises Her

Her children arise and call her blessed; her husband also, and he praises her.
—Proverbs 31:28, NIV

The book of Proverbs ends with a poem that describes an excellent wife. In the words of the wise man, the virtuous woman is married; she seeks the best for her husband; she is hard-working and takes good care of her household; she is generous to the needy; wise; she fears Yahweh, and finally, her children and husband praise her. Isn't it interesting that she is honored the most by those who know her best, namely, her husband and her children? I love the words of Ellen G. White in the little devotional, *My Life Today*. Quoting from page 197, we read, "The home should be to the children the most attractive place in the world, and the mother's presence should be its greatest attraction."

How is it that these children call her blessed? I believe it has to do with the example of their father. If he makes it his goal to honor her through his words and actions, showing her the respect she deserves, supporting her decisions and opinions, treating her kindly and tenderly, his children will follow his example, and it will be natural for them to treat her in the same way. If, on the other hand, he is disrespectful, undermines her, makes fun of her, and treats her badly, his children will begin to treat her the same way.

The woman who is treated in a kind, loving, and tender manner will respond accordingly. Mistreatment, neglect, or abuse will result in her spirit being quenched a little at a time and will ultimately destroy the woman, the children, and the home. It is a wise husband who determines to treat his wife like a daughter of God—respectfully, lovingly, patiently, and supporting and encouraging her. As he does this, she will grow and flourish, and he will end up with a stronger, happier, healthier wife and mother, and an improved home and family life. As he rises up and calls her blessed, his children will do the same, not only in appreciation for all she does but also in support of who she is. Thus, a positive cycle of mutual love and praise is set in motion.

Father God, help me to show appreciation, love, and praise toward my spouse. May I build them up, encourage and support them, not only because it is the right thing to do but also because I want to set a good example for my children.

A Friendly Relationship

*"No longer do I call you servants, for a servant does not know what
his master is doing; but I have called you friends, for all things
that I heard from My Father I have made known to you."*
—John 15:15, NKJV

The meaning of the word *servant* in this passage refers to someone who would be expected to obey blindly without being taken into their master's counsels. Jesus wanted to contrast this type of relationship with the one He had with His disciples, which was one of friendship. He left us a perfect example of servant leadership. While He is Lord, and we are His servants, He desires a relationship with us that is based on friendship, in which each one serves the other in a spirit of selflessness and joy.

Those who wish to assert their authority at home and expect everyone in the family to serve them blindly, while using certain biblical texts to prove their point, is neither a leader nor an example of Christ. They should realize this and look at how Jesus demonstrates what a good, healthy relationship should be like. He calls it friendship. In marriage, if we and our spouse are best friends, we will maintain a positive, healthy relationship. While it's great if we can begin our marriage with our spouse as our best friend, we can also grow in our relationship with our spouse so that they become our best friend, if they are not already so.

Another lesson we can take from this verse is the type of communication that should exist among friends—particularly if that friend is your spouse. Jesus told them, "All things that I heard from My Father I have made known to you." In a marriage, this can mean a couple of things, including sharing God's good news with our spouse. As we learn and grow personally in our spiritual walk, it is good to share with our spouse and with our children what we are learning. Let's not keep these jewels to ourselves.

Finally, there should be no secrets between us and our spouse. A good, healthy relationship is built on trust, and trust is built on open, honest communication. That level of intimacy is grown, one conversation at a time.

Thank You, Father, that Jesus is not only our Lord and Savior, He is also our very best Friend: the kind of friend that sticks closer than a brother. Bless our marriage, Lord, bless our home, and may Jesus' type of friendship reign in our most intimate relationships.

Preparing for the Race

Do you not know that those who run in a race all run, but one receives the prize?
Run in such a way that you may obtain it. And everyone who competes for the
prize is temperate in all things. Now they do it to obtain a perishable crown, but
we for an imperishable crown.
—1 Corinthians 9:24, 25, NKJV

To the inhabitants of Corinth the periodic games and foot races held more than a passing interest. The ancient Greeks were passionate about the preparation, the training, and the outcome of each race. It was a source of national pride. Participants had to swear an oath that they'd been in training for ten months; that they'd been faithful in following the strict diet and rigorous program. The imagery of running a race was a perfect one for Paul to use when referring to the Christian life, and it can just as appropriately be compared to marriage.

Preparation. Just as preparation was a key component in determining the outcome of the race, it is vital to the success of two people joining their lives together in marriage. During this time a couple must determine how to handle conflict, manage their finances, raise their children, and plan for their future together. Adequate preparation will help greatly when the uncertainty and strife threaten the home.

Healthy mental attitude. Runners all reach a certain point in the race that is referred to as "hitting the wall," when the pain seems unbearable and they feel they can't take another step. Those who finish the race anticipate this hurdle and mentally prepare to push through the pain to the finish line. So, too, in marriage it is vital to prepare well and to adopt a healthy mental attitude. That we will face challenges is certain. We will experience both days of discouragement and days of triumphs and joys. Through it all, we must keep our eyes on the final goal, on the prize, and strive to reach the finish line together. When we win that race, our reward will include the satisfaction of having made a wonderful lifetime together and providing our children with a lasting reward—the example and legacy of their parents' happy marriage.

Father, help us to prepare well for the race of marriage. And when we finish the course, may we receive from Your hands the crown of glory. At the same time, Father, may our children be blessed by watching our example so they, too, may run victoriously their own race of life.

Persevering to the End

Therefore I run thus: not with uncertainty. Thus I fight: not as one who beats the air. But I discipline my body and bring it into subjection, lest, when I have preached to others, I myself should become disqualified.
—1 Corinthians 9:26, 27, NKJV

Marriage can be compared to a marathon. It is definitely not a sprint! Running a marathon is more demanding, in some regards, than a sprint. Here are several things that are required:

Endurance. A sprinter trains to run his race in a short burst of speed. He hasn't much time, so he knows he must run as fast as possible as soon as the starter's pistol sounds. Some relationships can be compared to a sprint. They start with a burst of speed, include a short dating period, a rapid engagement, a fast-and-furious wedding and honeymoon, and end in a quick divorce. A marathon runner knows he has a long race ahead and learns how to keep moving forward at a steady pace, pushing through the pain and exhaustion, knowing the difficulties will end. He learns what it means to run with perseverance and how to endure to the end of the race.

Focus. Runners don't get distracted by the noise of the crowd or with the other runners pressing around them. They have one goal in mind—to finish the race. They discipline their minds and visualize crossing the finish line. So, too, good marriages are not distracted by the noise and opinions of others. They are not derailed by the busyness of life. They focus on the goal—creating a happy home and developing a close relationship with one another. They visualize, anticipate, and experience the joy of a successful marriage.

Support team. While running is an individual sport, in reality runners need a strong support team. They need others to help provide water along the way, others to cheer them on when they're tempted to quit, and those who encourage them during their training, the ones that lift them up when they are too tired or weak or hurt to go on. In marriage, we not only need each other, but we need the support and encouragement of family, friends, and our spiritual community. We need one another so we can go on to win the race together.

Dear Lord, please help us to focus on the goal, to endure through life's trials, and to find good friends and godly counsel to help support us in the race of life and marriage. Thank You for being beside us—all the way!

The Darkest Valley

Though I walk through the valley of the shadow of death, I will fear no evil; for You are with me; Your rod and Your staff, they comfort me.
—Psalm 23:4, NKJV

The words of Psalm 23 are probably among the most familiar and well-loved passages in all of Scripture. Quoted at gravesides, in movies, between friends, Psalm 23 has brought comfort and strength to countless people through the ages. And for good reason. The phrase "Though I walk" provides us with hope that even when we experience the trauma of death, as everyone ultimately does, God is with us. We don't have to walk this path alone.

The words "walk through" indicate movement. For believers this is a tremendous promise. We do not remain in the place of death. Though it may feel shattering and all-consuming in the moment, it is temporary. We will pass through it when Jesus comes to raise the faithful to life eternal. And even though we may be surrounded by the shadow of death, we don't have to be afraid of it, for it has no power over us. The shadows will lift. The sunlight of God's presence will break through and fill our lives with gladness once more.

As terrifying as dark valleys may be, it is encouraging to remember that our walk doesn't end in the valley of death. When the mountains press in on every side and disaster threatens to smother us; when we lose our loved ones to death and fear being alone in life, we have the assurance that we will pass through the valley. With Jesus as our Savior, we are never forsaken. We are never truly alone.

In the shepherd's psalm, the imagery of a Divine Shepherd offers deep comfort to people in distress. The rod and staff are symbols of God's power and authority. With them, the shepherds of old provided protection and guidance for their sheep. With their staff, they were able to rescue sheep that had wandered away. Our Divine Shepherd provides us with the hope and comfort of His presence and guidance.

Father God, our gentle, loving Shepherd, thank You that we don't need to fear death because Jesus has conquered it. And thank You that even when we or our loved ones have to taste death, it is simply a temporary state until Jesus the Conqueror of death calls us back to life eternal. Thank You, Father, for walking with us through that dark valley.

Correct, Console, and Charge

*Just as you know how we were exhorting and encouraging and
imploring each one of you as a father would his own children.*
—1 Thessalonians 2:11, NASB

In his letter to his spiritual children in Thessalonica, Paul paints a vivid
picture of his role as a spiritual father to these believers who were young
in their faith. There are multiple aspects to parenting, and Paul uses several
words in this verse to show that he was being a responsible father as he
disciplined and instructed these members who still had much to learn.
The Greek word used for children emphasized more than the believers'
immaturity, however. It also conveyed his affection for them.

The three words Paul uses to show his fatherly love for his spiritual children are *exhort, encourage,* and *implore.* Each of these words describes a
different aspect of parenting. Let's take a look at each one.

Sometimes the word *exhort* seems to carry a negative tone in our understanding, but its meaning is not necessarily negative. When we exhort our
children we influence them, direct them, and advise them with our counsel.
That's a good description of the role Paul held among the early church.

When we *encourage* our children, we affirm their best efforts, and where
they fall short we reassure them that with continued practice they will ultimately learn the skill, behavior, or reach the goal they're striving for. It's
difficult for anyone to grow and mature without receiving encouragement
from those whom they respect and admire.

Finally, when we *implore* our children we communicate that we are serious
about the thing we are asking of them. We're not making a casual request or
asking whether or not this is something they feel like doing. To implore can
also mean to pray for something.

There are times, as parents, when we have to reprimand, discipline, or
punish our children. While our goal is not to be vindictive or vengeful, no
child enjoys being disciplined. That's why it is important to use all three of
these aspects in disciplining our children. After we have exhorted them, we
should encourage and implore. While they need to be corrected, they also
need to be reassured that they are greatly loved. Tenderly correct them when
they do wrong, console them as they try to understand the process, and
charge them to do better next time.

*Heavenly Father, may we love and discipline our children in the same man-
ner You love and discipline us, and keep us consistent and kind.*

New Every Morning

It is of the LORD's mercies that we are not consumed, because his compassions fail not. They are new every morning: great is thy faithfulness.
—Lamentations 3:22, 23, KJV

These verses contain both a precious promise and a stirring challenge. We don't have to get too far along into the day before we've done something that deserves divine punishment. Sometimes even early in the morning our thoughts or careless actions toward the people closest to us are less than stellar. Our lives are living proof that it is only because of His mercies and compassions that we are not consumed. Thank God that His justice is always balanced with His mercy and His grace, or we would have been consumed long before now.

In the original Hebrew, the word for *mercies* conveys the following related aspects: grace, goodness, kindness, and compassion. When we say that God is Love—this is what we mean. He is good, gracious, and kind. The meaning of the Hebrew word for *compassions* is very interesting. It expresses a feeling of deep empathy, such as that of a mother's deep attachment and connection to her child. This is how God longs to be connected with His children.

Eugene Peterson, in his paraphrase *The Message,* expresses the thoughts in this passage the following way: "God's loyal love couldn't have run out, his merciful love couldn't have dried up. They're created new every morning. How great your faithfulness!" As His children, we are truly blessed! Our marriages remain intact in spite of what we have done to each other. Our families are still together even though we have not always been a good reflection of God's love. And the reason we're still together and have a marriage and a family is that God's mercies are abundant and never cease.

Take some time right now to thank God for His mercies toward you, toward your marriage, and toward your family. And then ask Him to help you understand and experience His deep love for you. Contemplate the fact that it is His love abiding in you that will help you display the same love and mercy toward those closest to you so that your marriage and your family may be a true reflection of His character of love.

Father God, thank You that Your mercies, Your compassions, are new every morning. Thank You for Your faithfulness to us, even when we have not been faithful to You. Help us to be more merciful and compassionate toward those closest to us.

Flee!

Flee sexual immorality. Every sin that a man does is outside the body, but he who commits sexual immorality sins against his own body.
—1 Corinthians 6:18, NKJV

In this passage, Paul urges us to *flee* sexual immorality. There's nothing passive about his instruction. Paul does not say, "Stand up and walk away from it." He commands us to "flee sexual immorality." It is imperative! And Paul is not alone in making sexual purity a top priority for believers. All the apostles shared the same concern, and both the Old and New Testaments are filled with counsel, instruction, and admonition for God's people to abstain from sexual immorality.

Remember the story of Joseph serving in Potiphar's household? This young man was seriously pressured by Potiphar's wife to have an affair. But his resolve was firm: "How can I sin against God?" One day she made sure they were alone and grabbed Joseph by his coat. His response followed exactly Paul's counsel and he fled the scene, leaving the irate woman holding his coat. Please note, he didn't stop to reason with her, nor did he simply stand up and walk away. He ran. Joseph recognized the gravity of her actions and the danger of the situation, and he fled to get away from her.

It is interesting to note that our verse for today is strongly connected to an often-quoted verse: "Or do you not know that your body is the temple of the Holy Spirit who is in you, whom you have from God, and you are not your own?" (verse 19, NKJV). This verse is used to remind us that we need to take care of our physical bodies by abstaining from certain foods and chemicals, and by eating properly and exercising. And it is exactly because our bodies are the temple of the Holy Spirit that we need to remember to flee from even a suggestion of sexual immorality.

Sexual promiscuity in any form, however subtle it may first appear, is truly all about self-gratification. Though Satan may weave an intoxicating web to draw us in, sexual immorality is contrary to God's command for us, and for good reason. When we obey Him, we give evidence of being His children by remaining pure and free from sin. That's why Paul doesn't simply suggest we stop but commands us to *flee* from it.

Father, may we remain pure not only to keep from sinning against our own body but because we don't want to betray the trust of others and sin against You.

Unselfish Relationships

Let no one seek his own, but each one the other's well-being.
—*1 Corinthians 10:24, NKJV*

How different would our relationships, our homes, and our churches be if we all followed this God-given principle? Remember, it was self-interest that led to self-seeking, which led to pride, which resulted in Satan claiming, "I will be like the Most High." Nothing good has ever come from it. All other sins flow from it. And we all are familiar with the innate desire for supremacy, for power, and for control that hides within our own hearts and minds.

When couples seek counseling because they are dealing with financial difficulties, it usually doesn't take long to discover that very often the conflict has come about because there is a basic disagreement on who should be the one to control the family finances. The same is true for issues arising out of how to discipline the children. In fact, the root cause for marital discord usually stems from both husband and wife feeling that they ought to be the one to have the final say on the matter. This is true even for issues in the bedroom.

The Bible is filled with excellent counsel for couples seeking to honor God in their marriages and in their homes. In Galatians 6:2, Paul writes, "Bear one another's burdens, and so fulfill the law of Christ" (NKJV). We are all burdened with something. What is it your spouse struggles with? Is there something you can do to lighten their load? When our focus moves from "What do *I* want?" to "What does my spouse need?" something changes. The hold that selfishness and self-interest has on us is broken. Again, Paul writes to the Philippians this time and says, in Philippians 2:4, "Let each of you look out not only for his own interests, but also for the interest of others" (NKJV).

By following these biblical principles, instead of seeking to supply our own comfort and convenience, we can change the whole dynamic and direction of our marriage. Where there is only conflict and tension, peace and harmony can reign. Instead of seeing only the failings and mistakes of our spouse, we will begin to see the beauty of who they really are: the special person we fell in love with at the start of our relationship.

Dear Lord, please remove this desire for control from me. It has no place in Your kingdom, and no place in our home. Help us to seek what is best for the other and bless our marriage and our family. Thank You, Lord!

Sharing Joy and Sorrow

Rejoice with those who rejoice, and weep with those who weep.
—Romans 12:15, NKJV

Joy shared is joy doubled;
Sorrow shared is sorrow halved.

How do we share joy and sorrow? We've all heard of *sympathy* and *empathy,* and while they are closely related, it is easy to confuse their meanings. Here is a definition so we can better understand them. When we empathize with someone it means we understand how they are feeling because we have experienced it ourselves and can put ourselves in their shoes. Sympathy, on the other hand, means acknowledging another person's emotional pain and providing comfort and assurance even if we haven't personally experienced what they are going through.

Empathy says, "I understand how devastating it is to lose your mother. My mother died last year and the grief is still so fresh."

In contrast, sympathy says, "I was sorry to hear about your car accident. Is there anything I can do to help you during this difficult time?"

Both empathy and sympathy find their source in compassion. If you are struggling to find compassion in your heart for someone, realize that the opposite of compassion is competition. Ask yourself if there is something you feel you're competing against regarding the person in this situation. Perhaps you need to take time to work through it with the Lord. The apostle Paul encourages us to sympathize and empathize with others. Paul says that when the love of God is in our hearts, we can freely rejoice with those who rejoice. We are not envious of them nor will we want to compete with them or rain on their parade.

When someone weeps, we don't need to insist they pull themselves up by their bootstraps or stop crying because it makes us feel uncomfortable. Instead, we are admonished to share their sorrow and acknowledge their pain when bad things happen. We're also encouraged to rejoice together when life is good and all is well. This is especially true in our marriage and family relations. Let us be sympathetic with our spouse, our parents, and our children. Let us show empathy with what they are feeling wherever we possibly can.

Father, help us to feel with others as well as to feel for others, and may we openly rejoice with those who rejoice and weep with those who weep.

Rescue, Heal, and Save

For "whoever calls on the name of the Lord shall be saved."
—Romans 10:13, NKJV

Paul chooses to specifically use the word *whoever*. Whoever includes everyone. Everyone who calls on the name of the Lord shall be saved. Not *may,* or *could be,* or *if they're lucky.* Everyone shall! It's an imperative. Everyone shall be saved when they call upon the name of the Lord. This has to be one of the most powerful promises we can claim—for ourselves and for those we love.

The word used for "saved" in the New Testament Greek can also be translated as rescued or healed. And while each of these words plays an important role in our salvation through the sacrifice of Jesus, they also have powerful implications for our marriages, our homes, and our families. There are countless circumstances in our lives where this verse offers us help. For instance, we are often asked if a marriage can be saved after infidelity has taken place. While infidelity is an indication that something is desperately wrong in the marriage, this verse promises that God can bring healing to our relationship even when trust has been broken. Notice, it doesn't promise that it will be easy or that it will occur overnight. Marriages that are facing problems have typically been struggling for some time. Don't be tempted to look for a quick fix. There may be much work that needs to be done to restore a broken relationship.

What about those who may be in the grip of an abusive relationship or shackled by an addiction? Remember, *whoever* means everyone. Whenever we call on the name of the Lord, He is present to help, to save, to rescue, and to heal. If you are caught in the crosshairs of brokenness right now, suffering at the hands of an abusive spouse, this promise is for you and for your children. Claim it. God is faithful, and even though we experience heartbreak in this life, we never have to face it alone. Ask the Lord to show you where to find the help and support you need at this time. Then pray for the courage to make whatever decisions may be necessary. Remember, He promises to save, to rescue, and to heal. You are not alone!

Father, we ask in the name of Jesus that You save, rescue, and heal us. You see our broken hearts and wounded homes. Draw close. Our need for You is very great. Lead us into the abundant life that You have promised us.

Givers and Takers

*Seek good and not evil, that you may live; so the L*ORD *God of hosts will be with you.—Amos 5:14, NKJV*

Christian psychologist Willard Harley speaks of the two sides of us that are fighting for control. The "Giver" is the side of our personality that wants to make the other person happy. It is our unselfish, loving, caring nature that desires what is good for the other and is even willing to be hurt, to be vulnerable, and to be unhappy if in the process the other person is happy. This side of our personality is very prominent during the time we are dating, during the honeymoon, and early in marriage; and it is the side that promotes true intimacy in marriage, an intimacy that can last a lifetime.

The "Taker," on the other hand, is the opposite side of our personality that wants to make sure we are happy, even if it makes the other person unhappy. This is the selfish, unloving, uncaring, sinful nature that desires what pleases us in disregard of the other person's needs. When the Taker takes over in our marriage, conflict becomes a regular part of life. If allowed to continue to dominate our relationship, the Taker will eventually lead us to withdraw from our spouse—emotionally, physically, spiritually—and at the end it could lead to the termination of our relationship.

What the prophet Amos suggests is that we not only allow but encourage the Giver side of our personality to dominate in our relationship so we will seek to do what is good for our spouse—and for others in our life—rather than evil (that's the Taker in our lives). When we seek to do what is good— which is also what Agape love, caring love, is all about—the promise from Amos is that God will be with us. This does not mean that there are times when God is not with us—God is everywhere and always with us as Matthew states in Matthew 28:20—but rather that His abiding, loving presence will be real in our relationship to make it a healthier, more intimate one—one that reflects His relationship with us, and one which reflects His plan for our lives.

Father, You desire that Your type of love reign in our relationships. Help me to seek what is good for my spouse so that I may reflect Your love to them and so that Your plan for our marriage and our home may be fulfilled in us today.

What Will I Answer?

I will stand my watch and set myself on the rampart, and watch to see what He will say to me, and what I will answer when I am corrected.
—Habakkuk 2:1, NKJV

The role of parents in the lives of their children has several similarities to the role the prophets played in the lives of God's people. The prophets compared themselves to watchmen, ever attentive and expectant of hearing a message from the Lord. Habakkuk implies a steadfast, persevering waiting and watching for the Lord. As parents we need the wisdom that comes from the Lord, and if we have a constant watchful expectancy that we shall hear from Him in answer to our request for counsel, we can expect He will respond to us. He does this in several ways: through His Word, by His Spirit, through the godly counsel of others, and through events that take place, what some people call *providence*.

Parents fulfill the role of the seer in the home—a term used to describe the role of the prophet who spent his life watching and waiting to see what God would tell him, for wisdom to know how to lead God's people. Parents do the same for their home and their children, waiting and watching for guidance from the Lord to impart to their household.

The role of parents is also as God's spokesmen. As head of the household the parent, and particularly the father, needs to lead his family to do what God wants them to do, what God's Word teaches we should do. It's important to keep in mind, however, that our role as God's spokesmen does not give us the right to speak as if we were infallible, flawless, or perfect. In fact, Habakkuk reminds us that if we are open to God's leading, there will be times when He will reprove us. "What shall I answer when I am reproved?" he asks. How we respond to God's reproof will be an opportunity for our children to see what being a Christian looks like in real life. A humble, contrite spirit will teach them important lessons about submission to God, accepting by faith that He knows what is best for us.

Father God, may we as parents represent You properly and faithfully to our family, especially to our children. Help us to wait and watch with patient endurance and a humble expectancy, demonstrating a living faith to the young ones who are watching us.

Walking in the Same Direction

Can two people walk together without agreeing on the direction?
—Amos 3:3, NLT

How important is it for husbands and wives, for families, to walk together in unity? "If a kingdom is divided against itself, that kingdom cannot stand. And if a house is divided against itself, that house cannot stand" (Mark 3:24, 25, NKJV). That's pretty important. It can mean the difference between the success and the failure of our homes. When we are united it means we're pulling together, in the same direction, toward the same goals. Being divided in our homes means exactly the opposite—each one is pulling in a different direction. A home can only last so long when that occurs before being torn apart.

Walking together in unity does not mean there is uniformity in every aspect of life. There is room in unity for diverse views and opinions without alienating family members, without our differences tearing the family apart. It's good, however, to have similarities in the important areas of life, such as the religious beliefs and principles we live by, values and morals that guide us, goals and attainments, family backgrounds, education, and principles of financial management. It is particularly important for there to be agreement between husband and wife on the principles they will use in child rearing and discipline even before they have children.

The idea that opposites attract is used as a way to explain that we are still individuals with differences. While it is true that opposites attract, it is also true that similarities help to bind us together. The expression, "Birds of a feather flock together," comes to mind. While we maintain our individuality when we marry, and we should, it again underscores the importance of having and sharing similarities with the person we marry.

Finally, the psalmist reminds us, "Behold, how good and how pleasant it is for brethren to dwell together in unity!" (Psalm 133:1). Let us benefit from each other's differences, enjoying the variety and interest it adds to our homes, and let us rejoice in our similarities for the unity and the strength it brings to our families. There is room for both. In fact, when there is a healthy blend of the two, we will have stronger, happier, more vibrant homes and families.

Father, bless us so we may benefit from our different strengths, but also bless us that we may find and marry the person with whom we have more similarities, especially when it comes to how we relate to You.

Praying for Our Children

Therefore we also pray always for you that our God would count you worthy of this calling, and fulfill all the good pleasure of His goodness and the work of faith with power, that the name of our Lord Jesus Christ may be glorified in you, and you in Him, according to the grace of our God and the Lord Jesus Christ. —2 Thessalonians 1:11, 12, NKJV

Praying for our girls began before they were born. Before they entered into the world, we prayed for that baby developing inside the womb. At each stage of life our prayers focused on different things. The prayers targeted the specific challenges that each stage of life brought to them: choices of friends, academic challenges, peer pressure, media choices, and so on. We quickly realized that as they grew, so did the importance of the choices they made. Academic challenges in elementary school gave way to college and career choices. Choosing childhood friends gave way to choosing a marriage partner. As the significance of choices increased, so did our prayers. Even now, as the parents of two young adult daughters, our prayers continue.

One of the most important gifts you will ever give your child is your prayers on their behalf. Your child will depend on those prayers. They will go forward into difficult circumstances with the knowledge that they are covered in prayer. As they face daily challenges, pray with them. Tell them that you will be in prayer as they take a math test or deal with a classroom bully. Prayer should be a part of everyday home life. Children should be taught to take all matters, great and small, to Jesus.

And, no matter how old your child gets, never give up praying for them! Prayers make a difference, and prayers change things! This is one of the greatest life lessons that you as a parent can teach your child. "Patiently, lovingly, . . . parents are to do their appointed work. . . . Constantly they must pray that God will impart His grace to their children. Never must they become weary, impatient, or fretful in their work. They must cling closely to their children and to God" (*The Adventist Home*, 208).

Dear Lord, thank You for giving me the privilege of being a parent. I pray that my children will be worthy of Your calling. I pray that they will live their lives in a way to glorify Your name. And, I thank You that Your grace is sufficient for them.

First Things First

But the Lord said to her, "My dear Martha, you are worried and upset over all these details! There is only one thing worth being concerned about. Mary has discovered it, and it will not be taken away from her."
—Luke 10:41, 42, NLT

It seems as if the laundry basket is always full, the dust settles constantly on the furniture, toilets need to be cleaned, and floors need to be scrubbed. And that doesn't even take into account the car shuttles to soccer practice, piano lessons, doctor appointments, and grocery store runs. The calendar is full, and it seems overwhelming to attempt to fit one more thing in. Where do we fit in the time to be with Jesus on our to-do list?

In Luke, Jesus reminds us that we give too much time and energy to things that are of little significance. Do we need to take another look at the *one thing* Jesus mentioned? "The 'one thing' that Martha needed was a calm, devotional spirit, a deeper anxiety for knowledge concerning the future, immortal life, and the graces necessary for spiritual advancement. She needed less anxiety for the things which pass away, and more for those things which endure forever. Jesus would teach His children to seize every opportunity of gaining that knowledge which will make them wise unto salvation. The cause of Christ needs careful, energetic workers. There is a wide field for the Marthas, with their zeal in active religious work. But let them first sit with Mary at the feet of Jesus. Let diligence, promptness, and energy be sanctified by the grace of Christ; then the life will be an unconquerable power for good" (*The Desire of Ages*, 525).

As our children see us model these priorities, they will incorporate them into their own spiritual walk. Let us keep our personal and family worship as the centerpiece of our plans for each day. Make this time a sacred commitment. Let's not allow anything else to push this time aside. This will always be a challenge—but making it a habit will make it easier to carry out.

As we commit to daily spending time together as a family at the feet of Jesus, as we reorder our priorities, we will end up discovering that our productivity, as well as our energy level, will actually increase as God blesses us.

Dear Lord, please help me set my priorities in a way that honors You. Keep the busyness of life from crowding and distracting me. May nothing prevent me from spending quality time with You each and every day.

Stealing Your Life

"The thief's purpose is to steal and kill and destroy.
My purpose is to give them a rich and satisfying life."
—John 10:10, NLT

John perfectly contrasts the intentions and actions of the thief and the Shepherd. The thief drops in randomly to steal and kill and destroy. His only desire is to further his own aims, and he does not have the best interests of the sheep at heart. The Shepherd is the polar opposite. The interests of the sheep are uppermost in His mind to the extent that in order to give them a rich and satisfying life, the Shepherd was willing to lay down His life for His sheep.

In the same way, the devil is only interested in how he can use us to further his own agenda. The more chaos and destruction he can bring into the lives of God's children the happier he is. His ultimate goal is to have us walk away from the Good Shepherd—to steer us off the narrow way and have us join the multitude on the wide road that leads to destruction. But as long as we stay in the care of the Good Shepherd, the devil cannot force us away from Christ.

Here are some of the ways the thief destroys relationships within our families.

He steals. If we allow him to, he steals our time when we become consumed with financial pursuits rather than spending time with Jesus and with our family. He steals our sense of safety when disasters strike and leave us reeling.

He kills. Unless we are intentional about keeping our marriage strong, he will do everything to kill it. Too many homes have fallen prey to his attacks. Fortunately, we have a Protector and Counselor. Our marriages and families can be strong, vibrant, and healthy as we allow the Shepherd to have control.

He destroys. After killing a marriage he destroys the lives of those involved—including those of our children. He destroys the example of a godly marriage and causes nonbelievers to think there is no difference between a Christian and non-Christian home.

How blessed we are to follow the Good Shepherd! Jesus came for the express purpose of giving us life, abundant life, satisfying life. With Jesus our marriage, our home, our lives can survive any attempt of the enemy to steal, kill, and destroy.

Father God, may the abundant life Jesus came to give us be the hallmark of our homes, our churches, and our communities. Help us to stick close to the Good Shepherd!

Magic Eyes

Then God saw their works, that they turned from their evil way;
and God relented from the disaster that He had said He would
bring upon them, and He did not do it.
—Jonah 3:10, NKJV

Several years ago, I read a story about marriage that illustrates the value of forgiveness. It goes like this:

In the village of Falken lived a long, thin baker named Fouke. Fouke was so upright that he seemed to spray righteousness from his thin lips over everyone who came to him. So, everyone preferred to stay away. His wife, Hilda, was short and round. Her soft roundness seemed to invite them in to share her warmth. She respected her husband and loved him as much as he would allow her; but her heart ached for something more from him.

One morning Fouke came home and found a stranger lying on Hilda's bosom. Fouke surprised everyone by keeping Hilda as his wife, saying he forgave her as the good book said he should. But, in his heart of hearts, he could not forgive her for bringing shame to his name. He only pretended to forgive her so that he could punish her with his righteous mercy.

His fakery did not sit well in heaven. So each time he would feel his secret hate, an angel came to him and dropped a small pebble, hardly the size of a small button, into his heart. The pebbles multiplied, and his heart grew heavy with the weight of them. Weary and hurt, he began to wish he were dead.

The angel came to him one night and told him how he could be healed of his hurt. There is only one remedy. "You cannot change the past. You can only heal the hurt that comes to you from the past. And you can only heal it with the vision of the magic eyes." He asked how to get the magic eyes. "Ask, and they will be given. Each time you see Hilda through your new eyes, a pebble will be lifted from your heart."

Finally, his pain drove him to ask, and the angel gave him the magic eyes. Hilda began to change, and he saw her as a needy woman who loved him. He invited Hilda into his heart again, and she came. And together they began their second season of humble joy.

Father, please give us the "magic eyes" we need in our marriage. Teach us to forgive, to see our spouse as You see them.

August

Pleasant Words

Pleasant words are like a honeycomb,
sweetness to the soul and health to the bones.
—Proverbs 16:24, NKJV

Let only pleasant words be spoken by parents to their children, and respectful words by children to their parents. Attention must be given to these things in the home life; for if, in their character building, children form right habits, it will be much easier for them to be taught by God and to be obedient to His requirements.

". . . Fathers and mothers, husbands and wives, brothers and sisters, do not educate yourselves in the line of vulgarity of action, word, or thought. Coarse sayings, low jests, lack of politeness and true courtesy in the home life, will become as second nature to you and will unfit you for the society of those who are becoming sanctified through the truth. The home is too sacred a place to be polluted by vulgarity, sensuality, recrimination, and scandal. . . .

"Indulge in no foolish talking in your house. Even very young children will be benefited by 'the form of sound words.' But idle and foolish words exchanged between father and mother will lead to the same kind of words among the children; while right, candid, truthful, and serious words will lead to the same in all the household and will lead to right actions also.

". . . When you speak angry words to your children, you are helping the cause of the enemy of all righteousness. The work of teaching should begin in childhood, not accompanied by harshness and fretting, but in kindness and patience; and this instruction should be continued through all their years to manhood and womanhood.

"Let every family seek the Lord in earnest prayer for help to do the work of God. Let them overcome the habits of hasty speech and the desire to blame others. Let them study to be kind and courteous in the home, to form habits of thoughtfulness and care.

"What harm is wrought in the family circle by the utterance of impatient words, for the impatient utterance of one leads another to retort in the same spirit and manner. Then come words of retaliation, words of self-justification, and it is by such words that a heavy, galling yoke is manufactured for your neck; for all these bitter words will come back in a baleful harvest to your soul.

". . . Words are as seeds which are planted" (*The Adventist Home*, 437–439).
Father, may our words be sweet and bring about a harvest of happiness.

A Soft Answer

A soft answer turns away wrath, but a harsh word stirs up anger.
—*Proverbs 15:1, NKJV*

When emotions are running wild, and words are about to fly about, here are six suggestions on how to say things more effectively to one another in order to help real dialogue to take place and make our homes the truly Spirit-filled havens that God intends them to be.

1. *Use a still, small voice.* Take a deep breath and speak in measured tones. A whisper is more effective than yelling. The spirit in your heart affects the tone of your voice. If you're filled with unresolved bitterness and resentment, it will come out in your voice. No one listens when you're shouting, but everyone does when you whisper. Watch your body language and eye contact. A certain demeaning toss of the head or look in the eye can make the hearer angry and defensive.

2. *Maintain your sense of humor.* It's amazing how a little humor can ease the greatest of tensions. Many conflicts can reach resolution by simply allowing ourselves to laugh at the circumstance and, more important, at ourselves.

3. *Address the issue.* Don't say irresponsible things about each other with the intent to hurt and demean. That's attacking the person, not the issue at hand. Address the issue; don't shoot down the individual.

4. *Don't bring up the past.* Let the past remain in the past. Don't bring up issues from years earlier and attempt to use them in the current conflict in order to win the verbal battle and bolster your position.

5. *Stay on topic.* Don't get off the subject by widening your argument to issues unrelated to the current conflict and discussion. This is easily done, and we must consciously guard against it. Remember, he who angers you controls you. Anyone can take away your freedom, but remember, the most important human freedom is your freedom to choose your attitude in any circumstance.

6. *Avoid statements that are impossible to defend.* One person may say, "I asked you to pick me up at school." The other may reply, "No, you didn't!" The first person responds, "Yes, I did!" This interaction is endless and fruitless. Make sure your statements are the truth.

Dear Lord, when emotions are running high, please help me to remember Your promise that a soft answer turns away wrath.

Choose Your Words Wisely

Like apples of gold in settings of silver.
—Proverbs 25:11, NIV

When learning the finer techniques in communicating with our spouse and our children, there are six fatal phrases to avoid:

1. *"You always . . ."* No one *always* does anything.
2. *"You never . . ."* Again, you cannot accurately use the word *never* about another person's behavior or choices.
3. *"You should/could have . . ."* How can you rationally discuss something someone *should* have done? Keep the conversation in the present.
4. *"Why didn't you . . . ?"* You can't rewind the clock. There is no way they can rewind the experience and fix what they have already done.
5. *"I would have . . ."* Now you're getting arrogant. "*I* wouldn't have made that mistake." This remark only separates you and your listener and breaks down any chance for productive interaction.
6. *"You make me . . ."* No one *makes* you! This one's a real dandy. Talk about taking away all responsibility for personal behavior. Instead of saying, "You make me . . ." say to the other person, "I feel . . ." and explain your emotions from your perspective.

Instead of using these six fatal phrases, use the following three fabulous phrases to replace them.

1. *"In the future . . ."* This is a proactive statement. It provides a positive position for a beneficial conversation and takes the defensiveness and sting of accusation out of your interaction. For example, "In the future, would you please leave my keys on my desk and not in the car?"
2. *"Next time . . ."* You cannot change what has already happened. There are no magic wands to magically erase a word or deed. Instead, try saying, "The next time you find out you will be late picking me up after work, I would really appreciate it if you would call and let me know."
3. *"What would have to happen . . ."* Open-ended questions give the other person a chance to respond. A person who is given the opportunity to think about their ideas, thoughts, position, or interest in a matter will be much more open to what you have to say.

Father, teach us to speak in such a manner that our words are as apples of gold in settings of silver.

The Power of a Woman

*The wise woman builds her house, but the foolish
pulls it down with her hands. —Proverbs 14:1, NKJV*

It is within a woman's power to build her house, her marriage, and her family, by the power of the words she chooses to speak—not only to her children, but primarily to her husband. With her words she can affirm and build up, or criticize and tear down. Many women don't realize that they hold this power, but they do. It is not theirs to manipulate, but should rather be a sweet influence that is felt in every area of the home and marriage.

Dennis Rainey, in his *Family Life Marriage Bible*, comments on this text: Every wife has the power to create or destroy her relationship with her husband. "The wise woman builds her house, but the foolish pulls it down with her hands." Every man needs his wife's respect. It is one of his deepest needs. He has others, but your respect—or lack thereof—impacts his whole life.

He goes on to say: "Respecting your husband includes really listening to him, not simply hearing the words that come out of his mouth. Take seriously what he says! . . . Some wives do not realize how powerful they can be in their husband's life when they truly respect their man . . . and a wife should look for ways to affirm and respond to her husband's leadership. It starts by praising him for those areas in which he deserves genuine respect."

I'm baffled at times to hear how some wives speak to and about their husbands and then complain that their marriage is not what they would like it to be or that they're not treated as well as they would like to be. Applying the golden rule, if wives begin by affirming and showing appreciation and admiration for their husbands, even for the smallest of things they say or do, it will build them up and encourage their man to be a better husband. Willard Harley writes that admiration and respect are among a man's most important emotional needs. Please note, these are valid needs and not merely selfish desires. Showing admiration and respect for your husband is a gift to them, but if practiced consistently, it will in turn become a gift you give yourself, your children, and your home.

Father, may we show and express more appreciation toward our spouse and thus meet their needs, and while doing so, may our marriage be strengthened.

Longing for Home

By the rivers of Babylon, there we sat down, yea,
we wept when we remembered Zion.
—Psalm 137:1, NKJV

I have lived in the United States for thirty-three years and have been adopted by this country and the people here. I am an American citizen, and love the U.S. as if I had been born here. But my heart is also in Colombia, where I spent the first eighteen years of my life and where I still have many relatives and friends. It is there I received the first part of my education, and where I have some of my strongest memories—the death of my father when I was fifteen years old, my sister's wedding, my group of friends, and many more.

I have been back home only four times in the last thirty-three years, one of them for my mother's death. The other three visits were vacations to see the family, and to get reacquainted with my home and my people. I don't know if all foreigners experience this, but I know that every time I come back from Colombia I go through a couple of weeks of deep sadness and a longing for home. I desperately want to be back with those I love, eat their food, enjoy their music, travel their roads, watch their sunsets, share their landscapes, and feel their warmth.

I wonder at times if Jesus ever had similar thoughts and feelings. He left heaven and was away from home for thirty-three years. He left a place where He was surrounded by love. There was no violence, anger, or hatred, and He had face-to-face communion with His Father, with the Holy Spirit, and with all the angels. While here on earth, even though He had a loving mother and stepfather and several friends, He also encountered the hostility of His step-brothers, the anger of the people, and the hatred of the authorities. I wonder how much He longed to be home!

I remember reading of Ellen White being transported to heaven in a vision. After coming out of the vision and witnessing the darkness and gloom of earth, she felt so sad. I'm glad we won't experience that after we leave heaven for the new earth because God Himself will be with us. In the meantime, as much as I long for my Colombian home, I long for heaven even more.

Father, we long for Jesus to return and take us home. Keep us faithful, and keep us looking up until then!

Invitation to Pray Together

For this cause everyone who is godly shall pray to You in a time when You may be found; surely in a flood of great waters they shall not come near him. You are my hiding place; You shall preserve me from trouble; You shall surround me with songs of deliverance.
—Psalm 32:6, 7, NKJV

I love the words of this psalm and see it as an invitation for couples to pray together. When the economy threatens to take our job, our house, our financial stability and security away from us, where do we turn to for help? And when we spend more time arguing than we spend in enjoyable conversation, when the thought of divorce swims in our heads like a piranha threatening to devour our home, who are we going to turn to? If we're in water up to our eyeballs and don't know how to swim, nothing will help save us more effectively than Jesus.

Praying as a couple, praying for each other, and praying together is our salvation. I have advised every couple that has come to me for counseling to do just that; it's one of the assignments I give couples in trouble if they are to receive the help they need for their problems. There are many benefits for couples when they pray:

1. As we come close to God, we are also drawn to each other.
2. It is a good time to pray for your spouse—it's hard to not have a good, positive attitude toward your spouse when you're praying for them.
3. It's good to know that your spouse is thinking about and praying for you.
4. It's a good time to confess to God, and to each other, our faults and frailties, to apologize, to forgive the other, and to receive forgiveness.

I have advised couples not to use prayer as a weapon or a finger-pointing device, to not pray, "Make him a good husband," or "Make her a good wife." Rather, pray that they may enjoy good health, that God's greatest blessings will fall richly on them, that they will enjoy God's protection, or that they may have a great day at work. These prayers, verbalized by your spouse, can bring great healing to your relationship.

Father, bless my spouse, this very moment. Bless them with health, with joy and peace, with the assurance of salvation and with the knowledge of Christ. Make them successful in their job, in their studies, and in their life. Protect them, and save them for Your kingdom.

Let Me Not Be Ashamed

*O my God, I trust in You; let me not be ashamed; let not my enemies triumph
over me. . . . Do not remember the sins of my youth, nor my transgressions;
according to Your mercy remember me, for Your goodness' sake, O L*ORD.
—*Psalm 25:2, 7, NKJV*

I find it encouraging to know that David was not the only one who faced
challenges, stumbled, and fell during his youth and pleads for forgiveness
in his later years. Sometimes those are sins of ignorance, at other times
sins of commission, or sins of omission. I was not raised in a Seventh-day
Adventist family, and I can look back at my youth and see a life tainted with
sins of ignorance—drinking and smoking—because that's what everybody
else did. I did not always apply myself to my studies, and I caused my parents
great aggravation, sadness, and pain. With David I can cry out, "God, do
not remember the sins of my youth," and I know that God's love and mercy
covers those times. And there were other sins, too, that have been forgiven
by God's grace and lovingkindness toward me.

What bothers me, though, is not the sins of my youth but the sins of my
adult life, after I came to know Him. Yesterday's sins. Today's sins. I can't
claim ignorance anymore. I can't claim inexperience, lack of maturity, or bad
luck either. My sin today is a sin of outright rebelliousness, something for
which I have no excuse. And so with David I also cry out, "My God, I trust
in You; let me not be ashamed; let not my enemies triumph over me." I don't
want to bring shame on my God or His cause, nor do I want to bring shame
to my wife and family, so I get up every morning to spend time with Him,
to study His Word, to talk to Him, and to listen from Him, so that I may be
changed from my selfish life of sin to His selfless life of love. If I fall and my
enemies rejoice it's sad enough, but when I sin and my enemy laughs at God,
it is a true shame.

*My God, I trust in You! Help me to live in such a way that I will not bring
shame on You or my family. Help me this day to live in such a way that there
will be no cause for me to be embarrassed for my actions or my words, and that
my family may never be harmed by them.*

Anger Management

Be angry, and do not sin. Meditate within your heart on your bed, and be still.
—Psalm 4:4, NKJV

Anger is a normal emotion, one that even God experiences. And while God's anger may be different than ours, it is still anger. David writes, "O Lord, do not rebuke me in Your anger, nor chasten me in Your hot displeasure" (Psalm 6:1, NKJV).

While anger is a normal emotion, we must manage it in a healthy way so it does not become sin and cause harm to anyone. According to marriage researcher and therapist John Gottman, during the heat of an argument, husbands tend to "flood" faster. By flooding he means that the blood "rises to the head" and prevents more "rational" thinking. Maybe this explains why anger in men so often develops into physical abuse.

We recommend that when either spouse begins to feel "flooded," they take a time-out. The key is to make sure there is a time limit to the time-out as opposed to an open-ended break. As the discussion begins to heat up, the husband may say, "I need to take a time-out; please give me an hour and then we can sit down and try to resolve it." Gottman's research shows that it takes at least twenty minutes for a person to calm down when they're in the middle of a discussion. To simply walk away would cause more harm as the wife feels like the issue has not been resolved and is being "stonewalled" by her husband. But a time-out can help both calm down, give them time to think about their own contribution to the issue at hand, and maybe come up with some possible solutions or compromises.

Many use relaxation techniques such as deep breathing, going for a walk, meditation, progressive muscle relaxation, listening to soft music, taking a warm shower, et cetera, to help them calm down before resuming the conversation. Denial or suppression of anger won't make it go away and will cause more harm to the relationship than dealing with the issue in a constructive way. So go ahead and be angry, if the case warrants it, but deal with it in a healthy way, and do not sin against your spouse, your children, other people, or God.

Father, thank You for the anger that makes us act in the face of injustice, evil, and sin. Help us to manage it in healthy ways that we may not become instruments of pain and destruction but agents of peace and healing.

Stumbling Blocks

"My breath is offensive to my wife, and I am repulsive
to the children of my own body."
—Job 19:17, NKJV

In our text for today we read of Job's sadness that even the close relationship he once enjoyed with his family has been affected by the smell coming from his body and from his breath. How does that apply to marriage today?

Willard Harley, in his book *His Needs, Her Needs,* talks about the ten most important emotional needs of men and of women. He says that in general terms, men have the same five emotional needs, and women have the same emotional needs, although men's emotional needs are in general not the same as those of women.

Understanding that, Harley says that one of the five most important emotional needs of men is physical attractiveness. By that he means it is important to a man that his wife keep herself physically fit through diet and exercise and wear her hair and clothing in a way that he finds attractive and tasteful. Harley also explains that if the attractiveness of your spouse makes you feel great, and loss of that attractiveness would make you feel very frustrated, you should include physical attractiveness in your list of important emotional needs. It's not right or wrong. It simply is an emotional need.

Among the various aspects of physical attractiveness, weight generally gets the most attention. While physical attractiveness can't endure as the basis for a relationship, it does meet certain strong needs that some people have. While weight is important, it is also important to have a healthy body image. Know what is realistic and be happy within those parameters.

Another area where physical attractiveness can derail romance and passion in marriage is personal hygiene. Even Job declares that "my breath is offensive to my wife," with which many women may identify. No wonder some couples may share a quick kiss! Other simple personal hygiene problems are not showering or bathing daily, not using deodorant, not brushing your teeth, not flossing them, not having them cleaned at the dentist regularly, not shaving, and not wearing clean clothes. While all of these seem so logical, so many seem to forget how important they are in order to maintain passion and romance in their relationship.

Father, help us to maintain cleanliness of our bodies, not just for health reasons, but also so that we may be able to maintain a healthy, passionate relationship with our spouse.

The Ministry of Presence

"So man lies down and does not rise. Till the heavens are no more, they will not awake nor be roused from their sleep. Oh, that You would hide me in the grave, that You would conceal me until Your wrath is past, that You would appoint me a set time, and remember me!"
—Job 14:12, 13, NKJV

It's amazing how well-intentioned, yet heartless, Job's friends are. They see their friend suffering through all of his losses, and yet instead of helping him through these tragedies, they assume a judgmental stance and set out to prove to Job that all he's experiencing is the result of his own sin, and if he would only repent, God might just forgive him. Their accusations do not bring any consolation to Job. In the same way, well-intentioned friends and relatives feel compelled to say something to their loved ones or friends who are terminally ill or who have lost a loved one, and at times use old clichés or explanations that do nothing to alleviate the pain. The result may be more pain and more confusion. Here are some suggestions to help with knowing what to say or do for a friend or loved one who is dying of a terminal illness.

The ministry of presence. Most people feel uncomfortable, maybe even afraid, to talk about death and dying. Therefore, when they hear that a friend, loved one, coworker, or schoolmate has been diagnosed with a terminal illness, they stay away. In reality, what you say is not what matters to the terminally ill person or their family, but rather the fact that you cared enough to come be with them. However, respect their privacy, and always call beforehand. If they are in a hospital, you must not only respect visiting hours but also be conscious of the fact that those visiting hours may be the only time the family gets to spend with their loved one. Make your visits brief.

Listen. More important than what you say is how much you listen. While most people's greatest fear is not knowing what to say, if you go prepared to listen and let the terminally ill lead in the conversation, you might find that death is not all that's on their mind. They just want someone to talk to.

Father, help us to be such instruments in Your hands that we may bring Your comfort, not so much by what we say but rather by what we do to help those experiencing illness, sadness, or pain.

When a Man Dies

"If a man dies, shall he live again? All the days of my hard service I will wait, till my change comes. You shall call, and I will answer You; You shall desire the work of Your hands." —Job 14:14, 15, NKJV

It's hard to know what to say or do for a friend facing a terminal illness. Here are four more suggestions you may find helpful.

Empathize, don't proselytize. If your friend doesn't share your beliefs, this is not the time to try to convert them. For instance, several of my patients talked about going to heaven after their death. Rather than lecturing on the state of the dead, I would say something such as, "As Christians we have a special hope, don't we?"

Offer practical help. The reality is that during these difficult times the challenge for the patient includes thinking about what needs to be done or asking someone to do it. It would be better to offer to do specific things for them—mow the lawn, wash clothes, or run errands such as grocery shopping. Sometimes an offer to stay with the person who is ill to relieve the caregiver for a few hours can be the welcome help they need.

Watch for special events. One of my patients waited until the day after his daughter's birthday, and the night he died he was so restless that his wife decided to sleep in the living room. When she woke up the next morning, he was dead. He had chosen not to die before or on his daughter's birthday, and he didn't want his wife to see him die. Others wait for birthdays, anniversaries, graduations, weddings, and other special occasions. Be aware of this fact as it may help you get an idea of when they might die.

Fear of dying or of death. One of my patients told me, "I'm not afraid of death; I just don't want to die in pain." Most people are afraid of the dying process. In his case I assured him that we in hospice would do all in our power to keep him comfortable and without pain. That assurance helped him relax and enjoy the last few days of his life. If the person you're visiting expresses such fears, clarify what the source of their fear is, and if they are unable to answer, ask someone who may be better able to answer.

Dear Lord, give me a heart of wisdom, love, and compassion. May I show Your love to my friend at this time.

Lie Down in Peace

In peace I will lie down and sleep, for you alone, LORD,
make me dwell in safety. —Psalm 4:8, NIV

Facing death is traumatic. It's not something that people have practice with—so how can we help those making the transition from life to death face it peacefully?

Help them to die in peace. In hospice we have learned that those patients who struggle the most in their dying process seem to be the ones who have strained relationships with people. It may help them to ask, "Is there someone you would like to see or talk to?" Offer to contact the person they'd like to speak with. If the other person is not willing to speak with the terminally ill patient, you can facilitate the expression of their feelings by offering options such as, "If you could talk to them, what would you tell them?" You may offer to help them write a letter that they can then choose to mail or burn it, thus symbolizing their having taken the step of reconciliation. Many patients wait to die until after they see someone they care about, so you could offer to help make the contact.

Another way to help them die in peace is to pray for and with them. The medical field has come to recognize the benefits of praying for those who are ill. We need not feel the obligation to pray for healing; it does not reveal a lack of faith, but recognition of the inevitable. When I pray with and for members or patients who are terminally ill, I pray for comfort and peace, courage and strength, hope and renewal of love for themselves and for their loved ones.

Instruments of peace. Dying can be a difficult and painful experience, or a special memory for their loved ones. You can be instrumental in making it as comfortable and comforting as possible by carefully doing for them what they need as they write the last chapter in their earthly life.

When you think of it, no explanation, no matter how good or theologically correct it may be, can take away a person's pain or fear. Walking through this difficult valley with your friend will require that you remain firmly grounded in God's love. Take time to fill your mind with His Word so you will have His peace to share with them.

Heavenly Father, please grant me Your peace as I walk with my friend through this valley. Please give them the assurance of Your presence and Your peace.

Talk Grief Away

"My soul loathes my life; I will give free course to my complaint,
I will speak in the bitterness of my soul."
—Job 10:1, NKJV

When I worked or volunteered as a hospice chaplain, and later as a grief and bereavement counselor, I reminded my families and clients that pain shared is pain divided. When we talk about our loss, our pain, our loved ones, we are sharing the load, little by little, with others who are stronger than we are at that point and who, hopefully, by listening can help us carry that heavy load until we are able to stand again on our own.

I have been asked often by people who want to help their friends or loved ones who are terminally ill or who have experienced loss of a relative, their job, their house, et cetera, what they should say to them. They're afraid to go visit their friend or loved one because, they say, "I just don't know what to tell them." What I always encourage them with is this: "The best thing you can do for them is to be there and show them that you're willing to just listen."

In talking about *The Inner World of Grief,* Elizabeth Kubler-Ross encourages those in bereavement to talk about their grief and to tell the story of their loss and their loved one who is no longer with them. Telling the story plays an important role in the healing process. It helps to dissipate the pain. Because of the enormous amount of pain in our stories, when we share them we dispel the pain, for sorrow shared is sorrow halved.

Bildad, Job's friend, got many things wrong, both about Job and about God. But the one thing he did get right were his words: "He will yet fill your mouth with laughing, and your lips with rejoicing" (Job 8:21 NKJV). What an incredible promise! Be assured that there will be a time when your friends or loved ones are ready to listen to words of encouragement and hope, and they will appreciate you reminding them that death is not forever, that grief and pain are not forever. That's the reason that Jesus came to this world—so that one day death, pain, and suffering will come to a permanent end.

Father, thank You that while we experience pain in this life, it, too, will come to an end when Jesus comes. May He return soon so we can enjoy the peace and the happiness You intended from the beginning.

Come Mourn With Me

Now when Job's three friends heard of all this adversity that had come upon him, each one came from his own place—Eliphaz the Temanite, Bildad the Shuhite, and Zophar the Naamathite. For they had made an appointment together to come and mourn with him, and to comfort him. . . . So they sat down with him on the ground seven days and seven nights, and no one spoke a word to him, for they saw that his grief was very great.
—Job 2:11, 13, NKJV

Job had lost everything he owned, but most tragic of all was the loss of his children. When he became physically ill, his wife had had enough and told him to "curse God and die." But then his friends came to be with him and to comfort him. They sat with him for seven days straight, without saying a word, just being there.

One of the most tragic results from the death of a child is the all-too-frequent demise of the marriage. Many couples simply can't handle their pain and end up drifting apart and eventually separating and divorcing. It is very difficult to offer support and encouragement to your spouse when your own heart is breaking. At the same time, nothing can bring a couple together like experiencing a loss and growing together out of it. My wife and I have gone through the loss of my mother and both her parents, and several other family members. Those times, as difficult as they have been, have strengthened our relationship and are part of our history that keeps us together.

But there are times when we need help from outside too. Job's friends teach a very important lesson: when visiting a grieving friend it is more important to just be there and to listen, rather than trying to speak. It is incredibly therapeutic and very cathartic for them to talk through their pain. When we share our pain with others, we all get to carry it together, which makes it easier and lighter for the one experiencing it. That's why being there for the mourner is your gift to them, the ministry of presence. Don't be afraid to be with those in mourning; it may be the best, the kindest, the most loving thing you can do for your friend.

Father, in the midst of our pain, You listen to us and come close to us to comfort us. Help us to learn from You. Thank You for healing our pain and carrying our burdens.

The Way to a Man's Heart?

So the king and Haman went to dine with Queen Esther. And on the second day,
at the banquet of wine, the king again said to Esther, "What is your petition,
Queen Esther? It shall be granted you. And what is your request, up to half the
kingdom? It shall be done!"—Esther 7:1, 2, NKJV

Esther was made aware of Haman's plan to destroy the Jewish people, and after a period of fasting and prayer she invited the king, her husband, to a banquet. After that banquet, she invited him to a second banquet the following night. It was at that banquet, when he was very pleased with the food, and with Esther, that she made her request on behalf of her people.

It's been said that the way to a man's heart is through his stomach. One of the things I appreciate about my wife is that since we were young and dating, she made efforts to learn from my mother how to cook those things that I like best. I have to say that she not only learned how to prepare some very typical Colombian food, but learned to make it very well. Pretty regularly she will prepare for me one of those special dishes which not only takes care of my appetite but also warms my heart.

Now, if a woman thinks that just by feeding her husband well she will be guaranteed his undying love, she's going to find herself with a very overweight man who simply likes the benefits of having a good cook living with him. There's more to it than just the food. It is not that men like to eat and want to have a woman to cook for them. What men appreciate is having a woman who loves them enough to cook for and take care of them. Statistics show that married people enjoy better health. Single men are notorious for poor health habits. Married men enjoy the benefits of a wife who cares about them, fixes healthy meals for them, and encourages them to take good care of themselves by exercising and going to the doctor for regular physical, eye, and dental exams. So really, a way to a man's heart is not through his stomach, but rather, the way to a man's heart is through her heart.

Father, thank You for the love of a wife, expressed through good food, but also expressed through loving, caring actions for her husband.

Selfish Demands

On the seventh day, when the heart of the king was merry with wine, he commanded . . . [that] Queen Vashti [be brought] before the king, wearing her royal crown, in order to show her beauty to the people and the officials, for she was beautiful to behold. But Queen Vashti refused to come at the king's command . . . therefore the king was furious, and his anger burned within him.
—Esther 1:10–12, NKJV

In the book *Conflict and Courage,* Ellen White writes, "When this command came from the king, Vashti did not carry out his orders, because she knew that wine had been freely used, and that Ahasuerus was under the influence of the intoxicating liquor. For her husband's sake as well as her own, she decided not to leave her position at the head of the women of the court.

"It was when the king was not himself, when his reason was dethroned by wine-drinking that he sent for the queen, that those present at his feast, men besotted by wine, might gaze on her beauty. She acted in harmony with a pure conscience.

"Vashti refused to obey the king's command, thinking that when he came to himself, he would commend her course of action. But the king had unwise advisers. They argued it would be a power given to woman that would be to her injury" (*Conflict and Courage,* 243).

Willard Harley, in his book *Love Busters,* cites selfish demands as one of the things that a spouse does to hurt the other and which damages the love that should exist between them. He defines them as, "Commanding your spouse to do things that would benefit you at your spouse's expense, with implied threat of punishment if refused." Instead of selfish demands, Harley recommends using thoughtful requests—respectfully explaining to your spouse what you would like and allow your spouse the option of granting or denying your request.

Vashti's response to the selfish demands of her husband, even if he was the king, showed greater respect to him than he showed to her. It is understandable that she was not pleased with his demands any more than any spouse today would be at the selfish demands of their spouse. A thoughtful request may not get you what you want, but a selfish demand certainly will not promote any warm, caring feelings toward you.

Father, selfishness and rebellion began the biggest battle ever in the universe; may they never be present in our marriage or family.

Guarding the Gates

The cities of the South shall be shut up, and no one shall open them; Judah shall be carried away captive, all of it; it shall be wholly carried away captive.
—Jeremiah 13:19, NKJV

The walls, the city, and the temple had been rebuilt, and the Law of Moses had been read to the people, who dedicated themselves anew to the worship of God. Now Nehemiah faced a new challenge as vendors were coming to Jerusalem to sell their wares on Sabbath. Even though he had warned them before, they continued to do so, so this time he ordered that the gates of the city be shut during the Sabbath hours.

We've heard about guarding the edges of the Sabbath and are familiar with the words by Ellen G. White, "We should jealously guard the edges of the Sabbath. Remember that every moment is consecrated, holy time" (*The Faith I live By*, 34). By the edges we mean the beginning and the end of this special day. As parents we have the responsibility to do all in our power to ensure that the sacred hours of the Sabbath remain untainted by outside influences.

As our girls were growing up, we switched to Sabbath toys, and Sabbath music, and Sabbath activities, and we enjoyed a good time of worship to welcome the Sabbath. We incorporated a few traditions like the lighting of the Sabbath candles, had Mexican tostadas, and for dessert we had doughnuts.

The other edge of the Sabbath, the sundown that marks its end, should also be marked with worship, and with a good time of family fellowship and prayer. There's no need to rush "out" of the Sabbath. Again, Jewish tradition teaches that the Sabbath is finally over when at least three stars are visible in the sky. There's a certain sense of sadness to see the Sabbath come to an end as the new week begins.

Guarding the edges of the Sabbath is like closing the doors in the winter in order to keep in the warmth of the home. I love the feeling of coming home and walking in from the cold garage into the warmth of the foyer. The warmth of my house greets me as I open the door and embraces me until the next time I have to go out. And that's how I picture the Sabbath—its warmth embracing me and protecting me from the bitter cold of the rest of the week.

Father, thank You for the warmth and the rest of the Sabbath day.

They Made It Clear

So they read distinctly from the book, in the Law of God; and they gave the
sense, and helped them to understand the reading.
—Nehemiah 8:8, NKJV

As the building of the city of Jerusalem and of the temple were finished, Nehemiah and the leaders recognized the need for a consecration of the people to God. Ezra, the scribe, stood before everyone gathered and read to them the words of the Book of the Law of Moses, the first five books of the Bible, or the Torah. As the people heard the stories and the regulations found in those books, they were moved in their hearts. But it wasn't enough to just read the Law. The Levites helped the people to understand it by explaining its content and meaning.

I encourage daily, regular reading of the Bible personally and at home. I encourage everyone to read through their Bibles every year. I have followed that practice for many years and have read through the entire Bible, in many different versions and translations, in two languages, by reading a section on every day of the year (with just a few exceptions), and doing so has enriched my life and opened windows of information, knowledge, and faith that I might not otherwise have had.

Beyond a reading of the Bible, though, there must be thoughtful study of selected passages, stories, and sections of the Scriptures for deeper understanding. Also, for daily family worship, at least a portion of the Scriptures should be read and discussed. It doesn't have to be a long theological dissertation and exegetical study of a passage, but at least a simple conversation of its meaning. Dennis Raney, Christian counselor and writer, advises that when we read the Bible to our children we should take the time to stop and explain the words and ideas they may have difficulty grasping. If needed, we can paraphrase the text to give them a simple explanation of what it is saying. Let them stop you and ask if they don't understand something.

Reading and studying the Bible as a family can be a source of great blessing. But we need to make sure we aren't just reading through it as quickly as possible, without helping everyone to understand what's being read. Let's grow together as families by studying God's Word. The lessons our children learn during these early years will stand them in good stead for the years ahead.

Father, help us to spend time daily with Your Word, to understand it, to meditate upon it, and to spend the time teaching others what we have learned from it, and from You.

Repentance for All

*"I pray, L*ORD *God of heaven . . . please let Your ear be attentive and Your eyes open, that You may hear the prayer of Your servant which I pray before You now, day and night, for the children of Israel Your servants, and confess the sins of the children of Israel which we have sinned against You. Both my father's house and I have sinned. We have acted very corruptly against You, and have not kept the commandments, the statutes, nor the ordinances which You commanded Your servant Moses." —Nehemiah 1:5–7, NKJV*

Nehemiah was saddened to know the ruined condition of Jerusalem and Judah, and he recognized that it was the result of the people's rebelliousness against God. The seeds of rebellion bore fruit in an unrepentant spirit among the people. Nehemiah did not let that stop him from petitioning Heaven on behalf of God's children. So he came aside and prayed the prayer in our text for today.

Nehemiah could have prayed for deliverance for himself and his family, but instead, he recognized that all had sinned and all were in need of repentance. That included himself and his family. Nehemiah demonstrated a truly humble spirit as he interceded for Israel. This gave power to his petition.

It is interesting how at times we pray for our loved ones, which we should do, and ask God to lead them closer to Him, and to bring them to repentance and to the place where they will be ready for His soon return. But somehow we don't always come humbly before the Lord in recognition of our own need for repentance, knowledge of God, and preparation for His return. Nehemiah prayed for his people but humbly also prayed and confessed his own sin. And the wonderful thing is that God heard his plea and granted his prayer, and Nehemiah was able to go back and lead in the rebuilding of the city and the reestablishment of the worship of God. Maybe our prayers will be the catalyst for a complete revival in our lives and in our homes, maybe even beyond to our churches and to the area where we live . . . and it all begins with being humble enough to recognize our own need for repentance and forgiveness.

Father, we, too, have sinned and have turned our backs to You. Won't You please grant us a humble spirit, Lord? Forgive our sin, cleanse us, and make us new. May we experience a renewed walk with You and with Your children.

It's Not Too Late

Thus Hezekiah ... did what was good and right and true before the L<small>ORD</small>
his God. And in every work that he began in the service of the house of God,
in the law and in the commandment, to seek his God, he did it with
all his heart. So he prospered. —2 Chronicles 31:20, 21, NKJV

From the time Hezekiah became king of Judah he began a spiritual reformation throughout the nation and also began to restore the temple and its services. Not only did he order the repair of the temple, with everyone's contribution, he also destroyed the worship of other gods and moved the people to rededicate themselves and their children to the worship of the true God.

As parents we know how critically important it is to lead by example in the worship of the Lord. No one notices more quickly than children whether or not their parents are practicing what they preach. Perhaps you may be tempted to think that since you have not been doing it as well as you ought that you should stop trying. After all, what's the point in trying if you know you'll probably fail again?

The story of Hezekiah's reforms can teach us that it is never too late to begin again. It is never too late to make changes in our personal devotional life or in our family worship. Begin today. Talk to your family, confess that you have not been faithful to His commands in that you have not been leading them by example in the worship of God, and share with them that you intend to begin again. Explain that you are making a new commitment to pray with and for them every day, and that you will be studying a portion of the Scriptures. Gather them together at a set time each day for family worship—and make it the happiest time of the day.

Don't let the devil defeat you. Think of yourself as the Hezekiah of your home, making personal and family reforms in order to bring a revival of the faith to your family. While you may encounter some resistance, if you do it kindly and lovingly, and persevere, the results will be better than continuing to neglect your personal and your family devotional life and daily commitment to God.

Father, forgive us for neglecting our time with You and for not leading our family in a daily experience of prayer and worship. Help us to begin again and bless our home.

Pride Consumes

In those days Hezekiah was sick and near death, and he prayed to the Lord; and
He spoke to him and gave him a sign. But Hezekiah did not repay according to
the favor shown him, for his heart was lifted up.
—2 Chronicles 32:24, 25, NKJV

Hezekiah did many good things in reestablishing the worship of God and His law, but he was by no means perfect. When he was sick, he asked for healing and his prayer was answered, but as a result his heart became proud, which caused him to make mistakes that cost him and Jerusalem a great deal. Fortunately, Hezekiah humbled himself again before God.

The Soviet dissident Alexander Solzhenitsyn wrote that "pride grows in the human heart like lard on a pig." Pride, it seems, can grow within the human heart without any nurturing or encouragement. Our hearts are prone to be proud.

I've often wondered about this thing we call pride, and it seems to me that there is a certain amount of joy we as parents have for our children, which can be considered healthy pride, but there is a point at which this healthy pride becomes unhealthy. When our children do well in school, when they are kind and polite, something good moves in our hearts. When someone compliments our children, something good stirs inside us and gives us a warm feeling. Would that be healthy pride? But when we become obsessed with our children's accomplishments, when we want to display bumper stickers every time our children win an award or get good grades or their name appears on the dean's list, has it become unhealthy pride? Are we using our children as pawns to tell the whole world how good we are as parents?

When we display pride for our children only when they accomplish something big, we may be sending them the signal that their worth is tied to those accomplishments. Some parents live their dreams through their children and thus are very happy when their children succeed and very disappointed in them when they don't do as they would wish them to do.

So, let's rejoice with our children in their accomplishments, but don't make them the goal or end of their lives. And let us not use our children to fulfill our dreams or as pawns against others so we can be exalted in our own eyes. It's better to be humble than to be humbled.

Father, teach us to be humble, even when our hearts burst with healthy pride.

The Marriage-Go-Round

Now Rehoboam loved Maachah the granddaughter of Absalom more than all his wives and his concubines; for he took eighteen wives and sixty concubines, and begot twenty-eight sons and sixty daughters.
—2 Chronicles 11:21, NKJV

Rehoboam was the king of Israel after his father Solomon passed away. Although he didn't marry or have as many concubines as his father, he certainly had more than God ever intended. The Scripture is filled with stories of men who had many wives even though it was never in God's plan for anyone to have multiple spouses. God does not condone polygamy, and in most countries it is illegal. And yet we have come to accept a different form of polygamy—successive marriages—punctuated with divorce in between. Celebrities seem to lead the way, although not exclusively, in the continual round of marriage and divorce.

Some examples include Elizabeth Taylor, Larry King, Billy Bob Thornton, Martin Scorsese, Charlie Sheen, Kenny Rogers, Tom Cruise, Kate Winslet, and Drew Barrymore. While some may say that it's only celebrities that change marriage partners so often, there are others who jump in and out of marriage just as much and as quickly. Some professions seem to be harder on matrimonial longevity, although it seems that no profession is immune.

One of the interesting facts that has come out of research is that each successive marriage tends to last for a shorter period than the previous one. Instead of finding marital bliss with more successive marriages, many people find out they were happier with their first spouse than they were with any of the others that followed. While there may be some romance and passion for a while in successive marriages and relationships, eventually the emptiness and dissatisfaction returns and leads to another divorce. How sad!

Rather than entering the marriage and divorce go-round, make every effort to make your relationship strong. Look for ways to meet one another's most important emotional needs, look for the best in each other rather than focusing only on the negatives. Instead of jumping ship on your spouse, thinking that someone else can make you happier, look for ways to make your spouse happy and to fulfill your marriage vows to live with them in sickness and in health until death do you part.

Father, we know that You hate divorce. Help us to cultivate a strong marriage so we have the blessing of a happy home and at the same time bring You the highest honor and glory.

Praise God for His Will

"And now, O LORD, the word which You have spoken concerning Your servant and concerning his house, let it be established forever, and do as You have said. So let it be established, that Your name may be magnified forever."
—1 Chronicles 17:23, 24, NKJV

David wanted to build God's temple and told Nathan the prophet, who encouraged him to do so. That night, God told Nathan to tell David not to build Him the temple he intended to. David's response is our Scripture for today, and it is a remarkable prayer of praise.

I think David's response was exemplary. He could have become angry or bitter that God didn't want him to build the temple for His honor and glory. He could have argued with God and made a case that because he had won so many battles for God and for Israel that he should be allowed to build this great monument to God. He could have become bitter and resentful; he could have rebelled; he could have become a stumbling block to the building of the temple; he could have acted like a bad loser or a politician after being voted out of office. He could have reacted in any number of negative ways.

What I love about this story is David's positive, indeed joyful, response to Nathan's message. It is no wonder that God calls David a man after His own heart. If we truly believe, and long for, God's will for our lives, and if we believe that His will always works out best, then we would do well to follow David's example in this story. When we don't get what we thought we might, especially when we were certain we knew God's will for us, then instead of becoming bitter or resentful we should praise God and thank Him. Don't be distressed when the job you wanted is given to somebody else; or when someone else makes a higher bid on the house you had your heart set on; or because someone else is now dating the person you wanted to date; or because the person you were dating left you to marry somebody else. Praise God it worked out that way! That means God has something more in store for you. Something better than what you wanted or longed for. It may not appear to be so at first, but it is God's best for you, without a doubt.

Father, today we echo David's words of praise for Your will in our lives.

Check Out the Family

And he walked in the way of the kings of Israel, just as the house of Ahab had done, for the daughter of Ahab was his wife; and he did evil in the sight of the Lord. —2 Kings 8:18, NKJV

Ahab's daughter, Athaliah, had a powerful influence over Jehoram. It was through her influence that Jehoram introduced the worship of Baal and many other evils into the kingdom of Judah. How does this apply to marriage? Take time to get to know the family from which your sweetheart was raised. As I work with couples preparing for marriage, I strongly recommend that they take their time and don't rush into a hasty marriage.

Take time to prepare for married life. Shakespeare said, "A hasty marriage seldom proveth well." It takes time to get to know another person well. Proverbs 21:5 says it well: "The plans of the diligent lead surely to advantage, but everyone who is hasty comes surely to poverty" (NASB). A wedding is a one-day event, but a marriage is a lifetime commitment. Take the time necessary to learn everything you can about the person with whom you plan to spend a lifetime.

Couples should focus on two key areas when getting to know one another. The first is getting to know your sweetheart's family. Don't make the mistake of thinking extended family doesn't matter. The fact is that we don't marry one person—we join ourselves to the entire family. Meet the potential in-laws. Spend time getting to know them. Observe how they interact with each other. Remember, an apple doesn't fall far from the tree. This family reared your potential mate, so you need to know who they are and what they believe. Only time will tell.

Second, get to know as much as possible about the one you intend to marry. It will take time to see how they handle conflict, jealousy, or failure, but it will be time well invested. What are their needs, likes, and dislikes? And are there any warning signs to look out for? Some of these characteristics are only revealed over time. They can include lying, placing blame on others, controlling how you spend your time and money, jealousy, or being abusive—physically, emotionally, and/or sexually. If any of these characteristics are apparent, run, and run fast! The person is not marriage material.

Father, help those preparing for marriage to take the time they need. May they look to You for wisdom, counsel, and discernment.

Spiritual CPR

*He returned and walked back and forth in the house, and again
went up and stretched himself out on him; then the child sneezed
seven times, and the child opened his eyes.* —2 Kings 4:35, NKJV

We don't know her name, but we know that she did all in her power for her child—this miracle child that had been born to her after Elisha had prayed. And now he lay dead. After going to find Elisha and requesting he come to her home to help her boy, she left the results to God. After Elisha's prayers, God graciously, miraculously brought her son back to life. Countless parents who have had to face the darkness of losing a child will understand her longing to receive back her child from death's grasp. To the brokenhearted, grieving ones, we have the promise of the resurrection which reminds us that one day, when Jesus returns, they will be reunited with their children in the most joyful family reunion ever.

I have always loved these words by Ellen G. White, which describe the resurrection morning: "The living righteous are changed 'in a moment, in the twinkling of an eye.' At the voice of God they were glorified; now they are made immortal and with the risen saints are caught up to meet their Lord in the air. Angels 'gather together His elect from the four winds, from one end of heaven to the other.' Little children are borne by holy angels to their mothers' arms. Friends long separated by death are united, nevermore to part, and with songs of gladness ascend together to the City of God" (*The Great Controversy*, 645).

So while we may not have a prophet today who has the power to bring our children back to life, we do have this promise, this scene depicted so beautifully, in which we will be reunited with our children who have died before us. I pray we may never have to go through the pain and separation that death brings about most cruelly in the loss of a child, but if we do, may we hold on to this scene and its promise. Jesus is coming to take us home with Him, where we will spend eternity with our children! And there will be no more death—ever again!

Father, the pain caused by the death of a child is unbearable. While the promise may seem a faint consolation, may we hold on to it, until that great and joyful reunion day!

The Pouting Adult and the Enabler

So Ahab went into his house sullen and displeased because of the word which Naboth the Jezreelite had spoken to him; for he had said, "I will not give you the inheritance of my fathers." And he lay down on his bed, and turned away his face, and would eat no food. —1 Kings 21:4, NKJV

King Ahab wanted his neighbor's vineyard, but Naboth wanted to keep it in the family. Ahab responded by pouting. Jezebel's response? She told him to cheer up because she would get the vineyard for him. She then wrote letters on Ahab's behalf, which falsely accused Naboth of cursing God and the king. Naboth was stoned, and Jezebel presented his vineyard to Ahab.

If it were not so tragic, this story would almost be comical. An adult pouting like a child because he couldn't have someone else's toy. We can almost imagine Ahab sulking, refusing to eat—normal reactions for a child who's not getting his way, but certainly not an age-appropriate response from Ahab. Then we have Jezebel, the evil enabler of her husband's immaturity. This suited her purposes, however, for then she could control him.

Sometime ago I heard of a guest psychologist who appeared on a show with Oprah. The topic up for discussion was marital relationships. The doctor made an interesting observation when he noted that when women treat their husbands like children, they will eventually stop finding them desirable, because a woman instinctively wants a man, and not a child, as a husband. There are women who seem to enjoy being in charge at home and controlling everything concerning their husbands. Treated as children, these unfortunate men end up feeling emasculated and forbidden to fulfill their God-given role as the head of the home. But these very women will eventually disrespect and be repulsed by their husbands without ever realizing that the blame lies at their own door: they are responsible.

If a man is to grow up, so he doesn't pout like a child when confronted with challenges and difficulties, he needs a supportive spouse, not one who will enable his moodiness. God designed woman to be a help-meet. The best help a woman can give her husband is to believe in him, encourage him, and express appreciation and admiration for him. And perhaps once in a while tell him to stop pouting.

Father, may we be true helpmeets to our spouses so that they will grow and mature as they help us grow and mature.

A Powerful Relationship

"You shall not intermarry with them, nor they with you. Surely they will turn away your hearts after their gods." Solomon clung to these in love.
—1 Kings 11:2, NKJV

Solomon, as wise as he was, married hundreds of women, many of whom were from the people God had forbidden Israel to have any relationship with. It was these women who led him to commit idolatry, the sin for which Solomon's children lost the kingdom God had given to David.

As we read of the lives of David and Solomon, both had several things in common: both were chosen to be kings of Israel, both were prophets, both were inspired, both did many good things for God and for His people, and both had multiple wives. The difference was that while Solomon worshiped the idols of his wives, David remained loyal to God. I think we can safely draw a few conclusions.

First, God knows the danger of entering into marriage with an unbeliever and forbids it. While many Adventists have led their spouse to God and to the church, the number who have left the church because of their spouse is alarming. Marriage is such a powerful emotional relationship that some may be driven away from God by their spouse. We observe the power of this relationship when Eve led Adam to sin by eating the forbidden fruit. Adam couldn't see himself without Eve and chose rather to die with her instead of trusting that God would do what was best for him.

Second, adultery must not be the worst of all sins. While we would not condone adultery at any time, at the same time we should not make it the un-pardonable sin and shun people who've fallen into adultery. In David's case, not only did he commit adultery but he tried to cover it with murder, and yet God called him a man after His own heart. Solomon had multiple wives, and hundreds of concubines, and yet God blessed him with great wisdom.

Finally, what God *does* take great offense to is idolatry—turning away from Him to worship other gods. Again, we do not wish to excuse adultery in any way, shape, or form. We do discourage marrying someone of a different faith, and we must never turn from God to worship idols, whatever and whoever they may be.

Father, may we always worship You and never idols, may we always be faithful to You and to our spouse, and may Your love always cover us.

Mom's Love

Then she said to him, "My lord, you swore by the LORD your God to your maidservant, saying, 'Assuredly Solomon your son shall reign after me, and he shall sit on my throne.'" —1 Kings 1:17, NKJV

These words were spoken by Bathsheba to King David when Adonijah, another of David's sons, tried to make himself king of Israel as his father neared his death. It's not unusual for a mother to look out for her children. In fact, second only to the love God has for us is the love of a mother for her children. That love is so special that God uses it as an illustration of His love for us in various places in the Scriptures.

Among the Jewish people, the love of mothers for their children is legendary and is credited for the great success of so many of them. They joke about the proverbial Jewish mothers who hold their babies in their arms and introduce them as, "This my son, Aaron, the doctor." And when they leave for school, the typical Jewish mother will make sure her children have their books while other mothers may be more concerned with seeing their children have their lunch.

In the Gospels, John and James's mother asked Jesus for a special place for her sons in God's kingdom—right next to Jesus. The other disciples were understandably upset, although perhaps it was because their own mothers didn't get a chance to be the first to ask Jesus the same question. We get annoyed, too, with mothers who are overly proud of their children and who expect the rest of us to feel the same way. We would probably do well to check to see that we don't fall into that category ourselves!

As a father who loves his daughters dearly, I may sound unfair in saying that the love of fathers is not shown as prominently as that of mothers. But the reality is that a special bond is formed between a mother and her child as she carries them within her own body for nine months. But that doesn't mean fathers cannot develop a strong bond with their children. King David wrote, "As a father pities his children, so the Lord pities those who fear Him. For He knows our frame; He remembers that we are dust" (Psalm 103:13, 14, NKJV).

Father, thank You for our children. Bless our relationship with them, and may our bonds, whether fathers or mothers, be strengthened with them each day.

The Most Painful Death

Then the king was deeply moved, and went up to the chamber over the gate,
and wept. And as he went, he said thus: "O my son Absalom—my son, my son
Absalom—if only I had died in your place! O Absalom my son, my son!"
—2 Samuel 18:33, NKJV

I have been told by those going through it that there is no more painful death than the death of a child, regardless of their age. As a chaplain, I remember being at the hospital with the mother of a stillborn child. A few months later, in another room nearby, I sat with the parents of a three-year-old. As a police chaplain, I had to give a family the news of the tragic motorcycle death of their seventeen-year-old son, and I've officiated at the funeral of a forty-five-year-old daughter who died of cancer. During times like these, the parents have told me again and again how the death of other family members had been painful, but nothing compared to the pain they felt at losing a child.

My dad died when I was fifteen years old and my mom when I was forty-two years old, and their deaths have affected me in different ways. As difficult as this loss is, it is normal to expect that at some point in time your parents will die. But your child? It feels unnatural. A disconnection with the natural order of life. Imagine how it must have been for Adam and Eve to lose a son at the hands of another son. Unimaginable! For David, the death of his first son with Bathsheba was excruciating. For God, the death of His Son Jesus is beyond anything the human can even comprehend. And yet, He experiences the death of so many of His children every single day!

That's why our heavenly Father understands our pain. During the difficult days following the death of a child, we can find comfort in Him who also lost a child. Unlike us, however, He bore the added pain that came with being the only One who could have stepped in and stopped the death of His Son. Our Father not only understands, He is the very One who brings healing and hope to our brokenness. We can trust our children with such a God!

Father, for those who are grieving now, please bless and comfort them, and may Your gentle, loving arms surround them during their time of mourning, and hold them until healing comes.

Brotherly Kindness

Then he bowed himself, and said, "What is your servant,
that you should look upon such a dead dog as I?"
—2 Samuel 9:8, NKJV

David promised his friend Jonathan that he would show love and kindness to all surviving members of the royal family. Mephibosheth, Jonathan's son, was the only survivor. He was afraid of David at first, but eventually David's kindness won him over, and he ate at the king's table for the rest of his life.

This story of brotherly kindness is a wonderful allegory of God's plan of salvation for us. Let's look at some parallels. Mephibosheth was crippled. In Jewish culture, any kind of disease or deformity was considered the direct result of that person's sin. Mephibosheth's deformed feet were viewed as evidence of his sin. Today, we are crippled by sin, yet the Lord says, "I have a place prepared for you. Enter into relationship with Me, and come and eat at My table for all eternity." Like us, Mephibosheth felt unworthy, yet he ate at the king's table for the rest of his days.

Even the man's name tells us something about him. In fact, he had two names: the first was Merib-baal, which means, "Baal is my lawyer." This name was so embarrassing to him that it was changed to Mephibosheth, which means "shame." If that were not enough, the place where he lived before coming to the palace was called Lo-Debar. In the Hebrew language, it meant literally "No-nothing" and described a place that was worse than nothing. Isn't that a fair description of our world today? The more we try to fix it with technological advances, the more we ruin it.

This man's condition is worthy of the intensive care unit in God's hospital. He was lost; he was crippled by sin; he had no social status, because ex-royalty is no royalty at all; he had a shameful name descriptive of his situation; and he was living in a place that was worse than nothing. And yet the king wanted to show him kindness. Likewise, the King of the universe looks at us and sees the state we're in and He longs to make a place for us at His table. "You're part of My family," He says. "Come and sup with Me." Who could resist such an invitation?

O Lord, thank You for Your lovingkindness in reaching down and lifting us up. Save us for Your kingdom, and may we all sit at the table You have prepared for us.

Promise of Restoration

*So David said to him, "Do not fear, for I will surely show you
kindness for Jonathan your father's sake, and will restore to you
all the land of Saul your grandfather." —2 Samuel 9:7, NKJV*

David gave Mephibosheth all the property previously owned by King Saul, and at the beginning of humanity's story, God gave Adam the Garden of Eden to care for and to be his home. Adam lost this gift when he disobeyed. Later, God promised Abraham that he would inherit the Promised Land, and through Abraham the promise has been passed to the remnant of all the ages. Paradise, given to Adam and his descendants, was lost at the Fall, but it will be returned to them at the establishment of God's eternal kingdom on earth.

Now, Mephibosheth could have refused David's kindness. He could have allowed his fear and skepticism to keep him from accepting this gracious gift. In the same way, God doesn't force us to accept His love. Sadly, there are many who refuse God's love. Ellen White writes, "There are those who have known the pardoning love of Christ and who really desire to be children of God, yet they realize that their character is imperfect, their life faulty, and they are ready to doubt whether their hearts have been renewed by the Holy Spirit. To such I would say, Do not draw back in despair. We shall often have to bow down and weep at the feet of Jesus because of our shortcomings and mistakes, but we are not to be discouraged. Even if we are overcome by the enemy, we are not cast off, not forsaken and rejected of God. No; Christ is at the right hand of God, who also maketh intercession for us. . . . He desires to restore you to Himself, to see His own purity and holiness reflected in you. And if you will but yield yourself to Him, He that hath begun a good work in you will carry it forward to the day of Jesus Christ. Pray more fervently; believe more fully. As we come to distrust our own power, let us trust the power of our Redeemer, and we shall praise Him who is the health of our countenance" (*Steps to Christ*, 64).

Father, thank You for Your plan to save us, as sinful and wicked as we may be. We accept Your grace and forgiveness, and by faith we claim Your gift of salvation and our new status as sons and daughters of the King of the universe.

September

The Influence of a Christian Family

For I know him, that he will command his children and his household after him,
and they shall keep the way of the LORD, to do justice and judgment.
—Genesis 18:19, KJV

The youth who are consecrated to God sway a mighty influence for good. Preachers or laymen advanced in years cannot have one half the influence for good upon the young that the youth, if devoted to God, can have upon their associates.

"The silent witness of a true, unselfish, godly life carries an almost irresistible influence.

"The unstudied, unconscious influence of a holy life is the most convincing sermon that can be given in favor of Christianity. . . .

"Every Christian family should illustrate to the world the power and excellence of Christian influences.

"The home in which the members are kindly, courteous Christians exerts a far-reaching influence for good. Other families mark the results attained by such a home and follow the example set, in their turn guarding their homes against evil influences. Angels of heaven often visit the home in which the will of God bears sway. Under the power of divine grace such a home becomes a place of refreshing to worn, weary pilgrims. Self is kept from asserting itself. Right habits are formed. There is a careful recognition of the rights of others.

"One well-ordered, well-disciplined family tells more in behalf of Christianity than all the sermons that can be preached.

"A lamp, however small, if kept steadily burning, may be the means of lighting many other lamps. Our sphere of influence may seem narrow, our ability small, our opportunities few, our acquirements limited; yet wonderful possibilities are ours through a faithful use of the opportunities of our own homes. If we will open our hearts and home to the divine principles of life, we shall become channels for currents of life-giving power. From our homes will flow streams of healing, bringing life, and beauty, and fruitfulness.

"The influence of a carefully guarded Christian home in the years of childhood and youth is the surest safeguard against the corruptions of the world" (*My Life Today*, 122, 124).

Father, may our home be one in which the light of Your presence dwells. May we pass on our passion to serve You and make You known to our children, and may they grow to love and serve You too.

Facing the Economic Giant

"You come to me with a sword, with a spear, and with a javelin.
But I come to you in the name of the LORD of hosts, the God of the
armies of Israel, whom you have defied. . . . For the battle is the
LORD's, and He will give you into our hands."
—1 Samuel 17:45–47, NKJV

While we don't face a physical Goliath, many of us face economic uncertainty, and sometimes just surviving can present a fearsome challenge. If you are struggling with your personal and family finances, here are some suggestions you may find helpful.

First, transfer ownership of everything to God. All we own are gifts from a loving Father—including the health and ability to earn a living. God gives to us not so we can hoard these blessings. He wants us to be pipelines of His blessing to others. When we are trustworthy, it makes it possible for Him to bless us even more. His ownership has a single goal: to use all of His resources to be a blessing to His children.

Second, remember to return God's tithe and give your offerings joyously. You don't have to understand how tithing works; you just need to know that it does. Try it and you'll soon experience the miracles. God's Word guarantees it!

Third, work hard. God intended for us to learn this important principle. According to His plan for the family, we are to earn our bread by the toil and sweat of our brow. Work is satisfying, molds character, and develops gratitude, appreciation, and value.

Fourth, make a realistic budget and keep accurate records. The culprit in family finance problems is not the big-ticket items. It is the steady drip, drip, drip of spending on little purchases that no one tracks. The absence of an accurate record of spending keeps many from making good financial decisions.

Finally, get out from under the bondage of debt. Your attitude toward money will make a huge difference in the success or failure of your family. Do you need to take immediate action? To get out of debt, pay your bills on time, get sound financial advice, and change your lifestyle. Determine to honor God with your finances, commit to being faithful to Him, and you will ultimately be victorious as you battle the economic giant.

Father, help us to be good stewards of all You've given us, and may we be faithful conduits of Your blessings to others.

Young and Chosen

*Samuel said, "Send for him; we will not sit down until he arrives." . . .
Then the LORD said, "Rise and anoint him; this is the one."*
—1 Samuel 16:11, 12, NIV

After Saul rejected God, Samuel was instructed to anoint the next king of Israel. God directed him to the home of Jesse, who made six of his seven sons parade before him. But Samuel did not choose any of them. After making inquiry, the prophet was told that the youngest son was out in the fields tending his father's sheep. Samuel asked to have him sent for, and when young David came into his presence, Samuel immediately identified him as the second king of Israel.

The youngest child in a family often has to endure much at the hands of their older siblings. In many cases, by the time the hand-me-downs reach them, they've been worn by so many older siblings that they look pretty bad. They have to compete with older siblings for everything from school, to sports, and even for their parents' attention, and for their entire life they are often seen as the baby of the family.

It's not unusual that from an early age, the youngest child learns to excel in areas where they don't have to compete with their siblings who are taller, faster, or more knowledgeable. Often the youngest child becomes the one who brings laughter into the home. This leads them to clown around, tell funny stories, and do all they can to make others laugh and thus be the life of every party. No wonder so many actors and comedians are the last-born of the family.

Paul wrote to young pastor Timothy: "Let no one despise your youth, but be an example to the believers in word, in conduct, in love, in spirit, in faith, in purity" (1 Timothy 4:12, NKJV). For those of us who have some of the characteristics of the last-born and enjoy humor and laughter, we can identify with David, who was a singer, and with the fact that his older siblings did not take him seriously (see 1 Samuel 17:28). But God doesn't see younger children or the last-born child as unnecessary, unskilled, or unimportant. In fact, with God's guidance, and the natural gift of laughter, a younger person can do great things—just look at King David!

Father, may our conduct be such that others may respect who we are and what we do and thus be able to help others come to You.

It Happens Even to the Best

Now it came to pass when Samuel was old that he made his sons judges over Israel. The name of his firstborn was Joel, and the name of his second, Abijah; they were judges in Beersheba. But his sons did not walk in his ways; they turned aside after dishonest gain, took bribes, and perverted justice.
—1 Samuel 8:1–3, NKJV

S amuel's sons were corrupt, and, like other religious leaders at the time, they took advantage of their position to exploit the people. The Israelites, on the other hand, wanted to be like the other nations and asked Samuel, the God-given leader of his time, to give them a king to reign over them. I wonder how Samuel felt when he heard this request. It certainly wasn't God's plan for His chosen people, and Samuel knew it. God understood clearly that it was Him they were rejecting—not Samuel. Yet He kindly tried to show them what they would get if they chose a human king for themselves instead of God.

As I visited with a pastor-friend over the weekend, we talked about PKs—pastors' kids. Even in the homes of the best of pastors, children have gone astray. Even in the home of a beloved, lifelong prophet like Samuel, his children walked away from God. How sad it is when godly parents lose their children to the world. It happens too frequently, and it is heartbreaking.

I recognize that it's not always a single event or situation but rather a number of these that drive them to take those steps. Maybe it's the frequent moving from one church, one community, and one school to another. Maybe it's leaving friends behind and being put in the position of meeting new ones only to leave them again a few years later. Perhaps it's the school or series of schools they attended. Maybe it's the various teachers and principals. Or maybe the church people, the conference, or the church in general. And perhaps the blame lies with us, their parents, who spent more time doing the work of the Lord than spending time with His and our children. Whatever it might be, we certainly recognize the challenges all of our children face. How much we need to keep our children—all of our children—in our prayers!

Father, I pray for our children, particularly our PKs, who are particular targets of the enemy. Guide all of our children, Lord, and save them for Your kingdom. May Your grace be sufficient for them.

The Other Woman in Your Marriage

And Boaz answered and said to her, "It has been fully reported to me, all that you have done for your mother-in-law since the death of your husband, and how you have left your father and your mother and the land of your birth, and have come to a people whom you did not know before."
—Ruth 2:11, NKJV

After the death of her husband and sons, Naomi returned to her homeland. While one of her daughters-in-law, Orpah, went back to her own home, Ruth, her other daughter-in-law, chose to travel with Naomi. Thus she joined her life forever to Naomi, to her God, and to her people. Ruth was devoted to the care of Naomi, and her devotion did not go unnoticed. Boaz, who was a relative of Naomi's, noticed Ruth's care and indirectly made provision to help them.

The close relationship between Naomi and Ruth is special but by no means unique. Many mothers-in-law have been especially loving, supportive, and kind to their children's spouse. In some cases, they have had a closer relationship with them than with their own children. The same has been the case with daughters- or sons-in-law toward their spouses' parents.

For some reason, mothers-in-law have received a bad rap over the years. While it may be accurate in some cases, it is not warranted in general. My wife and my mother had a very good relationship in spite of a language barrier, and I credit both for it. My wife was always very kind and respectful to my mother, and she learned from her how to cook many of my favorite dishes. My mother was careful not to usurp my wife's place as the lady of the home and the one who held first place in my life. In addition, both of them also were very generous with the time that I was able to spend with each of them.

Three simple but important keys that are vital in establishing a great relationship between in-laws include everyone making every effort to learn from the other—family history, tradition, customs, recipes, et cetera. Next, it is important to show respect for each person's position in their own home. Finally, watch carefully the time spent with each, giving preference to your spouse first while not neglecting time with your own parents.

Father, may we all be blessed with a loving, supportive relationship with our in-laws, whether they are our parents-in-law or our children-in-law. May we honor You in all our relationships.

Painful and Bitter

But she said to them, "Do not call me Naomi; call me Mara, for the Almighty has dealt very bitterly with me. I went out full, and the LORD has brought me home again empty." —Ruth 1:20, 21, NKJV

In just a few verses, we read of all the reverses that Naomi and her family suffered. First, they had to leave their home and become immigrants in a foreign country. Years later, she became a widow, and then the unthinkable: her two sons also died. The last of her sorrows came when Orpah, one of her daughters-in-law, left her to go back to her own home and people. About the only bright moment in the midst of all this darkness was when her daughter-in-law Ruth chose to stay with her. Together, Ruth and Naomi made the long journey back to Naomi's home. When they arrived, Naomi asked that her name be changed to Mara, reflecting the bitterness of her heart and life.

My parents were married twenty-eight years until the afternoon one day in early January when my father suffered a massive heart attack that took his life and left my mother a widow. For twenty-eight years they had lived together, traveled together, and raised six children. The shock of the sudden loss of her life-partner plunged my mother into the darkness, pain, and bitterness of widowhood. She lost a dangerous amount of weight, and her three children who were still at home became very subdued and masked their own pain so they would not cause her any further pain. From that day on, and for more than a year after, she wore only black mourning clothes. Such was her grief.

The longer a couple are married, the deeper their bond and love toward one another. It is no wonder that so many people die not long after the death of their spouse. It is a separation too great for some to bear. It is a privilege to walk through life together with a spouse who shares your love for the Lord and commitment to your family. What a blessing to be able to serve the Lord together. But we grieve not as those who have no hope. Because of Jesus—we shall see our loved one again!

Father, while the pain of death may separate for a time, I pray that our marriage may be such that we will live without regrets. May the memories we're building together carry us through the darkest, dreariest valleys of sorrow and pain.

Reversal of Feelings

Then Amnon hated her exceedingly, so that the hatred with which he hated her was greater than the love with which he had loved her. And Amnon said to her, "Arise, be gone!" —2 Samuel 13:15, NKJV

A mnon was the son of David who fell in love with his stepsister Tamar and plotted to have her come to his house under the pretense of being sick. While there, he forced her into intimacy with him, and then, having accomplished his evil plot, he despised her and rejected her altogether.

I wish more single young people, teens and single young adults, were familiar with this story. I think they would be really interested to learn that it follows the pattern of most premarital relationships. This may be particularly important for young women who surrender their virginity early in a relationship to show their boyfriend their love, or, out of fear they'll lose him if they don't. It may sound trite, but it is true nonetheless, that once a woman has surrendered herself, a man will often lose respect for her and will no longer be interested in pursuing the relationship further. While young people think that having premarital sex will bring them closer together, more often than not it becomes an insurmountable barrier that ultimately leads to the disintegration of the relationship.

Last year in the United States, more than four million unmarried heterosexual couples shacked up, in contrast to only half a million at the end of the supposedly free-spirited sixties. Though living together has become conventional, studies show that these unions, in contrast to marriages, tend to have more episodes of domestic violence against women and physical and sexual abuse of children. Also, the annual rates of depression among unmarried couples are more than three times those of married couples.

After living in a low-commitment relationship, it's hard for people to shift that kind of pattern when they consider marriage. Premarital sex and premarital cohabitation do not benefit the relationship; instead, it brings a host of problems and challenges that make it difficult to sustain the relationship. God's original plan for sex after marriage is best and healthiest and provides the best chances for lasting happiness.

Father, bless the young and single who are tempted to enter into relationships and practice premarital sex and help them to not fall into a sin which will bring about life-lasting difficulties and challenges. May they enjoy the best and healthiest of relationships before and after their wedding.

Listen to Your Parents

He went up and told his father and mother, saying, "I have seen a woman in Timnah of the daughters of the Philistines; now therefore, get her for me as a wife." Then his father and mother said to him, "Is there no woman among the daughters of your brethren, or among all my people, that you must go and get a wife from the uncircumcised Philistines?" And Samson said to his father, "Get her for me, for she pleases me well." —Judges 14:1–3, NKJV

Samson became obsessed with a woman from Timnah and insisted, against his parents' advice, that they get her for him. They objected because marriage with an unbeliever, a pagan no less, was strictly forbidden. But Samson was insistent, and his parents eventually gave in and made the appropriate arrangements for Samson to have her. As we read the rest of Samson's story, we see the terrible results of Samson insisting on his own way. Going against their wishes ultimately led to his involvement with a prostitute, Delilah, to his capture, and to his eventual demise.

While in Western culture we don't have arranged marriages today, I can't help but wonder how many people I know who would be better off if they'd only listened to their parents. It seems they believed that by stubbornly staying together they would eventually force their family to come around. They assume the objectors will ultimately come to love the other person.

In the material I provide to couples contemplating marriage, we look at their parents' and friends' reaction to the relationship. When their reaction is positive, the couple seems to do better. The opposite is also true of the couples who don't enjoy the support of their family or friends; it's like fighting an uphill battle as they begin to form their new relationship without the love and support of those closest to them.

While the family may not always be right in their feelings or opinions of your boyfriend or girlfriend, if there are negative feelings going into the relationship, chances are that they won't get any better later on. Listen to what your family and friends are trying to tell you; they are trying to help you, and they may be saving you from a life of hardship and pain.

Father, thank You for the wise counsel of family and friends. May we be attentive to what they have to tell us, especially if it concerns seeking to know Your will. We look to You for guidance and help.

Idle Words

*"All you need to say is simply 'Yes' or 'No';
anything beyond this comes for the evil one."*
—Matthew 5:37, NIV

Sometimes parents can drift into a style of discipline that amounts to little more than idle words. We've observed parents who threaten discipline with little action to follow their words. You've heard them too, I'm sure. Some use counting: "Jimmy, stop that! One. Two. Two-and-a-half." Children learn very quickly how to play that game and soon become proficient at it.

Others threaten discipline by repeating themselves: "Sissy, come here. Sissy, I told you to come here. Sissy, I'm not going to tell you again, come here. Sissy, I'm getting upset, you better come here." Other parents use their staccato voice and increasing volume: "Ronny, pick up your toys. Ron, pick up your toys. Ronald, pick up your toys! Ronald Arthur, I told you to pick up your toys! RONALD ARTHUR SMITH, YOU COME RIGHT NOW AND PICK UP YOUR TOYS OR I'M GOING TO . . ."

Do we think our children are ignorant of this game? They almost seem to memorize the script instinctively. Don't use idle words when it comes to disciplining your children. Save yourself from frustration and unnecessary tears. Set clear limits and make certain your children know what the consequences will be. Be sure that you let the consequences be determined according to the age and understanding capacity of each child.

When your child crosses the limit, and they all will at some point, apply discipline immediately. This will accomplish a couple of things. First, you can apply the discipline without losing your temper. Second, the child learns that you mean what you say and that you will follow through on the previously stated consequences. Never apply discipline without reassuring your children of your love for them. And always be consistent.

Idle words are also used when parents make promises they can't keep. Don't say, "If you get good grades, I'll buy you a car," when you may not be able to afford the car. When your child does get good grades and you don't fulfill your promise, you're teaching them that you can't be trusted. Those broken promises can never be undone, and your child will become completely unmotivated in working for good grades.

Father, help us to simply say "Yes" or "No." Keep us consistent, fair, and loving as we seek to raise our children in a manner that honors You. May we never make a promise we cannot keep. Help us to not speak idly.

The Sword of the Lord

*Then the three companies blew the trumpets and broke the pitchers—they
held the torches in their left hands and the trumpets in their right hands for
blowing—and they cried, "The sword of the LORD and of Gideon!"*
—Judges 7:20, NKJV

Gideon's large army had been pruned down to a very small number,
particularly when compared with the Midianite army. At Gideon's
signal, they broke the pitchers, blew the trumpets, and lifted the torches as
they shouted, "The sword of the Lord and of Gideon!" To the half-asleep
Midianite army, amid the noise, the sights, the lights, it must have seemed as
though they were being attacked by an army of thousands.

On a visit to Israel, we heard our guide tell the story of a lone Israeli tank
operator who accomplished a remarkable feat during the war with Syria over
the Golan Heights. He drove up to the ridge, fired against the Syrians, then
drove down, moved to another spot, and repeated the action again and again.
Down below, on the Syrian side, all they could see were tanks going up and
down and firing at them. They thought it was an entire combat unit. These
actions slowed things down just long enough for the Israeli army to reach the
Golan Heights in time to defend that strategic site.

Gideon's battle reminds me of the battles parents fight for their children.
At times we can become overwhelmed, but maybe that's why this story is
here, to remind us that if we blow the trumpet and lift up the torch (God's
Word), God will give us the victory.

"God does not always choose for His work men of the greatest talents, but
He selects those whom He can best use. . . . The Lord can work most effectu-
ally through those who are most sensible of their own insufficiency, and who
will rely upon Him as their leader and source of strength. He will make them
strong by uniting their weakness to His might, and wise by connecting their
ignorance with His wisdom" (Ellen G. White, *Patriarchs and Prophets*, 553).

"There is a lesson for us in the story of Gideon's army. . . . The Lord is
just as willing to work through human efforts now, and to accomplish great
things through weak instrumentalities" (Ellen G. White, *Conflict and Courage*, 127).

*Father, give us the courage to face this conflict and win the battle in Your
name and in Your strength so that we may enjoy the rewards of eternal life
together as a complete family.*

In One Generation

When all that generation had been gathered to their fathers, another generation arose after them who did not know the LORD nor the work which He had done for Israel. —Judges 2:10, NKJV

After the death of Joshua and his generation, things declined rapidly among God's people. They stopped their conquest of the Promised Land and left entire cities to continue their pagan worship. Before long they began to worship Baal. In one generation they went from following God to idol worship. Things can change rapidly in the span of one generation.

My mother's parents were the first Seventh-day Adventist converts in the city of Bucaramanga, Colombia, in South America. When her mother died, leaving her father to raise five young children alone, her father, overwhelmed by hospital debt, stopped returning tithe and ultimately left the church with all but one of his children. My mother converted to Roman Catholicism when she met my father, and although she did everything in her power to believe her new religion, she confessed to me many years later that she never really came to believe it. Nevertheless, she raised her children as Catholics. It was only after the death of my father, and our move to the United States, that she returned to the Adventist faith, and she and I were baptized on the same day in a church in Silver Spring, Maryland.

While some may wonder how the Israelites could abandon the faith of their fathers in one generation, I witnessed how easily it can be done. After my mother left the church, it only took a few short years before she went from being a Sabbath-keeping, Second-Coming-expecting Christian to a Sunday-keeping, idol-worshiping Catholic. With the birth of each of her children, she introduced us to this worship, and it became a part of our lives.

I am amazed at parents who've told me they don't want to force their children to believe as they do. They want to give their children the freedom to choose what to believe on their own. I'd like to encourage every parent to hold dear their faith and live it and teach it to their children from the time they are born so that they may grow up in it from their earliest days. If we as parents don't live our faith, we will quickly lose our children and all the generations to come.

Father, help us to live daily our faith, and may we transmit it faithfully to our children for generations to come.

The Best Choice

"Choose for yourselves this day whom you will serve, whether the gods which your fathers served that were on the other side of the River, or the gods of the Amorites, in whose land you dwell. But as for me and my house, we will serve the Lord*." —Joshua 24:15, NKJV*

This is one of the most recognized passages in the Bible, and it occurs in the latter part of Joshua's life. He recounts for the Israelites what God has done for them and reminds them one more time not to enter into relationships with the people of the land lest they "become a snare" for them. Joshua knew what would happen if they pursued that course of action. And God's people responded by promising Joshua that they, and their children, would remain faithful. Unfortunately, once Joshua died and was no longer there to set a living example of faithfulness, the children of Israel forgot their promise and forsook the Lord.

We should never underestimate the power of our influence on others— particularly as it applies to our own family. We can challenge our children to aspire to being faithful as often as we want to, but if our actions don't match our words, the challenge will not only go unheeded, it could well drive them to choose to walk away from God. It's not enough to talk the talk. We need to walk the walk.

In Sabbath School, we teach them to sing, "Oh be careful little eyes what you see, oh be careful little feet where you go." What do our children see when they look at us? We must realize that our children are watching us, and as parents we have to consider the power of our example on our children. Where we lead, they will follow.

Ultimately, each person is responsible for the choices they make. Our children included. But if we are not setting a godly example, the likelihood of their choosing a wayward path increases greatly. For our part, then, we must dedicate ourselves and our family to God; live uprightly with God's help; pray for and with them daily; and entrust them to the Lord with the expectancy that ultimately His grace will be sufficient for them, as it is for us.

Father, we choose You as our God and Savior and ask that You will draw close to our children. May they sense Your presence in their lives and choose to follow You this day as their God, their Savior, and the Lord of their lives.

More Time!

*Then Joshua spoke to the L*ORD *... and he said in the sight of Israel: "Sun, stand
still over Gibeon; and Moon, in the Valley of Aijalon." So the sun stood still, and
the moon stopped, till the people had revenge upon their enemies.*
—Joshua 10:12, 13, NKJV

These verses recount one of the most powerful miracles ever recorded in
the Bible. After Joshua prayed that the sun would stand still, it is recorded
that the sun indeed stood still for about a day. Then the kings fighting against
Israel were captured and executed. These wholescale destructions of entire
cities have often caused some to question God. *Is He simply acting like an
angry parent?* Let's consider several things.

Israel had no home at that time, and God wanted to provide them with
a home of their own where they could live in peace and worship Him. He
intended that this nation He had chosen would become a witness to the
whole world. The surrounding nations had become so depraved by sin that
their corrupting influence was not only spreading but it could, and in some
cases did, become a hindrance, a temptation, and a stumbling block to God's
people.

The heathen nations treated their own in a manner that was dehumanizing
and deadly. They had temple prostitutes, the women were treated as objects
to abuse and mistreat, children were abused and at times offered to idols; but
God could not permit this abuse on the innocent to go on forever. Without
the presence of Israel as a nation, the world was rapidly becoming like the
world before the Flood, and even though Israel was not always faithful to
God, its presence gave the rest of the world an opportunity to know God and
forsake their evil ways.

In reality, the destruction of these nations was more an act of mercy on
God's part than an act of anger. Today, families are facing temptations and
an enemy that is bent on their destruction. While we don't need the miracle
of stopping the sun in its tracks, we do need the light of God's presence in
our lives and in our homes. The world is growing ever darker and mankind
has all but forgotten Jehovah. His plan for His children is that we will shine
in this dark world and bring knowledge of Him to those dying without Him.

*Father, may we be aware of all You are asking of us, and all You want to
accomplish in and through us.*

The Word to Everyone

There was not a word of all that Moses had commanded which Joshua did not read before all the assembly of Israel, with the women, the little ones, and the strangers who were living among them. —Joshua 8:35, NKJV

After the defeat at Ai, Joshua discovered, and had to deal with, Achan's sin. The sin itself didn't seem to be terribly serious—a little pilfering. Was it really such a big deal? God thought so. And so did Joshua, who called all of Israel together to deal with the problem. In order to bring the people back to God, he read to them God's specific instructions. Today's text makes it clear that these words were read before all, but it specifically mentions women, children, and foreigners. Passages like these should show us that God intended equal treatment to all.

The short story, *The Yeshiva Boy,* written by Issac Bashevis Singer, tells the story of a young girl who defies tradition by discussing and debating Jewish law and theology with her rabbi father. When he dies, she cuts her hair, dresses as a young man, and sets out to find a yeshiva where she can continue to study the Talmud and live secretly as a male named Anshel. She has such a hunger for learning that she sacrifices everything just for the opportunity to learn all she can from the Bible and other Jewish scholars.

Through the years I've been privileged to learn from gifted women who have answered God's call in their lives. My life has been enriched by their knowledge, their wisdom, and their experience. Without these interactions, my life, my ministry, and my future would have been cheated of something invaluable. What a loss it would be if these women had never been allowed to express their opinions or to teach or lead others, simply because society or culture dictated.

Joshua taught the Torah to women, children, and foreigners, because before God we all are equal and must be treated thus. I pray for the day when we will all learn to treat each other and give each other equal opportunities to learn and teach, follow and lead, listen and preach, serve and be served, as God intended; we will all benefit and be blessed as a result.

Father, may we set aside the societal and cultural barriers that keep us from enjoying Your gifts through men and women for the benefit of Your people. May we achieve the equality with which You created us as male and female and thus honor You.

Spiritual Landmarks

" 'Take for yourselves twelve stones from here, out of the midst of the Jordan,
from the place where the priests' feet stood firm. You shall carry them over with
you and leave them in the lodging place where you lodge tonight.' "
—Joshua 4:3, NKJV

After spending forty years in the desert, the Israelites finally get to cross the Jordan into the Promised Land, and God instructs Joshua to choose twelve men to each carry a large stone into their camp. God's purpose in doing this was to create a memorial that would be a talking point with each generation. Whenever children asked about that pile of stones, they would be told about all the miracles God had performed on behalf of His people.

We would do well to take this lesson to heart. Why don't we make a big deal about some of the most important moments in our spiritual lives, particularly with our children? Why not have a celebration every time a person, particularly a young person, is baptized? Baptism is one of those spiritual landmarks that gives us a great opportunity to tell our children what God has done for us. Other spiritual landmarks are the Sabbath, a weekly opportunity to celebrate God's love; Thanksgiving (at least in Canada and the United States, where it is a holiday); birthdays and anniversaries.

We could also take time during Communion to explain to young children what this special service is all about. We could also celebrate each year on the anniversary of our baptism; it would be like a spiritual birthday of sorts. Any high spiritual moment should be marked with a celebration—the first time the person speaks to somebody about Jesus, the first person they lead to Christ and to baptism, their first Bible study with someone else, ordination as deacon/deaconess or church elder. For those who are called to the gospel ministry, ordination is a special spiritual landmark. For those getting married, that day is not only a special moment that marks the union of two people but it should also be a moment of spiritual renewal and thus another spiritual landmark.

Look for special spiritual highlights and turn them into life landmarks to reflect on during the challenging times that come to all of us. These celebrations give us the opportunity to reflect on God's goodness and love and will help anchor us firmly on solid ground.

Father, thank You for all those high spiritual moments in our lives when You show us a greater, brighter glimpse of You.

The Head and Not the Tail

"Now it shall come to pass, if you diligently obey the voice of the LORD your God, to observe carefully all His commandments which I command you today, that the LORD your God will set you high above all nations of the earth. And all these blessings shall come upon you and overtake you, because you obey the voice of the LORD your God." —Deuteronomy 28:1, 2, NKJV

As I write these words, I am returning home from my nephew's wedding. He was brought up with an alcoholic, physically abusive father. His mother, my sister, became an Adventist in his pre-adolescent years but later left the church. In his late teens and early twenties, he experimented with different lifestyles and religious views, and I have to confess that I really don't know exactly what he believes. It appears to be an eclectic mix of Eastern religions, Christianity, naturalistic views, personal observations, and probably a few other things.

My nephew met and married a lovely young lady from a nice Buddhist family. Yesterday they had a Buddhist wedding ceremony at midday, and later they had a second, generic wedding. At least that's how it was described by the man who officiated—an attorney friend who also happens to be a notary public and can officiate at wedding ceremonies. I'm reflecting on all that took place yesterday, which happened to be a Sabbath, as a young Buddhist girl officially married my former Adventist nephew with whom she had been living, in a generic wedding ceremony—a short, generic service that marked the beginning of their life together, at least officially. And God, the God of Creation, the God who established marriage and the Sabbath, was not invited to their wedding, or their lives, on His holy day.

I wish them well. I wish them a long life of happiness and joy, health and prosperity. And yet, I can't help but feel sadness as they begin to build a new home together without the firm foundation that is present when God is at the center of a marriage and a home. As I write these words, I can almost hear Moses telling the Israelites, "The Lord will establish you as a holy people to Himself." Who is your foundation? Whose people are you? On whom is you marriage, your family, being built?

Father, our Lord and our Foundation, may we be obedient to Your commands and build our lives on You so our marriage and our home will be firmly established forever.

The Lost Virtue

And he said to his men, "The LORD forbid that I should do this thing to my master, the LORD's anointed, to stretch out my hand against him, seeing he is the anointed of the LORD." —1 Samuel 24:6, NKJV

As a child, when I was in school, we all had to stand anytime a person of authority walked into the classroom. When the teacher walked in to begin class, we'd stand to show respect. This was done in each class all the way through twelfth grade. Respect! We were taught to show respect and to be polite to everyone. My parents taught us to greet everyone with a polite, "Good morning," or "Good afternoon," regardless of who they were.

My father-in-law was a perfect example of someone who demonstrated respect. One of the best tributes we heard at his funeral was from those men who had worked for him through the years. They spoke of him more like a father to them than simply their boss. I was the recipient of his respect as well. As a young man, dating his eldest daughter, he treated me like a member of the family from the first day I met him. He asked my advice, shared his thoughts and feelings with me, and talked about his concerns. After he was diagnosed with brain cancer, he had his will drawn up, and while the ladies were out shopping, he showed me his will and asked for my opinion. He wanted to be fair in the decisions concerning his estate. He was fair, and in the act of asking my opinion, he showed his care and respect for me.

Respect seems to be a largely lost virtue today. It's assumed that those in authority are always wrong. At least that's the message we transmit to our children. Teachers are wrong for giving too much or too little homework, or for not giving our children a higher grade, even if they didn't do the work that deserved that grade. Police officers are always wrong for arresting someone, even if that person hurt, killed, or threatened to kill them or someone else. It's as though we have reached a point where we believe we are the only ones who are right. Everyone else is wrong. That's why David's actions toward Saul are so important: you can show respect, even to your enemies, and leave the rest to God.

Father, help us to rediscover the lost virtue of respect and to teach it to our children.

The Art of Mourning

"You are the children of the Lord your God; you shall not cut yourselves nor shave the front of your head for the dead. For you are a holy people to the Lord your God, and the Lord has chosen you to be a people for Himself, a special treasure above all the peoples who are on the face of the earth."
—Deuteronomy 14:1, 2, NKJV

The other nations had peculiar and superstitious beliefs about dying and the dead. Some even worshiped dead spirits. The precise significance of the rituals mentioned here, the laceration and shaving the head for the dead, is unknown today. But cutting oneself was a sign of mourning. In contrast with the surrounding nations, the Israelites were to demonstrate their faith in the Lord by refraining from these pagan practices.

I think we have forgotten how to grieve well. We want to shortcut the mourning process, allowing only the shortest time possible for a person to grieve, before expecting them to be done with it. We define it, outline the different stages, and expect everyone to follow the script. And if they can't do that, then they should probably see the doctor for something to help numb the pain. Everyone mourns in their own way and in their own time. We need to stop trying to hurry the mourning period and find healthy ways to grieve.

During my years as a hospice chaplain, I witnessed the deaths of all my patients and observed how their loved ones mourned. I learned much about the importance of appropriate mourning. I learned to counsel people to keep from medicating themselves or their loved ones, as that only serves to delay or interrupt the healing process which mourning provides. For those who used alcohol, I recommended they stay away from it for at least four weeks in order to give themselves time to grieve appropriately and not to drink in order to numb the pain.

We can definitely say that hurting oneself is not appropriate. As we read above, God did not want His people to follow the customs of the people around them by cutting themselves. Some appropriate ways to mourn include talking to others about the one who has died, journaling, and looking out for opportunities to help others. Look for positive ways to manage your grief. Help is available and it is appropriate to accept help at this time.

Father, when the loss of a loved one touches us, help us to know how to mourn them in an appropriate and healthy manner.

To Orphans, Widows, and Foreigners

For the LORD your God is God of gods and Lord of lords, the great, mighty, and awesome God who is unbiased and takes no bribe, who justly treats the orphan and widow, and who loves resident foreigners, giving them food and clothing. So you must love the resident foreigner because you were foreigners in the land of Egypt. —Deuteronomy 10:17–19, NET

Many years ago we helped a friend of ours relocate across the country where the opportunities for work were better for her and her family. The Lord blessed us, and within a couple of weeks we found her employment, an apartment, and a car. A couple of months later, she invited a friend to relocate so they could help her as well.

When their friend arrived in town, she moved in with my friends. We helped her find employment and transportation. One Sabbath she came to me crying because my friends were treating her poorly. They were charging her more for the rental of one room than they were paying for the entire apartment. I became furious. We had helped them, at our own cost, and now they were taking advantage of someone else. I confronted them and their response was, "It's none of your business." When things got worse, we helped this lady find another place to live and went to the police when my friends were holding some of her belongings.

My personal experience, sadly enough, has been that many times those who are blessed with the opportunity of coming to America where they receive help from others do not behave in like manner with other newcomers. Instead, they mistreat, take advantage of, or abuse their own countrymen or other foreigners. Just as I was angered by this injustice, God is even angrier when foreigners, orphans, or widows are treated unjustly, and He will see that His justice is meted out against all offenders.

But, while we see the importance of treating the orphan, widow, and foreigner well, how do we treat our family? Our husband or wife? Our children? Are we treating them as outcasts? God calls us to love one another. Let's make sure that our wife and children are not emotional or physical orphans and widows; love them, treat them kindly, and take good care of them.

Father, thank You for treating us better than we deserve. Bless us so that we may be a blessing to others, those nearest to us, and also those who don't have someone to show them Your love.

An Immigrant's Heart

"When the Lord *your God brings you into the land of which He swore to your fathers . . . to give you large and beautiful cities which you did not build, houses full of all good things, which you did not fill . . . when you have eaten and are full—then beware, lest you forget the* Lord *who brought you out of the land of Egypt, from the house of bondage." —Deuteronomy 6:10–12, NKJV*

As an immigrant, I can identify with the Israelites. I grew up in Bogotá, the capital city of Colombia, on the northwest corner of South America. When we left Bogotá to come to the United States, our first home was in Takoma Park, Maryland. Living in America felt almost surreal, like living a dream. With my mother and younger brother, I visited the monuments and museums, rode the bus whenever it would take me up and down the streets, in total awe of the city's beauty and gorgeous architecture.

While I was working at the Capital Hilton Hotel, just three blocks from the White House, I was asked to open and close the curtain for a program presented by the Gridiron Club. As I did, up on the stage barely three feet away from me, stood Mrs. Ford, wife of the president of the United States, and her husband, the president, was just on the other side of the room. Mrs. Henry Kissinger and a lot of other powerful people were also there . . . I LOVE THIS COUNTRY!

Little by little we got ourselves situated, found an apartment, bought furniture and clothes, attended college, got married, and continued life like everybody else. We became part of the people, the culture, citizens of this country, contributing to its economy and well-being, voting, enjoying our privileges, and respecting the laws.

As immigrants, we have been given a great gift in coming to this country. It was here I received my faith, my family, and my education. Here we have been able to live and succeed, work and rest, travel and have fun. While having the heart of an immigrant, I am grateful for all we have and are—we have benefitted from the work of those who came before us, and God has been the One to provide it all for us. May we never forget the Giver or take the gifts for granted.

Father, we pause to thank You for all You have given us. Help us to always be thankful for all Your generosity.

Talk About Miracles!

"Only take heed to yourself, and diligently keep yourself, lest you forget the things your eyes have seen, and lest they depart from your heart all the days of your life. And teach them to your children and your grandchildren."
—Deuteronomy 4:9, NKJV

I arrived at the airport and went to the electronic ticket dispenser. There were no lines, and things were looking good for a trouble-free trip. Until I got my tickets. Printed on them were the words "No Seat Assignment." I knew what that meant. The plane had been overbooked by the airlines, and I was one of the lucky ones without a seat, unless someone didn't show up, and their seat was reassigned to me. I would have a short layover before taking a connecting flight to my final destination, and I was not particularly excited at the prospect of missing my connection. I was more than relieved when my name was called and I was given a seat.

In my line of work I travel a lot, and each time I fly, I marvel at the miracle of modern transportation. We may say it is the result of modern technology; and it is. I marvel that God gave us such incredible brains capable of creating this modern technology. I marvel that while anything could happen at any time and planes do crash and people do die, I am alive today, after having flown countless miles around the world, surrounded by thousands of people, driving on roads congested with traffic in two different countries. So many things could go wrong—yet I am safe, and I continue to live and work each day.

And what God, through Moses, is asking me to do in the verse above is to remember Him. To not forget Him through these miracles and build idols to modern technology, to the airline industry, or to my GPS. Praise God, I'm alive and safe, because He loves me and wants me to experience a new day with friends and family; to witness for Him one more day through my words and my actions.

Father, thank You for the miracles of safety during long journeys across the country or across the world. Thank You for the miracle of life we find in a flower, in a bird, in a child. Thank You for breath, and water, and air, and sight. Thank You for food and shelter and clothing and a job. Thank You for all of Your miracles for us, simply because You rejoice in our happiness.

Problem-Solving Skills

" 'You shall not show partiality in judgment; you shall hear the small as well as the great; you shall not be afraid in any man's presence, for the judgment is God's. The case that is too hard for you, bring to me, and I will hear it.' "
—Deuteronomy 1:17, NKJV

It is tempting to want to help our children make decisions based on the knowledge and experience we have. However, it was in trying and failing that we gained that experience in the first place. Trying and failing is where we learn the skills necessary to navigate life. When we take that away from our children we shortchange them. Instead, we need to give them the space, and the grace, to try and fail and eventually succeed.

I believe children should be allowed to solve their own problems. If parents are constantly helping them when they get in trouble, they will learn to expect their parents' help and will never learn to use good judgment. At home, allow your kids to work things out among themselves and only intervene when they have tried and have reached an impasse.

In the neighborhood, encourage your kids to work things out with their friends; don't go and try to solve their problems by talking to their friends or their friends' parents. This does not mean you allow others to hurt, abuse, or take advantage of your children. You need to teach, advise, and, most important, listen to them; this will be more useful to them. Concerning school, don't be too hasty to call and yell at the teacher because of something your child tells you; if they got a bad grade, maybe they deserved it; besides, no one has to always get good grades, and one grade that is not perfect can be an incentive to try harder next time.

So, don't rush to solve your child's problems; encourage them to learn to solve their own problems in a positive, constructive manner. Intervene only when they have tried but have not been able to come up with a fair, workable solution: that's where your own experience and life wisdom will be of greatest benefit. And don't always take your child's side; take time to listen, analyze, and observe, and then take the side of what is right.

Father, thank You for allowing us to make our own decisions and to solve our own problems; it us thus that we grow and mature. Help us to let our children grow and mature in the same way.

Boundaries and Borders

*Then the L*ORD *spoke to Moses, saying, "Command the children of Israel, and say to them: 'When you come into the land of Canaan, this is the land that shall fall to you as an inheritance—the land of Canaan to its boundaries.'"*
—Numbers 34:1, 2, NKJV

While at the borders of the Promised Land, God gave Moses and the Israelites clear instructions regarding their future. Before settling in their new land, God told them about the boundaries He had set for Israel, boundaries that defined their entire country as well as internal boundaries between the tribes. These boundaries were set so Israel would know how far to go in settling in their new country, and also so others would know not to trespass Israel's borders. The Lord knew His people would need these boundaries for their safety and protection.

Psychologists have defined three types of boundaries within family systems. First, permeable boundaries are open, or diffuse. Second, impermeable boundaries are closed, or rigid. And third, semipermeable boundaries are flexible, or porous. Relationships with permeable boundaries are ones in which togetherness is all important, individuality tends to be sacrificed, and relationships are all about feeling, thinking, and doing everything together. By contrast, impermeable boundaries are the exact opposite. They indicate relationships that are characterized by poor communication or no communication, as well as rigidity and indifference. Individuality prevails over togetherness. And the third type of boundary, the semipermeable boundary, is one that enables a healthy balance between togetherness and individuality. A person can be free to be himself and yet fully engaged as a member of the group. Semipermeable boundaries are characterized by open communication, a healthy sense of self, and the ability to distinguish between one's own thoughts, feelings, and problems and those belonging to others.

Each of these boundaries are appropriate in different circumstances. We need to determine which boundary is needed in each area of our lives. For instance, the boundaries between spouses may be more permeable than those between parents and children. Boundaries between friends should be more impermeable than those between members of the family. Appropriate boundaries encourage healthy relationships.

Father, thank You for the boundaries in our lives and relationships because they are there to protect us. May we be mindful of the boundaries of others and thus show them the respect and love they deserve.

A Long Journey

These are the journeys of the children of Israel, who went out of the land of Egypt
by their armies under the hand of Moses and Aaron. Now Moses wrote down the
starting points of their journeys at the command of the Lord. And these are their
journeys according to their starting points.
—Numbers 33:1, 2, NKJV

On many occasions Moses recounted for the children of Israel the journey from Egypt to the Promised Land. He reminded them of all the places where they had traveled and how the Lord blessed and protected them even during those times they spent complaining about God's leading.

I was born in Bucaramanga, in the South American country of Colombia, but only lived there for my first eighteen months when my family moved to the capital city of Bogotá. I remained there until my mother, younger brother, and I moved to the United States. Since living in this country, my journey has included living in Michigan, Maryland, Oklahoma, New Jersey, Virginia, Wisconsin, Delaware, and Minnesota. I'm a sort of Adventist gypsy, I guess, going from place to place wherever God leads.

Several years ago our daughters voiced their discontent at having moved so often, unlike their friends who'd grown up and gone to school with the same friends each year. While we recognized that moving often had its drawbacks, we also wanted them to appreciate all the opportunities we'd had as a result of our moves. So we made a list of all the places we had visited, all the things we had seen, and all the fun we had enjoyed. By the time we were finished, our travel-log of sorts covered several pages. Our girls realized how enjoyable our journeys had been and how much richer their lives were for having been to all those places. As they thought about their friends who'd never left their city or county, they kind of felt sorry for them as they realized how blessed they'd been to enjoy all their adventures.

And now, after all these years as we count the thousands of miles we've traveled, we recognize and appreciate God's protection over us. He is so good! And we have so many reasons to thank Him and praise Him.

Father, thank You for all the opportunities You have given us to travel and see so many different and beautiful places and for providing us with Your protection through thousands of miles. But most of all, Father, thank You for the time we have spent together while enjoying those various trips.

What's Your Inheritance?

And the LORD spoke to Moses, saying: "The daughters of Zelophehad speak what is right; you shall surely give them a possession of inheritance among their father's brothers, and cause the inheritance of their father to pass to them."
—Numbers 27:6, 7, NKJV

God cares for the widows and the orphans, so when the daughters of Zelophehad came to Moses asking for some inheritance, He told Moses their request was fair and to make provision for them. This is an important lesson. Too many make no provision for their families in the event of their death. If a person makes no legal arrangements prior to their death, those decisions will be left up to their loved ones or to the court, which would involve people who know nothing about their situation. Here are some examples:

If you have an accident and are unable to make decisions for your care, your family will have to. If you are in a vegetative state, your family will be asked to make the choice to discontinue life support—one of the most painful decisions for a loved one to make. But if you have your medical advance directives, then you will have made the choice yourself and the medical personnel will abide by that.

If you don't have a will, the court may not choose to place your children with someone of the same faith as you. They may be placed with a relative or with anybody else, regardless of their personal beliefs or their commitment to God. Do you want your children to be raised by someone who does not share the same beliefs as you?

Too many families are fractured after the death of a loved one because of inheritance disputes. While your will may not guarantee peace among your descendants, at least you will be the one to decide how your possessions will be distributed.

The most important benefit you can leave your family is the memories you create today. Make videos, take pictures, leave each member of the family something special; write letters, share your stories of family and of their upbringing so they will have something to retell their own children. Those memories may be the most valuable treasures you pass on to the next generation. Most important of all—pass along your faith. Earthly treasures will fade away, but faith in God and a personal experience with Him will continue for eternity.

Father, thank You for our children; help us to give them the inheritance that will last forever.

Flirting With Sin

Then Balaam answered and said to the servants of Balak, "Though Balak were to give me his house full of silver and gold, I could not go beyond the word of the LORD my God, to do less or more. Now therefore, please, you also stay here tonight, that I may know what more the LORD will say to me."
—Numbers 22:18, 19, NKJV

Balak hated God's people and came up with a scheme to get rid of them. He sent a delegation to the prophet Balaam with an invitation to come and curse Israel. Balaam replies, "I could not go beyond the word of the Lord my God." But then, instead of sending these messengers on their way, he invites them to stick around, while he takes the matter to the Lord. In spite of his noble words, it seems as if Balak's gold and silver proved to be very attractive after all. We know the rest of the story. Balaam chooses to bend the rules and override God's will.

What lessons can parents learn from Balaam's story?

Even though God had already told him not to go, Balaam went back to God to check just one more time. Didn't he know that God wouldn't change His mind? As we lead our households in the knowledge of the Lord, we must do so without wavering and going back on established truth. Follow a plain "Thus saith the Lord," and stick with it.

By allowing Balak's delegation to stay while he consulted with God, Balaam was flirting with sin. Eventually, the temptation led to full-blown sin. He was more interested in growing rich than in doing God's will. But we can't serve God and mammon. We cannot allow love for the things of this world, or even the pursuit of them, become our guiding principle while abandoning the pursuit of the will of God. If we allow temptation to linger it will become sin, and greed leads to rebellion.

Balaam's greed was also responsible for leading the Israelites to worship idols and to commit sexual immorality. With God's help, we must do everything possible to protect our families from the three sins that led to Balaam's downfall: greed, idolatry, and sexual immorality. With God's help—we can!

Father, thank You for reminding us through the story of Balaam that when we allow temptation to lead us away from You, we're acting dumber than a donkey. Help us to be wise, and protect our family from temptation.

The Challenges of Intercultural Marriages

Then Miriam and Aaron spoke against Moses because of the Ethiopian woman whom he had married; for he had married an Ethiopian woman. So they said, "Has the LORD indeed spoken only through Moses? Has He not spoken through us also?" —Numbers 12:1, 2, NKJV

Zipporah was concerned about the many responsibilities Moses had to face. She spoke with her father, and when Moses acted upon Jethro's wise counsel without first consulting Miriam and Aaron, they became jealous of him and blamed Zipporah for what they considered Moses' neglect of them. The fact that Zipporah was a Midianite was used by Miriam and Aaron merely as an excuse for rebelling against the authority of Moses. Zipporah was a worshiper of the true God. Moses did not violate the principle of non-marriage with the heathen when he took her as a wife, as his siblings claimed.

Marriage is a challenging thing regardless of who enters into it. Problems can be magnified between siblings for many reasons, including differences of opinion concerning intercultural marriage. The fact is that the more a couple has in common, the stronger the relationship will be. While success in inter-cultural relationships is not impossible and many couples have been very successful and happy, many others have encountered insurmountable challenges, which have caused or contributed to the demise of their relationship.

I speak from experience since I was born and raised in Colombia, South America, and my wife was born and raised in Virginia. Our upbringings were very different. We spoke a different language and followed a different faith. However, by the time we met and eventually married, our commitment to God and to each other, and the similarities we shared, were greater than the differences we had. Even so, we have had challenges from time to time due to our cultural differences. Praise the Lord, we have been happily married for many, many years.

Regardless of whom you choose to marry, look for common areas of strength and build on those. Be aware of the possible challenges you may face as a couple, some of which may come from your families of origin, and make a commitment to work through them together. Make the Lord your Counselor and you will walk in safe paths.

Father, help us to find more things in common than things to divide us, and help us to stay committed to each other and to You, until Jesus returns.

Journey With God

At the command of the LORD they remained encamped, and at the command of the LORD they journeyed; they kept the charge of the LORD, at the command of the LORD by the hand of Moses. —Numbers 9:23, NKJV

Precious promise—that God would be with His people during their travels. At night the pillar of fire reminded them that He was watching over them as their Light and Protector. In the day the cloudy pillar told of His love in providing shade in a dry and weary land. When the cloud moved, they moved. When the cloud remained still, so did they, demonstrating their obedience and faith in His direction.

I have pondered this text many times for we have moved so many times, to many different locations, in the course of working for the Lord. From the Southwestern cities of Oklahoma City and Muskogee, in Oklahoma, to the eastern United States in New Jersey, Delaware, and Virginia, to the Midwest in Wisconsin and Minnesota, and now to Silver Spring, Maryland. With many years left before we retire, who knows what other places He has in store for us?

I remember driving through Oklahoma, the setting sun hanging over the horizon like a huge ball of fire, never imagining that one day we would be working in that state. Once, while driving from Columbia Union College to New York City, I decided that I wouldn't want to live in New Jersey, yet we spent four of the best years of our lives in that state. When attending Andrews University Theological Seminary, we drove to Racine, Wisconsin, to visit some friends and never imagined one day, many years later, we would live and work there for seven wonderful years. While in Wisconsin we drove to Minneapolis to catch a Yankees-Twins game, and the thought never even crossed our minds that one day we would live in that same area.

As I reflect on these experiences, I can't help but wonder what God has in store for us next. And that's what we marvel at the most, knowing that no matter where we are, if God takes us there, that is home, and He will take care of us. As long as we follow Him and do His will for our lives, we will be blessed and happy. We can't wait to see what God has in store for us next!

Father, thank You for leading in our lives. We can hardly wait to see what You have in store for our future!

To Trust Him More

Then God remembered Rachel, and God listened to her.
—Genesis 30:22, NKJV

For years, Rachel had been pleading with God to give her a son, but she remained barren. It's hard for us to understand the level of her humiliation and desperation within our societal and cultural norms. For Rachel, there was no greater shame than in not being able to give Jacob a son. You can almost hear her bitterness as she demands of Jacob, "Give me children, or else I will die!" It must have been so hard to watch her sister become pregnant again and again, each time with a son for Jacob. How that must have stung!

Our verse for today doesn't imply that God had not heard Rachel all along. Neither does it imply that God had forgotten her. However, from Rachel's perspective, that's probably exactly how it seemed. If Rachel could have caught a glimpse of things from God's perspective, how differently would she have lived? With less bitterness and resentment? With greater peace and happiness? For in seeing the big picture she would have seen that God had His hand in the timing of Joseph's conception, birth, and life. His seeming delay was actually His invitation for her to trust Him completely in all aspects of her life. It's an invitation He gives to all His children, and it's our choice whether or not we accept it from His hand. And whether we accept it graciously or with resentment.

As for Leah, it must have been a very heavy burden to know that she was not loved, as was Rachel. Yet Leah chose to remain. She did not leave or divorce Jacob. Their children enjoyed living with their father and mother in what was essentially a large blended family. Once we have brought children into this world, as parents we must do everything we can to provide them with a loving home, doing everything we can to protect them, provide for them, and to help and encourage them. Life was not easy for either Leah or Rachel, but God was with them, and it was up to them to choose how to walk with Him.

Father, we don't always recognize Your invitation to us, to trust You more. And once we do, it's not always the easiest of invitations to accept. Help us, Lord, to realize that You truly do have our best interests at heart, and no matter how difficult today may be, You are walking beside us. Thank You, Lord.

First of All

"And you shall take the Levites for Me—I am the Lord."
—Numbers 3:41, NKJV

The firstborn have always had a privileged relationship with God, beginning with Adam in the Garden of Eden, the firstborn of the human race. In the book of Numbers, God reiterates that the Levites belong to the Lord in place of all the firstborn of Israel; it was their privilege to be chosen to enjoy the special honor of conducting the services of the sanctuary, taking care of and maintaining God's special place among His people. They enjoyed a unique relationship with God.

As the fifth child in a family of six, I understand all about the privilege the older siblings enjoy. In my home, when riding in our car, my mother was always seated by my father, and my sister, the firstborn, sat next to her. When my sister left home, the second-born took her place beside Mother. As you can imagine, it was a long time before I sat in the front seat; in reality, I rarely did, except at those times when I was the only one riding with my dad in the car.

We had similar seating arrangements at the dining table with my father at the head, my mother at his left, and the older siblings down the line. I sat at the far end. My older sister had her own room, while the rest of us shared rooms. Once she left, my older brother got his own room, and when he married, his room was given to the next in line. I eventually got my own room, but by then I was about thirteen years old and had been sharing a room with my younger brother for the past five years.

As I look back, it was not a matter of showing preference for any of us, it was a way of honoring and respecting us all individually and instilling in the younger siblings the same honor and respect for those older than us. Maybe that was part of what God was trying to instill in the Israelites; that the Levites were a special tribe in the same way the Israelites were chosen to be His special people. While we want to love our children equally, the birth order of our children gives us an opportunity to help them understand good, strong, healthy family dynamics and also lessons of respect and honor.

Father, thank You for teaching us to honor and respect those older than us.

October

Called to Be Like Jesus

*As he which hath called you is holy, so be ye holy in all manner
of conversation; because it is written, Be ye holy; for I am holy.*
—1 Peter 1:15, 16, KJV

The word of God is to have a sanctifying effect on our association with every member of the human family. The leaven of truth will not produce the spirit of rivalry, the love of ambition, the desire to be first. True, heaven-born love is not selfish and changeable. It is not dependent on human praise. The heart of him who receives the grace of God overflows with love for God and for those for whom Christ died. Self is not struggling for recognition. He does not love others because they love and please him, because they appreciate his merits, but because they are Christ's purchased possession. If his motives, words, or actions are misunderstood or misrepresented, he takes no offense, but pursues the even tenor of his way. He is kind and thoughtful, humble in his opinion of himself, yet full of hope, always trusting in the mercy and love of God. . . .

". . . The grace of Christ is to control the temper and the voice. Its working will be seen in politeness and tender regard shown by brother for brother, in kind, encouraging words. An angel presence is in the home. The life breathes a sweet perfume, which ascends to God as holy incense. Love is manifested in kindness, gentleness, forbearance, and long-suffering.

"The countenance is changed. Christ abiding in the heart shines out in the faces of those who love Him and keep His commandments. Truth is written there. The sweet peace of heaven is revealed. There is expressed a habitual gentleness, a more than human love.

"The leaven of truth works a change in the whole man, making the coarse refined, the rough gentle, the selfish generous. By it the impure are cleansed, washed in the blood of the Lamb. Through its life-giving power it brings all there is of mind and soul and strength into harmony with the divine life. Man with his human nature becomes a partaker of divinity. Christ is honored in excellence and perfection of character. As these changes are effected, angels break forth in rapturous song, and God and Christ rejoice over souls fashioned after the divine similitude" (*Christ's Object Lessons*, 101, 102).

O Lord, please do whatever You need to make me more like You! May my face shine with the light of Your indwelling presence!

A New Beginning

"He who is to be cleansed shall wash his clothes, shave off all his hair, and wash himself in water, that he may be clean. After that he shall come into the camp, and shall stay outside his tent seven days." —Leviticus 14:8, NKJV

For the people of Israel, having just left their captivity in Egypt, and on the way to establish their new home as an independent nation, the laws and regulations concerning health issues were specific and important for their well-being and survival. For anyone suspected of having leprosy, there were many cleansing rituals as well as sin-atonement rituals that had to be performed before the person would be allowed in camp. The steps for diagnosis, treatment, and reinstatement were long and tedious, but they ensured the safety of the people.

In marriage, even in the healthiest and happiest ones, there are times when mistakes are made and the results can cause a wound in the relationship. It may be something small and therefore easy to heal. But there are times and situations where the guilty party does something to hurt their spouse and their relationship, and instead of confessing and making restitution, the wound is ignored and left to fester. Like a physical wound that is not properly cleaned, the wound in this relationship will become infected, fester, and cause further pain that can end up poisoning the entire system.

In marriage, problems that are not dealt with are like leprosy. In the beginning, the infection is not easily detected. It may be felt, but it's not obviously noticed. If left untreated, however, it will begin to affect the nervous system of the relationship so that eventually, like leprosy, the emotions are numbed and cannot be felt. Eventually, the numbness may keep us from feeling the deepest wounds, but eventually the untreated disease will result in the loss of the relationship.

Leprosy does not have to be fatal. Appropriate medication can treat it so that it doesn't progress or kill the person infected. In marriage, confession and repentance are the best medicine. As we confess our sins to God and to one another, the diseases that kill healthy marriages can be eradicated and the relationship restored.

Father, forgive us for the times when we have hurt our spouse, and help us to be more sensitive to their needs in the future. And Father, help us to confess to them our sins toward them so that there may be total healing in our relationship.

Consecration

"And you shall not go outside the door of the tabernacle of meeting for seven days, until the days of your consecration are ended. For seven days he shall consecrate you." —Leviticus 8:33, NKJV

In Leviticus 8, we read about the process Aaron and his sons experienced before being set apart for the priesthood. They had to wash themselves. A physical cleansing helped prepare them for the spiritual cleansing that would follow. Then they were dressed in the beautiful priestly garments that had been specifically designed for them. The ritual for spiritual cleansing took place next, each aspect designed to symbolize that the blood of the sacrifice covered their sins and enabled them to serve and minister on behalf of the people. Finally, a seven-day consecration period took place. Only then could they officially begin the ministrations of the sanctuary.

The rituals and ceremonies surrounding the beginning of the Levitical priesthood remind me somewhat of the traditions and rituals involved in becoming husband and wife. On the wedding day, the man and the woman each go through a process of preparing themselves, including cleansing themselves. Then the couple, separately, gets dressed in their beautiful wedding clothes. Making their way to the church, the groom is careful not to catch sight of his bride before the ceremony. At last, the groom goes up to the front of the church with his best man and the pastor, and the rest of the wedding party march in. The bride enters, holding on to her father's arm, and marches down the aisle to join the groom. The wedding ceremony commences and they are pronounced man and wife, united legally and in the sight of God.

There is one more tradition that cannot be overlooked in this process of becoming one—the honeymoon. While some view it simply as a vacation, the honeymoon is the time when the couple consummates their marriage. From now on, they are one and their covenant must remain for as long as they live. The honeymoon serves as a way to seal their commitment to one another and, most important, to God, by fulfilling His plan for their lives of becoming one and by committing to not let anyone or anything come between them.

Loving Father, we rededicate ourselves to You this day, as husband and wife, to remain together, under Your will and blessing for the rest of our lives. May we walk together more closely with You every day until the day Jesus returns and we walk together with You for eternity.

Just What We Need

Then the children of Israel did so and gathered, some more, some less.
So when they measured it by omers, he who gathered much had nothing left
over, and he who gathered little had no lack. Every man had gathered according
to each one's need. —Exodus 16:17, 18, NKJV

After 430 years in Egyptian captivity, the Israelites had forgotten many things about worshiping the true God. One reason for this wilderness journey to the Promised Land was to give the Israelites the chance to bring them back to worshiping Jehovah. And one of the very first things God taught them was to keep the Sabbath day holy. If His people obeyed Him and honored the Sabbath day, He'd take care of all their needs. He gives the same promise to His children today.

From the very beginning, the week of Creation, God gave the same lesson to Adam and Eve. He created them on the sixth day, and their first full day of life was the Sabbath. They hadn't had opportunity to do any work yet, and God showed them that He would provide for all their needs. The Sabbath invitation was an invitation to rest in Him.

God's instruction to Moses was that the people were not to gather food on Sabbath but were to stay together as families and enjoy the day and God's blessings. Sabbath is not a day to do nothing. It's a day to enjoy God's blessings with our families, whether at home or with our church family—a day to remember that He takes care of all our needs, and a day to be refreshed, rejuvenated, and re-created.

This morning, as I write these words, it is Sabbath. Outside it is -15°F here in Maple Grove, near the Twin Cities of Minneapolis and St. Paul, with a wind chill somewhere between -25 and -30. And yet, inside our home it is warm. We have plenty of food, we have our cars in the garage ready to take us wherever we need to go, we have books to read and clothes to wear. On this Sabbath, like on every other Sabbath, God is taking care of our needs, and we're enjoying the physical, emotional, and spiritual rest we so much need and desire.

Father, thank You for the blessings of the Sabbath. May today be a glorious one for each of us, and may our families receive the greatest blessings on this day as we come to You and as You bring us closer to one another.

Death at Birth

"When you assist the Hebrew women in childbirth, observe at the
delivery: If it is a son, kill him, but if it is a daughter, she may live."
But the midwives feared God and did not do what the king of Egypt had
told them; they let the boys live. —Exodus 1:16, 17, NET

The Egyptians were worried that the Israelites would grow in number to such an extent that they would become an overpowering majority. In order to keep that from happening, they ordered the midwives to kill the male babies born to all Israelite women. The midwives, however, were God-fearing women and did not obey those orders, in spite of risking their lives to do so. And God rewarded the midwives for their actions.

So many look for reasons to excuse the objectionable, unethical, and immoral abuse and destruction of children under the guise of doing what's best, or most convenient, for others. The trafficking of children continues around the world. Children are sold to a life of forced labor as slaves. Others excuse abortion on demand for the sake of the women who do not wish to have babies, for victims of incest or rape, or for unwanted pregnancies for teen mothers. In some countries the birth of a baby girl is frowned upon, and in some places parents are penalized for having more than one child. As the wise man once said, "There is nothing new under the sun." Majorities still worry about the growth of minority groups who may one day overthrow them and become the ruling group. And so they excuse genocide in order to protect their culture, ideas, and way of life.

We are called upon to protect and help our children, not to harm them, either before or after birth. If children are a blessing from the Lord, how can we justify abortion on demand? And with so many childless couples, if someone has experienced an unexpected pregnancy, why not consider giving that child up for adoption instead of ending prematurely an innocent life? As much as God blessed the midwives for respecting the sanctity of life, so He blesses the people who respect the sanctity of life today by refusing to abort their children, even if unplanned.

Loving Father, thank You for the gift of children. May we always be loving toward them and respect the sanctity of life. Give wisdom and courage to those who are in the valley of indecision today regarding their unborn child. May Your grace be upon them, Lord.

Love Lifts the Load

They told him, "Joseph is still alive and he is ruler over all the land of Egypt!"
Jacob was stunned, for he did not believe them. But when they related to him
everything Joseph had said to them . . . Jacob's spirit revived. Then Israel said,
"Enough! My son Joseph is still alive! I will go and see him before I die."
—Genesis 45:26–28, NET

Although it's not specifically mentioned, but rather implied, Jacob's sons had to confess to him what they'd done to Joseph so many years before. Can you imagine how it must have been to receive such news? In a few other Bible versions, it says that "Jacob's heart fainted." This expression in the original Hebrew means "his heart was numb." He was stunned. Unable to respond as if he were dead. But once he knew it to be true, his heart was revived, and he set about making plans to go and see his son.

We know that Reuben was filled with sorrow when he discovered what his brothers had done to Joseph. While we don't know when the others began to feel remorse for their sin, I imagine that watching Jacob suffer terribly through the years for his loss would have touched their hearts deeply. How heavy the burden of unconfessed sin! Now, standing before their father, they might have been afraid that their confession would be so traumatic to Jacob that he might die. What relief it must have been to see his spirit revive—and to finally be rid of the burden of guilt!

Confession is always good, and when it comes to total honesty in a relationship, which includes emotional and historical honesty, it is vital. What happens when we carry a secret unconfessed is that a barrier is built in our communication with our loved one. It widens with time, destroying the emotional bond between family members. Secrecy destroys intimacy, and the consequences can be devastating. The resulting dishonesty is one of the main factors in destroying a relationship. Although it's never easy, why not confess and be completely honest and transparent? Honesty is one of the most important emotional needs that we as men and women have, and without which our relationships suffer. Pray that your spouse will be as gracious and forgiving as Joseph and Jacob were with the ten formerly jealous siblings.

Loving Father, give us the strength to confess our faults to one another in all honesty. And, if our spouse comes to us to confess, may we be gracious and forgiving. Please protect and keep our family whole.

The Unloved Spouse

Leah's eyes were delicate, but Rachel was beautiful of form and appearance.
—Genesis 29:17, NKJV

The words that describe Leah have been debated for many years by many commentators. The Hebrew word *rak,* translated "tender" in the King James Version, has usually been understood to mean "weak" or "dull." Some believe that Leah had soft blue eyes, which were considered to be a great blemish. The fact that Jacob was not attracted to Leah would indicate the contrast between the two sisters and perhaps Leah's eyes, as well as her personality, lacked the brilliance and lustrous warmth of Rachel.

After the wily Laban tricked Jacob into marrying Leah, it would naturally follow that Jacob would be resentful. In *The Story of Redemption,* Ellen White writes: "Jacob was not happy in his marriage relation, although his wives were sisters. He formed the marriage contract with Laban for his daughter Rachel, whom he loved. After he had served seven years for Rachel, Laban deceived him and gave him Leah. When Jacob realized the deception that had been practiced upon him, and that Leah had acted her part in deceiving him, he could not love Leah. Laban wished to retain the faithful services of Jacob a greater length of time, therefore deceived him by giving him Leah, instead of Rachel. Jacob reproved Laban for thus trifling with his affections, in giving him Leah, whom he had not loved. Laban entreated Jacob not to put away Leah, for this was considered a great disgrace, not only to the wife, but to the whole family. Jacob was placed in a most trying position, but he decided to still retain Leah, and also marry her sister. Leah was loved in a much less degree than Rachel" (89, 90).

There were constant disputes between Leah and Rachel over their marital rights, and with the addition of their two maidservants, and the birth of all thirteen children, tensions rose even higher. Leah desired the love of her husband—as every woman does. And Rachel resented having to share her husband with her sister—as any woman would. It's not difficult to see why God has never approved of polygamy. One thing's certain: married life wasn't what either Leah or Rachel thought it would be, and it certainly wasn't what Jacob had anticipated. Nevertheless, God did not forsake or leave them. His blessings flowed faithfully on.

Dear Lord, life's not always what we'd like it to be, but You are faithful. Help us to lean on Your faithfulness during life's trying times.

A Compatible Spouse

*"Swear by the LORD, the God of heaven and the God of the earth,
that you will not take a wife for my son from the daughters of the
Canaanites, among whom I dwell." —Genesis 24:3, NKJV*

As Abraham grew older, he wanted to be sure that the promise God made him of a long posterity would indeed be fulfilled through his son Isaac. Abraham was diligent in his desire that Isaac and his descendants would remain faithful to Jehovah and not be sidetracked by the practices and the people of the land. So he sent his servant back to the land of his father, with strict instructions on how to find a wife for Isaac from among his own people.

Even in an age of arranged marriages, Abraham understood the importance of seeking God's will when it came to selecting a life partner for his son. It mattered that they shared the same faith, for the more things a couple has in common, the more compatible they will be in the important areas of their life, including parenting, communication, conflict resolution, and financial management. Through the prophet Amos, God said, "Can two walk together, unless they are agreed?" (Amos 3:3, NKJV). After diligently seeking God's will, Eliezer found Rebekah and made Abraham's request known to her family.

The story of Isaac and Rebekah is one of the best-loved stories in the Bible. When Eliezer returned with Rebekah, "Then Isaac brought her into his mother Sarah's tent; and he took Rebekah and she became his wife, and he loved her. So Isaac was comforted after his mother's death" (Genesis 24:67, NKJV). Isaac loved Rebekah, which is every wife's longing, to be loved, cared for, nurtured, and protected by her husband. In turn, Rebekah comforted Isaac after his mother's death, which every husband longs for, to have his wife be his true comfort and encourager, sharing her strength during his most vulnerable moments.

When looking for a life partner, bring your longings before the Lord. Ask Him for wisdom and discernment, and trust both His leading and His timing. When you find someone, look for compatibility in the most critical areas of life, and know exactly what you're looking for. Finding someone who shares your love for God, your values, and your priorities will do much to help ensure a successful life together.

Father, what is Your will in this matter? I surrender my life to You and trust Your leading and Your love for me in all areas of my life. Thank You, Lord.

The Challenges of Blended Families

Therefore she said to Abraham, "Cast out this bondwoman and her son; for the son of this bondwoman shall not be heir with my son, namely with Isaac." And the matter was very displeasing in Abraham's sight because of his son.
—Genesis 21:10, 11, NKJV

Whenever man, or in this case, woman, steps in and takes matters into their own hands, things never end well. When young lives are involved, that becomes particularly sad. In Genesis 16, we read about the problems between Sarai and her servant Hagar. Sarai seems to have forgotten that it was her idea for Hagar to become pregnant in the first place. Once Sarai gave birth to Isaac, she made life unbearable for Hagar. As the boys grew older, we can only imagine the rivalry between the two mothers. Problems between the boys were probably exaggerated until Sarai demanded that Hagar and Ishmael be thrown out of the house. Turns out that Sarai's solution wasn't the best idea she ever had.

This story illustrates several dynamics that can be problematic to healthy family relationships and which come when we don't follow God's established plan for us. First, sibling rivalry. While every family will experience a certain amount of sibling rivalry, this problem can be much more pronounced in blended families and in families where adultery and divorce occur. The antagonism between Ishmael and Isaac was passed along to their children, causing great heartache and trouble, which continues to our day.

Second, blended families face some unique challenges. While some enjoy a smooth transition and go on to enjoy their family life, many more experience great turmoil, internally and outwardly. The Brady Bunch may make for good television viewing, but it's hardly the norm. Often, the challenges of the early days leave lifetime scars, affecting not only the immediate family members but resulting in deep pain and dysfunction for years to come. How tragic when these problems are never resolved and are left to complicate and damage the family for generations.

Whenever we violate God's plan for our life and our marriage, we bring on ourselves painful and lasting consequences for us, our spouse, our children, our families, and beyond. When tempted to take matters into our own hands, we'd do well to remember this story!

Our loving Father, thank You for our families. Please keep us from trying to force Your hand, or trying to work things out ourselves. May we trust You instead. Please help us and protect the unity and integrity of our home.

When Storms Threaten

And they came to Him and awoke Him, saying, "Master, Master,
we are perishing!" Then He arose and rebuked the wind and the raging
of the water. And they ceased, and there was a calm. —Luke 8:24, NKJV

Even Jesus needed a respite at times. Sometimes even a short break on a boat was what He did to step away from the crowds. On this occasion, a storm arose and threatened to capsize the boat. Many of the disciples were experienced fishermen, but though they used all their expertise and strength to try to navigate safely to the other side of the lake, they were overwhelmed by the storm.

Desperate, they called on Jesus to save them. When He ordered the storm to be still, a sweet peace immediately surrounded them as they made their way safely to shore.

This was not the only storm Jesus and the disciples would face, but here, as it would happen many other times, Jesus brought them the peace and safety they needed as well as the encouragement that strengthened their faith.

Every relationship faces conflict at some point. We are all different and try to get our own way at times. In marriage, the goal is not the absence of conflict but rather positive conflict management. As a marriage counselor, almost every couple that comes to my office feels overwhelmed and powerless to do anything to save their relationship from the problems that threaten to sink their family ship.

The same Jesus who calmed the fiercest storm can calm the storms of our lives. Turning to God should be a daily experience. It will prevent many of the storms in life and should be our first resort. We need to have daily devotional time individually, as a couple, and as a family. It is during those moments with God that our faith is strengthened, as well as our relationship with one another.

Do you have any storms in your life right now? Talk them over with Jesus; He will bring calm to your life. He often uses His people to help, so talking with a godly counselor might be just what you need. Don't wait until you are overwhelmed and the storms of life threaten to drown you. Seek help at the first sign of trouble.

Father, thank You that the storms of life don't have to drown us and that You are always with us ready to help us. Calm the storm and return to us the peace You so desire for us to enjoy.

Honor Your Parents

And Ham, the father of Canaan, saw the nakedness of his father, and told his
two brothers outside. But Shem and Japheth took a garment, laid it on both
their shoulders, and went backward and covered the nakedness of their father.
Their faces were turned away, and they did not see their father's nakedness.
—Genesis 9:22, 23, NKJV

This story often causes us to shake our heads and ask, "So what exactly did Ham do?" Did he simply walk in on his father's nakedness? Where is the sin in that? Did it warrant receiving Noah's curse? Many fanciful suggestions have been proposed, but the answer is pretty simple and holds some important lessons for families in learning respect and discretion.

It's helpful for us to understand that to the ancients it was exceedingly shameful for anyone to see their father naked. Ham apparently stumbled on this accidentally, but went out and exultantly broadcast the news to his brothers. What seems to be a trivial incident turned out to be a major event that would go on to impact these three brothers, and God's people, through hundreds of succeeding generations.

Ham's sin was in ridiculing his father for his nakedness and mocking his father in the presence of others. Although he may have accidentally seen his father's shameful condition, instead of protecting his father, he rejoiced in what he saw and gleefully shared what he'd seen with others. By contrast are the actions of Shem and Japheth. They walked in to where Noah lay, backwards so they would not see his nakedness, and carefully, respectfully, covered their father. In this way, they honored their father, rather than ridiculing him as Ham had done.

Ellen White gives us additional insights when she writes, "The unnatural crime of Ham declared that filial reverence had long before been cast from his soul, and it revealed the impiety and vileness of his character. These evil characteristics were perpetuated in Canaan and his posterity, whose continued guilt called upon them the judgments of God" (*Patriarchs and Prophets,* 117).

The Lord is very clear regarding His expectations of how children are to treat their parents. He wrote, "Honor your father and your mother" (Exodus 20:12, NKJV). What example are we setting for our children regarding the respect we show to our parents? Remember, they hear and see how we interact with our parents.

Dear Lord, may we show respect to our parents so clearly and beautifully that our children will have no doubts as to what parental respect looks like.

Words of Encouragement

That I should know how to speak a word in season to him that is weary.
—Isaiah 50:4, KJV

All around us are afflicted souls. Here and there, everywhere, we may find them. Let us search out these suffering ones and speak a word in season to comfort their hearts. Let us ever be channels through which shall flow the refreshing waters of compassion.

"In all our associations it should be remembered that in the experience of others there are chapters sealed from mortal sight. On the pages of memory are sad histories that are sacredly guarded from curious eyes. There stand registered long, hard battles with trying circumstances, perhaps troubles in the home life, that day by day weaken courage, confidence, and faith. Those who are fighting the battle of life at great odds may be strengthened and encouraged by little attentions that cost only a loving effort. To such the strong, helpful grasp of the hand by a true friend is worth more than gold or silver. Words of kindness are as welcome as the smile of angels.

"There are multitudes struggling with poverty, compelled to labor hard for small wages, and able to secure but the barest necessities of life. Toil and deprivation, with no hope of better things, make their burden very heavy. When pain and sickness are added, the burden is almost insupportable. Careworn and oppressed, they know not where to turn for relief. Sympathize with them in their trials, their heartaches, and disappointments. This will open the way for you to help them. Speak to them of God's promises, pray with and for them, inspire them with hope.

"Words of cheer and encouragement spoken when the soul is sick and the pulse of courage is low—these are regarded by the Saviour as if spoken to Himself.

"From age to age the Lord has been seeking to awaken in the souls of men a sense of their divine brotherhood. Be co-workers with Him.

"Speak as He would speak, act as He would act. Constantly reveal the sweetness of His character. Reveal that wealth of love which underlies all His teachings and all His dealings with men. The humblest workers, in co-operation with Christ, may touch chords whose vibrations shall ring to the ends of the earth and make melody throughout eternal ages" (*The Ministry of Healing*, 158, 159).

O Lord, this *is my prayer!*

The Loving Parent

"If a son asks for bread from any father among you, will he give him a stone? Or if he asks for a fish, will he give him a serpent instead of a fish? Or if he asks for an egg, will he offer him a scorpion? If you then, being evil, know how to give good gifts to your children, how much more will your heavenly Father give the Holy Spirit to those who ask Him!" —Luke 11:11–13, NKJV

The relationship between a parent and their children has a significant impact on their children's physical, emotional, and spiritual development. From the physical point of view, human children are totally helpless and dependent on others from the time they are born. Without the physical nurturing they receive from their parents, the child would die. As a child grows, their parents are responsible for providing them with good, nutritious food if they want them to grow up healthy. In our day, there is an increase in diabetes and hypertension among children, and this is directly linked to their diet.

From the emotional point of view, babies and children who experience healthy physical touch from their parents grow healthier emotionally. The words children hear from their parents have a great effect on their psychological and educational well-being. If their parents put them down, yell at them, tell them how dumb they are, or that they will amount to nothing in life, these words will negatively impact their fragile minds and lives. If, on the other hand, children hear words of love, encouragement, and affirmation from their parents, they are more likely to develop into stronger, healthier adults.

Finally, from the spiritual point of view, their relationship with their parents will either lead a child closer to or further from God. The love of a mother toward her children is used in the Bible as an example of the loving care God has for His children. The relationship of a father toward his children is also used as an example and helps form that relationship between their children and their heavenly Father. The message from today's text is that God's goodness to us is greater than even the best of parents.

Father God, help us to forgive our parents when they have fallen short of the ideal You have for them. Forgive us when we, as parents, have not been a good example to our children. Restore us all to the best relationship we can have together so that our children will experience physical, emotional, and spiritual health.

God's Love for the Widowed

*When the Lord saw her, He had compassion on her and said
to her, "Do not weep." —Luke 7:13, NKJV*

One can only begin to imagine the pain this woman must have been feeling as she prepared to bury her only son. As a widow, she had already lost her husband. In that society, he was not only her companion, but her sustenance, her identity, the one who gave her life value. In a land where men were the breadwinners, she had lost her financial stability, her social status, and her future security, but at least she had a son. He would provide her with consolation and companionship, with financial security, and with the assurance that she would have someone to take care of her in her old age. But now her son was dead, and her dreams and hopes were shattered, and her heart was broken with her overwhelming loss. With his death, this widow had no one left.

Throughout the Bible, we find many instances where God instructs His people to care for the widows. For instance, "You shall not afflict any widow or fatherless child" (Exodus 22:22, NKJV); and, "He administers justice for the fatherless and the widow, and loves the stranger, giving him food and clothing" (Deuteronomy 10:18, NKJV). Jesus' own mother was widowed. He had witnessed her sorrow at the death of her life-companion, Joseph, and so great was His love and concern for His mother that while hanging on the cross, Jesus made careful provision for her welfare, leaving her to John's care.

How often do we today overlook the widows in our congregations? Because they have family, we sometimes forget that they have special needs. We forget that God has commanded us to care for them. It is our responsibility, and privilege, to see that they are visited and taken care of. Even if we cannot provide for their every need, we can connect them to the people who can. And let us not forget the widowers in our communities and church families. They are in need of our love and support just as much as the widows.

Father, thank You for reminding us that You care about the widows. Thank You for making special provision in Your Word for the care and support of those who have lost their spouse. Open our eyes to the needs of the widows and widowers in our congregations and in our communities, and may we be an extension of Your love toward them.

The First Mission Field

"Return to your own house, and tell what great things God has done for you."
And he went his way and proclaimed throughout the whole city what great
things Jesus had done for him. —Luke 8:39, NKJV

The demoniac had been isolated from his family and from civilization, living in a cemetery until Jesus cast out the demons. Everyone was afraid of him because of his violent behavior. After Jesus released him from the demons who held him captive, this man's immediate reaction of gratitude was to follow Jesus, but Jesus wanted more than his freedom. He wanted freedom from sin for the man's family and friends. So He sent him home as a missionary.

One can only imagine the surprise of this man's family when they saw their beloved husband and father again. No longer was he wild and scary, but fully recovered, normal, healthy, peaceful, and full of life and joy. He didn't have to take them through a whole set of Bible studies. All he had to do was tell them what Jesus had done for him. His physical, emotional, and spiritual restoration was evident to all, and that was the most powerful sermon he could preach and that they could hear.

Ellen White writes, "No sooner is one converted than there is born within him a desire to make known to others what a precious friend he has found in Jesus. The saving and sanctifying truth cannot be shut up in his heart" (*The Desire of Ages*, 141). We all have our own stories of what God has done in our lives, and when we have the chance we want to tell others of His miracle-working power. Again, Ellen White writes, "Our work for Christ is to begin with the family, in the home. . . . There is no missionary field more important than this" (*The Adventist Home*, 35).

Let us not hesitate to let others see what God has done in our lives, to give testimony of His power through our behavior and our words. When we make mistakes, we must recognize them for what they are, repent, and seek forgiveness. When we do this, others will be drawn to God. They will know that if He can accept us with our imperfections, He can also accept and love them.

Father, reflect Your love through us that others may see not us but You shining through us, and that they may come to know, love, and serve You too.

Let the Children Come

Then they also brought infants to Him that He might touch them; but when the disciples saw it, they rebuked them. But Jesus called them to Him and said, "Let the little children come to Me, and do not forbid them; for of such is the kingdom of God." —Luke 18:15, 16, NKJV

In this story, Jesus is teaching in parables. Many people came to listen to Him and were immediately attracted to Him, not just because of His words but because of His loving, welcoming demeanor. It is His kindness and warmth that encouraged the parents to bring their children to be blessed by Him.

The disciples' response is interesting and somewhat understandable. With people pressing on Him from every side, and with such a busy schedule as Jesus had, they wanted to protect Him. Jesus was not a campaigning politician looking for a photo opportunity holding a child. The disciples felt that holding and blessing the children would distract Him from the important message He needed to present and the miraculous healing people were waiting for. But Jesus reminded them that on His priority list, children rate very high, and that we should remove anything and everything that may keep them from approaching Him.

We would shudder today if we were the parents bringing our children to be blessed by Jesus only to be met with such harshness on the part of His disciples. Of course, we're always more critical as we look at what others do and not so harsh with ourselves, even if we're doing the same thing. If we were His disciples, would we keep children from approaching Jesus?

When we make rules, policies, regulations, traditions, practices, or anything else more important than helping our children come to Jesus, we display the same attitude as the disciples did. When we fail to spend time with our children, teaching them through word and action about Jesus, we are keeping them from knowing Him. This is one of the reasons why daily worship, morning and evening, is so important to our children, because it is during these moments that we bring them to Him so they will come to know and love Jesus as their personal Savior. Invest in your children, and lead them to Christ, that they may become His disciples for life.

Father, forgive us when we have kept our own children from knowing You, and help us to do everything in our power, from this day forward, to lead them to You.

Now I Lay Me Down to Sleep

I lay down and slept, yet I woke up in safety,
for the LORD was watching over me.
—Psalm 3:5, NLT

King David was in danger, knowing that at any moment of the night he might be attacked. He was hunted and cursed by his enemies, but his trust in God was so great that David was able to lie down in peace. Because he knew that everything was in God's hands, he had a sense of complete protection. He was not being presumptuous. He enjoyed a calmness of spirit that can only come from God. For David, the last thoughts of the night were often the first thoughts of the day, and so it should be for us.

Countless children throughout the years have been taught to repeat the simple bedtime prayer, "Now I lay me down to sleep, I pray the Lord my soul to keep. If I shall die before I wake, I pray the Lord my soul to take."

Innocently, children have been taught that we have a soul inside of us which God might decide to keep for Himself. If we think about it, this idea could be scary for a child. Are we teaching our children that God is selfish, choosing each night which soul He will keep and which soul He will return to the child's body so he or she may awake?

As important as it is to pray with our children at bedtime, we need to make sure that we teach them to not fear God. Let us not scare them with the thought that He might decide to keep their soul. Instead, we can help them to enjoy a good night's sleep with the assurance of His watchful care for them while they sleep, and in the morning, teach them to thank Him for His protection during the night. When we do that, we will be teaching them gratitude for each new day. We will be teaching them that God is the Source of life and health. They will learn to express appreciation for those precious gifts. Maybe we could modify the child's prayer to say something like, "Now I lay me down to sleep, I pray the Lord my life to keep. And when I wake to see the light, I'll thank the Lord with all my might."

Father God, thank You for a new day of life and health, and thank You for watching over us last night as we slept.

Lost and Found

*" 'Then get a grain-fed heifer and roast it. We're going to feast! We're going to
have a wonderful time! My son is here—given up for dead and now alive! Given
up for lost and now found!' And they began to have a wonderful time."*
—Luke 15:23, 24, The Message

This is the third of the three parables dealing with the lost and found in
Luke 15. The plot is the same in all three: something/someone is lost,
and when it is found, there's great rejoicing. In the first two, there is a search
for that which was lost until it has been found. In this third one, the lost
comes back on his own.

I can't help but wonder about the family relationships, particularly the
ones that are not mentioned in the story. Where was the mother? Is it possible she had passed away? Maybe that's what affected this child and caused
him to be selfish. At that time, for a child to ask his father for their portion of
the inheritance was the equivalent to wishing the father were dead. Imagine
that for a moment. This young man stands before his father and says to him,
"Dad, I wish you were dead so I could have what belongs to me." That was
just as shocking to the ears of those who heard Jesus' story as it is to us today.

Psychological birth order theory states that the baby of the family tends
to be careless with finances. As the baby in this family, this young man certainly demonstrates bad financial skills. He took what his father gave him
and quickly wasted it on partying and loose living with his friends. It seems
evident that he was somewhat spoiled. He got what he asked for, after all.

It also appears that there was some sibling rivalry between the two
brothers. The younger one wanted to leave the confines of family life. It looks
as though the older brother was a typical first child—organized, responsible,
somewhat egotistical, and jealous of the younger brother who "took his toys."

Even the best of families face conflict and some degree of dysfunction, but
God can still help and bless such a family if we ask Him, and if we let Him.

*Father, thank You that Your Word is more than just a diatribe of theological
platitudes; it is a great study in the psychological principles of human relations.
Help me to use these principles to bless our family and the lives of others.*

The Worship of Sex

With one thrust he drove the spear through the two of them, the man of Israel
and the woman, right through their private parts.
—Numbers 25:8, The Message

After Balaam had pronounced blessings on Israel, he advised Balak on how to make Israel fall, by leading them to have sexual relationships with Moabite women. This would, in turn, lead them to worship their gods. An arrogant man brought a Midianite woman into a tent in broad daylight, flaunting his rebellion and disobedience in front of all the Israelites. When he was made aware of it, Phinehas, Aaron's grandson, drove a spear through them while they were having sexual intercourse.

Some Bible commentators have suggested that the tent Phinehas stabbed them inside of was the shrine of a priestess or cult leader. Phinehas must have seen all this as part of the sexual pagan ritual that was defiling the camp. A plague had broken out in the camp, and he knew that the only way to stop it was to put the guilty to death. So Phinehas took up the spear, and the plague was lifted.

Idolatry is abominable to God and is prohibited in the first four commandments. God also finds sexual misconduct abhorrent; in fact, He dedicates two commandments to that specific sin (the seventh and the tenth commandments). What then could be worse than a combination of the two by using sex as part of a religious cult or ceremony? This man had the audacity to do it so blatantly and arrogantly! If it had not been dealt with immediately, the entire congregation would have been contaminated and destroyed. This drastic measure saved Israel from being wiped out completely.

Since Satan could not get Balaam to curse Israel, he used trickery to make them abominable to God, resulting in the withdrawing of God's blessings from them. Satan is using the same tactics today with great success. The influence of electronic media continues to stealthily invade our lives. Scenes of intimacy, which should be reserved for the privacy of the marital bed, are portrayed with regularity in film and on television. Pornography, which used to be reserved to magazines and dark theaters, is widely available in the privacy of our homes or smartphones. Today's culture is sweeping us away into hedonism and idolatry. The only salvation we have is to die to sin so that we may live for God.

Father, keep me from the contamination of sin that will lead me to the worship of other gods.

Passion Under Control

Now those who belong to Christ have crucified the flesh with its passions and desires. —Galatians 5:24, NET

After giving us a list of what he calls the works of the flesh, Paul gives us a list of the fruit of the Spirit as a contrast, and then ends with today's text. We all have a war to fight against unholy, natural tendencies, appetites, and passions. To win this fight, we must make a decisive, firm, and irrevocable decision to surrender our hearts and wills to Christ so that He may cleanse not just our sins but also every tendency to sin. We need to make that decision every day, and sometimes many times throughout the day as temptations arise.

It is possible that we will get discouraged when we fail, when we try to defeat sin in our own strength instead of relying on God's power, or when we fail to cooperate with God (Philippians 2:12, 13). We may also run into the danger of becoming content with our present accomplishments or of measuring our progress by that of others around us.

Paul reminds us that "those who belong to Christ have crucified the flesh with its passions and desires." As Ellen White wrote to young people, "When we are clothed with the righteousness of Christ, we shall have no relish for sin; for Christ will be working with us. We may make mistakes, but we will hate the sin that caused the sufferings of the Son of God" (*Review and Herald,* March 18, 1890).

It can be very discouraging to know that our internal battle with sin does not get easier, nor does it go away until Jesus comes back for us. That is the reason why the final struggle, what we've come to call the "time of Jacob's trouble," will be more of a mental anguish, wondering whether we have confessed every sin in our lives. Obviously, the first thing is to live in such a way that we remain as close to Christ as possible, so that He may help us to overcome our sin, so that we may grow to hate sin. Secondly, when we do fall, as we probably will, we must ask for forgiveness so He may continue the process of sanctification in us.

Father, please help me to fight this fight. Rescue me from the downward spiral of sin, and set my feet on solid ground so that I may not fall ever again. I want to belong to You today and always.

Marriage and the Impending Crisis

Because of the impending crisis I think it best for you to remain as you are.
—1 Corinthians 7:26, NET

This chapter is one of the most extensive and influential chapters in the New Testament that deals with the subject of marriage, specifically targeted at those who are unmarried. Our text for today forms the basis for Paul's teachings on marriage.

Lest there be any misunderstanding, Paul does not advocate permanent celibacy for everyone nor divorce as a rule from God. His recommendation for those who are single is to be content with that state in life and to dedicate themselves to advancing God's cause, "because of the impending crisis." In his mind, the advantage to not being married is that a single person can give their full attention to God's work without the distractions that come with marriage. Married people must think not just of their own well-being but also the well-being of the person to whom they are married and the children they have conceived. It is understandable, therefore, that they cannot give their undivided attention to advancing the work of God.

Paul is not commanding the single to remain unmarried, and neither is God. He is giving them a new perspective, showing them the opportunities they have to advance God's cause. On the other hand, he tells those who are married to remain married and take good care of their families. They are not excused from service to God. On the contrary, the married can advance the work of God by caring for their families and in this way reach others for Christ.

While Paul believes divorce is not part of God's plan for us, he realizes it is permissible under certain circumstances. If a marriage comes to an end, one should not seek to begin another relationship. Again, his reasoning is that there's very little time until the end.

Paul obviously has a high regard for the soon second coming of Jesus and wants all of us to work hard at preparing ourselves and others for that event. He wants nothing and no one to distract us from that goal. He does not disparage, undermine, attack, or reject marriage in any way. He only reminds us that time is short and that, whatever our circumstance, we should strive to draw closer to the Lord even as His return draws nearer to us.

Father God, use me, whatever my circumstance, whether I am married or unmarried, to reach others for You.

Bless Your Family

Arrangements completed, the people all left for home. And David went home to bless his family. —1 Chronicles 16:43, The Message

David built a tent for the ark of the covenant and assigned the Levites to care for it and to lead in the services of the sanctuary. It was now time to bring the ark to Jerusalem, a symbol of God's presence in the midst of His people. There was a great spiritual revival that day. "So they brought the ark of God, and set it in the midst of the tabernacle that David had erected for it. Then they offered burnt offerings and peace offerings before God. And when David had finished offering the burnt offerings and the peace offerings, he blessed the people in the name of the Lord" (verses 1, 2, NKJV).

It wasn't enough for David to have a public celebration and a corporal revival in Israel. He understood the importance of maintaining that revival at home. "Then he distributed to everyone of Israel, both man and woman, to everyone a loaf of bread, a piece of meat, and a cake of raisins" (verse 3, NKJV). "And he appointed some of the Levites to minister before the ark . . . and to praise the Lord God of Israel" (verse 4, NKJV). As the services concluded and everyone returned to their homes to continue enjoying the blessings of the day, he returned home, not now as the king but as a husband and father, to bless his family.

How important it is for each of us as heads of household to not just simply enjoy the blessings that come our way when we participate in the church services from week to week. We can't just take care of the responsibilities assigned to us for the maintenance and care of the church and then go home and act as if we didn't know Him, the Lord of that church.

We must put David's example into practice more often. As we minister to the people in the church, we must be careful to not fail to minister to our own family and to be a blessing to them. The practice of our faith can't be limited to the walls of the church but must extend to the walls of our home. See what you can do to bless your family in word and action today.

Father, may my words and actions be a blessing to my family, and may we all experience a revival of our faith but also of our relationship daily. May our family life be a reflection of our relationship with You.

Don't Let Your Marriage Dry Up

Drink water from your own cistern, and running water from your own well.
—Proverbs 5:15, NKJV

Solomon warns us about the dangers of falling for a promiscuous woman. This warning should also apply to women, cautioning them against falling for the seductions of men. Sandwiched between are the words of today's text. Take the time to read the entire section, verses 15–20. I love Eugene Peterson's paraphrase of this passage: "Do you know the saying, 'Drink from your own rain barrel, draw water from your own spring-fed well'? It's true. Otherwise, you may one day come home and find your barrel empty and your well polluted. Your spring water is for you and you only, not to be passed around among strangers. Bless your fresh-flowing fountain! Enjoy the wife you married as a young man! Lovely as an angel, beautiful as a rose—don't ever quit taking delight in her body. Never take her love for granted! Why would you trade enduring intimacies for cheap thrills with a whore? for dalliance with a promiscuous stranger?" (Proverbs 5:15–20, *The Message*).

Solomon's counsel is to keep your own marriage strong and your wife happy. When you do, you won't want to have anything to do with another woman. There are several features in this passage that are particularly important. The well is symbolic both of marriage and of the intimacy it should have. Find your wife's body something to delight in, to enjoy. Never take her love for granted. As a warning, he reminds us that an affair with another woman will never compare to the fulfilment of true love or bring the satisfaction found in marriage.

We should also be wary of fantasizing about a relationship with other people. At the first signs of attraction to another woman, turn away before it's too late. Don't rationalize or excuse your actions by saying that your wife is not treating you well or that your marriage is unsatisfying. If this is how you feel, be careful not to say so to people of the opposite gender. This is only opening the door to temptation and sin. Repent, ask for forgiveness, and abide by the consequences of your actions.

Father, strengthen us against sexual temptation and sin, and bless our marriage that it may not just remain intact but that it may grow stronger every day. Help us to guard our hearts and minds against temptation. May the strength of our own marriages serve as an example to others.

Abba, Our Adoptive Father

*And because you are sons, God sent the Spirit of his Son into our hearts, who
calls "Abba! Father!" So you are no longer a slave but a son, and if you are a son,
then you are also an heir through God. —Galatians 4:6, 7, NET*

In this passage, Paul speaks of the role of the law in respect to sin and
sinners. He makes it clear that no one is justified by the law, because that
is not its role. Salvation is a free gift from God to all who believe. God's grace
not only saves us from the penalty of breaking the law but also grants us a
new status as adopted children. When we believe, we are saved and adopted
by God. It's a double status of sorts: we're already His children by creation,
and now we are His by adoption.

First, we are saved from the condemnation of the law; second, we are given
the status of adopted children of God. Now Paul adds a third item. If God is
our Abba, Father, then we are His heirs, and thus we have full access to all
that is His. Adoption is not a lower status than that of sons and daughters.
When people adopt a child, that child has the same rights and responsibilities
and enjoys the same privileges of natural-born children. Adopted children
are not second-class citizens but equal in every respect to those born to their
parents.

These passages are particularly meaningful for those of us who became
orphans at an early age and who have basically nothing, if anything, as a
material inheritance. Those who were adopted at an early age have formed
a relationship with their adoptive parents as though they had been born to
them. Those of us who lost a parent later in life had to learn to live without
that parent for the rest of our lives. But through Christ we are no longer
orphans. We have His Father as our Father. We are now His children by creation and by adoption, a double privilege. And as God's children, we have the
richest inheritance: God Himself gives us His life, which is eternal.

*Thank You, Abba, Father, that we can have a Dad again, that we can be
called Your children, and that You give us the same rights, promises, and privileges of any other child of Yours. We are no longer orphaned but rightly Your
children. And since You are eternal, we will never be orphaned again.*

A Home Divided

"Every kingdom divided against itself is laid waste, and no city or house divided against itself will stand." —Matthew 12:25, ESV

While Jesus uses the example of a kingdom, this principle can also apply to the establishment and maintenance of a permanent home. If we want to have a better chance at a lasting, satisfying marriage and family life, there are a few things we can do to ensure that outcome.

First of all, marry someone with whom you have a shared faith. The most personal, intimate part of a person's life is their spirituality. If you can't share that with your spouse because your faith is very different, how can you truly be one? Many studies have shown that the more differences that exist in a marital relationship, the greater the chance that they will lead to problems and even divorce. When you marry a believer, someone with whom you share your faith and spiritual beliefs, it will bring you closer and keep you close to each other and to God.

One of the most powerful tools God has given us to bring and keep us together as a couple and as a family is daily worship. As we study and pray together, not only are we drawn toward each other, but we're certainly drawn closer to God Himself. Weekly, habitual church attendance adds to the blessings of the daily family worship. When one or both parents stay home while the children go to church, it will prove detrimental to their children's faith.

Besides agreeing on faith beliefs, decisions at home should be made together. This is particularly true of financial decisions (tithes and offerings, home budget, expenses, investments, savings, etc.), and anything else that impacts the well-being of the family. This includes such things as the education of the children, buying a home or a car, and health care.

Another area in which there should be no division is the discipline of the children. The children's discipline should be agreed on by both parents together, and it should be done privately, not in front of the children.

If you don't want a house divided, spend quality time together in recreational activities. The memories we collect during these times keep us together and will remain even after death takes a loved one away. In fact, some of these memories go on through generations.

Father, keep our family together in the bonds of mutual love, and may we rest secure in the knowledge of Your love for us.

Selfless Love

Now there was a famine in the land, and Abram went down to Egypt to dwell there, for the famine was severe in the land. And it came to pass, when he was close to entering Egypt, that he said to Sarai his wife, "Indeed I know that you are a woman of beautiful countenance. Therefore it will happen, when the Egyptians see you, that they will say, 'This is his wife'; and they will kill me, but they will let you live. Please say you are my sister, that it may be well with me for your sake, and that I may live because of you."
—Genesis 12:10–13, NKJV

A bram had already shown his faith in leaving Ur with his family. Later, he would demonstrate his faith by his willingness to sacrifice his son of the promise, Isaac. Yet here, his faith in God's protection is weak. His love for his wife is weaker still. He seemed to be more concerned for his own safety than Sarai's. He was selfish, loveless, and faithless.

Several hundred years after this event, one of Abraham's descendants wrote some of the best words to husbands and wives: "Let nothing be done through selfish ambition or conceit, but in lowliness of mind let each esteem others better than himself. Let each of you look out not only for his own interests, but also for the interests of others" (Philippians 2:3, 4, NKJV). In his classic definition of love, Paul added that love "does not behave rudely, does not seek its own" (1 Corinthians 13:5, NKJV).

True love is protective of the other person. That's why abuse is a contradiction of love. Abusers will always blame the other person for the abuse, accusing them of being at fault, and rationalizing that it was the other person who made them do what they did.

Neglecting the needs of the family also demonstrates selfishness and a lack of true love. Love is not selfish; it does not look at what the other person can do for them but rather at what they can do for the other person. Love does not withhold itself emotionally or physically from the spouse but gives generously. Love aims to meet the emotional and physical needs of the spouse. Love moves one spouse to protect and help the other.

Father, help us to be less selfish and more loving. Help us to love and protect each other so that You may be honored in our relationship and that we may enjoy the type of relationship You planned for us.

Nothing Is Impossible

"Is anything too hard for the Lord? At the appointed time I will return to you, according to the time of life, and Sarah shall have a son."
—Genesis 18:14, NKJV

God first appears to Abram and gives him the promise that he would be a father of many nations and the father of the faith. God also assures him that his lineage would be directly through a son He would give Abram and his wife Sarai. What was Abram's first reaction? He "fell on his face and laughed, and said in his heart, 'Shall a child be born to a man who is one hundred years old? And shall Sarah, who is ninety years old, bear a child?' " (Genesis 17:17, NKJV). Later, God reaffirmed the promise to Abraham, and it was then Sarah's turn to laugh "within herself, saying, 'After I have grown old, shall I have pleasure, my lord being old also?' " (Genesis 18:12, NKJV). It is at this time that God speaks the words of our text for today, "Is anything too hard for the Lord?"

Some of us might have a difficult time accepting that what are impossibilities to us, God can turn into possibilities. There have been many times when couples come to us for help, at the end of their rope, when they feel there's nothing else that can be done to save their marriage. Those who are willing to give God another chance have experienced great changes and a rebirth in their relationships. Sadly, there have also been those who believe that not even God can save their marriage. In a way, they have laughed at God and His promises.

If nothing is impossible for God, and if we submit ourselves to Him, then He can and will heal our diseases, our troubled marriages, our deepest wounds. He can and will rebuild, heal, and reinvigorate our marriages in ways we thought were impossible. So don't give up on God, and don't give up on your marriage. God can make it something beautiful if you put your trust in Him.

God of the impossible, today I thank You for my marriage, for my spouse, and for my family. I thank You for taking two imperfect people and giving us a warm, loving relationship, one where we can help and encourage each other, one where we can love and strengthen each other, and one where we can honor and glorify You. God of the impossible, turn what we think is not possible into the miraculous reality of answered prayer.

Wives and Mothers

"But seek first the kingdom of God and His righteousness."
—Matthew 6:33, NKJV

In many a home the wife and mother has no time to read, to keep herself well informed, no time to be a companion to her husband, no time to keep in touch with the developing minds of her children. There is no time or place for the precious Saviour to be a close, dear companion. Little by little she sinks into a mere household drudge, her strength and time and interest absorbed in the things that perish with the using. Too late she awakes to find herself almost a stranger in her own home. The precious opportunities once hers to influence her dear ones for the higher life, unimproved, have passed away forever.

"Let the homemakers resolve to live on a wiser plan. Let it be your first aim to make a pleasant home. Be sure to provide the facilities that will lighten labor and promote health and comfort. Plan for the entertainment of the guests whom Christ has bidden us welcome, and of whom He says, 'Inasmuch as ye have done it unto one of the least of these My brethren, ye have done it unto Me.' Matthew 25:40.

"Furnish your home with things plain and simple, things that will bear handling, that can be easily kept clean, and that can be replaced without great expense. By exercising taste, you can make a very simple home attractive and inviting, if love and contentment are there.

"God loves the beautiful. He has clothed the earth and the heavens with beauty, and with a Father's joy He watches the delight of His children in the things that He has made. He desires us to surround our homes with the beauty of natural things.

"Nearly all dwellers in the country, however poor, could have about their homes a bit of grassy lawn, a few shade trees, flowering shrubbery, or fragrant blossoms. And far more than any artificial adorning will they minister to the happiness of the household. They will bring into the home life a softening, refining influence, strengthening the love of nature, and drawing the members of the household nearer to one another and nearer to God" (*The Ministry of Healing*, 368–370).

It is too easy, Lord, to become worn down and weary with life's duties and responsibilities. I am too easily distracted. Remind me, Father, to always keep my eyes on You, to seek You first, and all the rest will fall into place.

Honor and Obey?

"Now therefore, my son, obey my voice according to what I command you." . . .
*But his mother said to him, "Let your curse be on me, my son; only obey my voice,
and go, get them for me." —Genesis 27:8, 13, NKJV*

In his old age, Isaac asked his favorite son, Esau, to bring him his favorite meal so that he could then give his son the blessing for the firstborn. Rebekah wanted her favorite son, Jacob, to receive the blessing, so she plotted to get it for him through deceit. She told Jacob what to do to secure it and was willing to take Isaac's wrath and God's wrath upon herself if it would ensure that Jacob received the blessing. The sad thing is that she ended up paying for her actions by never seeing her son Jacob alive again.

The fourth commandment of God's law tells us, "Honor your father and your mother, that your days may be long upon the land which the Lord your God is giving you" (Exodus 20:12, NKJV). In many faiths and cultures, parents are honored, cared for, and obeyed by their children. The question is, How far should we take this command?

First of all, to honor our parents does not mean to obey blindly. There are some limits to what one can and should do in our desire to follow the spirit of this command. We can, and should, try to honor father and mother as long as it doesn't violate any of God's other commands or His will, as long as it doesn't lead to doing anything that's illegal, unethical, or immoral, and as long as it doesn't cause harm or injury to yourself or to others.

When we neglect our spouse in deference to our parents, we could be violating the spirit of this command. In the creation of Adam and Eve, God made it clear that once a couple is married, their spouse assumes the most important position in their life. As Scripture tells us, "Therefore a man shall leave his father and mother and be joined to his wife, and they shall become one flesh" (Genesis 2:24, NKJV). These words are so important that they are repeated three other times in the Bible: Matthew 19:5; Mark 10:7; and Ephesians 5:31. We must be careful to honor our parents while not neglecting our spouse.

Heavenly Father, thank You for the parents with whom You blessed us. May we honor them and show them respect, because by doing so we also honor You.

The Pain of Death

So Rachel died and was buried on the way to Ephrath (that is, Bethlehem).
—*Genesis 35:19, NKJV*

Chapter 35 of Genesis relates in rapid succession three deaths that impacted the life of Jacob and his family. First Deborah, Rebekah's nurse. In sorrow, Jacob names the tree under which she was buried *Allon Bacuth*, which means "oak of weeping."

The second death that impacted Jacob was that of his beloved wife Rachel. As she is dying, she names her son, Ben-Oni, or son of my sorrows, but Jacob, a true optimist, decided his youngest son should have a name expressing hope and courage, a name that would ever remind him of his joy at the birth of his twelfth son, rather than his sorrow at the loss of Rachel, so he names him Benjamin.

The third death that touched Jacob was that of his father Isaac. As far as we know, he left home after deceiving his father into giving him the blessing for the firstborn and never saw his mother again. Now, his joy at seeing his father again is short-lived.

These three deaths were transitional events in the life of both Jacob and his children. While the return to Canaan was a joyful event, these three deaths were a somber reminder of the ups and downs of life. Death is as much a natural part of life as are birth and growing up, since the fall of Adam and Eve. Nevertheless, it is one of the natural stages of life that has the greatest impact on our lives, particularly if it comes suddenly and unexpectedly.

At the same time, the death of a loved one presents us with the opportunity to draw closer together for mutual help, support, and encouragement. It also presents families with the opportunity to heal rifts that might have taken place in the past, and the chance to form strong bonds again.

Father, while death is normal in our lives, it is still painful. When the time comes for us to die, may we be ready, and may we rest in the knowledge that You will take care of our loved ones and bring them the comfort they need during those difficult days of adjustment. May You shelter our children that they may not suffer harm or danger, and may we never experience their death while we, their parents, are still alive. As You promise, may we all hear the voice of Jesus at His return, calling us to eternal life.

The Favorite Son

Now Israel loved Joseph more than all his children, because he was the son of his old age. Also he made him a tunic of many colors. But when his brothers saw that their father loved him more than all his brothers, they hated him and could not speak peaceably to him. —Genesis 37:3, 4, NKJV

The Bible text makes it obvious that Jacob loved all his children. In verse 14, we read that Jacob sent Joseph to look for his brothers to see if they were well. It is also clear that the brothers, although they hated him, did not want to murder him. When Reuben found out Joseph was gone, he tore his clothes in mourning.

Nevertheless, Jacob treated Joseph with more favor than any of his other children. His special treatment of the son of his best-loved wife showed a partiality that increased their jealousy. Jacob already showed favoritism toward Rachel, and now he did the same for her first child, and later, for Benjamin. The result was a sibling rivalry that continued even after their descendants had settled in the Promised Land, ending in the division of Israel in two.

It is not only unwise but unhealthy to favor one child over another. Special treatment toward one child creates jealousy, competition, and rivalry, and in some extreme cases it may even lead to death. Jacob should have known the consequences of favoritism as his own father, Isaac, favored his brother Esau and wanted to give him the blessing for the firstborn even though the prophecy, and promise, belonged to Jacob. As a result of his deceitfulness, he lived in exile for twenty years and was never able to see his mother alive again. Now, as a result of his partiality, he would not see his favorite son for almost as long.

We must do all in our power as parents to treat all our children as individuals of value, without favoring one over the other. We need to be fair to all, consider their differences, and encourage them in their strengths while helping them to grow where needed.

Father, You give us all the same opportunities for salvation, and You pour out Your blessings richly to all. Even when we misuse the resources You so plentifully give us, You continue to pour out Your richest blessings on us. Help us to be loving, patient, and kind to all our children, showing no favoritism to any one over the others, but loving them all equally as You love us.

November

The Family as a Missionary Field

Whatever your hand finds to do, do it with your might.
—Ecclesiastes 9:10, NKJV

Our work for Christ is to begin with the family in the home. The education of the youth should be of a different order from that which has been given in the past. Their welfare demands far more labor than has been given them. There is no missionary field more important than this. By precept and example parents are to teach their children to labor for the unconverted. The children should be so educated that they will sympathize with the aged and afflicted and will seek to alleviate the sufferings of the poor and distressed. They should be taught to be diligent in missionary work; and from their earliest years self-denial and sacrifice for the good of others and the advancement of Christ's cause should be inculcated, that they may be laborers together with God.

"But if they ever learn to do genuine missionary work for others, they must first learn to labor for those at home, who have a natural right to their offices of love. Every child should be trained to bear his respective share of service in the home. He should never be ashamed to use his hands in lifting home burdens or his feet in running errands. While thus engaged, he will not go into paths of negligence and sin. How many hours are wasted by children and youth which might be spent in taking upon their strong young shoulders, and assisting to lift, the family responsibilities which someone must bear, thus showing a loving interest in father and mother. . . .

"God designs that the families of earth shall be a symbol of the family in heaven. Christian homes, established and conducted in accordance with God's plan, are among His most effective agencies for the formation of Christian character and for the advancement of His work. . . .

". . . As the Lord's heritage, they will be qualified to take up the work where they are. A light will shine from such homes which will reveal itself in behalf of the ignorant, leading them to the source of all knowledge. An influence will be exerted that will be a power for God and for His truth" (*Testimonies for the Church*, 6:429, 430).

Dear Lord, please help us to train our children to be productive so their lives are lived serving You, for Your glory. May our home be a true reflection of Your love.

Bless Your Children

So he blessed them that day, saying, "By you will Israel bless, saying, 'May God make you like Ephraim and Manasseh.'" So he put Ephraim before Manasseh.
—Genesis 48:20, NET

As Abraham and Isaac had done before, so now Jacob pronounces a blessing, this time on Joseph and his children, whom Jacob claims as his own and after whom two of the twelve tribes are named thereafter. Giving a blessing was a custom in biblical times. Fathers would pronounce a blessing on their children, older people would bless the younger generation, and those with authority would bless those beneath them. It was this custom that led mothers to bring their children to be blessed by Jesus. By their act, they recognized Him as someone worthy of respect, as someone with authority, and as someone whose blessing on their children would be a special mark and privilege.

It seems that we have abandoned the practice of blessing our children for fear that we may be taking on God's role, or that we may be imitating other faith communities. Since it is a biblical practice, there's nothing wrong in implementing it. The question is not whether we should do it, but rather, when and how.

As to the when, if parents begins early enough, their children will grow up hearing them pronouncing blessings over them and will not be uncomfortable with it later in life. As I (Claudio) was growing up, it was a custom in our family that whenever we left home or ended a phone conversation with our mother, we would ask for her blessing, and her common response was to say, "God bless you, my child." To this day, as an adult and after more than fifteen years since her death, I miss hearing her saying those words to me. So, a blessing may be pronounced when you part company, when your children leave for school or work, when you end a phone conversation, an e-mail, or a text message, or before they go to sleep.

As to the how, the context may be a situation they may be dealing with, a blessing for protection, or on their studies, or for them and their children, et cetera. Maybe this would be a good time for you to revive this beautiful biblical practice.

Father, bless our children today, wherever they may be and whatever they may be doing. Protect them, and may they sense Your presence in their lives and turn to You, at this moment, as we think about them.

Love Protects Children

But when she was no longer able to hide him, she took a papyrus basket for him and sealed it with bitumen and pitch. She put the child in it and set it among the reeds along the edge of the Nile. His sister stationed herself at a distance to find out what would happen to him. —Exodus 2:3, 4, NET

Despite the Egyptians' plans to destroy the Israelite male children, Moses was born. He was cared for by his own mother, and the challenge of keeping him hidden became more difficult every day. Fearing that he would be discovered and harmed, she hid him in a basket, away from populated areas, and under the watchful care of his older sister.

All of us are shocked when we hear of parents abandoning their newborn babies in fields, inside boxes or plastic bags, left to die or perhaps hoping they will be found and saved. It is so unlike a loving parent to not want to care for and protect their child. In contrast, Moses' mother risked her own safety to ensure that her son survived.

How can we ensure the safety and protection of our children today? Sometimes we think that doing the bare minimum, providing them with food, clothes, and shelter, is all that's required. But children need so much more than just the bare necessities. In order to ensure good emotional development and health, you need to spend as much time with them throughout their growing years as possible. As protectors of your children, you need to provide them with a safe environment in which to grow up. This not only means a house where they will be sheltered from the weather but also keeping negative outside influences from coming in. This would include what the media brings into our living rooms, computers, and smartphones, and also the influence of friends and school.

Guarding and protecting our children also involves giving them an example that they can safely follow, and making sure we treat them with the respect we wish them to emulate. It means that we provide for their physical, emotional, and spiritual needs.

Father, as much as we wish to protect our children, it is not possible to be with them all the time. We pray that You surround them with Your protection, with Your holy angels, and with the guidance of Your Holy Spirit. May no harm or danger come their way, and through their life experience, may they see Your hand in their lives.

Dedicated Families

And Moses said, "We will go with our young and our old; with our sons and our daughters, with our flocks and our herds we will go, for we must hold a feast to the LORD." Then he said to them, "The LORD had better be with you when I let you and your little ones go! Beware, for evil is ahead of you. Not so! Go now, you who are men, and serve the LORD, for that is what you desired." And they were driven out from Pharaoh's presence. —Exodus 10:9–11, NKJV

Time and time again, Pharaoh refuses to allow the Israelites to leave Egypt. It's obvious he suspected they were going to leave for good, and he would not risk losing his work force. At first he told them they could hold their worship service in the land. Then he told them they could go in the wilderness, but not very far. Finally, he agreed to let the men go but not the women or the children.

It is clear that Pharaoh never really intended to allow the Israelites to leave Egypt and stubbornly tested God's resolve to free them from slavery. After each plague, the display of God's mighty power should have been apparent, but instead of submitting to God's command, he hardened his heart and refused to allow them to leave. God was not about to compromise with Pharaoh. He wanted to set His people free—all of His people.

When it comes to the worship of God, it is not enough for the men to do so without the participation of their wives and children. The worship of God must be part of family life. Studies show that children drop out of the church a lot faster when they attend church by themselves, or when they attend with only one parent. But when children attend church with both their parents, they tend to remain members of the church longer, many for a lifetime. Men are the priests of their household, and as such they should lead in the worship of the Lord both at home and at church. This worship experience cannot and should not be a personal, private experience only, but a family experience as well.

Loving Father, thank You for the opportunity You give us to be Your children, and that together as a family, we can worship You. Help us to set aside daily times for private and family worship and to dedicate ourselves and our families to Your service.

What God Did for Me

"And you shall tell your son in that day, saying, 'This is done because of what the Lord did for me when I came up from Egypt.' " —Exodus 13:8, NKJV

God had delivered the Israelites from their life of slavery in Egypt after a long struggle with Pharaoh. The annual Passover service was established not just as a celebration of their deliverance but as a teaching tool for future generations, particularly for children. Every year, as the family gathered around the Passover table and the children asked, "What is this?" the parents responded in two ways: The Lord delivered me from slavery (verse 8), and the Lord brought us out of slavery (verses 14–16). One is the personal experience, the other the corporate experience of deliverance from slavery.

The point of the annual Passover celebration or commemoration was not simply to have a national holiday. The Passover was designed to teach the children for generations to come about God's marvelous power of deliverance, and to remind them that they were slaves but God gave them freedom. Children are taught through songs, through food items, through games played, and through the questions asked that God displayed His power on their behalf.

The questions sprinkled throughout the Passover service reflect something that is very special not just for the Israelites but for all of us who have suffered under the slavery of sin. To the first question the answer is, "The Lord delivered me." This reflects the fact that salvation is first of all a personal matter. The second answer reflects what God has done for us as a people: God delivered us all.

While most of us do not celebrate Passover, the Communion service gives us the same opportunity to explain to our children what Jesus has done for us. As we consider the foot-washing part of the service, we can explain to them that Jesus gave us an example of humility and service: we need to learn to be of service to others. We can also explain to them what the bread and the grape juice represent, and most important, the sacrifice of Jesus accomplished for each of us as individuals and what it assured for us as a people— eternal life on the earth made new. "What is this?" is an open door for a deeply spiritual conversation with our kids.

Father, thank You for delivering me from the bondage of sin, and thank You for guaranteeing for us, through the death of Your Lamb, eternal life with You.

Always Burning

"And you shall command the children of Israel that they bring you pure oil of pressed olives for the light, to cause the lamp to burn continually. In the tabernacle of meeting, outside the veil which is before the Testimony, Aaron and his sons shall tend it from evening until morning before the Lord. It shall be a statute forever to their generations on behalf of the children of Israel."
—Exodus 27:20, 21, NKJV

The Levites had the responsibility of caring for and maintaining the sanctuary, including the seven-branched lampstand, which was to be kept always burning. To that effect, the priest would go in and replenish the oil and the wicks and ensure that its fire would never go out.

After the destruction of Solomon's temple, the Jewish people found some oil for the lamps and immediately got the light going again. They began at once the preparation for more oil so the light would continually be shining. While the oil they found should have lasted only a couple of days, according to their story, the fire lasted nine days, until the new batch of oil was ready. The celebration was great and gave way to the beginning of the annual commemoration of that event through the festival of Hanukkah, or the festival of lights, which takes place at around the same time as the Christmas season.

It is important that in the marriage and in the home the light always be burning. For instance, we need to keep the light of God burning at home by having daily, personal, couple, and family devotional time, and Bible study and prayer. As a couple, you must keep the light of love burning daily by practicing its manifestations as Paul listed them in 1 Corinthians 13. The light of romance must be burning daily as we look for ways to show our spouse through words and actions how much we love them and how much we care for them. The light of kindness and patience must burn daily, particularly when we are hurt by others, whether intentionally or carelessly. The light of forgiveness must burn daily to get rid of the darkness of resentment and hatred.

Let's keep our light burning at home and in our relationships so others may see it and find hope for their own families.

Father, help us to keep the light bright and burning at home. May this light burn so brightly that it will help to dispel the darkness in our lives and in this world.

Holy to the Lord

"You shall also make a plate of pure gold and engrave on it, like the engraving of a signet: HOLINESS TO THE LORD." —Exodus 28:36, NKJV

As part of the priestly garments, the high priest was to wear a breastplate which had a stone for each of the twelve tribes of Israel, and a turban with a gold plate engraved with the words, "Holiness to the Lord." The breastplate was significant in that "whenever Aaron enters the Holy Place, he will bear the names of the sons of Israel over his heart on the breast piece of decision as a continuing memorial before the Lord" (verse 29, NIV). As to the gold plate on the turban, "It will be on Aaron's forehead, and he will bear the guilt involved in the sacred gifts the Israelites consecrate, whatever their gifts may be. It will be on Aaron's forehead continually so that they will be acceptable to the Lord" (verse 38, NIV). God's people were to be on the mind and over the heart of the high priest whenever he performed his ministry in the sanctuary.

The role of the husband as the high priest of the family is also very significant. His family must be on his mind and in his heart every time he prays and every time he performs any act before God. His words and actions must be guided not only rationally but also emotionally, with the mind and the heart.

The words engraved on the gold plate attached to the turban—Holiness to the Lord—are a call and a challenge to purity, to be separated from any influence that would distract from service to Him, and to refrain from any thought, word, or action that is contrary to His will. Those words demonstrate a total, undivided commitment to God, which can only strengthen our commitment to our spouse. It was such commitment that kept Joseph from agreeing to Potiphar's wife's invitations. It was that commitment which kept Daniel praying when it was decreed that prayer was an act of treason. It was such commitment that kept Jesus faithful to His ministry all the way to the cross. It is such commitment we as husbands and wives are called to today, to be holy to the Lord, and wholly our spouse's.

Loving Father, today we dedicate and consecrate ourselves to You anew. We want to be holy to You, and we want to be wholly our spouse's. Strengthen us daily that this commitment we make today remain firm forever.

No Compromise

"Take heed to yourself, lest you make a covenant with the inhabitants of the land where you are going, lest it be a snare in your midst." —Exodus 34:12, NKJV

While it may seem strange to us that God would tell His people to go into the land He was giving them and completely wipe out all the people already living there, we must understand the reasons. The basis for this command is found in the text for today in its entirety. Making a treaty with those who worshiped other gods would lead to involvement in their sacrificial communal meals (verse 15), to intermarrying with their daughters (many of whom were spiritual and/or physical prostitutes to their gods) (Hosea 4:13, 14), and to making images to those false deities (Exodus 34:17; cf. 20:4), as they had already done with the making of a gold calf (Exodus 32:4).

It wasn't only the danger of rejecting God and accepting idols, it was what the worship of those idols would lead them to do. Temple prostitution and the sacrifice of children were only some of the practices of these heathen nations that Israel passed through. God was trying to protect His people from such horror. Sadly, in their blindness and stubbornness, the Israelites disobeyed God. They spared the people, entered into relationships with them, accepted their gods, and engaged in the rituals of child sacrifice and temple prostitution.

The application for us as parents today should be as clear: Don't compromise principle, and choose carefully what you expose your children to. I am amazed at how lightly parents today take the issue of their children's school or church attendance, among other things. They don't seem concerned with what their children are watching, playing with, or reading. The lessons from the Israelites should serve as a warning to all of us: Watch carefully what you expose your children to, what they read, what they watch, whom they associate with, and where they go to school. These decisions could have eternal consequences.

Father, today as during the Exodus, we as parents need all the wisdom You can possibly give us to make the right decisions. It may not be any more challenging to be a parent today than in other times, but this is our time, these are our challenges, and these are the decisions we have to make. So, please endow us with the courage, the strength, and the wisdom to do what is right, even if it's not popular with our children or others.

The Colors of Our Family

Of the blue, purple, and scarlet thread they made garments of ministry, for ministering in the holy place, and made the holy garments for Aaron, as the LORD had commanded Moses. —Exodus 39:1, NKJV

Moses gives a very detailed account of all the materials used for the building of the sanctuary, its furnishings, and the clothing worn by the priests. As he closes the book of Exodus, he now reviews again all that was made, how, and with what. The exquisite materials and colors must have made this portable structure not only beautiful but awe-inspiring. Just a look at the sanctuary, even from a distance, must have caused the people to pause and contemplate its significance as God's abiding place on earth.

It occurs to me that we, as members of the family, come from so many different places. We have different families, and our cultural, educational, financial, and racial backgrounds are varied, all contributing to make us who we are. It is as though God is an artist, skillfully weaving all these threads into a beautiful, colorful tapestry. That's why abuse of any kind is so damaging. It pulls at our heartstrings and God's, and stains the beauty of the family. That's why divorce is so traumatic. It tears and mars God's beautiful handiwork and causes deep wounds that can never be completely restored.

Whenever a sacrifice was performed, the priests were to sprinkle some of the blood on the altar and on the curtain dividing the Holy Place from the Most Holy Place, marring its beauty. I can only imagine what it must have looked like when, day after day, more blood was sprinkled on that curtain. The smell of coagulated, rotten blood must have added to the impact the defilement of this holy structure had on those who witnessed it. It was only at the end of the year, on the Day of Atonement, when the sanctuary was cleansed both physically and spiritually.

As families, we need the daily sprinkling of the blood of Jesus upon us. His perfect sacrifice will take our imperfect lives and make them a sweet aroma before His Father. It is indeed His sacrifice on our behalf that purifies us and guarantees for us eternal life. Only in His blood can we be a complete, beautiful, colorful family for Him.

Father, thank You for the beautiful weaving You've made of our family. Please make its beauty shine for Your glory and for our well-being.

Abraham's Tree

And Abraham begot Isaac. The sons of Isaac were Esau and Israel.
—1 Chronicles 1:34, NKJV

A *genogram* is a pictorial display of a person's family relationships and goes beyond a traditional family tree by showing the hereditary patterns and psychological factors that punctuate their relationships. I recall the words, "I, the LORD your God, am a jealous God, visiting the iniquity of the fathers upon the children to the third and fourth generations of those who hate Me" (Exodus 20:5, NKJV). While some look at this text as God's way of punishing succeeding generations for the sins of their fathers, what God was trying to show was that the sins, habits, or practices of one generation are transmitted to others and often get worse.

By studying King David's family, we can see at least three patterns that emerge. The first is their religious experience. God referred to David as "a man after His own heart" (1 Samuel 13:14, NKJV), but David committed adultery and murder. Solomon asked for wisdom and was granted the answer to his prayers plus riches and power, but then he married hundreds of wives who led him to mix the worship of God with that of pagan deities. His son, Rehoboam, ignored God altogether and practiced idolatry like the nations surrounding Israel.

A second pattern that emerges is their sexual sin. Much like people and rulers of the time, David married several wives and even committed adultery with Bathsheba before marrying her. His oldest son, Amnon, raped his half-sister Tamar. David's other son, Solomon, continued his father's pattern by marrying seven hundred wives and adding three hundred concubines to his harem (1 Kings 11:3). Following his example, his son Rehoboam had eighteen wives and sixty concubines (2 Chronicles 11:21).

A third pattern we see is the sibling rivalry and rebellion present in every generation. David had problems with his older brothers who didn't think much of him (1 Samuel 16; 17). Absalom, one of his sons, murders one of his brothers, Amnon, in revenge for raping his sister Tamar, and then rebels against his own father. Rehoboam, Solomon's son, continues this pattern of rebellion and disobedience to God, and so Israel is divided in two.

What negative patterns do you see in your family? It is in your power to stop them before the new generation continues them.

Father, may we learn from our past so we don't repeat with our children mistakes and sins that will continue for generations in the future.

For This Child I Prayed

"For this child I prayed, and the Lord *has granted me my petition which I asked of Him. Therefore I also have lent him to the* Lord; *as long as he lives he shall be lent to the* Lord." *So they worshiped the* Lord *there. —1 Samuel 1:27, 28, NKJV*

The situation between Hannah and Penninah, Elkanah's wives, was very tense. In that society, childlessness was seen as a curse from God. Penninah, who had several children, picked on barren Hannah, who must have felt singled out by God and others for unfair treatment.

But Hannah prayed for a child, and God granted her a son. In fact, she later had three more sons and two daughters (1 Samuel 2:21). Hannah evidently was a praying woman who continued to pray not just until Samuel was born but for her other children for as long as she lived.

Christian couples should pray for God's gift of children beginning with whether they should even have any or not. While children are a wonderful blessing and add so much to the joy of a family, they can also bring a lot of stress and heartache. Many marriages have fallen apart after the birth of a child.

Once the mother is pregnant, the couple should redouble their prayers for the life, health, and protection of both the mother and the baby inside her. These prayers should not only be offered up individually in the silence of our hearts, but aloud, as a couple. What a wonderful way for the growing baby inside the mother to get used to his parents' voices, by hearing them pray for him!

I am sure that Hannah followed the life of her son, Samuel, from a distance, and that she continued to pray for him daily. As he received God's call to be His prophet, she didn't stop, but rather prayed more earnestly than before. Praying for our children does not stop at their birth but must continue throughout their lives and ours. When they take their first steps or say their first words. When they go to school for the first time, or when they graduate from college. When they play with their friends, or when they marry their best friend. Pray for your children without ceasing.

Father, we pause right now to pray for our children. May they sense Your presence in their lives this day, and may they come to know You, love You, serve You, and share You all the days of their lives.

The Journey of Forgiveness

And to Joseph were born two sons before the years of famine came, whom Asenath, the daughter of Poti-Pherah priest of On, bore to him. Joseph called the name of the firstborn Manasseh: "For God has made me forget all my toil and all my father's house." And the name of the second he called Ephraim: "For God has caused me to be fruitful in the land of my affliction." —Genesis 41:50–52, NKJV

After Joseph's interpretation of Pharaoh's God-given dream of the coming fourteen years, Pharaoh elevated him to second-in-command of the kingdom. Because of the famine, Jacob sent all his sons, except for Benjamin, to find food that would ensure the survival of his family.

When his brothers arrived in Egypt, Joseph recognized them immediately and tested them to see if they still had the same feelings of rivalry and jealousy that led to his enslavement in Egypt.

Pharaoh gave Joseph a wife with whom he had two sons, whose names reflect Joseph's emotional journey. This journey encompassed so much: the love of his father, the hatred of his brothers, the temptation of Potiphar's wife, and the respect of Pharaoh. Now Joseph completed his experience with a journey of forgiveness.

A significant factor of this biblical story is forgiveness. The first step is always acknowledging and recognizing the hurt that took place. Joseph was obviously hurt by the feelings and actions of his brothers, by Potiphar's wife, and finally by Pharaoh's butler who forgot him in prison. Feelings of hurt may take us to a time of anger, and this is the second step toward forgiveness. By the time Joseph was made second in the kingdom, he was able to take the final step in this journey: healing. That last step is reflected in the names of his two sons, as seen in our text for today.

Forgiveness must be an integral part of every marriage and family, because conflict is inevitable and hurt will occur at one point or another. The difference between a relationship that survives and one that breaks apart is the ability to go through this journey of forgiveness so that healing may take place, so that intimacy is restored, and the relationship may flourish and thrive.

Father, help us to take this journey of forgiveness as soon as any hurt takes place, so that our relationships may not suffer and so that healing and growth may happen quickly. May we soon return to the intimacy You designed for us to have at home.

Respect the Unmarried

"If a man entices a virgin who is not betrothed, and lies with her, he shall surely pay the bride-price for her to be his wife. If her father utterly refuses to give her to him, he shall pay money according to the bride-price of virgins."
—Exodus 22:16, 17, NKJV

This section of the book of Exodus begins with a series of civil regulations for the newly freed Israelites. Our Scripture verses for today speak of enticing a young girl and taking advantage of her youth and naiveté to take sexual advantage of her. According to this law, anyone who takes advantage of a young girl should be obliged to marry her. In a parallel passage (Deuteronomy 22:23, 24), we learn that if she was betrothed to another, and she is intimate with another man, both she and the man should be put to death. The point of the law here mentioned is that a man should respect a single young girl. At the same time, this law states that marriage is an honorable thing and teaches that children should not marry without their parents' approval.

While women didn't seem to enjoy the equality with men that God designed, God did not want men to simply take advantage of the young and vulnerable. That's the reason why there are so many regulations regarding the orphan and the widow, and in our text for today, for a virgin girl. While girls could marry at an early age, they were to follow the regular customs regarding courtship, betrothal, engagement, and marriage. Men, for their part, were not to take advantage of a young girl but were required to take all the steps necessary to protect her and ensure her physical and financial protection.

We today must also ensure that the young and vulnerable are not taken advantage of, neither physically nor, more specifically, sexually. We should take every step and every precaution to ensure their safety. At the same time, we should be careful not to encourage early dating. Since the frontal lobe of the brain, which is the seat of judgment and decision-making, is not fully developed until about age twenty-five, early dating can be a great disadvantage to a healthy relationship. Finally, young people would do best to listen to their parents in these matters instead of going against their wishes and advice.

Loving Father, thank You for Your care and concern for the young and vulnerable, and for reminding us that marriage and sex are to be cared for in a sacred manner.

A Deeper Conversation

"Why do you not understand My speech? Because you are not able to listen to My word." —John 8:43, NKJV

In a comic strip, the wife says to her husband, "I know you believe you understand what you think I said, but I'm not sure you realize that what you heard is not what I meant." We may talk a lot, but we don't always communicate properly. In his book, *Making Love Last Forever*, Gary Smalley refers to five levels of intimacy in communication, moving from the superficial to the meaningful.

The first level, the most superficial one, is the use of clichés. "What's up?" or, "How are you?" fall into this category. In fact, if other people respond with a personal account of how they really are doing, we would probably become uncomfortable. If we are honest with ourselves, we don't really care to know the answer to this question.

The second level is that of facts. At this level we share basic information such as, "Traffic was heavy today," and, "Did you know Mike and Sue had a baby boy?" Much like level one, this is very shallow communication. It is safe because we're usually sharing information that is not important to either the speaker or the listener.

The third level is the level of opinions. At this level you may hear things such as, "It's warm today, isn't it?" or, "How can anyone like that music? I can't stand it!" We get to this level when we begin to trust others. When we trust, we make ourselves more vulnerable.

The next level takes us deeper as we deal with feelings. At this level we say things such as, "I was hurt when you forgot our anniversary." While opening up this way can be scary, it can help us reach a deeper level of love for one another.

The final, deepest level of healthy communication is that of expressing our needs. You may say things such as, "I just need you to listen to me for a few minutes." If we feel secure in our relationship, we will take the risk of really opening up.

While we can maintain a superficial relationship as we communicate at the first three levels, only in going deeper, into the fourth and fifth levels of communication, will we experience the richest, most satisfying of relationships.

Father God, help me to be a better listener and a more careful speaker so that my family and I may enjoy healthier communication.

The Other Side of Forgiveness

Confess your trespasses to one another.
—James 5:16, NKJV

Christian psychologist Garry Chapman writes that "good relationships are always marked by a willingness to apologize, forgive, and reconcile. The reason many relationships are cold and distant is because we have failed to apologize" (Gary Chapman and Jennifer Thomas, *The Five Languages of Apology: How to Experience Healing in All Your Relationships* [Chicago: Northfield, 2006], 22). He suggests that just as we have different love languages, we also give and receive apologies differently.

The first language of apology, *expressing regret,* is probably the most commonly used today. That's when we say something such as, "I'm sorry." We just have to make sure our expression of apology is sincere, that it is not generalized by saying something such as, "I'm sorry *if* I did anything to you," or following up your apology with the word "but," which might be an attempt to shift blame to the other person. Naturally, that makes them defensive.

The second language of apology is *accepting responsibility,* which happens when you say, "I was wrong." This is recognition of wrongdoing on your part. *Making restitution,* the third language of apology, is following the example of Zacchaeus (Luke 19), and is achieved by saying something such as, "What can I do to make it right?"

Chapman says the fourth language of apology is *genuinely repenting.* Repentance is recognition of wrongdoing combined with the honest intention to not repeat it. Chapman writes: "Most people do not expect perfection after an apology, but they do expect to see effort. When the spouse gives up quickly after a failure and reverts to old behavior with no further effort to change, the apology is considered insincere" (ibid., 86).

The final language of apology, writes Chapman, is *requesting forgiveness.* While you cannot demand forgiveness, you can invite your loved ones to extend to you that gracious gift.

Keep in mind that it is important that we each learn our spouse's needs and aim to fulfill them. Husbands and wives usually have different apology preferences, and therefore it's crucial that we learn our spouse's preferred method and use it as soon as we do anything that may have hurt them.

Father God, when I am wrong, please help me to recognize it and ask for forgiveness from my loved ones.

Not a Funny Yoke

Do not be unequally yoked together with unbelievers. For what fellowship has righteousness with lawlessness? And what communion has light with darkness?
—*2 Corinthians 6:14, NKJV*

English isn't easy to learn as a second language, and pronunciation is a particular problem. For the untrained ear, the words *piece, peace,* and *peas* sound amazingly similar, almost indistinguishable. For many, the words *cheap, chip, ship,* and *sheep* can turn tongues into twisted pretzels.

For those of us who speak Spanish as our first language, the letter *J* in English sounds like the letter *Y* in Spanish, making the words *yolk, yoke,* and *joke* challenging. Of course, we know that the yolk is the yellow part of the egg, a yoke is a wooden bar or frame by which two draft animals (such as oxen) are joined at the heads or necks for working together. And we all know a joke is something said to generate laughter. Understanding these three words can make a world of difference.

In our text for today, Paul warns the Corinthians to not fall away from the faith and bring pain upon themselves by bearing the wrong type of yoke. The word *unequally* presents a picture of one of the partners being less committed than the other, being less disciplined than the other, being weaker than the other. It's like rowing a boat with only one oar—you will end up going in circles. The yoke itself is an instrument that binds for mutual help and support so that both partners can work together and benefit each other as a result.

Sadly, many choose to marry outside their faith and find themselves carrying an almost unbearable burden. Marriage counselors and social scientists have recognized for many years that one of the most important ingredients in a marriage is the spiritual commitment to God and to each other that both spouses have. A marriage where two people don't share the same faith in God and hope in His salvation can weigh heavily on their lives and keep them from enjoying true intimacy and the kind of love God wants us to enjoy. Regardless of what language we speak, this unequal union is not a funny yoke!

Our heavenly Father, help me to make decisions concerning my future marital life very carefully, always keeping You at the center of my life and relationship. Help me to live my faith and my commitment to You so that both my spouse and I can be drawn closer to You and to each other.

A Sacred Circle

"As the Father loved Me, I also have loved you; abide in My love."
—John 15:9, NKJV

There is a sacred circle around every family which should be preserved. No other one has any right in that sacred circle. The husband and wife should be all to each other. The wife should have no secrets to keep from her husband and let others know, and the husband should have no secrets to keep from his wife to relate to others. The heart of his wife should be the grave for the faults of the husband, and the heart of the husband the grave for his wife's faults. Never should either party indulge in a joke at the expense of the other's feelings. Never should either the husband or wife in sport or in any other manner complain of each other to others, for frequently indulging in this foolish and what may seem perfectly harmless joking will end in trial with each other and perhaps estrangement. I have been shown that there should be a sacred shield around every family.

"The home circle should be regarded as a sacred place, a symbol of heaven, a mirror in which to reflect ourselves. Friends and acquaintances we may have, but in the home life they are not to meddle. A strong sense of proprietorship should be felt, giving a sense of ease, restfulness, trust. . . .

"How many dishonor Christ and misrepresent His character in the home circle! How many do not manifest patience, forbearance, forgiveness, and true love! Many have their likes and dislikes and feel at liberty to manifest their own perverse disposition rather than to reveal the will, the works, the character of Christ. The life of Jesus is full of kindness and love. Are we growing into His divine nature? . . .

"Picture a large circle, from the edge of which are many lines all running to the center. The nearer these lines approach the center, the nearer they are to one another.

"Thus it is in the Christian life. The closer we come to Christ, the nearer we shall be to one another. God is glorified as His people unite in harmonious action" (*The Adventist Home,* 177–179).

Dear Lord, what beautiful imagery: a sacred circle! Help us to encircle our family within this sacred space. May it be a safe place where each one is free to grow, and learn, and love. May we reflect Your character as we fix our eyes on You. Fill us with Your beauty and grace!

To Love and to Cherish

A man must love his wife as a part of himself.
—*Ephesians 5:33, TLB*

There is a story from the Jewish Talmud that has a wonderful lesson about love in marriage. An emperor said to Rabbi Gamaliel, "Your God is a thief, because it is written, 'The Lord God caused a deep sleep to fall upon Adam, and he slept; and He took one of his ribs.'" The rabbi's daughter said to her father, "Leave him to me; I will answer him." She then said to the emperor, "Give me an officer to investigate a complaint." "For what purpose?" he asked. She replied, "Thieves broke into our house during the night and stole a silver ewer belonging to us, but left a gold one behind." "Would that such a thief visited me every day," he exclaimed. "Was it not, then, a splendid thing for the first man when a single rib was taken from him and a woman to attend upon him was supplied in its stead?" she retorted (A. Cohen, *Everyman's Talmud,* 160).

How true. And how different our marriages would be if we treated our spouses as God's special gift to us. As careful as we are with gifts we receive from those we love, how much more careful should we be with the gift God gives us in our spouses.

In our text for today, Paul gives us another reason for cherishing our spouse: they are a part of ourselves. During the wedding ceremony, a miraculous thing happens as God unites the two into one. It's as if that rib God took from Adam's side was not officially his to take care of. Because our spouses are now part of us, we will want the same good things for them that we want for ourselves.

I'm afraid many feel that an occasional expression of affection is sufficient to keep the flame of love bright and strong. Not so. We must fuel our relationships daily so they may shine brightly. It doesn't have to be large, expensive things, but rather simple things like a compliment. Listen attentively, encourage them to have some alone time; but also plan for some time together, help around the house, and be quick to forgive. These actions serve to remind your spouse how much you cherish them.

Father God, I don't always appreciate the gift You have given me in my spouse, nor do I always show it to them. Help me to show my spouse how much I love and cherish them.

The Mother

"And He said to me, 'Behold, you shall conceive and bear a son. Now drink no wine or similar drink, nor eat anything unclean, for the child shall be a Nazirite to God from the womb to the day of his death.' " —Judges 13:7, NKJV

What the parents are, that, to a great extent, the children will be. The physical conditions of the parents, their dispositions and appetites, their mental and moral tendencies, are, to a greater or less degree, reproduced in their children.

"The nobler the aims, the higher the mental and spiritual endowments, and the better developed the physical powers of the parents, the better will be the life equipment they give their children. In cultivating that which is best in themselves, parents are exerting an influence to mold society and to uplift future generations.

"Fathers and mothers need to understand their responsibility. The world is full of snares for the feet of the young. Multitudes are attracted by a life of selfish and sensual pleasure. They cannot discern the hidden dangers or the fearful ending of the path that seems to them the way of happiness. Through the indulgence of appetite and passion, their energies are wasted, and millions are ruined for this world and for the world to come. Parents should remember that their children must encounter these temptations. Even before the birth of the child, the preparation should begin that will enable it to fight successfully the battle against evil.

"Especially does responsibility rest upon the mother. She, by whose life-blood the child is nourished and its physical frame built up, imparts to it also mental and spiritual influences that tend to the shaping of mind and character. It was Jochebed, the Hebrew mother, who, strong in faith, was 'not afraid of the king's commandment' (Hebrews 11:23), of whom was born Moses, the deliverer of Israel. It was Hannah, the woman of prayer and self-sacrifice and heavenly inspiration, who gave birth to Samuel, the heaven-instructed child, the incorruptible judge, the founder of Israel's sacred schools. It was Elizabeth the kinswoman and kindred spirit of Mary of Nazareth, who was the mother of the Saviour's herald" (*The Ministry of Healing*, 371, 372).

Thank You, Lord, for providing the strength needed to mothers everywhere today.

How Young Is Too Young?

For as a young man marries a virgin, so shall your sons marry you; and as the
bridegroom rejoices over the bride, so shall your God rejoice over you.
—Isaiah 62:5, NKJV

A young woman was pleading with tears streaming down her freckled face. After a six-month, whirlwind romance, the not-quite-eighteen-year-old was just into her sixth month of marriage. She had begged her mother to sign the permission forms so she could marry her twenty-two-year-old boyfriend. The pastor who married them told them they were perfect for each other, but before their first anniversary, they had filed for divorce.

Unfortunately, such tragedy happens all too often. Ellen G. White wrote of a young bride: "Poor girl! She married when but a mere child, needing her mother's care. It was an unhappy event. . . . This child was too young for a companion. . . . Already they are parted, she hating him most thoroughly and he without love for her" (*Testimonies on Sexual Behavior, Adultery, and Divorce* [Nampa, ID: Pacific Press®, 1989], 19).

Most divorces occur within the first five years of marriage. The strongest predictor of divorce is the age of the couple. The younger they are at the time of marriage, the greater their chances of divorce. The percentage of those divorced or legally separated who were fifteen to seventeen years of age or younger at the time of their first marriage is about three times more than the percentage of those divorced or legally separated who were twenty-four to twenty-six at the time of their first marriage.

I wish I had been the pastor who counseled this young couple. I would have offered them several premarital inventories and tests such as PREPARE/ENRICH, Taylor Johnson Temperament Analysis, and the Myers-Briggs Type Indicator. I would have asked them to read several books, and I would have spent at least six sessions over a period of two or three months in order to help them make a more well-informed decision on their marital future.

While there are many factors that play an important role in the success or demise of a marriage, one can at least minimize some potential problems by waiting until later to take this life-changing step. Unfortunately for this young couple, they were not privy to this advice. It could have prevented a lot of problems, headaches, and heartache.

Father God, help us to encourage Your people to wait, to prepare, and to continue to grow and mature until the right time.

Thanks-Living

I will give You thanks in the great assembly; I will praise You among many people. —Psalm 35:18, NKJV

Pecos Higgins was born on the Gulf Coast of Texas in 1883. At age six, some of his friends got him drunk. While still small, he worked on cattle ranches up and down the Pecos River. With only eight months of traditional schooling, he became one of the most colorful cowboy poets of the Wild West.

After two stays in the Texas State Penitentiary, he joined the 101 Ranch Wild West Show, touring North America and Europe. Unfortunately, Pecos Higgins drank enough whiskey over the next few years to fill up the Texas Dam. He married and divorced five times, bootlegged, cursed, gambled, and shot his way through half a century.

Amazingly, Pecos survived till the age of seventy-one, but as a battered, hopeless, drunken wreck. Some Christians found him on a deserted Arizona ranch. Through their loving care, Pecos met Jesus Christ as his personal Savior and Friend. He described his newfound joy: "I feel now like I imagine a little hound pup does when his eyes first come open. . . . I'm as happy as a fed pig in the sunshine." In discovering Jesus, Pecos also found a new attitude of gratitude.

We should do the same. It's so easy to focus on what's wrong in the world. There are wars and turmoil overseas. Closer to home, our job may not fulfill us and friends let us down. Children are sick or get bad grades. Our spouse is in a bad mood and the relationship seems broken. To cope with such negativity, we must develop an attitude of gratitude.

First of all, say "thank you" to everyone you appreciate: your mom, your kids, your friends, your spouse, your child's daycare provider, or the helpful woman behind the checkout counter. Learn to appreciate nature. Take a walk and give thanks for all the beauty you see, whether it's the stars above or the mountains in the distance. It also helps to remember those less fortunate. Even if you have car payments and college tuition weighing you down, many are far worse off. With gratitude for what you have, remember that it's always a great time to write a check, though small, to a favorite charity. Make it your goal to begin and end each day, each week, each month, and each year by expressing thanksgiving.

Father God, help me to be thankful for everything, even in the darkest of circumstances.

Surviving Thanksgiving Dinner

*It is good to give thanks to the L*ORD*, and to sing*
praises to Your name, O Most High. —Psalm 92:1, NKJV

Not every family's Thanksgiving dinner resembles a Norman Rockwell painting. While family ties can be close at this annual gathering, so can family tensions. The good news is that there are ways to make this celebration less stressful for yourself and your loved ones.

To begin with, you need to have realistic expectations. Sometimes we have preconceived notions of how the dinner should be, how people should behave, and how we should feel. If you go into your holiday celebration making fewer assumptions about what will unfold, you will be less likely to be disappointed and more likely to appreciate what everyone brings to the table—literally and figuratively. Forget perfection and be flexible with the rituals or traditions. Be open to new traditions, and don't do something just because you think it's expected. When it comes to those joining you at Thanksgiving dinner, don't try to change anyone, and treat people lovingly all year round. In other words, don't expect one dinner to compensate for a year's worth of neglect.

In addition, let other people help. It should go without saying that if you're a guest, help your host—but if you are the host, let your guests shoulder some responsibility for the holiday. For instance, you may choose to take turns each year hosting the dinner with other members of the family or with friends. While you're at it, make it a potluck: you provide the main course, the guests provide the sides. While some may choose to go to a restaurant, others may wish to spend part of the day volunteering and helping others. Take some time to find volunteer opportunities in your community.

Thanksgiving doesn't need to be a big production. Someone once told me that Thanksgiving is a day to feed and nurture one another, and it doesn't have to give us physical or emotional indigestion in the process. You might avoid conflict by refraining from disciplining other people's children and being critical. If possible, accommodate special dietary needs, and don't feel insulted if guests can't eat everything you've prepared. Remember to be flexible, to respect differences, and to relax and laugh when the unexpected happens.

Father God, may our Thanksgiving gatherings be a time to reflect, a time to rejoice, and a time to build new memories. Help us to use this annual event as an opportunity to strengthen our family bonds.

Thank You for My Family

*Therefore I will give thanks to You, O Lord, among the
Gentiles, and sing praises to Your name.* —Psalm 18:49, NKJV

While I didn't grow up with lots of worldly goods, I did enjoy the warm embrace of a loving mother and the example of a good, responsible father. Then a massive heart attack took my father's life when I was fifteen years old. Two years later, the U.S. Embassy in Colombia, my homeland, issued our legal papers, and we moved to our adoptive country, the United States of America. I suppose I could have concentrated on my losses: fatherless at fifteen; separated from home, country, and friends at seventeen. But a month after we arrived in the United States, we celebrated our first Thanksgiving, which helped us put our new life in perspective. Though separated from our homeland, we had a new home. We had lost family and friends, but we still had one another. Although we were away from the church of our birth, we found a new faith that provided us with greater hope. So in the midst of our negative circumstances, God provided us with many positives to focus on.

Matthew Henry, well-known Bible commentator, was robbed of his wallet. Understanding his duty to give thanks in everything, he meditated on this incident and recorded in his diary the following: "Let me be thankful, first, because he never robbed me before; second, because although he took my purse, he did not take my life; third, because although he took all I possessed, it was not much; and fourth, because it was I who was robbed, not I who robbed."

Keeping all this in mind, I am thankful too. I thank God first for my family with whom to spend these holidays. Second, because even when my wife and I don't see eye to eye, we have eyes to see the good in each other. Third, because even though our daughters don't always do as we wish, they're mature enough to make their own decisions. Fourth, because even though we may not have a perfect family—and who does?—our love for each other, our love for God, and His love for us keeps us together through life's most difficult times.

Consider this question: Have you expressed gratitude for your family? If the answer is No, there is no time like the present to begin.

Father God, thank You for Your love. Thank You for the life and health You give us daily and for the eternal life You have promised.

The Three Teams

So He came to Nazareth, where He had been brought up. And as His custom was, He went into the synagogue on the Sabbath day, and stood up to read.
—Luke 4:16, NKJV

You may not realize it, but a football team actually consists of three separate teams: offense, defense, and special teams. The offense's job is to move toward the goal and score as many points as needed to win the game. The defense is supposed to stop the opposing team from moving downfield and scoring. The special teams must help both defense and offense accomplish the goal of winning the game by defeating the opponent.

Parents need to approach the critically important task of raising their children in much the same way as a football team. We can compare a football team's offense to our influence at home. A winning home provides children with a healthy environment where they receive the nourishment and protection they need to grow up healthy and strong. It requires daily communion with God through Bible study and prayer so their spiritual nature may be strengthened and made ready for daily battles against the enemy of souls. Without a strong offense, the other two teams have an uphill battle.

We can liken church life to a football team's defense. It complements the home life, reinforcing the lessons learned beneath our roof in Sabbath School programs and meaningful worship services. This draws our children closer to God and into the fellowship of other believers their age. Paul wrote that we should not neglect "to meet together, as is the habit of some, but encouraging one another, and all the more as you see the Day drawing near" (Hebrews 10:25, ESV).

Church schools function in much the same way as a football team's special teams. Godly teachers and a committed staff can seal in the minds and hearts of our children the love of God and the hope of eternal salvation once the groundwork has been established at home and at church.

While we have compared the two here, the gridiron battles of sports cannot begin to compare to the war for our children's souls. May we take advantage of every minute and employ all three teams—home, church, and church schools—to make our young people winners in this life and for eternity.

Father God, bless our children that they may enjoy the benefits of the three teams—home, church, and church school—to help them for service in this world and for eternity.

The Best Family Vacation

To whom He said, "This is the rest with which you may cause the weary to rest,"
and, "This is the refreshing"; yet they would not hear. —Isaiah 28:12, NKJV

For several years our family saved up airfare miles on the credit card, hoping to visit a small town thousands of miles from our home. Sixty miles south of Madrid, we arrived at that special place, the town of Consuegra, from which our family derives its last name. The castle and seven windmills overlooking the town—even the city sign—are etched in our family memory bank forever. That's really what family vacations are about: an opportunity to build memories that, years later, keep us united, even when many miles separate us.

Even though the number of vacation days has grown from twelve to fourteen per year, most employees leave three or more of those days unused. Even while on vacation, they may still check e-mail or answer their phones.

Why not be more intentional about making your family vacation a real vacation? It might be an active getaway or one more relaxing. Active vacations may include hiking, snorkeling, or traveling to multiple places. In the United States, each state has unique vacation possibilities—start with the United States Capitol, museums, monuments, national parks, and any special attractions available. Outside the United States, without going too far, Canada is a wonderful country to explore. To the south, Mexico has great vacation places like Cancún and the amazing Aztec and Mayan ruins. Others may prefer a relaxing vacation in a cabin by a lake, camping, or on a beach someplace. Still others may choose to take vacation time to spend a week at camp meeting or on a mission trip.

Even Jesus recognized that we all need some time off and that it is good to just get away with those closest to us (Mark 6:31). About this event, Ellen White comments: "[Jesus] says to those who are worn and weary. It is not wise to be always under the strain of work and excitement, even in ministering to men's spiritual needs; for in this way personal piety is neglected, and the powers of mind and soul and body are overtaxed" (*The Desire of Ages*, 362).

So take a vacation with your family, and plan to make it the most enjoyable, memorable time you can. In doing so, you build unforgettable memories that last a lifetime.

Father God, help us to take time to rest and recharge our spiritual, physical, and emotional batteries.

Extreme Home Makeover

*Unless the L*ORD *builds the house, they labor in vain who build it; unless the L*ORD *guards the city, the watchman stays awake in vain. —Psalm 127:1, NKJV*

For several years, there was a show on television that surprised families with a complete home makeover. It was amazing to see how in seven days, a run-down, dilapidated house could be transformed into a mansion. We were moved by the stories of these families and sometimes even cried with them as they saw their new home for the first time.

While every parent wants to provide their children with the best home they can afford, it seems to me that we as parents have not always had our priorities straight. We may think that if we have the largest house, the most expensive vehicles, and all the latest toys and technology, our children's needs will be fulfilled. Conversely, we believe that if we are not able to provide them these luxuries, we have failed them. Perhaps we need an extreme home makeover, and it can begin with three simple things.

The first is worship. Set aside time each day to worship God as a family. Establish a habit of coming together every morning and/or evening in worship. The second step to a home makeover is prayer. While many go to church faithfully each week, they often go the rest of the week without talking to God at all. We need a makeover in daily communion with our Father. About this, Ellen White says, "They should make the season of family prayer a season of special interest, and in this way they will be obtaining an education that will fit them to become a benefit to the church" (*Review and Herald,* October 22, 1889). Notice that she is speaking specifically of family prayer and not just personal prayer.

Finally, let us invest in our children's education. This begins at home. It continues at church from week to week as we attend Sabbath School and the worship service, learning with and from others. It culminates in the experience of a good Christian school, where dedicated teachers share through their lives and words the love of Jesus.

We may not be able to change our humble dwelling into a large mansion, but we can transform our families into something that is truly out of this world.

Father God, eternal results begin with very small changes here on earth. Help us to experience a makeover in our home and family that will bless us forever.

NOVEMBER 27

The Miracle Eyes

"For I will forgive their iniquity, and their sin I will remember no more."
—Jeremiah 31:34, NKJV

Leafing through the pages of our wedding album recently, I looked into the faces of the two young people staring back at me. How young we were! Mere babes, really. Of course, we didn't think so at the time. Back then we looked at each other and saw only happiness, eternal youth, and the fulfillment of all our dreams. Such is the innocence of youth.

On my nightstand is a photograph taken on the day of our thirty-fifth wedding anniversary. How different we look! We're carrying a few more pounds, some wrinkles, and a little less hair with a sprinkling of gray. But our smiles are just as radiant, perhaps more so, which makes me realize that as much as I enjoy seeing the optimism of newlyweds, I think I prefer observing those who've been married for decades. Those are the faces that tell stories of battles lost and won; celebrations and disappointments; griefs and joys: a journey shared. There are often experiences that remain untold, however, and these include the struggles between husband and wife. It's not a bad thing for them to remain untold. In this social-media-crazed, hyperconnected world we live in—it is appropriate that some things remain solely between husband and wife.

I'm grateful my spouse doesn't feel a need to tell the world every time I mess up. I confess that I sometimes mess up frequently. Some of these messes are small and are easily cleared up, and it's important to take care of them as they happen. We've all experienced times when an accumulation of little messes end up resulting in a major catastrophe.

Then there are those mistakes that are not so small. These can be devastating to a marriage, especially if they result in a loss of trust or respect. Though our actions may bring about a crisis, it can provide an opportunity for deeper growth and healing. These times are never easy, but there's something that can help ease the heartache: the gift of forgiveness. Remember the way you looked at your spouse on your wedding day? The grace of forgiveness can help you see that love is a miracle and that mistakes can be forgiven.

Dear Lord, nothing hurts more between a husband and wife than betrayal. A loss of trust can devastate a home. Please grant me a forgiving heart that truly forgives and forgets—just the way You forgive me.

A Kiss for Good Health

Let him kiss me with the kisses of his mouth—for your love is better than wine.
—Song of Solomon 1:2, NKJV

A group of German psychologists, physicians, and insurance company representatives researching the secrets of long life and success made a surprising discovery. The answer is simple and free: kiss your spouse each morning when you leave for work. The researchers reported that people who kiss their spouses every morning have fewer automobile accidents on their way to work than those who omit the morning kiss. Morning kissers miss less work because of sickness and earn 20 to 30 percent more than non-kissers. According to the researchers, "A husband who kisses his wife every morning begins the day with a positive attitude."

The National Center for Health Statistics reported in 2004 that married people are healthier than non-married adults. There are two major theories for this. First, marriage may protect your health. For instance, married couples may have advantages in terms of economic resources, social and psychological support, and encouragement in healthy lifestyles. A second possibility is marital selection, the theory that healthy people get married and stay married, whereas less healthy people either do not marry or are more likely to become separated, divorced, or widowed.

But just as a healthy marriage is good for your health, an unhealthy marriage can be detrimental as it can be a source of enormous stress. A study of newlyweds found that hostile and negative behavior was associated with a decline in immune system response, causing a number of health consequences, such as slower wound healing and greater susceptibility to infections.

Intuitively, we know that a bad marriage is not good for your health, and researchers have found that divorce or cohabitation is not a better alternative. It is essential, therefore, to actively invest in the health of our marriage. When we do, we will not only be happier but we will be healthier too.

An online search can yield a large number of results showing the positive benefits of a good, healthy marital relationship, both to the spouses and to their children. We could spend lots of time reading those studies, but because I want to enjoy good health, avoid car accidents, earn more money, and have a healthier marriage, I'm going to stop here and go kiss my wife before we leave for work. Go ahead, you do the same.

Father God, help us to have a strong, healthy marriage for our benefit and as a blessing to our children.

Enjoy What You Have

So we, Your people and sheep of Your pasture, will give You thanks forever; we will show forth Your praise to all generations. —Psalm 79:13, NKJV

Someone has diagnosed the disease of modern Americans as affluence—either having too much or wanting too much. It seems that most people believe that if they cannot live like the Johnsons next door, they cannot possibly be happy. For many families, financial difficulties are the number-one problem they face, even if they have more money than most other Americans or most other people in the world.

The authors of the book *The Day America Told the Truth* discovered some disturbing trends in their research. When Americans were asked, " 'What would you give up to get ten million dollars?' 25 percent said they would abandon their family forever; another 25 percent said they would abandon God and the Church; 16 percent said they would leave their wives. In many homes, money has become king."

God is quite interested in this issue as well. The Bible has more than five hundred verses about prayer, around five hundred verses that discuss faith, but more than two thousand references to money and possessions! Of the thirty-eight parables in the Bible, sixteen of them—almost half—are about money.

Maybe we should be more interested in appreciating the things we have instead of wanting more. We could change our view of things by taking a few simple steps. First of all, transfer ownership of everything to God. Nothing really belongs to us; we are simply stewards. If we recognize this, then we should tithe and give offerings joyously. We don't have to understand everything about how tithing works; we just need to know that it does (2 Corinthians 9:6–8).

Well-being does not simply fall in our lap, so we need to work hard. God's plan is for us to earn our bread by the toil and sweat of our brow. Work is satisfying, molds character, and develops gratitude, appreciation, and value. A very practical step is to make a realistic budget and keep accurate records. The absence of an accurate record of spending keeps couples from making good financial decisions. At the same time, escape the bondage of debt. A familiar phrase from wedding ceremonies, "Till death do us part," has tragically become, "Till debt do us part."

Father God, You have given us so much, and compared to what millions around the world have, we are truly rich. Help us to be content with what we have rather than want what we don't have.

The Family That Eats Together

Now it came to pass, as He sat at the table with them, that He took bread, blessed and broke it, and gave it to them. Then their eyes were opened and they knew Him; and He vanished from their sight. —Luke 24:30, 31, NKJV

I remember coming home after school to the delicious aromas emanating from the kitchen. Immediately, my mouth would water as I envisioned what I smelled. A few minutes later, with all of us gathered around the table, we enjoyed another meal prepared by my mother's loving hands. As we shared the rice and lentils, the soup and the salad, we discussed that day's activities. I remember hearing about my brother's band practice, my sister's typing test, and my dad's endless stories and jokes. Research shows that those meals were not just nutritious to our bodies but they were also making a lasting impact on each of our lives.

There are many parents who feel that the most important thing is to have their children involved in as many extracurricular activities as possible. They shuttle the kids to sports activities, music lessons, and art classes, and in between they stop at a fast-food place for a quick bite. Studies show that the more often families eat together, the less likely kids are to smoke, drink, do drugs, get depressed, develop eating disorders, and consider suicide. They are far more likely to do well in school, eat their vegetables, learn big words, and know which fork to use.

Today's research reflects these words from yesteryear: "When the family gathers alone around breakfast or dinner table, the same courtesy should prevail as if guests were present. . . . Let the conversation be genial, and suited to the little folks as far as possible. Interesting incidents of the day's experience may be mentioned at the evening meal, thus arousing the social element. If resources fail, sometimes little bits read aloud from the morning or evening paper will kindle the conversation" (Ellen G. White, *The Health Reformer,* February 1, 1874).

Now that our daughters are living on their own, we look forward to each opportunity we have with them to sit down together to share a meal and good conversation, and to build lasting memories. So, turn off the TV, let the phone go unanswered. Instead, make every effort to enjoy at least one daily meal as a family, and rejoice in the glow of special moments.

Father, help us to guard the family meals as sacredly as the time of worship and rest.

December

Preparing for the Long Drive

*Lord, You have heard the desire of the humble; You will prepare their heart;
You will cause Your ear to hear. —Psalm 10:17, NKJV*

When our youngest daughter began driving lessons, we became acutely aware of how little actual training it takes for a young person to get their driver's license. In her case, she had to attend ten hours of classwork, then perform fourteen hours of on-the-road learning—half of those as a passenger watching another student drive. Essentially, in seven hours she was supposed to master the skills necessary to drive a car on the streets and highways of our country.

We, as parents, made sure she drove many more hours with us in the car, coaching her before we felt comfortable enough to allow her to take her first solo drive. Even then, we required many more hours driving by herself before she was allowed to drive, for short distances, with friends in the car. And yet most people spend more time preparing for a driver's license test than they do preparing for marriage. Indeed, in many cases the church has contributed to the increase of divorce rates by marrying people who are inadequately prepared for marriage.

For many years, our Catholic friends have been requiring all couples wishing to be married to go through a premarital preparation course. But non-Catholic churches have been more lax in their approach. The North American Division of the Seventh-day Adventist Church has been more intentional regarding this issue by recommending the use of the inventory PREPARE/ENRICH, and offering training to pastors everywhere in the use of this instrument. Couples taking the inventory receive the benefits of a computer analysis of their relationship, the *Building a Strong Marriage Workbook,* and several sessions with a trained pastor or counselor who can guide them through a discussion of some of the most important issues they will face. We encourage pastors not to marry couples unless they have had ample time to prepare them for the lifelong journey of marriage.

If you are considering marriage, ask your pastor to help you prepare for your life together before you become engaged. It gives pastors great satisfaction to perform the wedding service for couples who have made proper preparation and who are committed to the idea of marriage God's way.

Father, may those considering marriage take the time to prepare for their lifetime together with the help of a trained pastor or counselor so that they experience love for a lifetime.

Single in the Church—Part 1

"If you are wise, you are wise for yourself, and if you scoff, you will bear it alone."
—Proverbs 9:12, NKJV

We have talked to many unmarried people and asked them to share with us their experiences as Seventh-day Adventists.

One single adult shared that one of the positive things about not being married is that he has more freedom to decide to do things on the spur of the moment, without having to take anyone else into account. He can go home and relax without anyone asking him to do things or making demands on his time.

Another single adult shared that having time for herself provided opportunities to study for a graduate degree. She confessed that if she had been married she might not have been motivated to do so. She has been able to spend time as a missionary, once on very little notice, simply because the need was there and she felt God calling her. In addition, she has had plenty of time to think, pray, and read, which she loves, as an introvert.

What defines a person in the church? One single person said, "It is following Jesus with all my heart that defines me. If singleness is part of that, or if marriage or family is part of that, it is still simply a part; the true focus is Jesus." Several others said they have come to realize that the most important thing in life is not having a spouse but having a strong connection with Jesus. In the words of another active single disciple of Jesus, "I am interested to see but content to wait for whatever God may have planned for my future—with full assurance that either way I will receive my crown of life!" Many unmarried people who have devoted their lives entirely to Christ tell us that the ultimate goal for their lives is to be like Jesus. "Even though I would like to be married at some point," a single explained, "more than anything I want Jesus. If following Him means I stay single, then I wouldn't have it any other way. But if this path He is leading me on takes me to marriage, that's good too. I have learned that marriage is not the destination—Jesus is! That helps me to be content and gives me purpose, even when other others do not always understand."

Father, whether we are married or single, help us to focus first and foremost on our relationship with You.

Single in the Church—Part 2

But I want you to be without care. He who is unmarried cares for the things of the Lord—how he may please the Lord. But he who is married cares about the things of the world—how he may please his wife. —1 Corinthians 7:32, 33, NKJV

It's probably a given that most singles would like to find a spouse, yet some have been hurt by a bad relationship in the past, and others have simply not found the right person yet.

As if these challenges were not enough, many singles have to deal with the thoughtless comments and actions of other people, many of them members of the church they attend. They are even stereotyped as career driven or anti-marriage. Sometimes people seem to think that a single person has a lot of money to spend, and therefore expect more from them than from the married. The reality is that it is common for singles to have less money than those who are married. One single expressed a painful concern when she wrote, "I have noticed that some married people feel they shouldn't interact with single people because of something unspoken, that some are afraid the single person will have an affair and break up marriages. I know that happens, and I am sorry. However, somehow the church needs to have general friendship times with mixed groups."

Some singles have very strong family ties and are really doing fine, but many singles could use extra friendship and support. Many times single people wonder if they will have someone to sit with in church or if they will have to sit alone. They sometimes wonder if they will have something to do with other people on Sabbath afternoons or whether they will have to go home by themselves, again.

Unmarried adults in general plead for church members, married or unmarried, to respect them and not treat them as an anomaly of nature. Our challenge as church members is to see them as brothers and sisters and surround them with our love and support. We can make them our mission field not with the purpose of getting them married but rather with the goal of helping them grow into the image of Jesus Christ and be His disciples—a goal we should all have. We must be to them the family they need, the family God calls us to be.

Father, may those of us who are married be sensitive toward and inclusive of those in our church who are not.

What Does God Think About My Son?

God told them, "I've never quit loving you and never will. Expect love, love, and more love!" —Jeremiah 31:3, The Message

A s we were walking down the hallway of the church where we were having camp-meeting presentations, one mother approached us with her concern. "My son just told me he is attracted to men; I didn't know what to say to him. What does God think about my son?"

I wonder, what would Jesus say to this mother's son? I imagine the first thing He would say is, "I love you, and I want a relationship with you." We all struggle with the reality that we are sinners and, as a result, separated from God. But God loved us enough to send His own Son to show us His love for us, and He wants us to know that He will never give up on us.

I imagine Jesus would also tell this mother's son, "I know you struggle. I see how others treat you at times. Please never forget that My grace is sufficient for you." I think Jesus would also tell him, "I am not finished with you yet, and if you trust Me, I will help you through the challenges you face until you are a perfect reflection of Me. I don't just want you to be happy, I want you to be holy" (see Philippians 1:6).

As we listened to the anguished cry of this mother, we sensed her unspoken question: *Was it something we did that caused him to be this way?* In reality, though many point the finger at the individual or their parents, no one knows what causes homosexuality. Those who choose to point an accusing finger are pointing it indirectly at the God that created them. To this mother and her son, I imagine Jesus would say, "I'm not finished with you, or him, yet. But trust Me, your challenges of today pale in comparison with what I have in mind for you in eternity. Walk with Me, and I will one day soon take you to live with Me."

There are so many things Jesus would tell that mother's son, and us, and it all could be summarized in what the prophet Jeremiah wrote: "I've never quit loving you and never will. Expect love, love, and more love!"

Father, there are many things I don't fully understand—but I trust You. Continue to do Your work in our lives until we are a perfect reflection of You.

Traveling With GPS

"You shall follow what is altogether just, that you may live and inherit the land which the LORD your God is giving you." —Deuteronomy 16:20, NKJV

Several years ago we purchased a GPS. We chose "American Jill" as the voice that provides us with directions, and so we have come to call our GPS "Jill." I don't always follow Jill's instructions and sometimes find myself explaining to her why I've chosen an alternate route. Jill never argues with me but rather, in her always calm voice, tells me she's recalculating and then gives me new instructions to get to my destination.

In my lifelong journey to heaven, I have a GPS—God's Plan for my Salvation. God Himself has set the coordinates and the destination, and it is His calm, quiet voice that guides me each step of the way. There are times when, instead of following His perfect ways, I take a detour, choosing to go my own way. I rationalize it and try to explain to Him why I'm taking this side trip as though I'm trying to convince Him that I know better. He doesn't argue back but remains calm and simply draws up a new plan for me to follow. At times that plan is for me to make several right turns until I get back on the original road. At other times He tells me to make a U-turn—that is, to repent. He knows that the best way is not always the main highway, and instead He takes me through smaller, less traveled, but safer roads, for "broad is the road that leads to destruction, and many enter through it" (Matthew 7:13, NIV). And I know that if I follow God's Plan for my Salvation, I will reach my destination safely and faster. When I don't listen to His voice, I end up lost, afraid, and despondent. Following God may not always make sense, the way is not always clear, and at times it seems as if we're fighting against all the traffic going in the opposite direction. But I have found that GPS has never been wrong, and when I look in my life's rearview mirror, it all makes sense. I can clearly see God's loving hand guiding me and holding me, even when I've chosen to go my own way rather than trust in Him.

Father God, help us to listen closely to Your voice and follow Your plan for our salvation, so we may all reach the destination Jesus has gone to prepare for us.

Romancing Your Wife

I have come to my garden, my sister, my spouse; I have gathered my myrrh with my spice; I have eaten my honeycomb with my honey; I have drunk my wine with my milk. —Song of Solomon 5:1, NKJV

Our wives are often starved for affection, their most important emotional need, and even the smallest of efforts on our part can build the balance on our accounts in their love banks.

To begin with, your wife's schedule is probably full from morning to night. Help her to do the dishes, take out the trash, or make sure she never has to put gas in the tank. Give her flowers throughout the year, and not just on Valentine's Day or your anniversary. Give her flowers for no reason other than to brighten her day. The message you give her is that she's still number one!

Contrary to what we may think, it's best to never surprise her. Now, you can plan the surprise date, birthday party, picnic, or trip, but it would be best to tell her what you are cooking up. If she likes your idea, she will look forward to it and brag about you. On the other hand, if the idea is kind of a bomb and she would not like it, you get to rework the plan to her liking.

When it comes to sex, don't rush it. Your wife takes care of you in ways you sometimes don't even realize. Ask her questions about herself. What has she been thinking about besides the kids, money, health, or what she is making for dinner that night? What are her dreams for the two of you, or what are her personal goals? How can you encourage her as she works toward them? Intimacy is not just about the sex, it is about the heart. Sex is not the objective, but rather the reward both of you get to share. God created it both for our pleasure and as a healthy romantic connection.

A very important part of romancing your wife is to pray with and for her every day. Let her know you are praying for her in whatever challenges she may be facing. Also, let her know that you need her. When you are vulnerable with her, this builds trust and shows your confidence in her.

Father God, help me to romance my wife today as I did in our earliest days, and may we together reap the results in a strong, healthy, happy marriage for a lifetime.

A Memorable Anniversary

Let the heavens rejoice, and let the earth be glad;
let the sea roar, and all its fullness. —Psalm 96:11, NKJV

Wedding anniversaries are opportunities to celebrate one more year of life together, despite any challenges or troubles that may have come our way. Don't take them lightly, and don't take your spouse for granted. Make those occasions memorable.

Look your best. While this should go without saying, we get too comfortable and let go of our appearance as the years pass. Does she hate your beard? Trim it, or chop it off. Does he love it when you wear heels? Take them out of the back of the closet, dust them off, and put them to use. It may not seem like a big deal to you, but it will mean the world to your spouse.

Build anticipation for this important day by sending your spouse flowers, love notes, or little gifts leading up to your anniversary. It will set the tone for that special evening and will have them looking forward to the actual celebration.

Don't be predictable. To make this anniversary special, do the unexpected. While traditions are good, it might be better to once in a while change the pattern. Instead of going to the same place, eating from the same menu, or doing the same thing, plan something different. Spontaneity will keep the relationship fresh and new.

Take notes throughout your marriage on those things they have always wanted to have or to do, and see if you can make it happen for them. Open your ears and you will find that they are communicating every day what they would like.

Throughout the evening, let your spouse know how much you appreciate and cherish them. It is important for both husbands and wives to hear praise on occasion. Gratitude goes hand-in-hand with marital satisfaction, and the more appreciative you are, the happier you both will be.

Don't forget to capture the moment. You don't want to go through all this planning and preparation for it to last one night. Save little memorabilia from your anniversary celebration, such as ticket stubs and pictures. Put all those items in a memory book or box so you can be reminded of how special the day was.

These simple ideas will help you to fall in love with each other all over again and to remember your anniversary for years to come.

Father God, may we celebrate every year of our life together. Every year is an accomplishment, a joy, and a memory to treasure.

Single Parent but Not Alone

Behold, God is my helper; the Lord is with those who uphold my life.
—Psalm 54:4, NKJV

Parenting is not particularly easy. If you are a single parent, the challenges may seem like an insurmountable task. While the circumstances may vary, here are a few simple things that single parents can do to help minimize the stress in their lives and to increase the joy they find in parenting.

You do not need to parent your children alone. Partner with God. He is willing to co-parent with you. He treasures you and your children, and He awaits your invitation for Him to join you in your parenting journey. You also need to take care of yourself. There is a good reason why the instructions for airplane emergencies say, "In the case of a loss of cabin pressure, a mask will fall from the compartment above you. Place the mask over your own face before you place it over your child's." If you do not first care for yourself, you will find it difficult to care for your child.

If you are parenting alone, you are probably trying to maintain your home alone too. That means the laundry is piled high, there are dishes in the sink, the floor needs scrubbing, and there is the next meal to prepare. You may wish to keep your house in pristine condition, but keep in mind that the most important investment you can make with your time is connecting with your children.

You may also consider partnering with other single parents. You could trade child-care responsibilities to give each other time to be alone, time to run errands, or time for private reflection. It is also possible that other parents may have expertise in some areas that may be beneficial to the entire group. A single father may offer his services as a handyman in exchange for someone else fixing meals for his family. A single parent who is a teacher may be able to provide some after-school tutoring in exchange for house cleaning, yard work, et cetera.

While it may be very difficult, don't let bitterness or regrets gnaw at your heart. We all want to do our best. Don't allow yourself to feel guilty or to believe that you are not a good parent or are not doing enough for your children.

Father God, bless me, as a single parent, to be able to take care of my children who are also Your children.

God's Got Your Back

God is our refuge and strength, a very present help in trouble.
—Psalm 46:1, NKJV

Single parents face more challenges than those who are still married. But there are a few things that can help minimize the stress in their lives and increase the joy they experience in parenting.

Positive communication with your child's other biological parent, where possible, can be very beneficial for all involved. If you are able to work together as a team to do what's best for your child, despite your own differences, your parenting burden will be lessened, and your child will reap the benefits of having both parents actively involved in their life. This is not always an easy task, so it must be bathed in prayer. Also, do not fall into the trap of talking about your child's other parent in negative, hateful ways. It puts your children in a very difficult position.

Partner with your child's teachers. Because you are busy working to support your family and also taking care of things at home, one of the areas that may fall by the wayside is your child's education. Maintain regular communication with your child's teacher. Ask them to inform you about their grades, their homework, and ways in which you can help. Don't be hesitant to ask their teacher for suggestions or resources you can use to help your child. After all, you both want your child to be academically successful.

Take advantage of your faith community. Look for godly Christians from whom you can seek parenting advice and who will commit to partnering with you in prayer. Keep in mind that your children also benefit from having others involved in their lives. Look for role models for your children among the people in your church. As a single mom, your son needs positive male Christian role models, and as a single dad, your daughter needs positive Christian female role models.

Instead of wondering how your kids will possibly turn out OK in light of all your mistakes, take a deep breath. Remind yourself that God has promised to walk with you. Take hold of His hand and know that because He stands beside you, you are not alone!

Father God, my children and I need You during this very difficult time of our lives. Please help us to have the energy and strength as well as the emotional and physical support we need, and help me to maintain a positive relationship with my children's other parent.

God's Plan Is Still Best

Then God blessed them, and God said to them, "Be fruitful and multiply; fill the earth and subdue it; have dominion over the fish of the sea, over the birds of the air, and over every living thing that moves on the earth." —Genesis 1:28, NKJV

With the words of our text, God laid out His plan for humanity that one man and one woman, married and committed to each other, would be joined physically, emotionally, and spiritually in order to populate the earth and bring up children who would be His children too.

As we remember, when Adam and Eve ate of the fruit of the tree of the knowledge of good and evil, immediately their eyes were opened. What was once pure, enjoyable, and satisfying intimacy became shameful, corrupt, and, for many, an enslaving passion.

Sexual passion once threatened to destroy the fledgling Christian faith, so that the apostle Paul had to address the problem. In a letter to the church in Corinth, he wrote, "It is actually reported that there is sexual immorality among you, and such sexual immorality as is not even named among the Gentiles—that a man has his father's wife!" (1 Corinthians 5:1, NKJV). Paul wrote this letter in order to address this serious problem in their church, and also to deal with the subject of sinful sexual practices. In addressing other sexual practices not in accordance with God's original plan, Paul writes to the members of the church in Rome: "Even their women exchanged the natural use for what is against nature. Likewise also the men, leaving the natural use of the woman, burned in their lust for one another, men with men committing what is shameful, and receiving in themselves the penalty of their error which was due" (Romans 1:26, 27, NKJV).

If God's plan is still best, why is there so much misinformation and incorrect, even sinful practices? Parents are, or should be, the primary educators of their children in all aspects of their lives, including human sexuality. If parents understand correctly God's plan for sexual intimacy and identity, and they can teach the correct view to their children, they will be helping them to live in a way that will more closely follow the pattern established by God and enjoy lives and relationships that are safer, healthier, and more satisfying.

Father, may we learn more about this special gift you created for us and to use it responsibly and with joy within the bounds of our marriage.

God's Watch-Care

*Because thou hast made the L*ORD*, which is my refuge, even the most High, thy habitation; there shall no evil befall thee, neither shall any plague come nigh thy dwelling. For he shall give his angels charge over thee, to keep thee in all thy ways. —Psalm 91:9–11, KJV*

Angels are commissioned to watch in every family. Each one has the watchcare of a holy angel. These angels are invisible, but sometimes they let their light shine so distinctly that it is recognized. I believe this to be the case in the revealing you have had. This manifestation is teaching you that the Lord loves you, and that His angels are guarding you. You are kept by the power of God.

"Many things of like character will take place. This manifestation of light is to encourage you, as you say it has done, to do right. You have had a glimpse of the light of God, and let this greatly encourage your hearts, making you thankful. All of us should be thankful at all times for the truth that heavenly angels are watching us moment by moment. Very many, had they seen the light you have seen, would rejoice and be thankful.

"When you search the Scriptures, trying to be right and to do right, the angels who attend your footsteps are rejoiced. Angels of heaven come in a marked manner to those who respond to the evidence of the truth and try to obey it. And if these angels are not always seen, you are to remember that they are present just the same, only your natural eyes are not strengthened to discern the light. . . .

"The great trouble with us all is that we do not take time to think that heavenly beings are near us, to help us in our every desire to do right. Heavenly light has come very near to you. Evidence has been given you that the Lord has love for you and cares for you. You can take courage, and feel that you receive strength and grace to do all the good you are capable of doing. . . .

". . . A Christian is one who is daily learning of Christ, taking up the little duties of life, bearing others' burdens. Thus you will have union with Christ" (*This Day With God*, 160).

Dear Lord, remind us that You draw near as we seek to know Your will. Thank You for the light You shed on our way. May we share this blessing with others.

Giving and Having

"Everything I have is yours, and everything you have is mine."
—John 17:10, GW

While the words of our text refer to the relationship between the Father and the Son, they also serve as a good pattern for the type of relationship that husbands and wives should enjoy. Often we are asked questions that have to do with financial matters in marriage. Who should be in charge of the finances at home? How should money be spent? Should the husband and wife have separate bank accounts?

Once we enter into the marital relationship, not only are our bodies joined into one but so also should our possessions, our interests, and our future plans be united. There should be no such thing as "what's mine is mine, and what's yours is yours." When we begin to consider property, information, or even feelings as only a personal thing, not to be shared with the other, we prevent true and complete intimacy from taking place. In contrast, when we see everything as part of the communal property of our marriage, then we will use it to benefit the family.

Another area in which this concept can be understood has to do with our bodies. Paul wrote, "The wife does not have authority over her own body, but the husband does. And likewise the husband does not have authority over his own body, but the wife does." He then further expands this to include, "Do not deprive one another except with consent for a time, that you may give yourselves to fasting and prayer; and come together again so that Satan does not tempt you because of your lack of self-control" (1 Corinthians 7:4, 5, NKJV).

So much trouble could be prevented if we stopped thinking and acting as though what we have and what we are is our individual property and instead were more willing to give to our spouse all that we are and all that we have: our funds, our property, our bodies, our thoughts, our plans, our feelings! As this spirit of having and giving is shared between husband and wife, their relationship benefits and strengthens, blessing the entire family circle.

Father, may the same unselfish spirit that reigns in the Godhead reign also in our home and in our marriage. Since everything really belongs to You, keep us from assuming possession of what You give us, and instead help us to gladly share it with the person You gave us to be married to.

Single-Parenting Priorities

But if a widow has children or grandchildren, these should learn first of all to put their religion into practice by caring for their own family and so repaying their parents and grandparents, for this is pleasing to God. —1 Timothy 5:4, NIV

God gave instructions to His people to take care of the widows and orphans. Widows were allowed to glean the fields and gather some much-needed grain that would help put bread on the table. The early Christians took care of the widows in their midst, leaving an example worthy of our attention.

There are more single parents now than at any other time in history, and the challenges they face every day are daunting. Single parents have to care for their own household entirely on their own, and trying to fill the role of both parents, fixing meals, doing all the household chores, helping with homework, and attending parent-teacher meetings often becomes overwhelming. Taking an ill child to the doctor, or staying home with a sick child, can result in lost income or even possibly the loss of their job.

Today's text underscores the important role that churches should play in supporting widows and single parents with children and grandchildren. Please notice that it is more than just a nice idea. It is God's plan and ideal for His church. Do you have single parents in your church, in your family, on your street? Don't close yourself off from them. Ask the Lord what you can do to help lighten their load. The answers may surprise you.

Bake an extra batch of muffins and drop them by.

Offer to take their kids swimming or to the park.

Call them from the store and ask if there is anything you can pick up for them.

Pray for them.

Be a safe friend. Single people need safe friends.

While it is a difficult road, remaining single is often the better arrangement for single parents, and many times it's the only option. If you are a single parent, take courage, for God sees you and all your needs. Bring them before Him and wait on Him. If you know a single parent—you may be the way the Lord wants to answer that prayer.

Father, open our eyes to the needs around us. Give us wise and compassionate hearts. May we be the caring church You long for us to be. Comfort and strengthen single parents and grandparents and help them in their many and varied needs.

Parents as Disciple-Makers

"And these words which I command you today shall be in your heart. You shall teach them diligently to your children, and shall talk of them when you sit in your house, when you walk by the way, when you lie down, and when you rise up. You shall bind them as a sign on your hand, and they shall be as frontlets between your eyes. You shall write them on the doorposts of your house and on your gates." —Deuteronomy 6:6–9, NKJV

Moses' intention in giving this counsel to the Israelites was that every father would pass on God's instruction and law to his children. By writing these words in their hearts, they were committing to memory God's instructions to them. These were not truths designed to be heard in God's house but in each Jewish home. This was a fundamental part in the education of each Jewish household.

As a parent, one of the most important decisions you will make is in regard to the education of your child. You will need to consider the school to which you will send your child. What environment will they be exposed to for those hours during the day? Is it one that will mirror the same values that you want your child to emulate? It may be stating the obvious, but it is important to point out that the school atmosphere should support and reinforce the values that we as parents are practicing in the home.

In essence, parents must assume the role as the primary disciple makers for their children. This job is not to be left up to the Adventist teacher, the Sabbath School teacher, or the pastor. While the school and the church indeed support, encourage, and reinforce the home values, it is also true that you, as the parents, will be the most influential people in your children's lives.

This wise counsel in Deuteronomy reminds me that parenting is a full-time responsibility that I cannot pass off to someone else. It happens 24 hours a day, 365 days a year. It happens when I sit and when I stand, when I lie down and when I rise up. Parenting is a verb and not a noun. It is defined by the life I lead and by the example that I set.

Lord, I am weary and overwhelmed right now. Will You please help me carry this load? I'm looking to You for wisdom. Please increase my strength. And my faith. I love You, Lord.

God of the Second Chance

"For You cast me into the deep, into the heart of the seas, and the floods surrounded me; all Your billows and Your waves passed over me."
—Jonah 2:3, NKJV

Jonah's story is more interesting than any novel, TV show, or movie ever made. It has all the drama, adventure, passion, and excitement of a modern blockbuster. Within just a few chapters we read the life-or-death struggle of a very reluctant ministry worker and how God resolved his personal spiritual struggle and at the same time provided the only lifeline to a people doomed to die.

Jonah's experience inside the fish must have been frightening and a little sickening. First he is thrown out into the raging waters. Imagine how he must have felt, plunging into the angry ocean, gasping for fresh air and feeling his mouth and lungs fill with sea water. And then to be swallowed by a large fish. We don't know how big the fish was, but however large, the stench of gastric juices, the darkness, the pressure on his ears as the fish dove deeper, the sounds of a large beating heart would all be strange and frightening for anyone.

Jonah was obviously not unconscious during this entire ordeal. He might have slept some of the time from sheer exhaustion, but while he was awake he had plenty of time to consider his situation, his life, and his failures. When he finally realized what he had done, his rebellion and disobedience, he also came to recognize his love and dependence on God, and that if God had rejected him he would have been destroyed by the fish. So he prays a prayer of adoration, thanksgiving, and surrender. God's grace, His billows and waves, passed over Jonah. We could say that God baptized him and brought him out of the fish to enjoy a new life and a new chance at fulfilling the mission God called him to.

We don't have to go through all that drama to experience God's love and forgiveness. Right now, wherever we are, we can stop and allow the billows and waves of God's love and forgiveness to cover us and our families and to renew in us His call to mission, as individuals and as a family. He is the God of a second chance. Ask for it right now.

Father God, may Your love and forgiveness wash over me and over my family so that we may be renewed by Your Spirit and go on to fulfill Your mission for us.

Recharge Your Batteries

However, the report went around concerning Him all the more, and great
multitudes came together to hear, and to be healed by Him of their infirmities.
So He Himself often withdrew into the wilderness and prayed.
—Luke 5:15, 16, NKJV

No one was ever sought after by the crowds as was Jesus. They pressed about Him relentlessly so that He didn't have time to eat. More important to Jesus was the need to withdraw from the crowds to spend time alone in prayer with His Father. It was here Jesus found strength and courage to go forward to meet the demands of each day. In coming aside to pray, Jesus has set an example for His followers for all time.

Parents will especially understand how it feels to be constantly in demand! Have you ever felt that you needed to escape? Are you besieged with endless to-do lists and a calendar that is relentless? The verse above reminds me that Jesus Himself needed time alone. Wow! That gives me permission to withdraw and recharge my own batteries without feeling guilty.

Parenting is a lot of work. It makes great demands on our time and energy. These demands start before our children even get out of bed and continue long after they've fallen asleep. Jesus understands these demands. Many people besieged Him when they discovered He could heal the sick and perform miracles. There was no end to the ingenious ways they devised just to touch Him or get His attention (Luke 5:18, 19).

Jesus recognized the huge demand for His time and knew that the only way He could deal with this well would be in spending time alone with His heavenly Father to rest, pray, and recharge His batteries. It wasn't selfish; it was the most loving thing He could do for His children. It gave Him the energy and strength He needed to deal with their many issues. Your own need for time alone with God isn't selfish either.

Do your children witness you spending time in prayer and with the Word? Do they see that this is a priority in your schedule? Teaching your children this is one of the most important lessons that they will ever learn, and it will help keep you refreshed and recharged to meet the challenges of each day.

Dear Lord, please help me to slow down. I need to drink deeply from the springs of living water that flow freely from You Word. May this be my first priority each day.

We Have Sinned

*"We have sinned and committed iniquity, we have done wickedly and rebelled,
even by departing from Your precepts and Your judgments." —Daniel 9:5, NKJV*

In the entire Bible, we read of very few people we would describe as pure and blameless. Jesus, of course, comes to the top of the list immediately as Someone who was perfect and sinless in everything He did.

Two young men of the Old Testament, each taken to a foreign land, lived exemplary lives. Joseph was sold into slavery by his brothers, yet he maintained a strong connection with God and a positive attitude. God recognized his forgiving spirit and his desire to keep himself pure, and elevated him to a high position in the land.

Likewise, Daniel lived a life of no reproach. From the very beginning of his captivity, he exemplified a commitment to God and to the principles he had obviously learned at home. Like Joseph, he kept himself uncontaminated by the Babylonian culture, and as with Joseph, God blessed Daniel and elevated him to a position of authority in the royal court of Babylon.

Daniel's prayer of intercession in chapter 9 is interesting because, when he prays for his people, he includes himself in his confession of their rebellion. He doesn't say "they" have sinned, but rather "we" have sinned.

As parents, we certainly can't claim perfection. But what Daniel's prayer suggests to me is that while we can, and should, intercede for our children in prayer, we should include ourselves in those prayers. We, too, have sinned. We have failed God. We have rebelled. Our intercessory prayers should not just be a demonstration of our goodness compared to their failures but rather a recognition that as much as they are not perfect, we also have fallen short of God's ideal, that we also struggle with our fallen nature, and that we need His help as much as they do.

As we bring our shortcomings to God in prayer, we should also confess our failures and mistakes to our children. I don't believe they expect perfection of their parents or that they feel better when we act as if we know everything and never make a mistake. Being transparent and recognizing we also fall can help them as they face their own struggles.

Father God, help us to be more willing to recognize our shortfalls and confess them not only to You but to our children when we make mistakes in the way we treat them.

God's Not Finished Yet

*God is the one who began this good work in you, and I am certain that he won't
stop before it is complete on the day that Christ Jesus returns.*
—*Philippians 1:6, CEV*

It is God who begins and completes the work of grace in our lives. If it were left up to us, it would lie unfinished through eternity. Thankfully, it's not up to us. God has promised that He will begin—and complete—His marvelous work in us. God's not finished with any of us yet!

Growth takes time, and yet as parents we often expect perfection in our children overnight. Is it possible that our expectations—and demands—regarding our children are higher than those we ask of ourselves? While it's easy to forget that God is not finished with us yet, it may be even easier to forget that He's not yet finished working with our children either.

As adults we struggle with certain behaviors and continue to grow and mature spiritually throughout our lifetime. Remember, the text for today tells us that the work God is doing in our lives will not be complete until the day that Jesus returns to take us home with Him. Why should we demand anything other than that for our children? Why do we want them to overcome their challenges *now*?

Don't be impatient with your child. Focus on the positives. Look for areas in which you see growth, and take the time to affirm that in your child. If your child only hears about their faults, they will become discouraged, develop poor self-esteem, and not be motivated to attempt new things for fear of failure. It is through failures that we all learn. It is only in falling that we learn how to get up.

I'm thankful that I serve a God who never gives up on me. And we should never give up on our children. Paul reminds us in Philippians that God won't stop. Christ keeps working on our hearts and attitudes day after day. Ever patient and always gracious, He loves us and continually forgives us and allows us to start anew. His mercies are new every morning. Now, that's great news for us and for our children.

Dear Lord, please help me to exercise patience with my child. As I trust You to finish the work that You have started in me, may I be gracious with their shortcomings and immaturity. You're not done with any of us yet! Thank You, Lord.

Peer Pressure

But with me it is a very small thing that I should be judged by you or by a human
court. In fact, I do not even judge myself. For I know of nothing against myself,
yet I am not justified by this; but He who judges me is the Lord.
—*1 Corinthians 4:3, 4, NKJV*

Bullying and peer pressure are very real problems facing our children today. While it may be easy for us as adults to say things such as "Just ignore it" or "Pay no attention to them," it is not an easy thing that our children face. In fact, our glib response will tell them we have minimized the problem and will end up making it harder for them to cope with the issue, or even to talk to us about it. Be careful not to brush it aside without examination.

There is increasing pressure on our children from their peers, considerably more than we faced as children. They are judged by how they dress, what they eat, who they associate with, and what they look like. Our children want to measure up to the expectations of their classmates. They want to fit in and be part of the in-crowd. It is human nature to want to be accepted and have friends. However, oftentimes this pressure and the inability to be accepted have led too many young people to suffer deep depression and can even lead some to commit suicide. How can we as parents counteract this peer pressure?

As parents we need to openly discuss bullying and peer pressure with our children. Role-play various situations in family worships and discuss how to deal with them. Have your children come up with some scenarios. They may be the very situations your child is currently dealing with. This will give your child the tools they need to respond to these changes when they arise.

Have you talked with your child about how to deal with peer pressure and bullying? Are they currently facing these issues? Do they know that they have a safe place to go to seek help? Are you aware of the resources available to parents struggling to help their children in this situation?

O Lord, this world is such a different place to grow up in compared to when I was a child. Please give me a sensitive and wise spirit to know how best to help my child deal with these issues. May home always be a safe place and Your love be a strong tower.

Family Traditions

Now I praise you, brethren, that you remember me in all things and keep the traditions just as I delivered them to you. —1 Corinthians 11:2, NKJV

Every family has its own traditions, things that they have been doing for a long time, perhaps without even remembering how they began. In some families, Dad has his place at the table, or his favorite chair. During special occasions, they do things the same way. In my family, for instance, my daughters made me wear a red stocking hat as I passed out the presents to everyone at Christmastime. There are certain things we traditionally like to eat for Thanksgiving, or for Christmas, or for other holidays.

For many years, as our daughters were growing up, we had a traditional meal on Friday evening, which we all looked forward to enjoying together. Each of them had a particular flavor of cake they liked to have for their birthdays. Some families like to spend their vacation time in the same place every year, while others decorate their house for the holidays using decorations that have been passed down to them from relatives of long ago.

One the fun things that occurs when two people get married is learning to blend their traditions and perhaps even creating some news ones of their own. In my home, in Colombia, South America, for Christmas the centerpiece of our home was the manger scene. At my wife's home, here in the United States, the centerpiece was the Christmas tree. In Colombia, we didn't celebrate Thanksgiving because it is a holiday particular to the United States and Canada. Obviously, we have different patriotic holidays. But we learned to adapt to each other's culture and traditions, adopting some from each.

The key is to begin to cultivate your own traditions. Years later, as you look back, you'll realize you have been doing the same thing, in the same way, for several years. If you stopped doing it, you'd probably feel a sense of loss of sorts. What's important to remember is that those traditions, some passed down from generation to generation, are what glues our families together both to those close to us and to the extended family. And some of the most special traditions also involve our faith in God. Don't reject family traditions; treasure them.

Father God, thank You for all those traditions that bring so much joy. May we treasure them, as we treasure each other, and look forward to creating new traditions in our heavenly home one day soon.

A Quiet Father's Messages

"Joseph, son of David, don't hesitate to get married."
—*Matthew 1:20,* The Message

Have you ever noticed that of all the characters in the Christmas story, Joseph, the husband of Mary, is the only one whose speech is absent in the Scriptures? He is talked to, he is talked about, but not a single syllable comes from the mouth of Joseph, the adoptive father of Jesus. But what he did speaks so loudly that he didn't have to say a word.

First of all, Joseph obeyed God's word. When told his wife was expecting a child of Divine Providence, he accepted the news. When told to flee to Egypt, leaving everything and everyone behind, he fled. He obeyed God, even in painful circumstances. During their betrothal, Mary was found with child! By the time he found out, Mary was showing signs of pregnancy. Under the rules of the time, Joseph could have had her stoned for fornication or adultery. Instead, he decided to keep Mary's pregnancy a secret. It was particularly hard since he was a small-town carpenter, where business and reputation go hand in hand. Joseph's example shows that obedience to God can be painful.

Joseph also reminds us that we can obey God despite our fears. It's interesting what Gabriel told Joseph: "Joseph, son of David, don't hesitate to get married. Mary's pregnancy is Spirit-conceived. God's Holy Spirit has made her pregnant" (Matthew 1:20, *The Message*). When Joseph recognized what was going on, his fear of betrayal was replaced by a much deeper fear. It was the fear of the presence of the Holy God. When God says, "I'm going to disrupt your little habits, and your life will never be the same," we may become afraid like Joseph. But the God who can create fear can also remove it.

Another unspoken word from Joseph teaches us that we can obey God by staking everything on His word alone. Joseph gambled the rest of his life on a word from God that came to him in a dream. Last of all, Joseph, the silent man of Christmas, demonstrates the influence of obedience. It may well have been in that carpenter shop, as He watched Joseph, that Jesus was marked with the unwavering obedience that led Him to the cross.

If we parents can learn a special lesson this Christmas, it is this: Our quiet example of obedience to God and to His word, like Joseph's, is perhaps the best gift we can give our children.

Father God, may my actions and my words give my children the most positive lessons of obedience to You.

God's Love Remains

*For I am persuaded that neither death nor life, nor angels nor principalities
nor powers, nor things present nor things to come, nor height nor depth,
nor any other created thing, shall be able to separate us from the love
of God which is in Christ Jesus our Lord. —Romans 8:38, 39, NKJV*

Paul is saying, in essence, that there is nothing strong enough to separate us from God's love. Nothing in life or death, nothing supernatural—whether of this world or not, nothing in our past history or anything in the future, nothing in any direction we look, there is nothing strong enough, big enough, or scary enough to separate us from God! Nothing is stronger, sweeter, or better than God's love. It is eternal and will remain for all eternity.

The greatest gift you can give your kids is not the newest and best gadget the world has to offer; it is introducing them to Jesus, their best Friend. Giving them Jesus is the gift that will enable them to fall in love with their Creator. Your kids are going to be bombarded with messages and "gifts" from the world, and the "gifts" that the world offers are extraordinarily difficult to resist. In fact, without Jesus at their side, your children will find them impossible to resist. Introduce your kids now to the gift that keeps on giving: the love of Jesus!

As parents we need to take inventory of our priorities. If you asked your child what they thought was important to you, how would they answer? What occupies most of your time? If our children see us prioritizing our relationship with God, they will be encouraged to form their own relationship with Him. Do your children know that even if calamity or tragedy strikes and everything the world values is lost, there is one thing of value they will never be separated from?

How often do you talk about the love of Jesus in your home? Are you spending more time offering Jesus to your children, or do you allow the world's offerings to take precedence? The more of Jesus you show them every day, the less they will be attracted to what the world has to offer, no matter how bright or shiny it may be.

Dear Lord, may I give the gift of Jesus to my children. May they follow my example in seeking You first and always, and may they know You and grow in Your love each day, even as I strive to do the same.

A Lasting Inheritance

Woe to those who join house to house; they add field to field, till there is no place where they may dwell alone in the midst of the land! —Isaiah 5:8, NKJV

Here is one of the most interesting stories Jesus told. "The farm of a certain rich man produced a terrific crop. He talked to himself: 'What can I do? My barn isn't big enough for this harvest.' Then he said, 'Here's what I'll do: I'll tear down my barns and build bigger ones. Then I'll gather in all my grain and goods, and I'll say to myself, Self, you've done well! You've got it made and can now retire. Take it easy and have the time of your life!' Just then God showed up and said, 'Fool! Tonight you die. And your barnful of goods—who gets it?' That's what happens when you fill your barn with Self and not with God" (Luke 12:16–21, *The Message*).

Here's an interesting story that provides perspective. A wealthy man gave these instructions to be carried out upon his death. First, that his coffin be carried to the graveyard by the most eminent doctors in the land. Next, that the treasures he'd amassed be scattered along the roadside to the cemetery. And finally, that his coffin be left open and his hands be placed in plain sight of everyone.

When asked the reason why, he responded, "I want the most well-respected doctors to carry my coffin to show the world that they do not hold the ultimate power to heal. I want the road to be scattered with my wealth so everyone can see that no matter how much you accumulate on earth, it will ultimately remain on earth. And I want my hands to be seen so that people will be reminded that we were born empty-handed and we will die empty-handed."

While we can leave our families an inheritance that can help them establish their own future, there are things far more important we can pass on to them. Right now, we can be giving them of our time, building memories, sharing our faith in God, and helping them to develop good, well-rounded characters that will be a blessing throughout eternity. These are the things that are not perishable.

Father, help us to fill our barns—our lives—with more of You and less of self. Keep us from getting caught up in the race to earn more and own more. May we focus on what truly matters, and may our faith be our greatest treasure.

Don't Release the Water

The beginning of strife is like releasing water;
therefore stop contention before a quarrel starts.
—Proverbs 17:14, NKJV

Solomon's advice is so good and practical that we would do well to keep it in mind. Once strife begins, it is hard to stop it before it causes harm to our most important relationships. It is so much easier to stem the flow before it is too late. Benjamin Franklin was on target when he stated, "An ounce of prevention is worth a pound of cure." It is possible to learn how to resolve conflict before it starts. Here are some good questions to ask yourself: Is it a worthy battle? Is it really worth the conflict?

Anyone who has ever played basketball knows that during a game there is going to be what is called "incidental contact." Learn to pick your battles. Solomon writes, "Those with good sense are slow to anger, and it is their glory to overlook an offense" (Proverbs 19:11, NRSV).

Are we wrong? Be quick to say, "I'm sorry. I was wrong." These simple words will open a highway of opportunity for real discussion. If you are wrong, admit it. Sometimes we're wrong. By admitting it, we will stop the flow of conflict. Immediately.

Should we react or respond? When we react, we don't take time to think, we just act! There is a huge difference between reacting and responding. To react requires no intelligence, only instinct. But to respond, you have to get that three-pound chunk of gray matter in your head involved. Responding requires time. It takes a consideration of the facts. Only when you respond will you have a chance to resolve conflict. In conflict, too many of us react when we should respond. Be certain you respond; don't just react with a knee-jerk, thoughtless reply.

What difference is this going to make in my life in three days? What impact will it have in five years? Many times, answering these two questions will help you avoid what might have been a ridiculous conflict that is simply not worth the battle in the big scheme of things. In Philippians 2:14, Paul admonishes us to do all things without complaining and disputing. When you say the right thing in the wrong way, it becomes the wrong thing to say even though it might be right!

Dear Lord, when tempers are about to flare and words are about to fly, help me to take a moment to stop the contention before a quarrel begins.

Give Your Child the Best You Have

And they came into the house and saw the young child with Mary his mother;
and they fell down and worshipped him; and opening their treasures
they offered unto him gifts, gold and frankincense and myrrh.
—Matthew 2:11, ASV

A t this time of the year we enjoy reading again the story of Jesus' birth. We are reminded of the visit of the angel to Mary and Joseph, of Joseph's decision to proceed with his plans to marry the young pregnant girl, of their trip to Bethlehem, and of the birth of the Baby Jesus. Have you noticed that no matter how well we know that story, or how many times we've read it, we never grow tired of hearing it again and again?

The wise men from the East traveled far to see the little King. Theirs was not a trip borne out of curiosity; they knew the prophecies concerning the Messiah and understood their significance and the imminence of their fulfillment. So they set out to follow the star that would lead them to the newborn King. And they took gifts with them. The very best gifts they had, gifts of gold, frankincense, and myrrh. While our minds are amazed at the splendor of these gifts, we don't always recognize the gifts given to Jesus by Mary and Joseph.

The wise men brought rich material gifts. Mary and Joseph gave Him a happy home environment and the example of godly parents who worshiped Jehovah faithfully. While not blessed with earthly wealth, Mary and Joseph provided a home where Jesus was taught to pray, and He learned how to work hard and well in Joseph's carpenter shop.

Our materialistic society leads parents to believe that the more toys they give their children the happier they will be. I would suggest that the best gifts you can give your children are a stable, loving home environment that is conducive for your children to learn about God and become His little disciples. In practical terms, that means to have daily morning and evening devotional time and prayer with them, to worship every week together at church, and wherever possible to make sure they attend a church school until they graduate from college. The combined effort of home, church, and school is the best gift you can give them—a gift they can treasure throughout eternity.

Father God, help us to provide for our children not only materials things but, most important, the environment and opportunities for spiritual growth.

Camping With the Family

*And the L*ORD *spoke to Moses and Aaron, saying: "Everyone of the children of Israel shall camp by his own standard, beside the emblems of his father's house."*
—Numbers 2:1, 2, NKJV

In the camp of Israel, God wanted order and organization. Three tribes encamped on each of the four sides of the tabernacle. The sight of all those tents and the thousands of people around them must have been very impressive. While there was order and solemnity much of the time, there must have been lighter moments when children played and families sat together to eat or to talk about the events of the day. It was a forty-year-long family camping trip!

I remember one camping trip in particular with my family. My dad had a tent made for our family, and it was large enough to hold all eight of us. It was made of heavy canvas, and the support was made of regular plumbing pipes. It was a headache! But once the canvas monster was finally set up, it was pure joy. On this trip we camped in an open field alongside the river.

The open field was a place where cows pastured, so we had to be careful where we stepped. We threw the dried-out cow patties onto the fire because we had been told they would serve as mosquito repellent. During that weekend, it was hot some of the time, rainy at times, and cool at other times. But it was always enjoyable. I remember swimming in the crystal-clear water of the river, eating freshly caught fish, sitting at night by the fire, and looking up at millions of stars we normally couldn't see from our city home.

Forty years later, I still remember that weekend fondly, including having to tow my future brother-in-law's car home. He and my sister were not yet married, so it was most embarrassing for him, even though no one said anything to make him feel bad. It's time spent together where our most precious memories are created. Not everyone enjoys camping, but there are many things families can enjoy doing together. My wife and I enjoyed traveling with our daughters, and we visited forty-five of the fifty states and several countries outside of the U.S. We treasure every memory we have collected through the years. Make time to build memories for your children. They will last a lifetime.

Father, help us be more intentional in setting aside time to be together as families in relaxing, memorable moments.

Misleading Eyes

"There is no one greater in this house than I, nor has he kept back anything from me but you, because you are his wife. How then can I do this great wickedness, and sin against God?" So it was, as she spoke to Joseph day by day, that he did not heed her, to lie with her or to be with her. —Genesis 39:9, 10, NKJV

Joseph had been sold into captivity by his brothers, but God blessed him, and while a slave he proved faithful to his master, Potiphar. The captain's wife, however, was attracted to Joseph and enticed him to be intimate with her, something Joseph immediately and repeatedly refused on the grounds that he would be offending God and betraying his master's trust. She became angry, falsely accused him before her husband, and Joseph ended up in jail as a result.

When a person is bent on sin, nothing seems to deter them. Such was the case with Potiphar's wife. Her sin began with her eye: She "cast longing eyes on Joseph" (verse 7, NKJV). She was truly daring and shameless in her interactions with Joseph. By her wanton looks and unchaste desires, she had already committed adultery with him in her heart.

Joseph knew the principles that were later written by Solomon. He knew that treasuring God's Word in his heart would be his salvation, "to keep you from the evil woman, from the flattering tongue of a seductress" (Proverbs 6:24, NKJV). He knew not to "lust after her beauty in your heart, nor let her allure you with her eyelids" (verse 25, NKJV). He understood clearly the dangers, "for by means of a harlot a man is reduced to a crust of bread; and an adulteress will prey upon his precious life" (verse 26, NKJV). He was aware that passion is like a fire in his chest that burns clothes and all (verses 27–29).

Had Joseph fallen to the enticements of this woman, the results would have been disastrous to him, to his family suffering under the famine, and for the survival of the people of God's promise. Just a few moments of sin can bring results that last much longer.

Father, give us the strength to not yield to temptation in any form. Shield our eyes from wandering into dangerous territory, and keep them focused instead on You. May we always be faithful to You and to our spouse for the sake and benefit of our families and to maintain Your honor and glory before the universe.

How to Grow in Grace

God is able to make all grace abound toward you; that ye, always having all sufficiency in all things, may abound to every good work. —2 Corinthians 9:8

Many are longing to grow in grace; they pray over the matter, and are surprised that their prayers are not answered. The Master has given them a work to do whereby they shall grow. Of what value is it to pray when there is need of work? The question is, Are they seeking to save souls for whom Christ died? Spiritual growth depends upon giving to others the light that God has given to you. You are to put forth your best thoughts in active labor to do good, and only good, in your family, in your church, and in your neighborhood. . . .

"The youth may be free in Christ; they may be the children of light, and not of darkness. God calls upon every young man and young woman to renounce every evil habit, to be diligent in business, fervent in spirit, serving the Lord. Jesus will help you, so that you need not remain in indolence, making no effort to correct your wrongs or improve your conduct. The sincerity of your prayers will be proved by the vigor of the effort you make to obey all of God's commandments. You may move intelligently, and at every step renounce evil habits and associations, believing that the Lord will renovate your heart by the power of His Spirit. . . .

"Do not excuse your defects of character, but in the grace of Christ overcome them. Wrestle with the evil passions which the Word of God condemns; for in yielding to them, you abase yourself. Repent of sin while Mercy's sweet voice invites you; for it is the first step in the noblest work you can do. Strive for the mastery with all the powers God hath given you.

"The path of the just is a progressive one, from strength to strength, from grace to grace, and from glory to glory. The divine illumination will increase more and more, corresponding with our onward movements, qualifying us to meet the responsibilities and emergencies before us" (*My Life Today,* 103, 104).

Father, may we learn to walk in the light, as children of light, and so set a living example for our own children to follow. May we allow You to transform us and be an encouragement to the little ones who are following in our footsteps.

When Children Struggle

But the children struggled together within her; and she said, "If all is well, why am I like this?" So she went to inquire of the Lord. And the Lord said to her: "Two nations are in your womb, two peoples shall be separated from your body; one people shall be stronger than the other, and the older shall serve the younger."
—*Genesis 25:22, 23, NKJV*

Isaac was forty years old when he married Rebekah, and sixty years old when Esau and Jacob were born. By today's standards, he was advanced in years for both marriage and parenthood. We are not told how much younger Rebekah was, but it took them twenty years before they had children. As happy as they were to be parents, their children brought them heartache and trouble even before they were born. Rebekah asks herself, "Why is this happening to me?"

The children had very different characters and personalities. Jacob bargained with Esau for his birthright and then tricked his father Isaac into giving him the blessing that belonged to the firstborn. He had to leave home to escape his brother's anger, and as far as we can tell, he never saw his mother alive again.

For Isaac, parenting was no easier than it is for parents today. While this is no consolation, it helps to know that we are not unique in our parenting struggles. As we get closer to the second coming of Jesus, the challenges of raising godly children become more difficult as temptations increase exponentially.

Our hope rests in the same God who helped Abraham and Sarah, Isaac and Rebekah, and Jacob and Rachel; the same God and Father who helped Mary and Joseph; the same God who helped James and Ellen White; the same God who helped our parents. As difficult and challenging as the task of parenting is, and as painful as it is at times, we have not been abandoned by our heavenly Father. He knows our struggles, He understands our pain, He helps us, and He blesses us and our children.

Loving Father, how much pain and heartache we ourselves have caused You, even though You are the perfect Parent. Forgive us for hurting You, and help us to be better children. And now that the tables have turned and we are the parents, help us to love and care for our children as You would, as You do, so they may grow to love You and accept You as their Father and their God.

Unity at Home

"Every kingdom divided against itself is laid waste, and no city or house divided against itself will stand." —Matthew 12:25, ESV

As Jesus healed people and cast out demons, some among those who witnessed the events accused Him of doing it by the power of the devil. The verse above is Jesus' response to those accusations. Basically, Jesus asked, What benefit is there for the devil to cast out his imps? How does it help a government or kingdom when there is infighting? The implied answer is that unity is stronger than divisiveness.

While Jesus used the example of a kingdom, these principles can also apply to the relationships at home. Here are a few things we can do to make sure our home is not divided.

Marry someone who shares the same spiritual priorities as you. The most intimate part of a person's life is their spirituality. If we can't share that with our spouse because our faith is very different, it makes it difficult to truly be one. When we marry someone with whom we can share our faith and spiritual beliefs, it will bring us closer and keep us close to each other and to God.

Worship together. One of the most powerful tools God has given to bring and keep us together, as a couple and as a family, is daily worship. As we study and pray together, not only are we drawn toward each other but we're drawn closer to God Himself. Weekly, habitual church attendance accomplishes the same affect and is a wonderful example for our children.

Decisions that affect the home should be taken together. This is particularly true of financial decisions such as tithes and offerings, home budget, expenses, investments, and savings. Other areas of joint decision-making should include such things as the education of the children, buying a home or a car, health, diet, medical care, and so on.

An important area where husband and wife need to be in agreement is in regard to how the children should be disciplined. This should be done long before the children are born, and as they grow, it should be done privately, not in front of them.

Spend quality and quantity time together. The memories we collect during these times keep us together and remain even after the children leave home, or death takes a loved one away. Often, the sweetest memories are treasured and passed on from one generation to another.

Father, keep our family together in the bonds of mutual love and within Your arms of love.

Do You Need Help?

When Jesus heard that, He said to them, "Those who are well have no need of a physician, but those who are sick." —Matthew 9:12, NKJV

Jesus spoke these words after being criticized for calling Matthew, a tax collector, to be one of His disciples. No one was hated more than tax collectors. They were considered the worst of sinners. But Jesus didn't distinguish between big sinners and small sinners. All need His grace and salvation equally. In fact, those who don't recognize their need of a Savior are in the greatest danger of losing out on eternal life.

Often couples don't seek help for their marital difficulties until it is too late, or almost too late. It is no sin to look for help for your relationship, any more than it is to go to a doctor when you are ill. Here are warning signs that your family may need to find help from a professional.

You go over the same issues again and again with no resolution or closure. The constant cycle of repeated arguments about the same problems is a clear sign things aren't working and you need help.

There is physical and/or emotional abuse. There is never a good reason for abuse to be tolerated. Don't allow this behavior to continue without getting help and finding safety. Physical, emotional, and verbal abuse should never be accepted as a way of life.

You pretend to respect a family member whom you do not really respect. This is an indication of a serious problem. One dysfunctional family member rules the rest of the family, usually by fear.

You're afraid to say certain things in your family. When you don't feel comfortable sharing your feelings and thoughts without being criticized, or bullied, something is terribly wrong.

You have a recurring wish that you were out of your family or had never come into it at all. All of us occasionally wish we weren't in a family or marriage, but when it becomes a daily obsession, there should be deeper consideration as to its reason and impact.

You ignore or excuse signs of bad behavior in a family member. Bullying, giving orders, pulling rank, indifference to the feelings of others are signs of this malady.

Father, help us to recognize when we need help before it's too late to save our family or our marriage. Help us to seek it and please lead us to wise and godly counselors.

Topical Index

Scriptural Index

3:5 .... Oct. 17
4:4 .... Aug. 8
4:8 .... Aug. 12
10:17 .... Dec. 1
18:49 .... Nov. 23
23:4 .... July 18
25:2, 7 .... Aug. 7
32:6, 7 .... Aug. 6
35:18 .... Nov. 21
46:1 .... Dec. 9
54:4 .... Dec. 8
79:13 .... Nov. 29
90:3, 5 .... June 17
90:14 .... June 2
92:1 .... Nov. 22
96:11 .... Dec. 7
102:1–3, 8 .... Mar. 7
103:13 .... June 15
113:9 .... June 20
127:1 .... Nov. 26
127:2 .... May 20
127:3–5 .... May 17
133:1 ....Apr. 30
136:1 .... June 29
137:1 .... Aug. 5

Proverbs
1:5 ....Feb. 27
3:5, 6 ....Jan. 21
3:5, 6 ....Apr. 25
3:27 .... May 19
5:15 .... Oct. 23
9:12 .... Dec. 2
11:24 .... May 12
12:1 ....Feb. 28
13:10 .... May 14
14:1 ....Aug. 4
14:21 .... May 7
15:1 .... July 1
15:1 .... Aug. 2
16:24 .... Jan. 19
16:24 .... June 26
14:24 .... Aug. 1
17:14 .... Dec. 24
17:22 .... May 3
22:6 ....Feb. 1
23:7 ....Apr. 29
24:26 .... Mar. 30
25:11 .... Aug. 3
27:23 .... May 2

31:28 .... July 14

Ecclesiastes
3:1 ....Apr. 9
4:9 .... Jan. 26
4:9–11 ....Feb. 20
7:12 ....Apr. 26
9:10 .... Nov. 1

Song of Solomon
1:2 ....Nov. 28
4:10 .... June 3
5:1 .... Dec. 6
5:16 .... May 22
8:7 ....Apr. 7

Isaiah
5:8 .... Dec. 23
28:12 .... Nov. 25
30:15 ....Apr. 4
50:4 .... Oct. 12
62:5 .... Nov. 20

Jeremiah
2:32 .... May 16
13:19 ....Aug. 17
31:3 .... Dec. 4
31:34 ....Nov. 27

Lamentations
3:22, 23 .... July 20

Ezekiel
20:31 .... June 24
36:26 ....Apr. 20

Daniel
9:5 .... Dec. 17

Hosea
1:2 ....Feb. 10
2:19, 20 ....Feb. 11
6:6 ....Feb. 25

Joel
2:28 .... Mar. 15

Amos
3:3 ....Feb. 16
3:3 .... July 27

5:4 ....Feb. 17
5:14 .... July 25

Obadiah
1:17 .... May 18

Jonah
1:1–3 .... June 30
1:12 .... June 28
2:3 .... Dec. 15
3:10 .... July 28

Micah
4:3 ....Feb. 14
4:5 ....Feb. 15
6:8 .... June 27
7:7 .... June 21

Nahum
2:1 ....Feb. 23

Habakkuk
2:1 ....Feb. 9
2:1 .... July 26
2:4 .... May 13
3:17, 18 .... June 23

Zephaniah
1:12 .... May 15
1:13 ....Apr. 28
3:12 ....Mar. 14

Haggai
1:6, 9 .... May 29

Zechariah
4:6 .... June 11

Malachi
2:16 ....Jan. 4
2:16 .... June 6

Matthew
1:20 .... Dec. 21
3:17 .... June 19
5:37 ....Sept. 9
6:2 .... May 30
6:7, 8 .... May 9
6:19–21 .... June 4
9:12 .... Jan. 15

NOTES

NOTES

NOTES

NOTES

NOTES